United Nations'

Global Straitjacket

A straitjacket is used in the medical and judicial fields to restrain an individual from hurting himself, herself, or others. A straitjacket is a jacket with very long sleeves into which a person is fitted so that the opening is in the back. The sleeved arms are then crossed over the stomach and the excess length is used to tie the sleeves in the middle of the back, unreachable by the tied person. This prevents him or her from harming anyone and from defending himself or herself—if he or she had to.

Cover design: Joan Veon *(RACINE, WISCONSIN)*
Cover art: John Bonner

All Scripture quotations are from the King James Version of the Holy Bible.

THE WOMEN'S INTERNATIONAL
MEDIA GROUP, INC
P.O. BOX 77
MIDDLETOWN, MD 21769
301/371-0542 www.womensgroup.com

ISBN 1-57558-38

United Nations'

Global Straitjacket

Joan Veon

01-1915

The logo is taken from the 1987 television series "Amerika" which depicted the "take over of America by the U.S.S.R." Interestingly enough the film used the above flag (without the British flag) to symbolize the merger. It became very apparent to Joan that there **is** a merger taking place on three levels: 1) government—through re-invented government/communitarianism/the third way (chapter two); 2) environment—through sustainable development (chapter four), and 3) economic — through globalization (chapter five). It is the United Nations which provides the structure for this merger under the guise of "peace."

In her first book, *Prince Charles: The Sustainable Prince*, Joan traces the power between the United Nations to the British royal family. Prince Charles works behind the scenes affecting global governmental policies and in facilitating the radical United Nations environmental agenda of sustainable development which has now been adopted by both governments and businesses world-wide (chapter two). This book is a handbook on the many facets of world government today. It begs for our response as to *how we shall stand in the gap.*

Dedication

I dedicate this book to my friends:

Craig Buchanan—a friend whose ideas usually involve work!
Jean Guilfoyle—we met in Cairo, my first U.N. conference
Dr. Noah Hutchings—a man of vision, faith, and integrity
Bob Klicker—a concerned businessman and American—
thanks for your help
Lois Leigh—a dear friend who has helped me
for a number of years
Linda Liotta—a kindred spirit and an encourager
Phil and Barbara Marchetti—without whose help my computer and
office would not run
Bernadette Marx and Eda Kavanagh—their encouragement was
essential
Ann Michael—a dear friend who is standing in the GAP
Bob Michael—a special friend
Pat Ramirez—my sister and my friend—
her helping hand has saved me more than once
Eunice Ray—a woman with ideas and a vision
Col. Ron Ray—a soldier of the Cross and
a highly decorated veteran of the Vietnam War
Judith Reisman—her inspiration and confidence in
me is appreciated
The Women at the Trust—Thank you, thank you, thank you
for your love and support
Rod Veon—my husband and my best friend

In Memorial:
Jack McCoy—a dear and true friend—So Long Jack!
Mary Wagner—an elegant and humble servant of the Lord

Table of Contents

POLITICAL STRUCTURE

Glossary of Abbreviations

APEC—Asian-Pacific Economic Council
ATF—Bureau of Alcohol, Tobacco and Firearms
BIS—Bank for International Settlements
BLM—Bureau of Land Management
BOE—Bank of England
BOJ—Bank of Japan
CBN—Christian Broadcasting Network
CFR—Council on Foreign Relations
DEA—Drug Enforcement Administration
ECB—European Central Bank
ECLAC—United Nations Economic Commission for Latin America
 and the Caribbean
ECOSOC—Economic and Social Conference of the United Nations
EIB—European Investment Bank
EMU—Economic Monetary Union
EO—Executive Order
ERM—European Rate Mechanism
ESCB—European System of Central Banks
EU—European Union
Ex-Im Bank—Export-Import Bank of the U.S.
FBI—Federal Bureau of Investigations
FDIC—Federal Deposit Insurance Corporation
FEMA—Federal Emergency Management Agency
FRB—Federal Reserve Bank
FTAA—Free Trade Areas of the Americas
G7—Group of Seven
G8—Group of Eight

G-10—Group of Ten

GATT—General Agreement on Trade and Tariffs

GDIN—Global Disaster Information Network

IAEA—International Atomic Energy Agency

IASC—International Accounting Standards Committee

ICC—United Nations International Criminal Court

ICC—International Chamber of Commerce

ICITAP—International Criminal Investigative Training Assistance Program

ICLEI—International Council for Local Environmental Initiatives

ICSID—International Centre for Settlement of Investment Disputes

ICTR—International Criminal Tribunal for Rwanda

IDB—World Bank Inter-American Development Bank

IFRC—International Federation of Red Cross and Red Crescent Societies

IMF—International Monetary Fund

IMO—International Maritime Organization

INL—State Department's Bureau for International Narcotics and Law Enforcement Affairs

IOSCO—International Organization of Security Commissions

MAI—Multilateral Agreement on Investments

NAFTA—North American Free Trade Agreement

NATO—North Atlantic Treaty Organization

NDPO—National Domestic Preparedness Office

NGO—Nongovernmental organizations

NOW—National Organization of Women

NPR—National Performance Review

OAS—Organization of American States

OCHA—Office for the Coordination of Humanitarian Affairs

OECD—Organization for Economic Cooperation and Development

OJP—Office of Justice Protection

OPIC—Overseas Private Investors Corporation

PAHO—Pan American Health Organization

PCSD—President's Commission on Sustainable Development

PDD 63—Presidential Domestic Directive 63

PPP—Public-private partnership

PWBLF—Prince of Wales Business Leaders Forum

RIIA—Royal Institute of International Affairs

SEICUS—Sex Education and Information Council of the U.S.

SUI—State Use Industries

TLC—Trilateral Commission

U.K.—United Kingdom

U.N.—United Nations

UNA—United Nations Association

UNCED—United Nations Conference on Population and Development

UNCTAD—United Nations Conference on Trade and Development

UNDP—United Nations Development Programme

UNDPI—United Nations Department of Public Information

UNEP—United Nations Environment Programme

UNESCO—United Nations Education, Scientific and Cultural Organization

UNFPA—United Nations Population Fund

UNICEF—United Nations Children's Fund

UPU—Universal Postal Union

WB—World Bank

WBCSD—World Business Council for Sustainable Development

WEDO—Women's Environment and Development Organization

WEF—World Economic Forum

WFC—World Food Council

WHO—World Health Organization

WIPO—World Intellectual Property Organization

WMO—World Meteorological Organization

WTO—World Trade Organization

YWAM—Youth with a Mission

Author's Introduction

Note: There is a tremendous amount of information in this book on the global agenda, groups, organizations, players, philosophy, modus operandi, and charts to help you "connect the dots." I write from a Christian world view. While this may or may not be compatible with yours, the information provided is strategic for anyone who loves the Constitution and values the freedoms provided for us in it and the Bill of Rights. As a result of the concentration of material, you may have to read the chapter a second time in order to assimilate all of the details, and you may wish to re-read the chapter summary after reading the chapter. Because of the length of this book, the first four chapters provide you with the infrastructure, philosophy, and players and are imperative, along with chapter ten.

The focus and desire of this book is to help you, the reader, understand the day and hour so you can determine how to respond and "stand in the gap." This is a book about world government and the infrastructure which has been set in place above the individual nations during the last sixty years.

As I contemplated writing about that which explained the governmental structure from my eyes as an independent international journalist who has covered over thirty-three United Nations and U.N. related conferences in the last five years, I realized that the world we now know will have to be changed as a result of some planned and managed catastrophic event to catapult us from "unofficial world government" into what has been termed "the new world order" or "official world government."

Truly, it does not make any difference what that catastrophic event will be, since this book is about awareness—understanding the structure of world government and then our response—how to stand in the gap. The purpose for writing it is to: (1) explain the infrastructure of world government today and how it is affecting our lives, our quality of life, our finances, and our freedom and, (2) to reveal to those who want to stand in the gap that the time is now to prepare spiritually in order to stand. We are living in uncertain times.

I believe that any planned and managed catastrophic event will be a "spiritual Armageddon," for it not only brings to fruition the stated goals and objectives of the United Nations, but it could signal the end of the way of life as we have known it in the United States. Unless you have a complete understanding of the events and objectives of the internationalists, i.e, the "one worlders," which are explained in this book, you will not have a vision of what is required. That is very simply—to stand in the gap. Should you miss this opportunity, you might miss the whole purpose for your being as any planned and managed catastrophic event presents a very unique opportunity for those who diligently seek Him to be used at this very critical day and hour. What I have written is not easy, it is not fun, but I believe it is a very accurate picture of what is to befall the world. Your job is to "sift and weigh" the information and determine what you think is relevant and ask God to reveal truth to you so that you may be found faithful.

In my first book, *Prince Charles: The Sustainable Prince,* I show how the signing of the United Nations Charter is the forum that will be used to bring America back under the control of the British Empire and into world government. Those waiting to fight the same kind of war for independence that our forefathers fought at Valley Forge, Yorktown, and Trenton, will be disappointed. Those days have been superseded by the computer, which has brought us into a "seamless" electronic world with no borders. This seamless world is further sewn together by hundreds of laws that our Senate has passed, such as the Tax Reduction Act of 1980, which tore financial barriers on an international basis, the North American Free Trade Agreement (NAFTA), and the 27,000-

plus-page General Agreement on Trade and Tariffs (GATT) (now the World Trade Organization), and a multitude of other laws that integrate us with the other countries of the world into a "new world order" which is world government. Furthermore, this seamless web has been strengthened by the immense powers given the United Nations (U.N.), the World Bank (WB), the International Monetary Fund (IMF), the World Health Organization (WHO), the World Trade Organization (WTO), and many other U.N. agencies and commissions. All of this activity has and is taking place above the national/federal level at the international level. There is and has been a blackout of what is transpiring at this level and we, as a nation, unfortunately have no knowledge of how it affects us. As a result, we have been put in a straitjacket—a global straitjacket.

A straitjacket is used in the medical and judicial fields to restrain an individual from hurting himself, herself, or others. A straitjacket is a jacket with very long sleeves into which a person is fitted so that the opening is in the back. The sleeved arms are then crossed over the stomach and the excess length is used to tie the sleeves in the middle of the back, unreachable by the tied person. This prevents him or her from harming anyone and from defending himself or herself—if he or she had to.

Because we have little working knowledge of what is transpiring on the international level, we have not been able to defend against the philosophical tyranny that has eroded our sovereignty. In addition, what is being done is sugarcoated so that to the untrained and unsuspecting ear, it "sounds good." Unfortunately, our Congress and president have aided and abetted the march into a "new world order" by agreeing with the need for America to become a one-world government instead of remaining a sovereign nation. This action has not occurred only in the Clinton administration but goes back to Presidents Woodrow Wilson and Franklin Roosevelt, and every president since—Republican and Democrat. On April 20, 1970, an article appeared in the *Anaheim Bulletin* entitled "Executive J—The United Nations is given full diplomatic recognition of being a *sovereign world government*." The article stated:

Historians of the future may point to March 19, 1970, as the day when the United States of America became an arm of a One World government. It happened quietly, unnoticed by the press, in a Senate chamber only partly filled, as a few Senators waited their turns. . . . [The floor speaker stated]: "The Senate will proceed to vote on Executive J, first session, 91st Congress, the Convention on the Privileges and Immunities of the United Nations." At the end of the count, the vote showed 78 yeas and zero negatives, with 22 senators absent. So it was that the United Nations would no longer be honored as a mere "International Organization." It now has the status of full diplomatic recognition as a *sovereign government*.

You see, not only have the people of America been put into a straitjacket, but so have the people of the world.

To many, the "world government" idea is a fleeting one that will take much time to fulfill. For many years I had heard the expression "new world order," which was popularized by George Bush at the time of the Gulf War. But since no one had really defined what it meant, I thought it was a concept "up in the stratosphere." It was not until I went to my first United Nations conference in Cairo, Egypt, that I came face-to-face with the reality of world government.

One year later in September 1995, I covered the first Gorbachev State of the World Forum, which was held in San Francisco. Numerous workshops were held for the very prestigious participants (CEOs from multinational and transnational corporations, delegates, and representatives from nongovernmental organizations). Because I was press, there were a number of workshops off-limits to me. However, my colleague, Linda Liotta, purchased the tapes to the forum. In one of the workshops entitled "The New Architecture of Global Security: Global Decision-Making and Sovereignty," a key participant, international law professor Saul Mendlovitz (who has written many books on international law and world government) said:

I believe I am a citizen of my own society and a citizen of the world. . . . Let me tell you the other myth. What does myth mean? I take this from Webster's. . . . "This is the story of a people, its origin, its beliefs." What is the myth we are attempting in this room and at this conference? We are attempting to create the myth of planetary objectives. We are attempting to bring about a planetary community. I think we are timid in not talking realistically about local citizenship and world government. I know all the reasons for using the term "governance" rather than government. I see no way out of the next century without an extraordinary amount of chaos, dislocation of the human race, environmental degradation of the worst sort, without government within governance. . . . I am not a world Federalist but I see no way out of government at the global level.

For years as a pro-lifer I was involved at the local level, specifically in the school system. I was gravely concerned about abortion, condom distribution in the schools, the family-planning textbooks that were being chosen for those specific classes, etc. As a businesswoman I thought I was informed, rather sophisticated, and effective at the local level. It was not until I went to Cairo that I realized that I knew absolutely nothing about the government at the international level and how ineffective I was, because all of the ideas and concepts being discussed in Cairo were already being implemented in Montgomery County, Maryland, where I lived at the time. It was in Cairo that I realized how "dumbed down" we are. We—the Joe averages—have been dealt a double "whammy" as we endure a higher cost of living and a faster pace of life that leaves very little time to consider political matters—locally, nationally, or globally—as we have been left out of the informational loop on purpose so that we would not be in a position to understand or discuss what is being set up on the international level, what it means, and how it affects us. By the time we figure it out, they hope it will be too late. This is another reason for writing this book.

I remember attending a workshop in Cairo sponsored by the

Sex Education and Information Council of the United States (SE-ICUS) in which participants were espousing all of the sexual freedoms children should have. To any law-abiding, moral American, it was an unspeakable travesty. (Ask Dr. Judith Reisman, who wrote *Kinsey, Sex and Fraud* and *Kinsey: Crimes and Consequence,* about the perverseness of Alfred Kinsey and how he was used to change American values to those of an alley cat. All one has to do is listen to the sexual exploits of the president to know how effective Kinsey has been. SEICUS is directly connected to the University of Indiana where Kinsey did all of his research!) I then decided to ask a very direct and bold question of the young man reading a twenty-page document about these "freedoms" children should have. Those in the room were outraged at my audacity for even asking such a personal question. I responded, "If he is telling us it is okay for our children (under ten) to have sex with whomever they wish, then why can't I ask him how he likes his sex?" Needless to say, I disrupted the entire workshop. Afterward, about twenty English-speaking Egyptian youths gathered around me and asked why I was mad enough to ask such a question. When I told them that most Americans do not agree with what was being said, that they did not know this conference was being held, and that they knew nothing about the United Nations, the Egyptians were aghast. You see, they thought that knowledge of what the United Nations is saying and doing was commonplace in America, and if Americans went along with the agenda, then they would too. Unfortunately, most people are in the same place I was in before Cairo, with no knowledge of the international level and structure of world government that exists and is waiting for the right time to be revealed at the community level (see chapter two).

In an effort to get informed since Cairo, I have attended more than thirty-three U.N. and U.N.-related conferences dealing with the environment, and social and economic issues. The infrastructure of world government is very far advanced. What is missing are the "teeth." You see, until the "teeth" are put in place, you and I will be able to live normally with a sense of freedom and protection of our freedoms. Once the teeth are in place, our lives will change because world government will then be in a position to overpower anyone who disagrees with the agenda. Our freedoms will change, the ability to buy and sell will change (instead of dollars, we may use electronic money), and the availability of food, water, energy, clothing, tools, equipment, etc., will also change as it will be controlled (sustainable development—see chapter four). We will probably go into a military police state to enforce not only all of the new rules and regulations, but to protect the resources of the planet.

I have found, unfortunately, that the United States Constitution has been and is being replaced by the United Nations Charter, that the Bill of Rights is being replaced by the United Nations Declaration on Human Rights, and that a new world constitution is being drafted (and has been for a period of time) called the Earth Charter. Many of our leaders, from the president on down, constantly refer to the U.N. Charter. On December 10, 1998, Bill Clinton issued Executive Order 13107 which establishes a federal agency to enforce compliance with all U.N. human rights treaties, even those that have *not* been ratified by the Senate. This executive order does three things:

1. It protects through the Constitution human rights treaties that have not been ratified;
2. It makes U.N. doctrine the legal standard for all U.S. policy and legislation; and
3. It creates a powerful new federal oversight agency that has the task of monitoring both state and federal laws to ensure compliance with the ratified and unratified U.N. treaties.

At the September 20, 1999, opening of the U.N. General Assembly, Secretary-General Kofi Annan stated that there is nothing in the U.N. Charter [which] "precludes a recognition that there are rights beyond borders." What we are seeing is that our "interconnectedness" is being expanded at every turn so that we all become responsible for each other which is collectivism.

Since 1948, some sixty human rights treaties and declarations have been negotiated, and include the Convention on the Prevention and Punishment of the Crime of Genocide, the International Convention on the Elimination of All Forms of Racial Discrimination, the Convention on the Elimination of All Forms of Discrimination Against Women, the Convention on the Rights of the Child, and many others. Our Constitution gives us unlimited and inalienable rights—rights that come from God, not government, and they cannot be taken away. When you define what a "right" or "human right" is, you have just limited the number of rights a person or country has.

This book will address a number of the components of the one-world government agenda. After considering how this global philosophy is seeping into society through the Hegelian dialectic, we will look at the governmental structure of the United Nations and international law. In chapter two we will consider the various components that constitute the new form of government that has been set up in place of the Constitution. Our federal government, which has been reinvented in the last six years through the leadership of Vice President Al Gore, is set to transfer all remaining power down to the communities—a bottom-up form of power versus a top-down approach as stated in our Constitution. What remains of the federal government will be dissolved through a national emergency as power is transferred to the international level—the United Nations.

Then, as it pertains to economic and natural disasters, we will consider in chapter eight how our fire/rescue/emergency management services have been and are in the process of being interconnected globally to not only better protect the citizens of the world against a disaster, but to also track down terrorists. In a recent speech, FBI director Louis Freeh provided the Senate with a description of a domestic terrorist. His definition helps us to understand reasons for the local to the global police, fire/rescue infrastructure.

Finally, we will consider the International Criminal Court, which was set up in 1998, after fifty years of hard work and maneuvering.

For the first time in history, this court will have the power to *transcend the sovereignty of individual countries and arrest someone if, according to the claims of special interest groups,* that person is guilty of a crime against humanity, a war crime, or genocide. Written within the International Criminal Court document is the process by which any individual can be deemed a terrorist. Nongovernmental organizations—any of the accredited United Nations NGOs—have the power to go to the ICC, present documentation, and have a person arrested. The case of Augusto Pinochet should be watched very carefully. Anyone who might be considered a terrorist now has a place to be tried.

During the summer of 1998, we saw the stock market drop two thousand points for a short period of time, only to regain all of its lost territory in a three-week period in October after Congress passed the Omnibus Budget Act which gave additional powers to the International Monetary Fund (IMF) and the World Bank (WB), as well as eighteen billion dollars to the IMF. After this power was transferred, the stock market recovered as if nothing happened. We were subjected to an incredible orchestration from powerful authorities worldwide as to the severe serious situation which America and the world was in. If the stock and currency markets of the world can be manipulated, what else can be manipulated for the objectives of those who manipulate world government?

Furthermore, you will read about the "new" political agenda called communitarianism or the Third Way which basically is "reinvented communism." In this philosophy, individualism and individual rights have to fade away. In commenting on this, George C. Lodge writes:

> Individualism is the epitome of the American dream, but in many ways its dreamlike characteristics have hidden the fact that the United States was and increasingly is a communitarian country. Individualism continues to be remarkably resilient (to buffeting by communitarian practices), as 1995 Republican rhetoric revealed. "They are," says Samuel Huntington, "at the very core of

> [our] national identity. Americans cannot abandon them without
> ceasing to be Americans in the most meaningful sense of the
> word—without, in short, becoming un-American." This is why the
> transition [to communitarianism] requires a good deal of crisis,
> and realistic leadership that can interpret the crisis accurately to
> make it useful instead of wasteful.
>
> —Lodge, 93–94

The purpose of this book is to expose and explain, and to help those who will be "end-time servants" (*see Appendix A*) to prepare to stand in the gap in whatever way they are directed by the Lord. This is not a how-to book, but a "for-your-information-only" book. Hopefully it will prompt those who want to be used of God to understand the truth about current events and to help them prepare mentally, spiritually, and emotionally for the days ahead.

This book is not all-encompassing. In order to be so, it would have to be at least five times its current size. The agenda of world government, i.e. the United Nations, is so big, vast, deep, and broad that once you understand the agenda, you will see it in your neighborhood, your school, your church, the newspapers, and local, federal, and international politics. It is so pervasive, it stinks to high heaven. In Cairo, I was amazed to pick up a brochure that listed all of the follow-up meetings across the United States that were already planned to carry the Cairo Programme of Action (agenda) further. I had no idea that there were nongovernmental organizations like Planned Parenthood of America, SEICUS, Zero Population, etc., already positioned to carry the U.N. agenda of abortion and condom distribution into the schools, family planning clinics, etc., across America.

I do not have time and space to discuss outcome-based education or school-to-work and their part in a global educational program or regional government. The U.S. is divided up into nine regions. The government we know will dissolve into "regional government" which pigtails into U.N. regional government, world religion, the World Trade Organization, a world army, or NATO.

On many occasions, I have asked myself why more people don't recognize what is happening around them. In reading Jeremiah, I found my answer. In 5:21 it says: "O foolish people, and without understanding; which have eyes, and see not; which have ears, and hear not." Then in Jeremiah 13:17 it says: "But if ye will not hear it, my soul shall weep in secret places for your pride." Other verses confirming Jeremiah 5:21 include Deuteronomy 29:4, Ezekiel 12:2, Psalm 115:5, Luke 8:10, Psalm 53:2, Isaiah 42:18–20, Isaiah 6:9–15, and Acts 28:31. It is as a result of an individual's pride, rebellion, and foolishness, that he cannot see, hear, or understand. Jeremiah states in 17:10: "I the LORD search the heart, I try the reins, even to give every man according to his ways, and according to the fruit of his doings." I believe that this applies even to Christians, for there are many Christians who cannot see, hear, or understand the day and the hour.

Dear reader, you must determine, much like those who have gone before us, just what you should do and how you should stand. There is no recipe or procedure manual for what you must do, only examples of those who have gone before us. This book is not written to create fear, but to inform so you may be bold. You must determine what truth is. I do not ask you to take my word for it, but research *my* research and ask God to show you His Truth. There is a difference between fear and faith. Of the spies who searched out the Promised Land, only two brought truth—"We can defeat the enemies, God is with us"—while the others said, "They are too big—they are giants, there are a lot of them, and we can't do it." This book is to help you understand the giants we face. Caleb, one of the original spies who God favored because "he wholly followed the Lord my God," was eighty-five years old when he asked Joshua for his inheritance according to what Moses had promised. He was given Hebron, which was the land of the giants. By faith, he possessed the land (Josh. 14).

Interestingly enough, Jesus Christ was *born into* world government. The early church certainly understood the rules of Rome and worked around and through it without becoming part of it or adding to it. In contrast, the end-time church is *going into* world government without knowing or understanding their agenda, and therefore blind as to the hour and how to stand in the gap. It is this lack of understanding which makes them ripe for compliance. This compliance equates the selling of their birthright!

Each of us has a role to play in end-time events. You must protect your mind, heart, and soul so that you do not miss your opportunity to stand in the gap. This is the last reason for why I wrote the book. If we understand the day and hour and the philosophical/ spiritual battle at hand, we then know how to pray and God will tell us what we need to do to stand in the gap.

> Then Mordecai commanded to answer Esther, Think not with thyself that thou shalt escape in the king's house, more than all the Jews. For if thou altogether holdest thy peace at this time, then shall there enlargement and deliverance arise to the Jews from another place; but thou and thy father's house shall be destroyed: and who knoweth whether thou art come to the kingdom for such a time as this?
>
> —Esther 4:13–14

Foreword

Moving the World Electronically into World Government

CHAPTER SUMMARY

In the aftermath of Y2K, many have been wondering exactly what all the hype was in the first place. Was Y2K real or imagined, was it built up to provide a cover for the real agenda and/or were we hoodwinked? The following combines my views before and after December 31, 1999/January 1, 2000.

—Joan Veon

In the last five years I have covered, as a reporter, thirty-five U.N. and U.N.-related conferences on a number of continents. It was my first conference in 1994 which made me realize that we are in a time of world government. It is my opinion that while the beginnings of world government began long ago, I believe the current world governmental infrastructure was begun between 1941 and 1943, with the passage of the United Nations Charter by the United States government in 1945 as its official birthday. In this regard, I have authored two books. The first, *Prince Charles: The Sustainable Prince*, deals with the behind-the-scenes role of the British royal family and their power and influence on the United Nations agenda as a way of bringing America back under their control. The second, *The United Nations' Global Straitjacket*, is a handbook dealing with the political, economic, and environmental aspects of the world governmental structure which has been erected on the international level above us. All that is needed to bring this understanding into the forefront of everyone's understanding on the local level, in my opinion, is a planned (because everything is planned), managed catastrophic event to make the transition from the world we know in America which is based on the United States Constitution to that of recognizable world government based on the United Nations Charter.

In the first edition of *Global Straitjacket*, I projected that Y2K would do which have not been fulfilled (yet), will be fulfilled in a different way, or will never come to pass are:

1. It would present an excellent opportunity to move the United States and the world into "official" world government, that is we are currently living in world government, but because all of the people have yet to recognize it, a planned, managed and catastrophic event would be needed in order to effect a change in how we are governed from the Constitution to one of world government through the United Nations (fulfilled in a different way);

2. Put into effect all of President Clinton's Executive Orders (not yet). You don't issue orders unless you have a purpose and a reason. In this case, we will have to wait and see, and;

3. Cause starvation in third world countries (hopefully will never happen).

In view of the fact that the lights never went out on December 31, 1999, exactly what did happen through the Y2K process?

For two years the United States and the world prepared to fight a common enemy—one which has no face, borders, parliament, or president. We were told that as a result of poor programming back in the 1960s, insufficient space was made in computer memories for the rollover of the years into a new millennium. This problem was called "Y2K." We were told that if the hardware and billions of lines of software code were not fixed, the world could find itself in chaos. In 1997 *Newsweek* printed an article entitled "The Day the World Shuts Down" in which it listed all of the sectors of society—industry, the military, banking, medicine, communications, and electrical utilities—that are dependent on computers to run and microprocessors to facilitate the computer process. The article pointed out that buildings could shut down, air traffic control systems could go dead, the entire financial infrastructure could go haywire, military preparedness could be adversely affected, billing systems could get lost, and cardiac monitors in hospitals could get shut down (*Washington Times,* October 17, 1998, A2).

On the heels of a growing awareness two Y2K books came out which became bestsellers. Explaining the problem in a logical manner, one author, Michael S. Hyatt, offered three scenarios based on a survey of thirty-eight computer experts and year 2000 researches of what they predicted. The results pointed to either a blackout or a complete meltdown of the entire system. On top of that, numerous executive orders were issued which could shift the power of government to the Federal Emergency Management System in the case of a catastrophe.

In response to this ominous threat, the president issued Executive Order 13073 establishing the President's Council on Year 2000 Conversion in February 1998. The council is comprised of representatives from more than thirty major federal executive and regulatory agencies and charged with outreach into the public and private sectors, both domestic and internationally. John Koskinen was appointed to head up the council, a position which was given cabinet-level status. Since this posed a global threat, the United Nations held two well-attended Y2K conferences in December 1998 and June 1999 for all of the nation-states. They also set up the International Y2K Cooperation Center and a steering committee to fight this common foe. Furthermore, they instructed each nation-state to appoint a Y2K national coordinator who would be not only their country's liaison, but would be the key contact person for other countries, governments, agencies, organizations, and corporations as well.

BACKGROUND

While writing *Global Straitjacket* in late 1998-early 1999, I concluded in the middle of writing it that Y2K was going to be serious since it appeared to have all of the necessary requirements for a "planned, managed, and catastrophic event" to catapult us from "unofficial" world government, with the form of government and way of life which we have known, into "official" world government, where the rules we live by and the government structure we have known is replaced with new rules using the infrastructure which has been put in place since 1945 on the international level. As you see, I was incorrect when it came to a physical transfer, because Y2K was a transfer of the world from individual nation-states to a new electronically interconnected world which uses wires, computer processors, and electricity to cement the individual countries together!

From June 1998 until September 30, 1999, I believed Y2K was going to be very serious. My whole understanding underwent a "sea change" when I attended the 1999 Annual IMF/World Bank Meeting in Washington, D.C. At that key meeting where everything of importance is discussed, Y2K was a non-event—there were no rumblings or undertones about it. Since this was the last major economic conference for the year, and in light of several other high-level economic meetings earlier in the year where Y2K was a non-event, I concluded just that—a non event. If the "big boys" who run the world's monetary system were not concerned, then there was no reason to be concerned. Furthermore I realized these same "big boys" probably were not going to go out of 1999 on a market down, but they were going to go out on a major upswing (right before the IMF/World Bank meeting, the market dropped to a low for the year). I then realized and predicted that we would have one of the strongest bull markets ever. Furthermore, I made this statement at a number of conferences, on radio, and wrote about it in my September economic newsletter.

THE AGENDA

When there were no meltdowns, blackouts, or incidents of any kind on December 31, it was declared on national television, "The Y2K bug has been met and conquered." This statement, along with reading Y2K czar John Koskinen's press briefing provided me with new insight as to the real agenda behind the Y2K scare. I was correct with regard to "The Report from Iron Mountain" and a number of other observations, but I was obviously wrong with regard to a physical transition into "official" world government. Exactly what did Y2K do?

In addition to the things mentioned above, Y2K provided a once-in-a-lifetime opportunity for the nation-states of the world who were not Internet savvy to get wired. It provided an opportunity to transition business and government into a new working relationship which compliments reinvented government. It sets up an electronic network (brains) which is unparalleled in all of history. It spurred the economies of the world and set the tone for a cashless society, all of which facilitate world government and control.

When a new house is built, the foundation is laid, then the structure and roof are added on. The wiring allows for the structure to have power and for the builder to choose the type of power which that house is going to use. Y2K was the wiring of the house, as the structure has already been built for some time. Y2K provided the excuse to transfer the world from individual nation-states into an electronically knit world—a world which is now ONE and which includes both governments and corporations. Beginning January 1, 2000, we entered world government electronically!

A follow-up question then is, "Were we misled or deceived by our government as to the seriousness of the situation?" While each person will have to decide for him or herself, I believe Y2K had to be painted as being serious (and we are told that it was) in order to have sufficient reason to get Americans to agree with Congress that the money had to be spent. Telling American's that the real reason for Y2K is to get the world wired or telling them that we have to spend money to fight the Y2K bug because of all the damage it will do creates that unifying desire to "meet the enemy eye to eye and win"! With regard to foreign countries, many of them do not have and cannot provide the basics for their people, let alone spend monies on getting wired. In order for them to justify the re-positioning of critical dollars, a global problem had to be created.

This picture begins to make sense when you look at how the United Nations painted Y2K. It does appear that Y2K provided a once-in-a-lifetime opportunity for the nation-states of the world who were not Internet savvy to get wired. In a speech at the second U.N. conference on Y2K in June 1999, U.N. Deputy Secretary-General Louise Frechette said in part,

The Threat

The millennium bug threatens to disrupt finance, trade, shipping, telecommunications, air traffic control and other vital public services such as electricity and natural disaster preparedness. It casts a shadow over issues of peace and security.

The Solution

The International Y2K Cooperation Centre was created with re-markable speed following the [U.N.] meeting in December 1998. The number of countries with a Y2K plan and a national coordinator has risen. New coalitions are being forged among business, industry, governments, and international organizations. Such solidarity and problem-solving shows the United Nations in action. Working groups [have] forged innovative partnerships with all available expertise, including the private sector and academia; and it has facilitated the efforts of the Secretariat and wider United Nations family to create an electronic organization. Ambassador Ahmad Kamel [of Pakistan] helped all of us harness the Internet, e-mail and other new communications technologies to our global mission of peace, development and human rights.

The Goal

We must all continue to take advantage of what the new technologies have to offer—for diplomacy and development, for advocacy and education. We must all pursue a vision of a new century in which all people are [technologically] empowered.

From this speech, it becomes clear that the need to battle the "Y2K bug" was basically an excuse and opportunity to synchronize the whole world electronically in order to bring the lesser developed countries into the electronic age—a different agenda than what we had been told by the American press starts to emerge.

So what did Y2K do? Let's take a look at what was said by Koskinen at several press briefings in early January as well as look at several publications.

1. Electronic Network or Brains. The press briefings which John Koskinen gave in the first few days of this new millennium provided us with the real truth of what Y2K was—an excuse to "wage war" in order to integrate the world using an electronic medium which can only further erase borders, and make us ONE, facilitating global integration in a new way for a new century.

Koskinen outlined the following ways we were integrated (my word, not his):

A. *The United States created the $50 billion Information Coordination Center (ICC).* The ICC, which now is at the center for state and local governments, the private sector, multinational and transnational corporations, and our federal government to interact on a daily basis in order to coordinate all systems from an electronic basis point. In other words, it appears that the electronic brains of the global system was created in the United States to monitor and coordinate all of the perceived electronic problems in the world!

The ICC was established, designed, and run by General Peter Kind. It is an information collection mechanism focused on dealing with information from around the world, the country and various levels of government. Koskinen organized more than twenty-five task forces to reach out to industry groups, corporations, the United Nations, and foreign trading partners. He has collected confidential industry information to assess the potential Y2K risks (*Washington Post,* December 16, 1999, G8). Reports sent to the center came from all federal agencies, domestic agencies, the Federal Reserve Board, every area of the executive branch, and FEMA.

In explaining the vastness of the ICC, Koskinen said:

What we have [en]capsulated here in the Information Coordinator Center is a unique operation. Communication going on, back
and forth, with not only all of our embassies, but national coordi-
nators in over 100 countries around the world, all freely exchanging information back in forth for now, which is the final step in a
long process of exchanging technical information and advice over
the last couple of years. We have begun to look at the question of
how we can build on this sort of unprecedented amount of cooperation and work together.

Koskinen further boasted, as reported in *USA Today,* "Solving Y2K
proved that I can run the world with four people."

Interesting to note, at the 1996 United Nation's Habitat II conference, the secretary-general of that conference, Dr. Wally N'Dow
declared: "Now what we are doing here is building . . . the global
brain." N'Dow was discussing the cooperation found in partnerships with governments, corporations, and civil society. When you
"wire" this global brain, you get a powerful interconnectedness
which cannot be taken apart.

B. *On May 22, 1998, the Policy on Critical Infrastructure Protection program was released* which set up the "National Infrastructure Protection Center (NIPC), which includes the FBI, the Secret
Service, other federal law enforcement agencies, the Department
of Defense, and the intelligence agencies, which are all ordered to
cooperate with the NIPC." We will live in a totally controlled society where everyone cooperates for the sake of one another.

C. *Financial markets were coordinated from an information
standpoint both nationally and globally.* Every major financial institution created a Y2K committee. At the Bank for International
Settlements (BIS) in Basel, Switzerland, they held several Y2K coordinating meetings. The Market Authorities Communication Service was established for financial authorities and involves, and has
involved for some time, periodic conference calls between central
bankers and market regulators on a regular basis to determine at
key critical times if there were or are any issues which needed to

be discussed and dealt with (chapters five, six, and seven).

In short, if you could encapsulate what transpired, it would be that an x-ray was taken of every aspect of life, business, industry, manufacturing, communications, defense, police, fire, rescue operations, water, electric, gas, coal, natural resources, hospital services, the operations of local, county, municipal, state, and federal governments in order to determine how to change the system from what it was to meet that of twenty-first century global governance using technology.

2. Partnerships. Joe Lockhart, White House spokesman, said this about Y2K: "I think the Y2K success story to date is very much a testament to the government working in partnership with local governments, communities, and corporations."

At the heart of Bill Clinton's "Reinventing Government" program begun in 1993 is a new form of government which is based on partnership—public-private partnerships, which is a marriage between government, business, and non-governmental organizations (NGOs). In the old days, this was known as fascism. Throughout the United States, this new governmental form has been replacing representative government, rendering politicians nothing more than paper pushers as the multinational and transnational corporations use their deep pockets to fund projects which heretofore had been the responsibility of county, local, municipal, state, and federal governments.

For example in the area of utilities, there are thirty-two hundred independent electric utilities in which electric power is generated—fifty-one percent by coal, twenty percent by nuclear energy, fifteen percent by gas, and ten percent by hydro. In order to come together, it required numerous levels of interaction: the Department of Energy (federal government), the Federal Energy Regulatory Commission to coordinate Y2K remediation efforts, the Nuclear Regulatory Commission, the Rural Utility Service, the Environmental Protection Agency, the Securities and Exchange Commission (federal agencies), the North American Electric Reliability Council (non-federal entity, state public utility commission), along with the American Public Power Association, the Electric Power Research Institute, the National Rural Electric Cooperative Association, Edison Electric Institute, the Nuclear Energy Institute, and the Canadian Electric Association (associations/institutes) (Source: *Senate Special Committee on the Year 2000 Technology Program*, published February 24, 1999). Most of the associations represent electric companies.

With regard to state and local government, in addition to the fifty state governments, there are three thousand sixty-eight county government jurisdictions, and approximately eighty-seven thousand other local government jurisdictions in the United States. In order to help these governments deliver police, fire, and emergency medical services response, financial support networks, welfare, and Medicaid, unemployment insurance, basic utilities such as water and wastewater, sanitation and local transportation, numerous intergovernmental councils and professional organizations were engaged: the National League of Cities, the National Association of Counties, the International City/County Management Association, as well as the National Governor's Association which focused on state, local, and private-sector coordination and on establishing a common agenda" (*Senate Special Committee on the Year 2000 Technology Program*, 113). In addition, you will see that there was an interconnectedness which occurred between the local fire, police, and rescue, and the global level. This was facilitated by the Federal Emergency Management Agency (FEMA), and a number of international fire, police, and rescue organizations.

We were told that in order to defeat the Y2K bug, it was necessary for government and business, industry, and manufacturing, along with their respective associations to come together and form partnerships in order to "fight it," when it now appears to be clear that the real reason was to wire the world.

In early January 2000, Koskinen said:

We have private sector associations and industries headquartered right now in federal agencies working together hand in glove, exchanging information, to make sure that, if there are any issues, we all deal with them immediately. Again, we have been doing that for the last 18 months or so, [and] we hope that there are productive ways to continue and build upon this infrastructure that now exists but it won't happen automatically. We have connectivity and information exchange, both ways, going on between the federal governments, state and local governments, and private sector industries across the United States.

Lastly, there were several other permanent partnerships which were created to fight Y2K. U.S. Energy Secretary Bill Richardson and his Russian counterpart created a permanent partnership in the area of energy (*Washington Post*, January 4, 2000, A13). In addition, the United States and Russia created a joint team to monitor Y2K from the U.S. Space Command at Peterson Air Force Base in Colorado Springs. This agreement was set up under an agreement signed in 1998 by Defense Secretary William Cohen and his Russian counterpart, Marshal Igor D. Sergeyev. Ultimately the experiment begun will evolve into a permanent Joint Warning Center to be built near Moscow and staffed by officers from both countries (*Washington Post*, December 31, 1999, A29).

3. Provided Corporations with a Leading Edge for the 21st Century. *Business Week* declared that the "Y2K Bug Repellent Wasn't a Waste," as it

ultimately it forced some companies to rethink the role of technology. With new, more "robust" networks in place, companies can take full advantage of the Web and e-commerce to streamline their businesses and reach new markets. [It] forced companies and government agencies all over the world to get rid of buggy old software and aging hardware and invest in new technology. Now systems are in place to provide a solid foundation for all sorts of new online systems for e-commerce and e-government.

Furthermore, it allowed some companies to now hook up all their employees to the Net for the first time, making it possible to share information and coordinate activities of different operations. The government was able to get rid of around twenty percent of their old systems. DaimlerChrysler got rid of fifteen thousand old computer programs and made it possible for two-thirds of its plants to connect with each other on the same network for the first time, all for a cost of $260 million. Technology departments had new discipline imposed by Y2K. Marriott's Y2K czar, Ina Kamenz said, "We've got tougher standards in place for the installation, purchase and care of technology" (*Business Week,* January 17, 2000, 35). Lastly, e-commerce reduces the cost of doing business. Overall most industries will save between five and fifteen percent.

4. Spurred the Economies of the World—An Economic Substitute for War. It was the Kennedy administration which commissioned fifteen hand-chosen men who were experts in their own chosen fields to come together and determine what would have to change in America if we were to enter a permanent time of peace. This top secret report was published by one of the fifteen whose identity to this day is still unknown. Their conclusions stated that we would have to find another enemy than our fellow man. They suggested the environment. Since war is an economic stimulus, they determined that ten percent of our Gross Domestic Product would have to be wasted per year. They suggested a number of ways to do that: a space program, medical research, free housing for the poor, etc.

In the first edition of *Global Straitjacket,* I suggested that the cost to fix Y2K would more than pay for any global war. To fight this enemy, the United States government spent over $8.5 billion and the country, as a whole, spent $100 billion. In comparison, the cost of the Vietnam War was $300 billion over a ten year period. Our legislature made numerous arrangements to accommodate the problems multinational and transnational corporations would encounter. Special legislation was passed giving them immunity from Y2K lawsuits. Small companies were given a special one-time tax write-off, limited to $40,000, for the expenses they would incur in fixing their antiquated and obsolete computer systems. Furthermore we assisted numerous foreign countries, including Russia and China. The global cost is estimated at $600 billion.

To what do we credit NASDAQ's stellar rise of 85.6 percent? I believe it was a combination of the spending to "fix" computers, i.e. to bring the rest of the nation-states on line, as well as a birthing of a new electronic era in business, industry, society, and politics.

The performance of the stock market reflects spending to stimulate the economy in the absence of war, as 1999 witnessed the greatest rise in our stock market's history since 1914. Besides the NASDAQ, the Dow was up twenty-five percent, and the Standard and Poor up nineteen percent. It only took thirty-eight trading days for the NASDAQ to climb from three thousand to four thousand. Internet stocks were hot at the beginning and end of 1999. The cover of the seventieth anniversary edition of *Business Week* in October 1999 showed two hands edged in yellow to simulate a power surge with the two index fingers extended to meet. The cover read, "The Internet Age." In 1998 Charles Schwab emerged as the giant of online trading, controlling thirty percent of the market and half of the assets in online accounts. In an effort to catch up, Merrill Lynch & Co. and Morgan Stanley Dean Witter were both working on plans to be offered later in 1999. Instead of television commercials telling you to call their representatives, brokers are now competing for online traders. The December 27, 1999/January 3, 2000, *Business Week* reflected what happened in 1999 as it read, "Smart Investing for the Internet Age Where to Invest."

What is the product which the Internet stocks are touting? Is it tangible like steel, automobiles, food, or housing? No, it is knowledge—an intangible something you cannot see or show, but something that gives you the edge over your competition. This alone has prompted politicians and economists alike to call it the "new economy" as all of the rules for business, the economy, and investing are changing. Does the price/earnings ratio still have relevance in the new economy? Time will tell.

The rash of Internet initial public offerings made millionaires of people. At the end of the first trading day after E-Loan went public, the stock rose one hundred sixty-four percent, increasing its value to $1.4 billion. VA Linus shares went public at $30 and rose to $299 per share in ten days, making the company worth more than $9.5 billion—more than Black and Decker, the steelmaker USX, or Wigley (*Financial Times,* December 21, 1999, 14).

In commenting on the 1999 market rally, Allen Sinai, chief global economist at Primark Decision Economics said, "The powerful rallies, and particularly the strength in the NASDAQ, is a sign of the global economy picking up and continued prosperity in the United States. There is no end in sight."

Those looking into the future now predict that besides smart toys, a smart card, smart computers, and cars will be "smart appliances" where the refrigerator will be able to tell you which items you need to reorder. Time has moved from that of a graceful society where there was time to be polite and to smell the roses to one of real time in which knowledge is not only instant but power.

5. Set the Tone for a Cashless Society. In a society where everything is cashless—American Express, Visa/MasterCard, etc., where we can go anywhere and obtain cash through our check cashing card, where everything can be done through the telephone or by Internet—the next thing to be fully changed is the monetary system. In 1999 there was a concerted effort to make gold obsolete. In 1998 a number of central banks declared their intentions to sell up to fifty percent of their gold holdings in order to diversify and invest in interest-producing investments. This prompted the value of gold to drop to a twenty-five–year low of $255 an ounce. In response, a number of highly indebted poor countries were caught in a global squeeze as their indebtedness far exceeds the proceeds received from their gold mining sales. Is gold obsolete? For those who understand the possibility of the electronic age to "lose account records," they also know the need to own gold.

The bottom line? While an electronic system increases production, reduces costs, eliminates waste, and basically makes everything sustainable, it is also capable of tracking every individual, rendering them nothing but individual production units with value for as long as they can produce.

CONCLUSION

In the first edition of *Global Straightjacket,* I wrote that Y2K would: (1) require global compliance in ways that companies would never adhere to as they now had to account to numerous government agencies; (2) cause local, state, national, and international agencies to interact with each other about disaster relief and other issues which comprised a new level of global cooperation, all of which were needed for global government (chapter eight); (3) present a multitude of problems for which the U.N. and its nation-states must find solutions; (4) provide an excellent opportunity to merge the world's policemen, firemen, emergency management systems, military forces, national guardsmen, etc.; (5) transfer wealth from the rich countries to the poor countries (chapter eight); (6) reinforce the implementation of "reinvented government" at the community level (chapter two); and (7) equate the economic stimulus of war without a real war through the expenditures of monies, a goal which "The Report from Iron Mountain" said would be necessary in the absence of war (chapter four). It appears that all of the above is "right on the money."

Koskinen said:

We view this, not only in the federal government, not only in the state and local governments but in the private sector around the world, as a great accomplishment, meeting what I continue to believe is the most significant management challenge the world has faced in 50 years. Y2K has taught all of us that the amount of reliance that we have on information technology now, the fact that the famous global economy is increasingly linked electronically, and over the next 5 to 10 years, all of that reliance, and all of that interconnectedness will increase, not decrease. If nothing else, the whole question of information security will become more and more critical to everyone around the world, not just the United States.

Lastly, in addition to a major rewiring of the world so that we are all on the same "electrical system," the celebrations which we witnessed on television on December 31, 1999, and the comments made by those who moderated sent a clear message—"We are one." On the PBS station which I watched, the moderator said: "In a sense, the lines between nations and borders are our own contrivance. As we go from capital to capital tonight to ring in the new millennium, we can see that we are one on earth—we are one people united." The songs sang worldwide had a common theme—"peace." Even the Queen of England joined in the celebrations at the Millennium Dome, singing a peace song. Bill Clinton in his millennium address called for a "just and lasting peace."

Tell me, were we hoodwinked? We must keep our options open as we may not have seen the last of Y2K since Executive Orders mean something and the ICC means something.

Chapter 1

The Hegelian Dialectic
and the New World Order

CHAPTER SUMMARY

My grave concern is that the Christian community—at the time in
history when it should "stand in the gap"—will be unwittingly processed through the Hegelian dialectic into world government without even realizing it.
—Joan Veon

This chapter will introduce you to the "Hegelian dialectic" which
is named after its originator, Frederic Hegel. It is the process which
the communists and Marxists have adopted as a way of gradually
changing the opinions of people and society. This "step-by-step"
process has been adopted by all levels of government and is used
as the "visioning process" in town meetings by county and city
land planners, and by other groups and organizations implementing the global agenda. As a result, American society has been moved
away from the concepts found in the United States Constitution to
those in the United Nations Charter. All of this has been done so
smoothly that people who are not cognizant of the Hegelian dialectic process are unaware. A great example is some of the Satur-
day even programs in which reporters from both sides review the
week's events.

I point out that in trying to alert a number of well-known Christian and family organizations about the United Nations and their
activities, I was not successful in getting their attention or response.
This then led to great concern over the blackout on world govern-

ment which is apparent. Either they are so high up they cannot see below their noses, or they understand the agenda they are protecting, which means that what they are doing is *containment.* By restricting the information, the real response that one would have is reduced. Our response to hold back unrighteousness has been contained while evil has flourished.

For years, many Americans have been blind to the activities happening all around them. These activities are described in this book and will put us in great bondage. My grave concern is that the Christian community, at the most critical time in history, when they should be alert so the can *stand in the gap,* unwittingly will be processed through the Hegelian dialectic, into world government without realizing they have agreed to it.

In order to protect yourself, in order to stand, in order to fulfill your God-given mandate, you must be familiar with the very complex and evil agenda which has been woven together on the international level—the level which in world government operates. This is not the time to be asleep but alert, for "the devil as a roaring lion seeketh whom he may devour."

INTRODUCTION

In the last four and a half years while covering the United Nations, I have come face to face, on a regular basis, with communism, fascism, and socialism. I found, as a result of my own ignorance, that I could not identify those "isms" and therefore could not identify the true meaning of what was being put forth in all of the United Nations documents I was reading. While I understood the goal of world government to be behind everything the United Nations was doing, I did not know how—what *modus operandi*—they would use to convert people from a capitalistic system where the individual is the master and molder of his own destiny undergirded by personal property rights reinforcing his claim to that destiny, to one of complete control where man does what the State directs, when the State directs, and in the process gives up his freedoms and private property so the State could better direct its use. I then found that the *modus operandi* being used for this transition was called the "Hegelian dialectic" which is comprised of three parts: the thesis, antithesis, and synthesis. It was Friedrich Engles, a German philosopher, who developed what is now called the Hegelian dialectic in the mid-1850s.

> Hegel basically said that ideas repressed bred its opposite and the two merged into a synthesis which in turn produced its own contradiction. This philosophy took the name of dialectic materialism: dialectical because it incorporated Hegel's idea of inherent change, and materialism because it grounded itself not in the world of ideas, but on the terrain of social and physical environment.
>
> —Heibroner, pp. 134–35

I immediately understood that the concepts being espoused at the U.N. were not concepts which I had grown up with or been taught. I saw that everything at the U.N. was constantly changing. There were always problems. It appeared that the U.N. could not fix anything, for they were always "refixing." Little did I know "the fixing" was part of the plan as a way to further their agenda and gain more power. I first heard the word "consensus" in Cairo when I attended my first U.N. conference in September 1994. When a journalist asked for a definition, he was given a ten-minute answer which didn't make sense but included the phrase, "everyone agreed on something in the document and therefore that was consensus." Another word I heard at these meetings was "diversity."

When I covered the United Nations Social Summit in Copenhagen in March 1995, then Secretary-General Boutros Boutros-Ghali said that change had three steps, "profound change, cosmetic change, and status quo," but he was offering an alternative, "constant change." He said: "You need continuous change. . . . To act . . . you must maintain a mobilization between all three for continuous change." It was at that conference that I first heard the phrase "paradigm shift."

Recently I interviewed Dean Gotcher, an expert in the Hegelian dialectic. Mr. Gotcher explained that the Hegelian dialectic is a specific psychological method used with diverse groups to "dialogue to consensus." He said Hegel's process, which was revolutionary in his day, has now become the basic tool for developing and supporting the universal world view of the New World Order. All forms of socialism (fascism, communism, existentialism, positivism, pragmatism . . . globalism) are unthinkable without the aspects of Hegel's formula.

THE HEGELIAN DIALECTIC—
A TOOL OF THE NEW WORLD ORDER

In the book *Spiritual Politics* by Corinne McLaughlin and Gordon Davidson (Ballantine Books, New York, 1994), the authors cite the importance of the Hegelian dialectic as being the process whereby

> we have to go to a higher level and transcend the polarities [opinions and differences that people have]. It was Hegel's view that all things unfold in a continuing evolutionary process whereby each idea or quality (the thesis) inevitably brings forth its opposite (the antithesis). From that interaction, **a third state emerges in which the opposites are integrated, overcome, and fulfilled in a richer and higher synthesis.** This synthesis then becomes the basis for another dialectical process of opposition and synthesis [emphasis mine].

Dean explained the Hegelian dialectic this way:

> The process is built on three stages which are more complex than what we are seeing with outcome-based education, total quality management, and school-to-work. There is the **thesis,** which is you and your position, and is based on facts and what you believe [God]. **Antithesis** is somebody who's different from you. For example, the moment the two of you, who are different, are in the same room, there's a potential relationship. However, the only

way you can get to it is **synthesis** [agreement in the relationship]. You and the other person have to put your differences aside for the sake of a relationship and try to find facts or elements in your belief systems which are in harmony. **This process of changing your position to blend with someone else basically is how socialism works.** Eventually if that becomes your agenda—the dialectic way of thinking, a socialist cosmic mind—it puts *aside* anything that gets in the way of the relationship.

A mind-changing technique that is used is the Delphi technique (see Appendix A).

In other words, the Hegelian dialectic is the process used to get a person to change their beliefs to match those who want them to change their beliefs. A simple example would be the person who tells his virgin lover, "If you loved me, you would show me by . . ."

The Hegelian dialectic is all around us. Every time the absolutes of the Christian faith are attacked, it eventually leads to a change in values when the person involved gives in and sacrifices their values for the sake of the relationship or situation. For example, to many senior Americans nudity in any form is repugnant (and it should be). However, the younger generation thinks nothing of partial or total nudity in a movie or in an advertisement. What happened? The Hegelian dialectic. People moved from their absolute position to one of complacency and consent over a period of time. As Hollywood exposed a little more and nothing was said by the public, they continued. How many people oppose *Cosmopolitan* or the yearly swimsuit issue of *Sports Illustrated?*

What is happening in the world is dialectic—we have been processed over a period of time from being a republic (Constitution) to a democracy (John Kennedy started popularizing that term) to one of world government—all unknowingly, of course. If I had not attended any United Nations conferences, I would not be able to recognize *most* of the concepts based on world government that are being forced on the American people. *WE THE PEOPLE* are being taken from the position of *thesis*—Constitution, individual freedoms,

personal property rights, and free speech—to one of *antithesis*—
the United Nations Charter and Declaration of Human Rights, collective action for the good of the whole (elimination of individual
needs), limited personal property rights for the sake of the environment, and politically correct thinking, all of which create a new
structure, the *synthesis*. What I have just defined is socialism and
is incorporated in Al Gore's "Reinventing Government" program.

**My grave concern is that the Christian community—at the
time in history when it should "stand in the gap"—will be unwittingly processed through the Hegelian dialectic into world government without even realizing it.** You say, "How could this happen?" The answer is, since the Christian church is not knowledgeable about the international level of government, it is not in a position to recognize how our freedoms are being lost. When a planned
catastrophic event is used as the excuse or reason for why the structure and way of life in America has to change, it will agree and
cooperate, not realizing it has just been processed through the
Hegelian dialectic from constitutional government to world government, thus giving up its God-given rights for man-made and
controlled rights.

THE CURRENT CHRISTIAN & FAMILY STATES OF AFFAIRS

The following is something I do not normally speak about. However, I feel that it is extremely important and needs to be disclosed in
order to make a very serious point. All of the following is firsthand
experience.

While attending conferences subsequent to the U.N. Conference on Population and Development in Cairo, all that I knew about
life, Bible prophecy, and politics came into question. What I dis-
covered was a very far advanced form of world government, which
I was told by many Bible prophecy experts was not yet here. If I
thought that was difficult, I had a more shocking wake-up call when
I learned that our greatest enemy is not the other side, but ourselves and those on "our" side. For example in intelligence work, I
am told that the most important thing to know is who your enemies

are. Intelligence experts have an expression, "Your friend is your enemy and your enemy is your friend." How is that for logical thinking! However, the prophet Elijah certainly knew that his enemies were not only the king, who did not want to hear what God wanted him to know, but all of the prophets (false) who surrounded the king and said everything was fine. I found that we have more false prophets than we know. Unfortunately, some of the biggest names in Christendom are questionable.

Cairo

In September 1994, I attended my first *international* conference sponsored by the United Nations—the U.N. Conference on Population and Development in Cairo. There I came to understand that the international level of leadership—the level above the federal or national level—was very far advanced in the establishment of a world government structure. What I saw, heard, and experienced as a naive American was shocking to my whole system of values and knowledge. Everything I believed on the national level was a lie when I considered the international level where world government was operating! In addition, I heard our political leaders—from Al Gore to my (former—I moved) congresswoman Constance Morella—discuss concepts and philosophies against which the American people would rebel if they knew about them. My only consolation, or so I thought, was that the Christian Broadcasting Network (CBN) was there. I was so excited and pleased to know that this conference was being reported to many. I assumed CBN was exposing world government. It did not.

I came home from Cairo very upset as a result of what I had seen and experienced. And I became livid when I read the major newspaper accounts of what they said had occurred. It was then I realized that all of the mainstream media was conducting a blackout on the truth about what these conferences were and how far advanced world government is.

Since I brought home a suitcase full of U.N. materials, I felt the need to put together my first briefing book, *U.N. Conferences and*

Goals: How They Will Affect the Family, the Church and Society. I asked God what I should do with it, and felt the need to mail it to every major Christian organization. It went to everyone you or I would normally think of—Focus on the Family, Concerned Women for America, Charles Stanley, D. James Kennedy, the American Family Association, etc. I did not send it directly to them; I used people with connections. For example, a good friend of mine who has written several nationally recognized books and knows Dr. Kennedy personally, was kind enough to write a cover letter and mail the briefing book to him.

From all of these organizations, I received one response—from the Family Research Council. They promised to put it in their research files.

Because I live near Washington, D.C., I called CBN and asked to speak to the gentleman who was in Cairo. When he answered the telephone, I told him that I had put together a briefing book on the U.N. and that the next U.N. conference, the Social Summit (to be held in Copenhagen in March 1995) would unveil a world tax. I asked if I could see him. He was interested and so we went to lunch. During lunch I went through my briefing book and explained how far advanced the U.N. agenda was and its quest for world government. He was sincerely shocked to see the big picture and commented that he had "no idea that it was this far." He then looked around to see who was close to us and who could listen in. When I pressed him to get CBN to go to the next U.N. mega-conference in Copenhagen, he said, "I need to tell you something off the record." He said, "Pat Robertson isn't fighting the new world order any more, he has joined it." I looked at him and told him, "You haven't told me anything that I did not already know. You only confirmed it." Unfortunately, I had begun to see a disturbing trend within the Christian community.

I had never been a journalist or reporter before going to Cairo and therefore did not know how to get credentialed by a news media. A friend of mine, at the time, who was instrumental in raising my awareness about Cairo, was a member of a Southern Baptist church. Before I knew it, I was credentialed by the *Southern Baptist Press* to go to Cairo. The only way you can attend these conferences is to be credentialed as a journalist or as a nongovernmental organization. The *Southern Baptist Press* said they wanted a short report on Cairo. As a result of my experiences, I wrote a rather lengthy report which I felt was necessary in order to explain the whole agenda of world government. The *Press* told me it was too long. I then took that same report, reduced it, and divided it up into two reports, which was in line with what they wanted. It was never published. I was told that they felt their readers "would not be interested."

Copenhagen

During the course of researching the U.N. from their materials, I stumbled upon information about the U.N.'s desire to press for a world tax in Copenhagen, the site of their next mega-conference. The John Birch Society was represented in Cairo by one reporter. When I uncovered the "alternative agenda" to get the world to consider a world tax, I called him and asked if his group was sending him to Copenhagen. He told me "no." I told him he had to go because I had uncovered the real agenda, which was a world tax. He was immediately interested. He asked if I could fax him my research. I both faxed and "overnighted" it, along with my briefing book showing the whole agenda. He called me back and asked if he could use it. I thought about it and responded, "I don't have the outlet that you do to get the news out. Go ahead." *The New American* did a special report on the global tax. I would have been pleased, except that they forgot to even credit me as a source. I again was learning something about the "conservative right."

I pressed other groups and organizations to try and get them to go to these conferences. I had no response. In fairness to the Southern Baptists, Dr. Richard Land, who heads up their Christian ethics division, and another man attended the Social Summit in Copenhagen. While I understood the agenda, they did not, nor did they take the time to read my briefing book (at their request, I sent them a second because they had misplaced the first), nor did they try to figure out firsthand what was going on. When I asked one of the ladies who accompanied me to Copenhagen what they were doing, she replied, "Joan, it is really sad. They walk around all day with their coats on staring at walls [lots of propaganda posters on the walls]." Since the U.N. hosts many workshops to inform and teach their world view, I asked if they were going to any of the workshops. *That* they did not know. Dr. Land subsequently decided to leave the conference early, as there "was nothing really happening."

Beijing

As the Fourth Women's Conference in Beijing (September 1995) approached, I spoke with Focus on the Family senior vice president Tom Minnery with whom I had been corresponding regarding the United Nations. Mr. Minnery was going to Beijing. I was ecstatic. After speaking with him, I faxed him a note that there would be no way that he would *not* see the world government agenda, as it would hit him in the face. I wrote that I hoped the focus of the ministry would change in order to help people understand what is really going on in the world. "Focus" came back, talked about how horrible the women's agenda was, and dropped the whole subject of the real agenda—world government.

Bill Bright

For many years my husband and I supported three Campus Crusade for Christ missionaries. In addition, we had given large (what we consider large) amounts for the support of the *Jesus* film. We believed in the ministry. However, I had an experience while trying to tell Bill Bright about the United Nations and world government that completely threw me off guard. Several years ago at a National Religious Broadcasters conference in California I attempted to give him a copy of my briefing book, *The United Nations and Its Global Agenda for the Environment, Economy, and Family* (which

Hearthstone published). He quickly called for his wife Vonette by turning his back on me so that I could not see his expression and handed me off to her as soon as he could. Vonette, who was very gracious as I explained where God has led me, basically made some "air-puffed" promises and concluded our discussion. This rattled me, as I did not expect to be treated like some kind of weirdo. I was wearing one of my most expensive suits and did not think I looked or sounded like one!

Either these people in high places are so high up they cannot see below their noses, or they understand the agenda they are protecting. If it is the first, they are in big trouble with God! If it is the second, they are in big trouble as false prophets and, therefore, in big trouble with God! There are those who would say they probably don't understand the agenda. I would have to counter with the fact that they operate on the international level and interact with very powerful politicians and businessmen. When you become acquainted with the international firsthand, it is very apparent.

Property Rights Groups
On the other side of the spectrum from family groups are the property rights groups. Environmental Conservation Organization (ECO) which actively works under an umbrella organization, Sovereignty International, is looking to make a difference at U.N. conferences. In fact, I had an extensive conversation with Henry Lamb of ECO/Sovereignty International who told me in July 1998 that they want a "seat at the U.N. table." I told him there was no way possible for them to have a seat without giving up their position and consenting to the U.N. agenda. He differed. I asked him if he had read *Prince Charles: The Sustainable Prince,* in which I outline the powers behind the U.N., and he said he had read it. I told him he was siding with an antichrist power and that having a seat would be joining them. Either we stand or we fall. It is one or the other. There is no compromise with evil—with those who would take our freedoms and then put us in a straitjacket where we cannot defend ourselves.

Containment

In October 1995 I was referred to a woman who has been studying world government for many years. Virginia Meves, a former medical missionary, and I met at a restaurant near the Milwaukee airport. Within five minutes of our meeting, she was able to help me understand what I had not been able to put into words. I told her how difficult it was to travel to all of these conferences and learn about an agenda for world domination in conflict with our Constitution (and based on the U.N. Charter). I explained that what was even worse was the fact that Christian and family groups were not interested in understanding the hideous agenda, and that it appeared that the conservative groups were not interested either. I had tried and tried, but was getting nowhere with them. In one word she said it all. As I expressed my frustration with all of these groups, which could be our "salvation," she said, "Don't you know they have their own agenda, which is **containment!**" It was as if a pie hit me in the face.

Containment means that your knowledge and understanding is limited and/or your energies are taken off of the real agenda—world government. Yes, I am a pro-lifer, but if you get rid of the U.N., you can get rid of abortion, family planning, and the homosexual agenda, because this is part of their sustainable development agenda to reduce the population. By focusing on the pro-life agenda, many people who could be instrumental in getting rid of world government spend their energies, emotions, and money fighting something that is not the **real** problem. They are caught up in an activity that **consumes** their minds and thoughts so that they do not see the real problem! Isn't that what Satan did in the garden? He took Eve's mind off of the real situation and painted a more palatable picture for her?

There are some Christian groups that are involved at the international level. A number of them are recognized missionary groups. One such organization, which I was amazed to see in Cairo, is World Vision. I remember one U.N.-sponsored conference held in Washington, D.C., in which World Vision had a booth. When I tried to have a conversation about spiritual things, the young lady manning the booth could not comprehend my comments. I thought that was strange. Having seen World Vision now at many other U.N. conferences, I now look at them as a chameleon—they are whatever you want them to be or whatever they want you to think they are. It *appears* that they have roots in the New World Order system and work very closely with the U.N.

Recently I was quite upset to read a letter from my husband's niece. This sweet young woman, who desires to do the right thing and serve the Lord, wrote us a letter explaining that she felt compelled, after serving a year with Youth with a Mission (YWAM), to attend a five-month course at their University of the Nations. Alarm bells went off as I read the title of the course, "Foundations of Community Development." What was a Christian organization doing teaching community development? The community development I was familiar with was that of the United Nations. YWAM was using the same term. In speaking to her before she left for South Africa, she misinterpreted my concern as criticism. I told her it was only concern as a result of where I had been and what I understood. When I finally asked her to define community development, she said, "We will be learning how to go into tribal villages and teach the natives about clean water, hygiene, sanitary conditions, and how to survive." I said, "You have just explained the United Nations agenda, as well as that of the Peace Corps [same agenda and goal]." She told me I was wrong. At my request, she sent me their college catalogue. Unfortunately, my assumption is correct. Too many red flags went up as I read the catalogue and course descriptions.

For example, part of the course description for a class entitled "Community Technology Systems" reads:

Water, food, energy, buildings, communication, transportation, and sanitation systems are basic for essentially all communities. It is the purpose of this school to look at the scientific and technological aspects of each of these infrastructure systems and determine relationships between the systems. Also, the impact of the technology infrastructure on the natural environment is illustrated, and methods of resource stewardship and sustainable development are discussed.

—*Youth with a Mission*, 181–82

The only definition I know of sustainable development comes from the United Nations. There is no other.

The Rise of Bible Prophecy

In 1970 a book about Bible prophecy, *Late Great Planet Earth* (which was to sell millions), came on the scene. I remember reading it. It had a very great impact on me. While we are all interested in what the Bible has to say about the future, the problem is that we all interpret words in the Bible differently and therefore there are a multitude of opinions about what is going to happen. I find it interesting that the *Report from Iron Mountain* (discussed in chapter four) was published in 1968, the first environmental conference was held in 1972, and Bible prophecy catapulted to global prominence in the early 1970s.

I have studied Bible prophecy for a number of years, read many books, and listened to all of the Bible scholars talk about what is going to happen. As a result of attending several U.N. conferences, everything that I believed about Bible prophecy has come into question. It is not the Bible that is in question, it is the understanding that most Bible scholars have, which does *not* include knowledge of the international level— **the specific agenda of the United Nations** and its various committees, agencies, and commissions. **How can scholars write about Bible prophecy when they don't have the full picture of current events?** They may "catch" something here or there, like the Economic Monetary Union (EMU) and the euro, but unless they have a complete picture, they cannot accurately make "predictions" about the future. What I do believe is that I need to be faithful on a daily basis, working out my own salvation with "fear and trembling," looking to serve God through personal holiness, and looking to stand in the gap when evil rears its ugly head! To do this, knowledge of the international level is needed.

CONCLUSION

A planned, managed catastrophe appears to be **the catalyst**—the straitjacket—to bring in world government for those who can't see it now. *As I have said on a number of occasions, currently it is the infrastructure which is being put in place. And at some point in time, the "teeth" of world government will be apparent for all to see.* As a result of the conferences I have covered, I have written about the various parts of the global infrastructure—economic, environmental, social, and legal. *A planned catastrophe will unveil all of that. In order to make the transition from individual nation-states to world government, a major catastrophe will be needed.*

As a result of this catastrophe, we will also be able to identify the false prophets who will tell us we need to go along to get along. Just as the Israelites first cried for deliverance from the bondage of Egypt and later looked for escape from Roman tyranny through the birth of the Messiah, I believe the end time "Remnant" will come as world government through the U.N. is unveiled.

All of this reminds me of the German theologian Dietrich Bonheoffer who broke with the Lutheran Church in Germany when they agreed to work with Hitler. Will this planned catastrophe be the downfall of the church, i.e. the mass of Christianity in America?

Lastly, we need to be prepared for uncertainty by being physically prepared, mentally alert, and spiritually ready to stand in the gap. Please see Appendix B, "The End-Time Servant."

Chapter 2

The History, Players, & Philosophy of Tyranny

CHAPTER SUMMARY

They say history repeats itself. We are in a time period when we can look back and look ahead and see how history is repeating itself. The players have always used deception and distortion—a trick first used by Satan in the Garden of Eden. The names of the players have changed, but the goal has not—complete control of the heart and soul of the earth. The process by which this is accomplished is called plunder and is an old political tool. As a result of the French Revolution, the French economist, statesman, and author, Frederic Bastiat wrote a pamphlet called *The Law* in which he analyzed how France was being plundered and was in the process of turning to socialism. His writings apply to America today as we are being plundered!

In 1902 the British aristocrat Cecil John Rhodes died, leaving a vast gold and diamond fortune and instructions for how to use it to bring America back under British rule. His trustees came up with the League of Nations. In 1920 America refused to be a part of the League and it basically was forced into obscurity until 1945 when the United Nations was birthed in San Francisco and then ratified by our Senate in August 1945. Today, those who share the vision of Rhodes are known as "Rhodes Scholars." Because Rhodes understood the importance of education, he set up the Rhodes Scholarship Fund in Oxford, England, to "educate" those men and women from around the world who might not be the smartest, but who were made of the right material to inculcate them with his vision so that they might become leaders in their respective countries and carry on his dream. In America, Bill Clinton is the first Rhodes Scholar to become president, and numerous appointees in his cabinet are also Rhodes Scholars.

The successor organization to Rhodes trustees are known today as the Royal Institute for International Affairs (RIIA). Its foreign branches include the Council on Foreign Relations (CFR) in the United States and others around the world. Powerful men are behind these organizations who share the vision of Rhodes. Many CFR members serve in government and in key positions throughout American industry—manufacturing, service, media, foundations, education, etc.—and are also in the military.

The agenda for the vision of a world united with Britain is funded by powerful corporation foundations such as the Carnegie Endowment for International Peace, the Rockefeller Foundation, the Ford Foundation, the Mellon Foundation, etc. This has been borne out by the findings of the Reese Commission, a special committee to investigate tax exempt foundations in the early 1950s.

In the last six or seven years, there has been a concerted movement spearheaded by Vice President Al Gore at the behest of President Clinton to "reinvent government." To use Clinton's words, "to change the way our governments work to fit a different time, and . . . come together behind our common purpose" (January 1995).

Reinventing government means:

1. downsizing and shifting power from the federal level to the local level, i.e. the community level which includes communication associations and churches;
2. changing the balance of power by shifting responsibility from Congress to the executive branch and its agencies (Bureau of Alcohol, Tobacco and Firearms [BATF], Environmental Protection Agency [EPA], National Park Service, Forest Service , Drug Enforcement Agency [DEA], National Guard, National Security Agency [NSA], and the President's Council on Sustainable Development [PCSD], to name a few); and

3. establishing public-private partnerships to become the new nucleus of government.

Public-private partnerships were first introduced on the global level at the United Nations conference in Istanbul called Habitat II in June 1996. It basically is what it says it is: first, it is a partnership to make money—a profit; second, it is compromised of public and private players. The public players include all levels of government: local, county, state, and federal governments in addition to foreign governments and U.N. agencies. The private players include nongovernmental organizations which support the U.N. agenda, such as environmental and pro-abortion groups as well as multinational and transnational corporations. Together these organizations set up a new organization—in many cases it is a nonprofit corporation to run the particular venture they are in charge of. Whoever has the most money, controls the venture—and that certainly isn't government.

Interestingly enough, the direct tie-in with the British royal family is Prince Charles and his Prince of Wales Business Leaders Forum, which is setting new political policies for many countries of the world by establishing public-private partnerships. When you consider that our new "reinvented government" uses public-private partnerships as its new foundation, what Prince Charles is really doing is establishing *governmental policy on a global level!*

Lastly, the shift of power to the local level is in line with a new political mode of thinking which we are told is new. This new political "movement," we are told, actually goes back to Aristotle, Voltaire, and Diderot, and today is supported by Mikhail Gorbachev, Tony Blair, Bill Clinton, Al Gore, Bill Bradley, Newt Gingrich, and Jack Kemp!! It basically is "reinvented communism."

The battle for the soul of the world has been brought down to the community level from the aspirations and machinations of the globalists. The fight for political control of your community will pit national constitutionalists against global communitarians or those who support the Third Way!

INTRODUCTION

In 1837, President Abraham Lincoln gave a speech in Springfield, Illinois, in which he recognized that no foreign power or combination of foreign powers "could by force take a drink from the Ohio or make a track on the Blue Ridge. At what point, then, is the approach of danger to be expected?" Lincoln said: "If it ever reach us, it must spring from among us, it cannot come from abroad. If destruction be our lot, we must ourselves be its author and finisher. As a nation of freedom, we must live through all time or die of suicide" (Church, 252).

Today many people think and feel that something is wrong with America. They cannot determine exactly what is wrong, when it went wrong, and what it means, but they know something is wrong. What Americans don't realize is that our country and its laws granting us freedom and rights are being taken from us—plundered. As you read this chapter you will understand that our Constitution has not only been bypassed, but it is in the process of being shredded by those who have been elected to office to uphold it. Plunder is tyranny.

The plundering of America—robbing her of life, liberty, and the pursuit of happiness—is a very old plan that is very far advanced. What we are about to experience in the near future is the result of this plunder. Because the day and hour is late, this is written to help you quickly understand the BIG picture so that you may be wise and pray effectively to stand in the gap. In order to tie in the past with the present, we need to look at history (for history repeats itself), the players (those who are robbing us), and the philosophy by which these players are perverting our laws and leaving us without any recourse.

HISTORY

The French Revolution

In 1850 the French economist, statesman, and author Frederic Bastiat wrote a pamphlet called *The Law* in which he explained how France was in the process of turning to socialism. He went on to analyze the socialist fallacy and explain how socialism must inevitably degenerate into communism. Some of his writings quoted below help us to see how America is walking in the same footsteps as France did during the French Revolution.

The beauty of the United States Constitution with its Bill of Rights is that it recognizes that our laws are based on natural, God-given rights. As such, they cannot be taken away and are inalienable, which means they cannot be transferred to another. Bastiat wrote: "These natural rights include the right to defend his person, his liberty and his property. They are basic requirements of life and the preservation of any one of them is completely dependent upon the preservation of the other two" (Bastiat, 6).

The right to defend our natural rights is protected through common force, which is given to us through the law. Common force is to do "only what the individual forces have a natural and lawful right to do: to protect persons, liberties, and properties; to maintain the right of each and to cause justice to reign over us" (Bastiat, 7).

> With these natural rights come privileges as well as the responsibility to protect them. When government respects its citizens, their labor and the fruits of their labor, then people are allowed to live in peace and harmony. As long as government respects the wants of its citizens, their satisfactions will develop in a logical manner. There will not be a great displacement of capital, labor, and population caused by bad or repressive legislative decisions.
>
> —Bastiat, 8

However, when the law has been used to destroy its own objective, it will destroy the rights that its real purpose was to respect and it will place the

> collective force [of the government] at the disposal of the unscrupulous who wish, without risk to exploit the person, liberty, and property of others. [When this happens,] government has con-

verted plunder into a right in order to protect plunder. . . . Plunder is when man seizes and consumes the products of the labor of others.

—Bastiat, 10

When the law becomes an instrument to plunder,

it erases from everyone's conscience the distinction between justice and injustice. No society can exist unless the laws are respected to a certain degree. Slavery and tariffs are plunder. Slavery is a violation, by law, of liberty. The protective tariff is a violation, by law, of property. There are two kinds of plunder: legal and illegal. Illegal plunder, such as theft or swindling—which the penal code defines, anticipates and punishes—[this] can be called socialism because it is not the kind of plunder that systematically threatens the foundations of society. The war against illegal plunder has been fought since the beginning of the world.

—Bastiat, 20

Legal plunder can be committed in an infinite number of ways: tariffs, protection, benefits, subsidies, encouragements, progressive taxation, public schools, guaranteed jobs, guaranteed profits, minimum wages, a right to relief, a right to the tools of labor, free credit and so on. All these plans as a whole—with their common aim of legal plunder—constitute socialism (122). How can you use the law to oppose socialism? And when once the law is on the side of socialism, how can it be used against socialism? There are only three ways to settle it:

1. The few plunder the many—limited legal plunder;
2. Everybody plunders everybody—universal legal plunder; and
3. Nobody plunders anybody—this is the principle of justice, peace, order, stability, harmony, and logic (23).

There are three systems of plunder: (a) protectionism, (b) socialism [which includes national socialism and fascism], and (c) communism. These are all from the same plant but at different stages of its growth. Legal plunder is more visible in communism because it is complete plunder, and in protectionism, where the plunder is limited to specific groups and industries (27). Justice is only achieved when injustice is absent (28).

As a result of over a hundred years of planning, America, like a ripe piece of fruit, is ready to fall. We are being plundered and yet no one really understands "the seriousness of the day and the hour." A planned catastrophe will create just the right opportunity for the final plunder when all of life as we know it will vanish—overnight— it will be "gone with the wind."

How could this plunder occur unless it was planned and deliberate? Those who have planned it have done so in secrecy. They have used deceit and deception to call black "white" and "white" black. Who are these "players of plunder"? Cicero said: "A nation can survive its fools, and even the ambitious but it cannot survive treason from within. An enemy at the gates is less formidable, for he is known and he carries his banners openly. But the traitor moves among those within the gate freely."

Cecil Rhodes

In 1902 British aristocrat Cecil John Rhodes died, leaving a vast gold and diamond fortune. Mr. Rhodes owed his fortune, later called the DeBeers Consolidated Mines, to support from Lord Rothschild and Alfred Beit, one of the two most powerful men in Africa. As explained in his "Confession of Faith" Rhodes left instructions for his trustees to find a way to bring America back under British control. In order to carry out his wishes, Cecil Rhodes set up a secret society, which is mentioned in the first five of his seven wills.

In the fifth [will] it was supplemented by the idea of an educational institution with scholarships, whose alumni would be bound together by common ideals—Rhodes's ideals. The (Rhodes) scholarships were merely a facade to conceal the secret society, or more accurately, they were to be one of the instruments by which the members of the secret society could carry out his purpose. The purpose, as expressed in the first will (1877), was "the extension of British rule throughout the world, the perfecting of a system of emigration from the United Kingdom and of colonization by energy, labour, and enterprise. . . . The ultimate recovery of the United States of America as an integral part of a British Empire, the consolidation of the whole Empire. . . . The inauguration of a system of a Colonial Representation in the Imperial Parliament.

—Quigley, 33

His trustees, who were themselves members of the British aristocracy, came up with the idea of a "League of Nations" which fulfills the "Imperial Parliament" requirement in which all countries would join under the banner of "peace." The United States Senate refused to ratify this treaty and the League was forced into obscurity in Switzerland until 1945. As a result of World War II and the determination to end war, representatives from around the world worked for months to fashion the Charter of the United Nations, which was passed by our Senate in August 1945.

During his life, Cecil Rhodes was influenced by his mentor, socialist John Ruskin (on whose grave is the swastika, the symbol of the Thule Society to which Hitler belonged) (Cuddy, 3). Ruskin was one of Rhodes' professors at Oxford University. Over sixty years later, another student of world government—a Rhodes scholar by the name of William Jefferson Clinton—would give credit in his first inaugural address to his mentor, Professor Carroll Quigley from Georgetown University, who was one of the people responsible for his appointment as a Rhodes scholar.

Professor Quigley wrote about the secret workings of the movement known today as "world government" or "the New World Order" in his thirteen hundred-page tome, *Tragedy and Hope*. He wrote:

This myth, like all fables, does in fact have a modicum of truth. There does exist, **and has existed for a generation, an interna-**

tional Anglophile network which operates and to some extent, in the way the radical Right believes the Communists act. In fact, this network, which we may identify as the Round Table Groups, has no aversion to cooperating with the communists, or any other groups, and frequently does so. I know of the operations of this network because I have studied it for twenty years and was permitted for two years, in the early 1960s, to examine its papers and secret records. I have no aversion to it or to most of its aims.

—Quigley, 950

PLAYERS

People

Quigley went on to give a history of the Round Table Groups, which were "semi-secret discussion and lobbying groups" that included the "Eastern Establishment" or the Round Table Group in the United States. These groups were organized by men like George Louis Beer, Walter Lippmann, Frank Aydelotte, Whitney Shepardson, Thomas W. Lamont, Jerome D. Greene, Erwin D. Canham of the *Christian Science Monitor*, and others (950).

Quigley mentions many other well-known names. He wrote:

Since 1925 there have been substantial contributions from wealthy individuals and from foundations and firms associated with the international banking fraternity, especially the Carnegie United Kingdom Trust, and other organizations associated with J. P. Morgan, the Rockefeller and Whitney families, and the associates of Lazard Brothers and of Morgan, Grenfell, and Company. The chief backbone of this organization grew up along the already existing financial cooperation running from the Morgan Bank in New York to a group of international financiers in London led by Lazard Brothers.

—Quigley, 951

Organizations

At the end of 1914, it was apparent that the system which Rhodes trustees had set up needed to be extended. The front organization in Britain would be called the Royal Institute of International Affairs (RIIA), and in New York, the Council on Foreign Relations (CFR), founded in 1921. Quigley goes on to note how the American branch exerted much influence through five American newspapers—the *New York Times*, the *New York Herald Tribune, the Christian Science Monitor,* the *Washington Post*, and the *Boston Evening Transcript* (953). Also, powerful men who were behind the formation of the CFR—J. P. Morgan, John D. Rockefeller, Paul Warburg, and Jacob Schiff—were the very same men who had engineered the creation of the Federal Reserve System in 1913.

In 1972 the Trilateral Commission (TLC), a sister group to the Council on Foreign Relations, was founded by David Rockefeller and Zbigniew Brzezinksi. "Tri" means three, and the commission's goal is to bring together people from the Western Hemisphere, Europe, and Asia. The commission proposes that "close Trilateral cooperation in keeping the peace, in managing the world economy, in fostering economic redevelopment and alleviating world poverty will improve the chances of a smooth and peaceful evolution of the global system" (Epperson, 232).

The Council on Foreign Relations has over three thousand members, and as of 1993, more than six hundred seventy of its members served in key positions across America: executive branch, 25; judicial branch, 5; legislative branch, 26; State Department, 63; Defense Department, 29; other cabinet departments, 12; independent agencies and corporations, 22; foundations, 83; media, 229; and corporate members, 185. Three presidents have been members of the Council on Foreign Relations, with Bill Clinton a member of both the CFR and the Trilateral Commission. Other names in government who participate in the council include former Secretary of State Warren Christopher, current Secretary of State Madeleine Albright, Secretary of Defense William Cohen, former CIA director John M. Deutsch, U.S. representative to the United Nations Richard Holbrooke, ambassador to Japan Walter Mondale, USAID administrator J. Brian Atwood, Secretary of the Treasury Robert Rubin, Supreme Court Justices Sandra Day O'Connor, Ruth Bader Ginsburg, and Steven G. Breyer, U.S. Senators Christopher Dodd, Bob Graham, John Kerry, Joseph Lieberman, Daniel Moynihan, Claiborne Pell, Larry Pressler, Chuck Robb, John D. Rockefeller IV, and Olympia Snowe along with Representatives Howard Berman, Jim Leach, Bob Torricelli, and former U.S. Representative Newt Gingrich (Grigg, W. N.).

Members from the media include all of the major television networks, many large city newspapers, and many business magazines and newspapers such as *Business Week, Forbes, Fortune, Money, Newsweek, Wall Street Journal.* Syndicated columnists Kenneth Adelman, Eric Breindel, Zbigniew Brzezinksi, William F. Buckley, Jr., Jimmy Carter, Georgia Anne Geyer, Richard Grenier, Jesse Jackson, Jeane Kirkpatrick, Henry Kissinger, Jessica Matthews, Jane Bryant Quinn, and Tony Snow, to name a few.

Corporate members include one hundred eighty-five multinational and transnational corporations such as American Express, Amoco, ArcherDaniels Midland Company, Arco, General Electric Company, IBM, Johnson and Johnson, Lehman Brothers, Lockheed Martin, Procter & Gamble, Royal Bank of Canada, Shell Oil, Tenneco, TimesMirror, and TRW. Many of these companies work with the Prince of Wales Business Leaders Forum.

Foundations
Foundations affiliated with the CFR include the Carnegie Corporation of New York, the Ford Foundation, the Heritage Foundation, the John D. and Catherine T. MacArthur Foundation, the Rockefeller Brothers Foundation, Rockefeller Family Fund, and the Rockefeller Foundation. Many of these foundations, along with others, fund many of the activities of United Nations-related studies on how to expand the global agenda. In 1990 powerful environmental groups that have been instrumental in changing personal property rights all over America, such as the Nature Conservancy, the National Wildlife Federation, the World Wildlife Federation, the Greenpeace Foundation, and the Sierra Club, etc., were funded

primarily by foundations such as the Richard King Mellon Foundation, which donated $23.5 million, John D. and Catherine T. MacArthur Foundation, $23.3 million; the Pew Charitable Trusts, $14.5 million; the Ford Foundation, $12.9 million; the Rockefeller Foundation, $10.9 million; and the Andrew W. Mellon Foundation, $6.3 million. (These foundations are also funding their agenda to change the world via grants to nongovernmental organizations, most of which are accredited by the United Nations, as well as private schools—primary, secondary, and college level. Many of the key United Nations reports which have been used to expand their agenda have been funded by these foundations) (Arnold, 592).

The Reese Committee

In the early 1950s, Congress set up the Special Committee to Investigate Tax Exempt Foundations, called the Reese Committee, after its chairman Congressman B. Carroll Reese of Tennessee, to find out how powerful foundations were and what effect they were having. In 1953 the committee filed its report with the House Committee on Tax Exempt Foundations. The findings in their report shook the very core of our republic. The *New York Times* wrote: "The incredible fact was that the huge fortunes piled up by such industrial giants as John D. Rockefeller, Andrew Carnegie, and Henry Ford were today being used to destroy or discredit the free-enterprise system which gave them birth" (Wormser, vii)

What is a tax-exempt foundation and who usually sets one up? For example, how would a family like the Ford family get out of paying the estate taxes that would reduce their vast fortune by sixty-five to seventy-five percent? By setting up a foundation and creating two types of stock: voting and nonvoting stock. The Ford Foundation was set up in 1946 and received about ninety percent of the stock of the Ford Motor Company, which was all nonvoting stock. Since the Ford family had no control over the company due to the nonvoting portion, this was a legal transfer and therefore they paid no estate tax on that stock. Meanwhile the family retained voting control of the company and had the satisfaction of knowing that even the nonvoting stock was in friendly hands.

—Wormser, xi

As the Reese Commission found:

Foundation activity has nowhere had a greater impact than in the field of foreign affairs. It has conquered public opinion and has largely established the international-political goals of our country. A few major foundations with internationalist tendencies created or fostered a varied group of organizations which now dominate the research, the education, and the supply of experts in the field. Among such instruments are the Council on Foreign Relations, the Foreign Policy Association, the Institute of Pacific Relations, the United Nations Association [cofounded by Eleanor Roosevelt], and many conferences and seminars held by American universities on international relations and allied subjects. It would be difficult to find a single foundation–supported organization of any substance which has not favored the United Nations or similar global schemes; fantastically heavy foreign aid at the burdensome expense of the taxpayer; meddling in the colonial affairs of other nations; and the American military commitments over the globe.

The influence of the foundation complex in internationalism has reached far into government, into the policymaking circles of Congress, and into the State Department. This has been effected through the pressure of public opinion, mobilized by the instruments of the foundations, through the promotion of foundation-favorites as teachers and experts in foreign affairs; through a domination of the learned journalist in international affairs, through the frequent appointment of State Department officials to foundation jobs; and through the frequent appointment of foundation officials to State Department jobs.

—Wormser, 200

At least one foreign foundation has had a strong influence on our foreign policy. The Rhodes Scholarship Fund of Great Britain, created to improve England's international public relations, but not registered here as a foreign agency, has gained great influence in the United States for British ideas.

Just as there have been interlocks between a "concentration of power" in education and in social–science research in domestic areas, there has been a similar combination in the field of foreign policy. The major components of the concentration in internationalism have been the Carnegie Corporation, the Carnegie Endowment for International Peace, the Rockefeller Foundation, and recently, the Ford Foundation.

This opinion is shared by Mr. Spruille Braden, former assistant Secretary of State who wrote to Rene Wormser and said, "I have the very definite feeling that these various foundations you mention very definitely do exercise both overt and covert influences on our foreign relations and that their influences are counter to the fundamental principles on which this nation was founded." Mr. Braden referred specifically to the Carnegie Endowment, the Rockefeller Foundation, the Ford Foundation, the Rhodes Scholarship Trust, in addition to the Foreign Policy Association, the Council on Foreign Relations, the Institute of Pacific Relations, and the United Nations Association, all part of what the committee majority called a "concentration of power" (Wormser, 212).

There is a saying: "Lies unanswered become [in people's minds] the truth. Lies by the government to the people are accepted as truth. However, lies answered with truth are discarded." Continuing with what Cicero said about what a nation can survive:

> But the traitor moves among those within the gate freely, his sly whispers rustling through all the galleries, heard in the very hall of government itself. For the traitor appears not a traitor—he speaks in the accents familiar to his victims, and wears their face and their garments, and he appeals to the baseness that lies deep in the hearts of all men. He rots the soul of a nation—he works secretly and unknown in the night to undermine the pillars of a

city—he infects the body politics so that it can no longer resist. A murderer is less to be feared.

These men, along with other individuals of the same ilk, have been orchestrating our move into world government. Do they know what they are doing? I am sure there are a few who do not really understand the BIG picture, while many of the others know full well what they are doing. Their motive? Power, possession, money, and the soul of the world.

REINVENTING GOVERNMENT

Introduction

In 1989 when Bill Clinton was governor of Arkansas, he became chairman of the Democratic Leadership Council (which is affiliated with the Progressive Policy Institute and the Smith Institute of London), which was created to develop the "third way" philosophy and a "third way" governing agenda. "Many of the New Democratic themes and ideas, developed during his chairmanship, have defined the 'third way' in America and as president, he has put them into action" (From).

In commenting on what the third way is, the editors of the left-wing magazine *Dissent* wrote:

> The idea of a third way for the left has a long history and many incarnations. In times past it most often meant a left-wing politics that was neither revolutionary communist nor social democrat reformist; instead it sought radical transformation through deep democratic commitments. The third way is being discussed by centre left governments across Europe and by Bill Clinton.
>
> —*Dissent,* 67

When he ran for the presidency, he promised change, and one of the things he said he wanted to change was government. On March 3, 1994, Clinton announced: "We intend to redesign, to reinvent, to reinvigorate the entire national government" (*Washington Times,*

March 4, 1993, "Government Waste Targeted"). The article said that his remarks were aimed at government waste and inefficiency, which is a half-truth. Gore added: "It's time we had a new customer service contract with the American people, a new guarantee of effective, efficient, and responsive government" (notice we are customers, not citizens). On December 18, 1994, Clinton asked Gore to "reinvent government." In his State of the Union address in January 1995 Clinton announced a "New Covenant":

> Our New Covenant is a new set of understandings for how we can equip our people to meet the challenges of the new economy, how we can **change the way our government works** to fit a different time, and . . . come together behind our **common purpose.** The New Covenant approach to governing is as different from the old bureaucratic way as the computer is from the manual typewriter. The old way dispensed services through large **top-down,** inflexible bureaucracies. The New Covenant way should shift these resources and decision-making **from bureaucrats to citizens** [bottom-up], injecting choice and competition and individual responsibility into national policy. The **old way was centralized** here in Washington. The New Covenant way must take **hold in the communities** all across America, and we should help them do that. Our job . . . is to empower people to make the most of their own lives and to enhance our security here at home and abroad. We should rely on **government as a partner** to help us do more for ourselves and for each other [emphasis mine].

In response to the president's New Covenant to reinvent government, Republican Speaker of the House Newt Gingrich, whose motto has been "devolution of government," decided not to provide any official or unofficial response. Governor Christine Todd Whitman (N.J.) conceded that there was a need to put "smaller, more effective government into action, stating that the people want less government, lower taxes and less spending from their federal government" (Whitman, A29).

The bold words in Clinton's speech basically outline the change from a centralized, top-down form of constitutional government to a decentralized, bottom-up approach, with power being shifted to the community. Furthermore, it would be changed by partnering, i.e., public-private partnerships. What he did not explain is that this change is part of Agenda 21, the U.N. agenda for sustainable development and democracy.

In order to understand the meaning of what Clinton was really saying, we must first review the background and history of "reinventing government." A fuller explanation is vital because vast numbers of Americans heard nothing wrong, but everything which sounded right in Clinton's speech. The use of self empowering terms: common purpose, citizens, communities, partners with government, and decentralization which lured them in.

History

Questions that should be asked are: Where and when did "reinventing government" begin? Who started it? How did public-private partnerships impact reinventing government? What part does the United Nations' Agenda 21 play? At what point did reinventing government begin to be the "final piece" in the destruction of the world system and the emergence of global corporate fascism and tyranny?

In my five years of researching the United Nations and in reading its documents, I have not seen the phrase "reinventing government." However, that does not mean the United Nations was not planning it. What I have found is that many times the United Nations and its related agencies use words with hidden meanings. In other words, you and I would assume that they use a word in the normal way we use it. That, however, is not the case. Most of the U.N. terms have their own peculiar meaning and, therefore, frequently used words such as "democracy," "decentralization," "capacity building," and "public–private partnerships" could very well mean or describe "reinventing government" and indeed do.

In looking to understand "reinventing government" we must

analyze the agenda behind it. I have narrowed the history down to two sources: Prince Charles, the Prince of Wales, who works behind the global scenes helping to set in place the radical agenda of the United Nations and *United Nations Programme of Action Agenda 21*.

Prince Charles, the Prince of Wales

To many, Prince Charles is only a polo player. However, in researching the U.N., I found that he is a very powerful and central player in the U.N. fora and behind the world scenes. As such, he has been instrumental in the passage of the *Programme of Action Agenda 21*, which perverts God's design for man having dominance over the earth by putting the earth over man. This new paradigm establishes man as equal to a plant or animal. Prince Charles has been instrumental not only in developing the business side of public-private partnerships, but in community governance. As it turns out, all of his activities reinforce "reinventing government." In response, all good-thinking people should be asking themselves, "Just who is Prince Charles and where does he get his power?"

While the prince's global and environmental activities began in 1968, we will begin with 1988. That year, Prince Charles was a key speaker at a three-day conference in Pittsburgh called "Remaking the Cities." This conference was convened by the American Institute of Architects and the Royal Institute of British Architects. Sponsors included numerous foundations and corporations in the Pittsburgh area. This conference is very important because of its tie-ins with Agenda 21, reinventing government, sustainable development, and public-private partnerships. In his keynote address, the Prince said:

> In Britain we have been learning a lot from the United States experience and we have been trying to adopt many of your partnership approaches to our peculiarly British problems. . . . Now through **partnerships between the public and private sector,** possibilities and opportunities for the future are being identified.

When all is said and done, it seems to me that the most essential feature of this whole debate is how to **recreate communities.** Man seems to function best in small, recognizable units—hence **the village—where he is part of a community of people** to which he can relate (emphasis mine).

—*Remaking the Cities,* 176

Other key speakers, such as conference chairman David Lewis, provide us with additional understanding: "This conference is about democracy." Roderick P. Hackney, president of the Royal Institute of British Architects said, "So a partnership of enterprise is what I'm calling for, a partnership between builders, professionals, and politicians—local, state, and national."

In 1990 Prince Charles again was instrumental in calling for an international conference of another kind, which was the impetus for the formation of the Prince of Wales Business Leaders Forum (PWBLF). The PWBLF consists of over two hundred multinational and transnational corporations that set up public-private partnerships around the world and who have been key in spawning the corporate governance debate. After all, if corporations are going to partner with government, then they need their own rules for "governing." Held in Charleston, South Carolina, this conference, "Stakeholders: the Challenge in a Global Market," brought together over one hundred chief executive officers of major multinational and transnational corporations from thirteen countries to discuss

[t]he rising expectations of "stakeholders"—shareholders, customers, employees, suppliers, national governments and local communities—in the fast-changing political and business world of the 1990s. Business participants explored the business rationale for action on these key issues in the communities in which they operate around the world.

—PWBLF, 5

The conference was followed by a seminar, entitled **"Building Urban Communities,"** on how **"private and public sectors could work**

in partnership with local communities to revitalize urban areas" (emphasis mine). In his keynote speech, Charles raised several questions that happen to be at the heart of reinventing government: "Business is at a crossroads. Does it enter new markets like cowboys on the frontiers? Or does it take a more sophisticated approach? You need to share your ideas about the challenges of our changing world." He asked how business can "tackle the challenges facing us: population, poverty, hunger, mass migrations, the conflicts over diminishing natural resources—unless we take a longer term view? **Governments can't do it by themselves"** (Jarrell, 3A)(emphasis mine). Today the Prince of Wales Business Leaders Forum partners with various agencies of the United Nations system as well as many different governments and multinational corporations around the world (see chapter five). The PWBLF has mobilized corporations, government, nongovernmental organizations, hotels, and the youth in various global and environmental projects worldwide, which involve public–private partnerships, implementing Agenda 21, biodiversity, and sustainable development. This should be seen as a major offensive to promote tyranny.

In 1996 the Prince of Wales Business Leaders Forum published its first book, *Business as Partners in Development*. Its purpose is to "spread good practice on how responsible business and local communities can work together to meet goals of sustainable development." This 280-plus-page book outlines what multinational and transnational corporations are doing to work with communities as well as implement Agenda 21. Their chapter on "Corporate Governance and National Competitiveness" opens with a quote from Al Gore's speech at the United Nations Social Summit in March 1995:

> We in the United States have come to recognize that it is time to abandon our old model [current form of government] for combating poverty, based on heavy government intervention through massive bureaucracies. We are working now to create a more vital relationship between the government and the people [reinventing government].

The chapter provides ten principles for reinventing government, which include: (1) catalytic government: steering rather than rowing; (2) community-owned government: empowering rather than serving; (3) competitive government: injecting competition into service delivery; (5) customer-driven government: meeting the needs of the citizens, not the bureaucracy; and (7) decentralized government: from hierarchy to participation and teamwork. All of these are being implemented in America.

Because the Prince of Wales partners with the United Nations Development Programme (UNDP) and the World Bank (WB), I went through a number of UNDP's reports beginning with 1990. While the 1990 report talked of equalizing the disparity between the rich and the poor, it did not address reinventing government. I then referred to the *1993 Human Development Report,* which discussed "democracy, people's organizations, nongovernmental organizations, and the need to decentralize government for equality" (*1993 Human Development Report,* 75–76).

In that report, the UNDP states:

Decentralizing governance increases local decision-making. It can take several forms: (1) horizontal decentralization which disperses power among institutions at the same level, (2) vertical decentralization, which allows some of the powers of central government to be delegated downwards to lower tiers of authority—to states in federal countries, then further down to regional and local governments or to even village associations.

—Ibid, 66

Decentralization of government is part of reinventing government because it is the transfer of power from the federal level to the local level—the communities—the village! To use Newt Gingriches words, "a devolution of power" (shades of Hillary Clinton!!). It should be remembered that the words being used sound good, but the underlying meaning is devolution—a transfer of power from national centralized control to global centralized control via public-private partnerships.

Agenda 21

In the Preamble of this radical, earth-changing document, it states:

> No nation can achieve this on its own; but together we can—in a **global partnership for sustainable development** [please refer to chapter four for an in-depth discussion of sustainable development]. This global partnership must build on the premises of General Assembly Resolution 44/228 of 22 December 1989, which was adopted when the nations of the world called for the United Nations Conference on the Environment and Development, and on the acceptance of the need to take a **balanced and integrated approach to environment and development questions.**

Furthermore, it states that in order to achieve the above,

> States have decided to establish a new global partnership . . . and that sustainable development should become a priority item on the agenda of the international community. It is recognized, that for the success of this new partnership, it is important to **overcome confrontation** [objections which countries may have] and to foster a climate of genuine cooperation and solidarity [communitarianism].
>
> —Earth Summit, Agenda, 21, 19, emphasis mine

Overcoming confrontation is another place where the Hegelian dialectic will be used. Overcoming confrontation leads to communitarianism.

Furthermore the preamble calls for public-private partnerships: "Governments, business and industry, including transnational corporations, should strengthen partnerships to implement the principles and criteria for sustainable development" (Ibid, 15).

In 1995, then U.N. Secretary-General Boutros Boutros-Ghali wrote *An Agenda for Development* in which he guided the U.N.'s objectives. He said that peace and development were the twin themes of international cooperation. He called for new partnerships between governments. He said development is comprised of: "environment, peace, the economy, society and democracy." He further singled out sustainable development as "preserving the availability and rationalizing the use of the earth's natural resources and the interconnections between the environment, society, the economy and political participation." He clarified by stating: "Sustainable development must be strengthened as a guiding principle of development [which requires] partnership" (37).

Lastly, he concluded the book by writing:

> The battle for people-centered sustainable development will be won or lost not in the corridors of Governments, but in every hamlet and home, in every village and town, in the daily enterprise of every member of the global community and every institution of civil society. The Charter of the United Nations begins with a pledge by 'we the Peoples . . .' (103).

You see this is where the real philosophical battle will be waged— the constitutionalists against the communitarians (one-worlders) in your community.

In April 1995, the United Nations General Assembly held a one-week special session on the role of public administration (democracy or "reinventing government"), which addressed areas of "sustained economic growth, the promotion of social development, facilitating infrastructure development and protecting the environment, promoting public-private partnerships, managing development programmes and maintaining a legal framework for development." At that time it was announced that the issue of public administration and development be included as a regular item on the General Assembly agenda and the Economic and Social Council, and that the Group of Experts on Public Administration and Finance, which has been meeting since 1983, be redesignated the Committee on Public Administration and Development (Press Release GA/9056, 12 April 1996).

Public-Private Partnerships

I first heard the term public-private partnership (PPP) when I at-

Chart 2–1

Public Private Parnerships

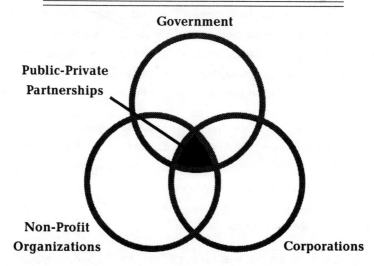

tended the June 1996 United Nations Habitat II conference in Istanbul, Turkey. The first time I read the conference's Programme of Action, I missed it completely. After I returned from Istanbul, I went back over the document and was shocked at its prominence. I spent six months trying to figure out what it was and I even conducted several interviews with people at the U.N. and other agencies.

A public-private partnership is exactly what it says it is. First, it is a partnership that is a business arrangement, and it is *for profit*. This arrangement is sealed by a formal business agreement or contract. In business a partnership provides its partners with the most flexible arrangement for doing business that there is. A partnership can have two or more partners and it can have several layers of partnerships, all of which are interrelated. Secondly, a public-private partnership has partners that are both public, meaning government, and private, meaning individuals, corporations, foundations, and/or nongovernmental organizations. Historically, such deals were considered glaring conflicts of interest and, as such, not in the best interest of the people.

The public partners include all levels of government from local government to county, state, regional, and federal government, in addition to international agencies and foreign governments. Private partners, as mentioned, include a wide range of nongovernmental organizations. These can include any corporations of substance—national, multinational or transnational corporations, and nongovernmental organizations like Planned Parenthood, the Sierra Club, the Nature Conservancy, World Wildlife Federation, the local "do-gooder" foundation, and the Ford, Rockefeller, and/or Carnegie Foundations. **In Chart 2-1 I have diagramed the components of a public-private partnership.**

Examples of public-private partnerships include sewer systems, power plants, water facilities, computers in classrooms, renovations to the Washington Monument, and many other similar projects. When you see these three words, know that our Constitution and representative government are being destroyed.

It should be noted that there is a new form of "governmental arrangements," which now governs society called "corporate governance." This has come about as a result of the new and prominent role which corporations are playing in helping to govern society. It fits in very well with public-private partnerships. There are some concerns, however, with the growing power of multinational and transnational corporations as they are trying to pass their own constitution called the "Multilateral Agreement on Investment (MAI) which would allow corporations to sue countries if there is any political instability for losses they incur in doing business.

Interestingly, at the Democratic Leadership Council conference on "Progressive Governance" held on April 25, 1999, the German socialist prime minister Gerard Schroeder said:

> The internationalization of economies, should it not be followed by an internationalization of politics? We have to include the private business community. They should have their liberties, the freedom of choice and the freedom to make decisions they consider right.

When you bring these entities together, where does the power lie?

With the deepest pockets. Is that government? No, it's business—another form of transfer of power and destruction of our American form of representative government. As a result, representative government disappears. Perhaps we should remember that our forefathers in the Declaration of Independence singled out "taxation without representation." This is exactly where we are with the rise of public-private partnerships—**taxation without representation!** What this means is that as corporations gain more and more power, their "circle" will become much larger than the other circles. Government will become less significant and in time, a hollow structure. Please see Chart 2-2. Those wealthy families who want to recreate the United States to suit their purposes and who are members of the Council on Foreign Relations and the Trilateral Commission and whose foundations fund the New World Order army of nongovernmental organizations, have just accomplished their goals—a transfer of power and the elimination of the Constitution! They are now in control. The economic agenda is orchestrated by them as well. This "new" concept just happens to fulfill Prince Charles statement, "governments can't do it by themselves." When business and government partner or marry, they have just entered into a fascist relationship. For further information, please refer to my book, *Prince Charles: The Sustainable Prince.*

Bottom line, when you marry government and business, all of the *existing* rules of law and government change as the checks and balances of our Constitution no longer pertain. When corporations rule the world financially and politically, only those who espouse the corporate philosophy will have a job. Want to keep your job? You may have to sell your soul. The door is wide open for anything—politically, socially, and economically. Plunder is tyranny.

Reinventing Government in the United States

The core central program of reinventing government is the national partnership for reinventing government, the National Performance Review (NPR). Proponents have set the tone and the agen-

Chart 2–2
The End Result of Public-Private Partnerships

Government

Nongovernment organizations (Empowered)

Multinational Corporations/
Transnational Corporations
—Rockefeller
—Carnegie
—Ford
—Mellon

In time, those industrialists who empowered the NGOs will "rule the world" through "reinvented government."

da for reinvention with the four principles: (1) cutting red tape, (2) putting customers [citizens] first, (3) empowering employees to get results, and (4) getting back to basics. They have built their reforms on a philosophy of "empowering" government workers to make better decisions.

Having abolished the ten thousand-page federal personnel manual, those in charge of reinventing government are committed to bottom-up decision-making. According to Donald Kettl, for the NPR two ideas were central. First, the reinventers argued implicitly the need to **transfer power from Congress to the executive branch.** Second the Clinton reformers argued explicitly that government employees needed to be empowered. "This approach implies a **transfer of power from Congress to the bureaucracy"** (Kettl, 32). Congress is being bypassed through a transfer of their power to the executive branch, which is comprised of not only the president but agencies like the Forest Service, Department of Defense, Department of Energy, Department of the Interior, Bureau of Indian Affairs, Bureau of Land Management, Fish and Wildlife Service, and National Park Service. These agencies have jurisdiction "over nearly half of the 760 million acres of eleven western states—and 87 percent of all federal lands outside Alaska. Nationwide the Bureau of Land Management (BLM) oversees 270 million acres; the U.S. Forest Service, 190 million" (Conniff, 11) (see Chart 2–3).

In 1998 President Clinton issued Executive Order 13083 which dealt with the subject of "federalism." It went as far as to redefine what "state" was so that it included all types and levels of government, delineated between the Constitution and "federalism" and allowed the president to declare a national emergency which would give the FEMA the power to direct federal, state, and local governments and control all communication facilities, power supplies, food supplies, etc. The Conference of Governors told Clinton they would not support this E.O. since they were not consulted.

In August 1999 a new "federalism" Executive Order 13132 was signed which mirrors a number of bills which were submitted by the 106th Congress to support its concepts. Unfortunately, as you read through these proposed bills, they basically "international-ize" terminology—instead of using words or phrases which are "national" in scope, it gives words a much broader definition. The E.O. is a "rewrite" basically of the Constitution by redefining the levels of government, words, and the powers of government. Furthermore, it is an empowerment of the federal agencies and therefore lends itself to "reinvented government."

In order to teach and reinforce our new form and structure of government, Johns Hopkins University in Baltimore is offering a Masters in Government in which a number of classes cover the reinvention of American government, privatization, and "America by Experiment and Design."

On Chart 2-4 is a conceptual diagram of constitutional government. Note that the circles depicting thirty thousand nongovernmental organizations and thirty-seven thousand multinational and transnational corporations with a worth of $5.5 trillion which operate outside of government and in their own sphere. In other words, the balance of power has shifted, destroying the checks and balances in the Constitution at the local level, and therefore destroying representative government. This power shift is a philosophical shift to a completely new form of government. It is a merger between government, corporations, and nongovernmental organizations. Charts 5 and 6 will show you the inversion of the "constitutional" pyramid and how through public-private partnerships, the power has shifted to within the constitutional pyramid, which now has become a new form of government. To show how this shift between government and business is progressing, the *Financial Times* stated that the United States government is no longer the world's largest borrower and that the balance was shifting to "top U.S. companies stepping into the void left by dwindling Treasury issuance which has fallen 20% since its peak in 1996. At the same time, U.S. corporations have embarked on a huge borrowing spree: bond issuance by companies has surged by 490% this decade." They went on to state that this is "spurring important changes in the market" (*Financial Times*, July 15, 1999, 18).

Chart 2–3

Devolution of Government

(no checks & balance)

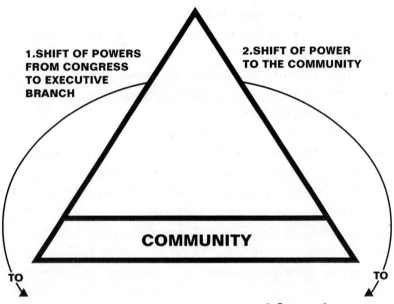

1.SHIFT OF POWERS FROM CONGRESS TO EXECUTIVE BRANCH

2.SHIFT OF POWER TO THE COMMUNITY

COMMUNITY

TO

TO

1.(Some) Executive Branches

> Bureau of Alcohol, Tobacco and Firearms
> Environmental Protection Agency(EPA)
> National Park Service(NPS)
> USDA Forest Service
> Fish and Wildlife Service(FW)
> Bureau of Land Management(BLM)

Drug Enforcement Administration(DEA)
Federal Bureau of Investigation(FBI)
Bureau of Indian Affairs(BIA)
International Development Cooperation Agency
International Trade Commission(ITC)
National Guard Bureau
National Security Agency(NSA)
Neighborhood Reinvestment Corporation
Peace Corp
President's Council on Sustainable Development

2.Community
- National Education Assoc. (NEA)
- County agencies: environment, zoning, health and human services, housing and community affairs, etc.
- NGOs: Sierra Club, Audubon Society, Nature Conservancy, Planned Parenthood, World Federalists, etc.
- Local representatives of bureaucracies—DEA, FBI, EPA, BATF, etc.
- Community Associations

Chart 2–4

Government Under the Constitution/Bill of Rights

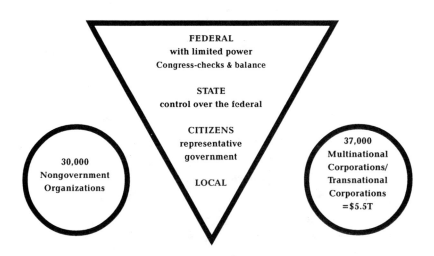

FEDERAL
with limited power
Congress-checks & balance

STATE
control over the federal

CITIZENS
representative
government

LOCAL

30,000
Nongovernment
Organizations

37,000
Multinational
Corporations/
Transnational
Corporations
=$5.5T

**REPRESENTATIVE GOVERNMENT
WITH CHECKS AND BALANCES
BY AND FOR THE PEOPLE
BIBLICALLY BASED PHILOSOPHY-MAN DOMINION OVER
EARTH
THE INDIVIDUAL-TOP DOWN**

Chart 2–5
"Reinvented Government"=
Communitarianism=
The Third Way=
"Reinvented Communitarianism"

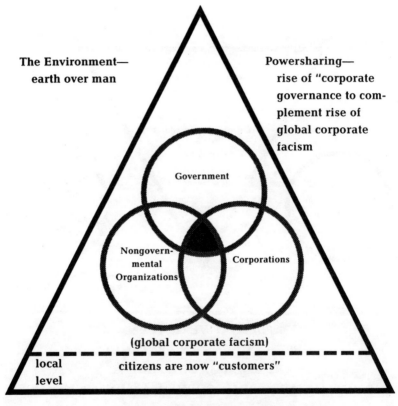

The Environment—
earth over man

Powersharing—
rise of "corporate
governance to com-
plement rise of
global corporate
facism

Government

Nongovern-
mental
Organizations

Corporations

(global corporate facism)

local
level

citizens are now "customers"

rule by public-private partnership
no representative government
no checks and balances
power shifted from federal to "community-owned government"
rise of communitarianism or rule for the "common good"
group rights—"bottom up"

Chart 2 © copyright 1999 TWIMG, Inc.

Chart 2–6

The Results of
"Reinventing Government"

"We intend to redesign, to reinvent, to reinvigorate the entire national government."

—President Bill Clinton, 3/4/93

Constitution

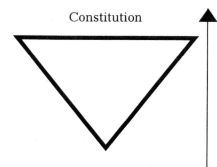

STRONG CONSTITUTION
AND
BILL OF RIGHTS

Executive Order 13083
Federalism

For NPR*, two ideas were central: first the reinventors argued if implicitly, **the need to transfer power from Congress to the executive branch . . .**

Changes the "sovereign powers granted to the states" so that the **federal agencies have control over the states.**

Second, the Clinton reforms argued, much more explicitly, that the government employees need to be empowered. . . . **This approach implies a transfer of power from Congress to the bureaucracy** and, within the bureaucracy, from top level to lower-level officials.
—*Inside the Reinvention Machine Appraising Government Reform*, Kettl and Dilulio, 32

Executive Order 13107
U.S. Compliance with U.N. Human Rights Treaty

LOSS OF CONSTITITION
TO NEW
"DEMOCRATIC GOVERNANCE FOR
21ST CENTURY"

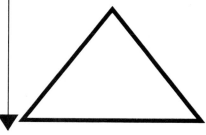

TYRANNY!!

In preparation for the inversion of our Constitution, on December 10, 1998, Bill Clinton issued Executive Order 13107 which establishes a federal agency to enforce compliance with **all** U.N. human rights treaties, even those which have **not** been ratified by the Senate. This executive order, which gives precedence to the United Nations Declaration on Human Rights, does three things:

1. It protects through the Constitution human rights treaties which have not been ratified;
2. It makes U.N. doctrine the legal standard for which all U.S. policy and legislation must meet; and
3. It creates a powerful new federal oversight agency which has the task of monitoring both state and federal laws to ensure compliance with the ratified and unratified U.N. treaties.

Since 1948, some sixty human rights treaties and declarations have been negotiated and include the Convention on the Prevention and Punishment of the Crime of Genocide, the International Convention on the Elimination of All Forms of Racial Discrimination, Convention on the Elimination of All Forms of Discrimination Against Women, Convention on the Rights of the Child, and many others. Our Constitution gives us unlimited and inalienable rights—they come from God, not government, and they cannot be taken away. When you define what is a "right" or "human right," you have just limited the number of rights a person or country has.

The bottom line is that the balance of power is destroyed as you move from constitutional government to a bottom-up form of government. On page 97 of *An Agenda for Development 1995,* Boutros Boutros-Ghali stated it this way, "The United Nations emphasizes bottom-up, country-driven programming of development assistance resources, without conditionalities."

By making governments accountable to citizens, democracy makes particular governments more responsive to popular concerns. By providing channels for participation of people in deci-

sions which affect their lives, democracy brings government closer
to the people. Through decentralization and strengthening of community structures, local factors, relevant to development decisions
can more adequately be taken into account.

—Boutros-Ghali, 47

If we take this one step further, even though the federal government is being shrunk, that does not mean the expense of the federal government is shrinking. On October 20 our Senate passed the
$500 billion Omnibus Budget Bill. In February 1999 it was an-
nounced that we would provide considerable support to rebuild
Honduras and Guatemala, which was hit by Hurricane Mitchell.
On March 5 it was announced that we would provide foreign aid to
help Russia and other countries prepare for Y2K. The unfair acts by
Britain enumerated in the Declaration of Independence which were
protected by our Constitution are now at the center of change. When
you consider the public-private partnerships and the United Nations Biological Diversity Treaty, it appears that we are reverting
back to feudalism. All of these vast expenditures increase our tax
burden. Therefore, I have extended the inverted pyramid one step
further.

In 1933 Franklin Roosevelt, a 33rd degree Mason, added the
all-seeing eye to our dollar bill. If you look again at the inversion of
the Constitution and compare it with the "eye of Horus" on the
back of our currency, there appears to be a resemblance!

Bottom-up Government Is Communitarianism or the Third Way
It used to be that only the groups who used the word "family" or
"community" were pro-life. However, in the last several years the
other side has adopted the same language as the pro-life family
groups, with a new emphasis on "community." I did not think anything about this until I attended the conference on Reinventing
Government in January 1999 where Al Gore and other world leaders referred to "we the people" as customers instead of citizens.

In looking to understand what is meant by community, I stumbled upon a new political philosophy, "communitarianism." When you understand the tenants of this new middle of the road approach, it basically is a new marketing concept for the old communistic form of thinking. It's "reinvented communism" at its finest! In chapter four you will read how sustainable development, a new environmental philosophy of the United Nations, is a merger between communism and capitalism. Communitarianism appears to be its moral, philosophical, and social equivalent.

Communitarianism rejects both authoritarian practices and individualistic ideas. It sets out principles for how the community—which is decentralized government (from the bottom-up)—should be governed. It maintains that no one opinion should be dominant as individuals are encouraged to act for the "common good" of the community. As such, social and political practices are to be reformed in relation to their contributions to the development of "sustainable forms of community life" (when you see the word "sustainable," it refers to the environmental philosophy of sustainable development).

There are a number of people who attribute communitarianism as part of their own genius. One is Amitai Etzioni who wrote *The Spirit of Community,* George C. Lodge who wrote *Managing Globalization in the Age of Interdependence,* and another is Henry Tam who wrote *Communitarianism: A New Agenda for Politics and Citizenship.* I believe it is safe to say that they have the same idea of community as the new central political force, but different ideas about why it is needed and how to bring it about.

In 1990 one of the founders of communitarianism, Amitai Etzioni, invited fifteen ethicists, social philosophers, and social scientists to explore and discuss the ills of society. He writes:

We were troubled by pressures to be labeled either conservative or liberal, pro-life or pro-choice, for or against the death penalty. We were troubled by the finding that many Americans are rather reluctant to accept responsibilities. We were distressed that many Americans are all too eager to spell out what they are entitled to, but are all too slow to give something back to others and to the community. We adopted the name *Communitarian* to emphasize that the time had come to attend to our responsibilities to the conditions and elements we all share, to the community,

—Etzioni, 14–15

However, fellow communitarian Henry Tam writes that the movement goes back to Aristotle, Francis Bacon, Voltaire, Diderot , John Stuart Mills, and more recently in the twentieth century, Leonard Hobhouse, an Oxford philosopher, and John Dewey, an American educationalist. "They shared a deep commitment to develop liberal ideals and to combat the distortion of those ideals" as they pertained to individualism. Lodge states that Stalin and Hitler were communitarians (Lodge, 123). With this in mind, I think one can conclude that the communitarian form of government is in itself authoritarian—no opposition to their way of thinking.

So what is their purpose? Etzioni writes:

The communitarian movement—which is an environmental movement dedicated to the betterment of our moral, social, and political environment—seeks to sort out these principles. And Communitarians are dedicated to working with our fellow citizens to bring about the changes in values, habits and public policies that will allow us to do for society what the environmental movement seeks to do for nature: to safeguard and enhance our future. . . .

We have a moral commitment to leave for future generations a livable environment, even perhaps a better one than the one we inherited, certainly not one that has been further depleted. The same observations hold true for our responsibility to our moral, social, and political environment.

—Etzioni, 2–3, 10–11

Without offering a source as to where they will get their values, Etzioni says that communitarianism is a *social movement,* looking to "restore the moral voices of communities (and the web of social bonds, the communitarian nexus, that enables us to speak as a community) . . . to encourage one another to live up to our social responsibilities." Etzioni says that society is in a "state of increasing moral confusion and social anarchy." "As communitarians we also recognized a need for a new social, philosophical, and political map."

Lodge affirms the environmental by saying: "Global forces such as commercial competition and the requirements of ecological survival are pushing national systems in the direction of ideological convergence—differences among the various forms of communitarianism appear to be diminishing" (91). Furthermore, he adds to his definition five dimensions, of which some overlap with Tam and Etzioni. They are:

1. equality;
2. consensus, which may be imposed autocratically by fiat or arrived at through democratic and participative means, rights and duties of membership in the community whereby the community has an obligation to assure certain human rights;
3. community needs versus individual needs which can include public-private partnerships between government and business;
4. the role of the state (versus the community) to define community needs; and
5. holism which is the "consciousness of the interrelatedness of all things" (Lodge, 113–120).

Etzioni points out that they must be on the right road because so many people have joined them as they have been given favorable response. These supporters are from both the Democratic and Republican parties and include Al Gore, Daniel Moynihan, Dave Durenberger, Alan Simpson, Bill Bradley and former Secretary of Housing and Urban Development Jack Kemp. Henry Tam points out something very interesting—communitarianism is not just in America, but is worldwide (surprise, surprise)! In the former Soviet Union "Mikhail Gorbachev, who led the way in dismantling authoritarian rule in his country, . . . maintains that the world must look beyond individualism for a sustainable alternative to authoritarianism." In addition, the Prince of Wales Business Leaders Forum is cited as being supportive of communitarianism:

> There are signs that increasing numbers of businesses are ready to adopt communitarian practices to enable them to act as responsible corporate citizens. Some business leaders are supporting research into how corporate responsibility can be enhanced in practice.
>
> —Tam, chapter seven

It is interesting to note that all of the above activity is happening at the same time on a global basis and that it is a fulfillment of U.N. Charter principles!!

So how will these proponents of this new social environmental movement change society? They state that they will use communities on the local and national levels as the main conduits of a moral revival (Etzioni, 19). (This just happens to fit in with reinvented government.) Furthermore, they have four platforms in which they will change society: (1) the family, (2) schools through education, (3) social webs of communities which provide neighborhoods, work, and associations with social and moral order, and (4) values which change as the community changes (this is the same as the third way) (248). Etzioni states, "Our agenda, by necessity, is as complex and compassing as the problems we face. We aim to change values, to alter mindsets, and to promote public policy that services the commons" (249–50).

One of the ways, he says, to "curb authoritarianism and right-wing tendencies is to stop the anarchic drift by introducing carefully calibrated responses to urgent and legitimate public concerns." Calling liberty "ordered," he says that the success of the democratic experiment is built on "shared values, habits and practices that assure respect for one another's rights and regular fulfillment of personal, civic, and collective responsibilities" (255–56). The community must develop moral values which are "nondiscriminatory, generalizable, justified in terms that are accessible and understandable, i.e. instead of claims based on individual or group desires, citizens would draw on a common definition of justice." Lodge concurs with the need to curb authoritarianism by writing, "Individualism argues for voluntary consensus; the communitarian believes that it may be necessary to secure consensus through coercion (e.g., prisons)" (Lodge, 123–124).

The center of all social justice, Etzioni states, is:

> the idea of reciprocity: **each member of the community owes something to all the rest, and the community owes something to each of its members. This does not mean heroic self-sacrifice; it means the constant self-awareness that no one of us is an island unaffected by the fate of others** (264, emphasis added).

British prime minister "Tony Blair's version of the third way amounts, rhetorically speaking, to 'neither-nor.' That is to say, neither state socialism nor libertarian conservatism, positively, it is communitarian" (Ryan, 77). If the true nature of communitarianism hasn't hit you in the face by now, you need to re-read this section. This is "reinvented communism" at its finest! What does that say about our government?

To show how funny this is to Bill Clinton and his cronies at the Democratic Leadership Council, Italian prime minister Massimo D'Alema was making a point about hidden words and their meaning. He said:

> We belong to the Socialist International, and I am aware that this word is somewhat sensitive here—(laughter)—and I can see that we have avoided using this word. But we should prevail over this fear of words because when we move from the words to the actual facts and actual experiences, we discover [them] to be closer and more similar.

President Clinton, laughing, replied: "I'm not sure I would have you here, Massimo, if I were running for re-election."

In a communitarian community, the community is to take its value from the collective beliefs and persuasions of the community. I find it most interesting that during the time communitarianism was "taking root" among the intelligentsia of the world leaders, that Bill Bennett wrote *The Book of Virtues,* a composite of "great moral stories." Bennett writes:

> In teaching these stories, we engage in an act of renewal. We welcome our children to a common world, a world of shared ideals, to the community of moral persons. In that common world, we invite them to the continuing task of preserving the principles, the ideals, and the notions of goodness and greatness we hold dear.
>
> —Bennett, 12

Bennett then goes on to employ the Hegelian dialectic:

> People of good character are not all going to come down on the same side of difficult political and social issues. Good people—people of character and moral literacy—can be conservative, and good people can be liberal. We must not permit our disputes over thorny political questions to obscure the obligations we have to offer to all our young people in the area in which we have, as a society, reached a consensus: namely, on the importance of good character.
>
> —Bennett, 13

Combining Greek mythology, fables, favorite moral stories, with the lives of famous people, and the Bible, Bennett writes that the experience was "mind opening." Interestingly enough, he opens his book with a quote from Plato's *Republic.* This book was hailed by all of Christendom's leaders as a good book to have. Is Christianity being processed through the Hegelian dialectic?

It should be noted that communitarianism, the third way, and the emphasis on community, where we all share and take care of one another, is *not* the same set up in Acts 2:45–46. *Dake's Annotated Reference Bible* says:

> Many thousands of goods were cared for without charge at the feasts of Jerusalem. Therefore, a sort of community of goods was no strange thing in Jewry at such times. This community idea was carried farther and longer than at a feast. Multitudes were staying longer due to the revival making it necessary to provide for the people. Many sold their possessions (not necessarily their homes, but extra possessions) in order that everyone could be provided for.
>
> —*Dake's Annotated Reference Bible,* New Testament, 142

I think it is time to ask ourselves, "Just who are these people?" and "Who is giving them the power to change society and mold it in their image?" While they state the community must be non-biased, the truth is that leadership demands an opinion—apparently it will be theirs. But this is where you come in. This is the reason for this book. To help you understand the real agenda.

SUMMARY

The final straw in changing the U.S. Constitution is seen in the Clinton administration's efforts to "reinvent government." In his January 20, 1999, State of the Union address, Clinton gave a very long speech using phrases that he did not define. If you understand the international agenda, you will see that his speech was an outline of the final integration of America with the other countries of the world as we adopt global programs that coincide with what other countries have established in social security and school-to-work programs; building a global financial system for the twenty-first century; finding common ground on which business, workers, and environmentalists, farmers and government can stand together; calling for a new round of global trade negotiations to expand exports of services, manufacturers, and farm products; building new partnerships for peace and security, with the U.N. playing a crucial role; and expanding NATO. Clinton went on to address the environment and communities. He called for the introduction of a twenty-first century crime bill to "deploy the latest technologies and tactics to make our *communities* even safer," and called for a new clean air fund to help *communities* reduce pollution, and tax incentives to spur clean energy technologies. He called for the expansion of "open space" and the preservation of land across America "from the most remote wilderness to the nearest city park." This, along with the First Lady's efforts to preserve historic places in every town across America for the millennium celebrations.

Clinton thanked Vice President Gore for a

> government that is a progressive instrument of the *common good*, rooted in our oldest values of opportunity, responsibility and *community*, . . . determined to give our people the tools they need to make the most of their own lives in the twenty-first century, a twenty-first century government for twenty-first century America.

Twenty-three times he used the phrase "twenty-first century" either by itself or in conjunction with a description, such as "twenty-first century seniors, twenty-first century economy, and twenty-first century schools.

CONCLUSION

The problem we are faced with is this: our forefathers came to America to flee tyranny of all sorts. They created our Constitution and the checks and balances between the executive, judicial, and legislative branches. As a result of concerted efforts by the British to recapture America, as well as their control of the United Nations and its global agenda for world control, the rise of public-private partnerships, reinventing government, and communitarianism (a new word for communism), I think it is clear that the twenty-first century is going to be challenging. Once our form of government and Constitution are completely dismantled, the checks and balances to protect our rights will also be dismantled. Clearly we are reverting back to feudalism where we become serfs—people without a voice whose only asset is what they are capable of producing! Where can we go to start all over again? What is our recourse? What are our rights?

What Boutros Boutros-Ghali wrote is quite correct. The major philosophical battle will be the third way, or communitarians versus constitutionalists. It will be up to you to oppose the communitarians by voicing your opinion and standing strong to show your neighbors that their choice is basically the Constitution and individual rights or communitarianism and the group [human] rights.

This book is written to help you understand that the philosophical battle ahead of you is not only spiritual warfare at its finest, but universal legal plunder!

The Political Structure

Chapter 3

The United Nations

CHAPTER SUMMARY

In this chapter we will consider the structure of the United Nations. It has all of the components of government. According to an article which appeared in the April 20, 1970, *Anaheim Bulletin,* the U.S. Senate voted on March 19, 1970, to give the U.N. "full diplomatic recognition as being a **sovereign world government."**

Whenever the U.N. General Assembly meets, the resolutions they pass help to expand the field of international law. Article 13 of the U.N. Charter gives the General Assembly the duty of initiating and promoting international political cooperation and encouraging the progressive development of international law. Types of international law include: municipal law; rules of jurisdiction (extradition and immunity); international environmental law; human rights law; international court of justice, which renders opinions; law of war and law of force; international law governing the sea, waterways, polar regions, and outer space; international economic law, such as the International Monetary Fund, World Bank, NAFTA, and the International Labor Organization; international civil aviation and international communication, not to mention international postal law.

The term "democracy" used by the U.N. does not mean the kind of "democracy" we have in America, for we are supposed to be a republic. The United States Constitution and Bill of Rights are being replaced by the United Nations Charter and the U.N. Declaration of Human Rights. Most recently Bill Clinton issued Executive Order 13107, which implements into our legal structure U.N. human rights law.

The U.N. has a socialistic purpose—a transfer of wealth from the "rich" (us) to the "poor" (those whom they have kept in poverty). However, if Russia or China are examples of working socialism, it does not work since those in power end up allocating monies to finance the lifestyle to which they have grown accustomed.

The U.N. Charter adheres to the concept of "collectivism" which says that the group is above the individual. Under communitarianism or the merged concepts of collectivism and individualism, the individual no longer exists, but we are to work for the "collective good of the community."

Lastly, the U.N. states that they are working for world peace. Peace to the U.N. means no opposition to their agenda. John Cecil Rhodes left his fortune to find a way to bring America back under Britain. His trustees came up with the concept of a "League of Nations." When our Senate refused to go along with this idea, America experienced a crash in 1929 and the Second World War. In 1945, our Senate ratified the U.N. Charter. In my opinion, when the U.N. Charter was ratified is when the world officially entered "world government" and America reverted back to British rule.

". . . and by peace shall destroy many" (Daniel 8:25).

INTRODUCTION

My understanding of the U.N. has always been vague. I don't recall studying the U.N. in school. If we had spent any kind of time on it, I would have remembered. What I do remember is taking an orange box around to neighbors at Halloween to collect money for the United Nations Children's Fund (UNICEF) to feed the poor children of the world. In 1990 I thought it strange that President George Bush had to ask the United Nations for permission to bomb Iraq since we are a sovereign country, or so I thought. Even the news media did nothing to evoke my interest in the United Nations. I remember reading about a U.N. conference on human rights which was held in 1993, but the news article was not very long and hence I did not think anything of the organization. That level of knowledge remained the same until I attended the 1994 United

Nations Conference on Population and Development (UNCED). There I saw and realized that the United Nations is world government! Since then I have seen an increase in the number of daily articles on the United Nations as well as on radio and television.

THE STRUCTURE OF THE UNITED NATIONS

The American people have been told that the United Nations was born out of two world wars and a desire for peace. We have also been told that the United Nations is a forum for countries to discuss their differences. However, to the unsuspecting eye, the U.N. has become more than just a forum for discussion. One only has to study the U.N. organizational chart that follows (Chart 3-1) to see that it has a distinct governmental structure.

The United Nations has set global policy for all countries to follow. The agreements coming out of the U.N. General Assembly become international legal code, which transcends national law. The U.N.'s structure is quite vast, comprising the same kind of commissions, agencies, and committees as you would find in any national government. Every member state contributes annual dues based on a very complicated formula which takes into consideration the wealth, income, economic power, and population (to name a few components) of a country. Each country has an ambassador appointed to handle its affairs and to vote at the U.N. In the United States, the U.N. ambassador and other liaisons to the United Nations are housed at the Department of State. The United States has been the largest contributor to the United Nations by way of dues, appropriations, and payments. Lastly the United Nations has its own army composed of troops from all of its member states.

So what **is** the United Nations? To answer that, we must consider what governments are and what a treaty is. According to Noah Webster's *American Dictionary of the American Language,* government is: "The exercise of authority; direction and restraint exercised over the actions of men in communities, societies or states; the administration of public affairs, according to established constitutions, laws or usages, or by arbitrary edicts."

Chart 3-1
The United Nations System

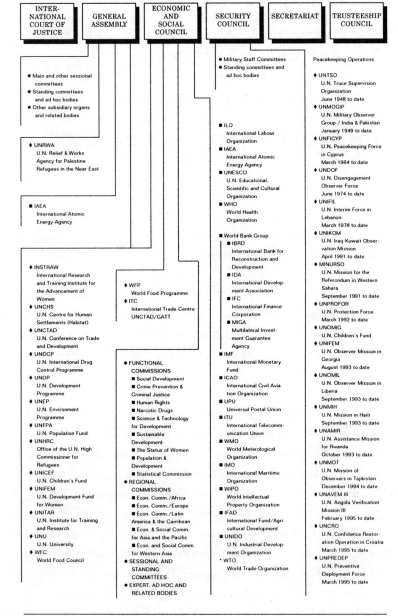

INTER-NATIONAL COURT OF JUSTICE	GENERAL ASSEMBLY	ECONOMIC AND SOCIAL COUNCIL	SECURITY COUNCIL	SECRETARIAT	TRUSTEESHIP COUNCIL

SECURITY COUNCIL
- Military Staff Committees
- Standing committees and ad hoc bodies

■ ILO
International Labour Organization
■ IAEA
International Atomic Energy Agency
■ UNESCO
U.N. Educational, Scientific and Cultural Organization
■ WHO
World Health Organization
■ World Bank Group
  ■ IBRD
  International Bank for Reconstruction and Development
  ■ IDA
  International Development Association
  ■ IFC
  International Finance Corporation
  ■ MIGA
  Multilateral Investment Guarantee Agency
■ IMF
International Monetary Fund
■ ICAO
International Civil Aviation Organization
■ UPU
Universal Postal Union
■ ITU
International Telecommunication Union
■ WMO
World Meterological Organization
■ IMO
International Maritime Organization
■ WIPO
World Intellectual Property Organization
■ IFAD
International Fund/Agricultural Development
■ UNIDO
U.N. Industrial Development Organization
* WTO
World Trade Organization

Peacekeeping Operations
♦ UNTSO
U.N. Truce Supervision Organization
June 1948 to date
♦ UNMOGIP
U.N. Military Observer Group / India & Pakistan
January 1949 to date
♦ UNFICYP
U.N. Peacekeeping Force in Cyprus
March 1964 to date
♦ UNDOF
U.N. Disengagement Observer Force
June 1974 to date
♦ UNIFIL
U.N. Interim Force in Lebanon
March 1978 to date
♦ UNIKOM
U.N. Iraq-Kuwait Observation Mission
April 1991 to date
♦ MINURSO
U.N. Mission for the Referendum in Western Sahara
September 1991 to date
♦ UNPROFOR
U.N. Protection Force
March 1992 to date
♦ UNOMIG
U.N. Children's Fund
♦ UNIFEM
U.N. Observer Mission in Georgia
August 1993 to date
♦ UNOMIL
U.N. Observer Mission in Liberia
September 1993 to date
♦ UNMIH
U.N. Mission in Haiti
September 1993 to date
♦ UNAMIR
U.N. Assistance Mission for Rwanda
October 1993 to date
♦ UNMOT
U.N. Mission of Observers in Tajikistan
December 1994 to date
♦ UNAVEM III
U.N. Angola Verification Mission III
February 1995 to date
♦ UNCRO
U.N. Confidence Restoration Operation in Croatia
March 1995 to date
♦ UNPREDEP
U.N. Preventive Deployment Force
March 1995 to date

GENERAL ASSEMBLY
- Main and other sessional committees
- Standing committees and ad hoc bodies
- Other subsidiary organs and related bodies

♦ UNRWA
U.N. Relief & Works Agency for Palestine Refugees in the Near East

■ IAEA
International Atomic Energy Agency

♦ INSTRAW
International Research and Training Institute for the Advancement of Women
♦ UNCHS
U.N. Centre for Human Settlements (Habitat)
♦ UNCTAD
U.N. Conference on Trade and Development
♦ UNDCP
U.N. International Drug Control Programme
♦ UNDP
U.N. Development Programme
♦ UNEP
U.N. Environment Programme
♦ UNFPA
U.N. Population Fund
♦ UNHRC
Office of the U.N. High Commissioner for Refugees
♦ UNICEF
U.N. Children's Fund
♦ UNIFEM
U.N. Development Fund for Women
♦ UNITAR
U.N. Institute for Training and Research
♦ UNU
U.N. University
♦ WFC
World Food Council

ECONOMIC AND SOCIAL COUNCIL
♦ WFP
World Food Programme
♦ ITC
International Trade Centre UNCTAD/GATT

● FUNCTIONAL COMMISSIONS
  ■ Social Development
  ● Crime Prevention & Criminal Justice
  ■ Human Rights
  ■ Narcotic Drugs
  ■ Science & Technology for Development
  ■ Sustainable Development
  ■ The Status of Women
  ■ Population & Development
  ■ Statistical Commission
● REGIONAL COMMISSIONS
  ■ Econ. Comm./Africa
  ■ Econ. Comm./Europe
  ■ Econ. Comm./Latin America & the Carribean
  ■ Econ. & Social Comm. for Asia and the Pacific
  ■ Econ. and Social Comm. for Western Asia
● SESSIONAL AND STANDING COMMITTEES
● EXPERT, AD HOC AND RELATED BODIES

♦ United Nations programmes and organs (representative list only)
■ Specialized agencies and other autonomous orgs. within system
● Other commissions, committees, and ad hoc and related bodies
* Coop arrangement between U.N. and WTO are under discussion

We must then compare the structure of the United Nations to a form of government (Liotta). The U.N. has:

1. *Ruler/Head of State*—The Secretary-General is appointed in secret by the Security Council as opposed to being elected by the entire governing body, which includes the General Assembly, or by international popular ballot.

2. *Governing body*—The General Assembly and the Security Council. The General Assembly is comprised of 186 ambassadors from the U.N. member states. The Security Council consists of five permanent members: China, Russia, Britain, France, and the United States. Within the Security Council is the Military Staff Committee which has always had a representative from Russia as its chairman. The United Nations has:

   a. The ability to create international law. It has been the primary originator of international law since its inception.

   b. The power to make treaties. While there are many, many treaties that have been signed and agreed to by the countries of the world, they all fall into several classes:

      1. Human Rights Instruments, such as the International Declaration of Human Rights, the United Nations Rights of the Child, the Declaration to Eliminate all Forms of Discrimination Against Women

      2. Environmental Rights Instruments, such as the Rio Declaration, Agenda 21, the Law of the Sea, and the Convention on Climate Change

      3. Peace Instruments, such as Salt I and II, Outer Space Treaty, and the nuclear-weapons Non-Proliferation Treaty of 1968

      4. Equitable and Environmentally Sound Development, such as the Programme of Action of the United Nations International Conference on Population and Development, 1994.

3. *Source of Income*—Dues of member-states (U.S., Great Britain, etc.), voluntary gifts (Ted Turner's recent $1 billion gift over

ten years), fees from U.N./World Bank services, and proposed world taxes.

4. *Currency*—Presently the International Monetary Fund has Special Drawing Rights, which is a form of liquid money that is used among IMF members, and which was created by the IMF in the 1960s.

5. *Treasury and/or Banking System*—Is comprised of the World Bank and the IMF. Overseeing the control of the world's monetary system is the Bank for International Settlements, which is not part of the U.N. system, but is the "central bank's bank."

6. *Court and Legal System*—Currently the United States is not a member of the International Court of Justice—the World Court. There are numerous efforts to get our Supreme Court to appeal to the World Court in order to give it recognition. Also evolving is an International Criminal Court, which is favored by the U.S.

7. *Policing Mechanism*—Interpol and U.N. Peacekeeping Troops— The United States has been instrumental in sponsoring several international police academies around the world.

8. *Military Force*—U.N. peacekeeping troops—The United Nations has its own army comprised of troops from all of its member states. The U.N. armies fight wars to keep the world at peace. It appears that the definition of peace which the U.N. operates on is "no opposition to their agenda."

9. *Bureaucratic Agencies*—The U.N. system has a bureau for every level of human and governmental oversight common to any governing body: World Health Organization (WHO), United Nations Conference on Trade and Development (UNCTAD), World Food Council (WFC), World Intellectual Property Organization (WIPO), World Meteorological Organization (WMO), International Atomic Energy Agency (IAEA), Universal Postal Union (UPU), International Maritime Organization (IMO), United Nations Children's Fund (UNICEF), and United Nations Education, Scientific and Cultural Organization (UNESCO), to name a few.

10. *Flag*—The U.N. flag.

11. *Oath of Allegiance*—Every U.N. employee takes an oath in which they swear allegiance to the United Nations.
12. *Charter*—U.N. Charter signed in 1945 by our Senate.
13. *Constitution*—Currently there are actions being taken to create an "Earth Charter," which would govern the people of the planet. Mikhail Gorbachev, co-chair of the Earth Council, is one of the leaders in developing such a document.

HISTORY OF THE UNITED NATIONS

The United Nations Charter is what birthed the U.N. and was the product of months of deliberations in 1945 in San Francisco. All Americans—or constitutionalists—should note that the U.N. Charter does not reflect any of the values or principles found in our Constitution. Whenever you see reference to the Charter, it is in the context of various laws being passed to conform American law to it. Alger Hiss, who served President Roosevelt as director of the State Department's Office of Special Political Affairs in charge of all post-war planning, led the American delegation to the founding U.N. conference. Mr. Hiss also accompanied President Roosevelt to Yalta, where he served as the "top international organization specialist." Others on the American delegation included Noel Field, Harold Glasser, Irving Kaplan, and Harry Dexter White (who founded the IMF and World Bank, and who also was convicted as a communist spy). Alger Hiss became the first secretary-general of the United Nations, and in 1950 was exposed and convicted as a Soviet spy. Because the statute of limitations had run out, he ended up being convicted of lying to Congress about his affiliation with the Communist Party. Upon his death several years ago, it was confirmed that he indeed was a communist spy. When I had the opportunity to interview Daniel Cheever (special assistant to Alger Hiss at the U.N. founding conference) at the U.N. Fiftieth Anniversary in San Francisco in 1995, he told me that Alger Hiss was an exceptional man to work for and that he never saw anything improper about him. Before I knew that Dr. Cheever had this kind of affiliation to Hiss, I had observed him to be someone who is either very naive or truly believes that the United Nations is an honest and just organization which is of, by, and for the people. Daniel Cheever wrote a book about the United Nations, *Organizing for Peace,* which is considered an epic in the international peace community.

SECRETARY-GENERALS ARE SOCIALISTS

All other secretary-generals since Alger Hiss have been socialists— Trygve Lie from Norway, Dag Hammarskjold from Sweden, U Thant from Burma, Kurt Waldheim from Austria (who was also a member of Hitler's Third Reich), Javier Perez de Cuellar from Peru, and Boutros Boutros-Ghali of Egypt. I have no knowledge at the present that Kofi Annan of Ghana is a socialist, but given the background of his predecessors, I would imagine he, too, is a socialist. Americans should consider this aspect since we provide the U.N. with twenty-five percent of their operating budget from our tax dollars.

Also, there are a number of efforts under way to strengthen the United Nations system by giving it more power. There are, however, a number of actions that increase and strengthen the United Nations Charter as it currently is. Four of them are: international law, democracy, the transfer of wealth, and collectivism.

THE UNITED NATIONS CREATES INTERNATIONAL LAW

International law is the "glue" for all of the U.N.'s efforts and is part of Article 13 of the Charter. Just as each country has its own set of laws—civil, criminal, familial, and commercial—so, too, does the U.N. International law is about three hundred years old. It was originally based on the law of nature coming from divine authority—the law of God. However, Hugo Grotius (1583–1645), a Dutch jurist, historian, and diplomat, guided the development of international law based on natural law, or universal reason (coming from man). His writings are considered the foundation for modern international law (Henkin, xxiv). According to Edison W. Dick of the United Nations Association–USA (UNA–USA) Board of Governors:

> More international law has been developed through the U.N. system during the past fifty years than in the entire history of man-

kind. The U.N. has been directly responsible for the conclusion of more than 465 multilateral agreements covering virtually every area of state [government] interaction and human endeavor from the Law of the Sea to narcotic drug control, from the environment to international trade and copyright law, from arms control to the advancement in women's rights. . . . The development of international law to the extent we know it today would not have been possible outside the framework of the U.N. . . . Each major organ in the U.N. has made a significant contribution to the body of international law and indeed to fashioning the rule of law. The U.N. General Assembly has directly influenced the substance of contemporary international law. In fact, Article 13 of the U.N. Charter gives the General Assembly the duty of initiating and promoting international political cooperation and encouraging the progressive development of international law.

The U.N. chartered international law, which is created by treaties, customs, general practices of law, decisions from the World Court, and academic writers. Article 38 (1) of the Statute of the World Court upholds all of these as sources of international law. Interestingly enough, unlike American law, academic writing, developed under U.N. encouragement, is a source for the creation of law. United Nations international law is comprised of all of the same areas of law any individual country covers, except that U.N. international law is "above national law or transcends it." In addition, every time a U.N. Programme of Action is agreed to at a U.N. conference (five thousand are held yearly), it is codified into international law.

In Chart 3-2, you will see the types of international law, which includes municipal law; rules of jurisdiction (extradition and immunity); environmental law; human rights law; international court of justice; law of war and law of force; international law governing the sea, waterways, polar regions and outer space; international economic law, such as the IMF, World Bank, NAFTA, and International Labor Organization; international civil aviation and international communication; not to mention international postal law.

In order to bring together the national and international levels of law, national laws must be changed. It was the Final Platform [agenda] for Action for the Fourth Women's Conference held in Beijing, China, in September 1995 that requested that all nations

> review national laws, including customary laws and legal prac-
> tices in the areas of family, civil, penal, labour and commercial
> laws in order to ensure the implementation of the principles and
> procedures of all relevant international human rights instruments
> by means of national legislation. . . .

For example, in the Habitat II Programme of Action, Action Item #145 stated:

> Innovative approaches and frameworks [laws] for international
> cooperation in the development and management of human set-
> tlements [cities] must be sought and developed to include the
> active participation of all levels of Government, the private and
> corporate sectors, non-governmental organizations and commu-
> nity-based organizations [PPPs] in decision-making, policy for-
> mulation and resource allocation, implementation and evalua-
> tion.

EXECUTIVE ORDERS SUPPORT INTERNATIONAL LAW

If you compare American laws or bills pending in the U.S. Congress with U.N. resolutions and treaties, you will see that our national laws are being "internationalized," that is, rewritten to conform to international law. This is why Americans are having more and more difficulty telling the difference between Democrats and Republicans. In some cases, actual language from the U.N. Treaty or resolution is inserted into congressional bills and law. It is unfortunate that our court system and/or our Congress are unwilling to halt this ominous change. What is not being introduced by law is being implemented through executive orders.

Bill Clinton's Executive Order 13107 on human rights is an example. Another example is illustrated by the following anecdote.

Chart 3-2

MUNICIPAL LAW INT'L LAW OF TREATIES

Article 13 of the Draft Declaration of Rights and Duties of States adopted by the Int'l Law Commission of 1949. "Every State has the duty to carry out in good faith its obligations arising from treaties and other sources of int'l law and may invoke provisions in its constitution." p. 149

INT'L LAW—RULES OF JURISDICTION, EXTRADITION & IMMUNITY

Int'l law has not yet developed a comprehensive set of rules defining with reasonable precision all forms of jurisdiction that may be exercised by states and other int'l legal persons. Rather, int'l law has given principal attention to the reach of a state's jurisdiction—legislative, judicial, or executive—in criminal matters.

INTERNATIONAL ENVIRONMENTAL LAW

The Earth Summit approved three documents: Rio Declaration on Environmental/Development, Non-Legally Binding Authoritative Statement of Principles for a Global Consensus, and Agenda 21. Signed 2 treaties: Climate Change and Biological diversity. All of these far-reaching agreements and pacts constitute the emerging area of Environmental Law.

HUMAN RIGHTS LAW

Int'l Human Rights Law encompasses the three principle instruments as well as other bodies of principles and customary law CEDAW, plus 22 additional human rights conventions: Universal Declaration of Human Rights. The International Covenant on Civil and Political Rights and the Int'l Covenant on Economic, Social & Cultural Rights called the "International Bill of Rights."

AIR AND SPACE LAW INT'L CIVIL AVIATION INT'L COMMUNICATIONS

PLUS: International Postal Law, Int'l Telecom & Satellite—INTELSAT, Weather, Health and Agriculture, Shipping, World Health Organization and Atomic Energy. Each of these areas has a corresponding U.N. agency or are part of ECOSOC.

INTERNATIONAL COURT OF JUSTICE

—The court can render advisory opinions to the U.N. upon request.
—The U.S. is not member to the World Court which the U.N. wants all members to accept their compulsory jurisdiction.
—Currently there are recommendations for an International Criminal Court.

INTERNATIONAL LAW: Definition—"International law lays down the foundation of the objectives, procedures and functions of international organizations, which, in turn, strengthens international law through enforcement, development, and codification of existing rules. . . ." Although the agreements reached by the League of Nations were not binding, the United Nations is a much stronger body in which the General Assembly of the U.N. is both 'a political and semi-legislative organ. Although its resolutions are not legally binding, they are more often than not observed by the Members . . . and may contribute to the development of new rules of international law. Many international conferences attended by representatives for almost all the states are, in effect, law-making bodies, they have indeed adopted numerous treaties and conventions binding upon the governments.
—William L. Tung, International Organizations Under the United Nations System

LAW OF WAR LAW OF FORCE

Law of War and Control of Weapons: 1. Regulation of Conventional, Biological and Chemical Weapons. 2. Int'l Humanitarian Law. 3. Law of War and Environmental Protection Arms Control and Disarmament

INT'L LAW: OF THE SEA. WATER-WAYS. POLAR REGIONS AND OUTER SPACE

Law of Sea signed after 14 years of negotiations to establish a "new legal order for ocean space." It is considered a "Constitution for the Oceans" and covers 25 subjects. Sets up a Law of the Sea Tribunal and the Enterprise, a profit making venture on mining the sea. Polar Regions include Antarctica. Outer Space encompasses Moon, other celestial bodies, Geostationary Orbit, etc.

INTERNATIONAL ECONOMIC LAW INTERNATIONAL MONETARY LAW INTERNATIONAL TRADE AND DEVELOPMENT LAW

Int'l Economic Law has been defined as "All the int'l law and int'l agreements governing economic trans-actions that cross state boundaries or otherwise have implications for more than one state . . . movement of goods, funds, erosions, intangibles, technology, vessels or aircraft." The Bretton Woods Institutions—IMF and World Bank are part of Int'l Economic Law. Some others include GATT and GATT Commodity Agreements on Wheat, Coffee and Rubber, NAFTA, UNCTAD and the Group of Seven. In addition, the Int'l Labor Organization, ILO, is part of Int'l Law. There are movements to establish an International Security and Exchange Commission. Each region of the world has its own economic commission.

While returning home from the Group of Seven meeting in Lyon in 1996, I met a Belgian attorney who was working with the Capital Markets Forum in London. This group is working to change American law to conform to international law in the area of the global investments settlement system. He told me that they were seeking to pass a new version of Article 8 of the [U.S.] Uniform Commercial Code. He said that by producing model legislation to introduce in each *state,* they would be able to facilitate this law change in just a few years, instead of the ten to fifteen years necessary through *federal* channels. This example also demonstrates another method to violate the constitutional process—going straight to the more local level. Wally N'Dow, the Secretary-General of U.N. Habitat II, held in June 1996, calls this "glocal" action. "Glocal" is a combination of global and local. It is also a good example of the Hegelian dialectic of the merger between the global level and the local level.

DEMOCRACY

Our country was founded as a republic and not a democracy. The following is a simple comparison:

Republic	Democracy
Government is based on law	Man's government—Humanism
Representative government people elect officials who are accountable	Direct government—no absolutes reason replaces righteousness
Limited government	Centralized government
Property rights are secure	Taxation is a form of social control
Individual liberty	License to do what you want— restricted freedom (U.N. Declaration of Human Rights)

| Stewardship and free enterprise | Collectivism—socialism—government controls goods |

In analyzing the term "democracy," which is a buzz word for U.N. advocates, I asked then Secretary-General Boutros Boutros-Ghali at the 1995 U.N. Social Summit in Copenhagen what democracy meant to him. He replied:

> I believe that the United Nations is based on democracy. The concept of **equality between all the member states**—that Andorra or Santa Marino have one voice equally to a superstate like the U.S., China, or India—so this is the first idea. The second idea is that we are adopting a basic principle, which is the participation of people, which is **the respect of human rights but a different form of democracy has to be decided by the member states.** We cannot impose a certain democracy on each country. The third important idea is that we must not limit our quest for democracy within our member states **but defend democracy among member states that have an authoritarian regime** at the world level because more and more we will have global problems which cannot be solved by one or two or three member states but need international community (emphasis mine).

Democracy, as explained by Dr. Boutros-Ghali, a member of the Socialist International, is contrary to the Constitution of the United States, yet this is the philosophy that is being supported by our government. In addition, the United Nations uses a parliamentarian form of government. It does not use our two-party form of government.

Everything that the United Nations is doing is geared at erasing all of the borders and boundaries between countries. We are all **one.** We all have the same goal—whether you want it or not. With the Clinton administration came something called "politically correct thinking." This phrase basically says if you don't agree, it is you who are wrong, not them. What happened to freedom of speech?

Little by little it is being taken away.

Interestingly, the U.N. was formed in 1945, but there were numerous agencies formed before the U.N. was formed. In Chart 3-3 you will find a summary of some of the organs, agencies, and commissions. You will see, as you read what their purpose is, that they are acting as a type of world government in that their programs are for the "people of the world" and have been approved by the General Assembly in which the U.S. has given their consent. If this is true, then the U.N. makes our Congress a bunch of high-paid paper pushers who are traitors to the United States Constitution.

UNITED NATIONS GOALS

The U.N. has many goals. All one has to do is read some of its documents. For example, the *1994 Human Development Report*. published by the United Nations Development Programme, called for a world tax. This has been discussed for a number of years, and appears to be getting close as the number of international taxes has increased. Even at the 1998 Group of Seven meeting in Birmingham, England, there was a huge demonstration by U.N. supporters, which included calling for a tax on international currency transactions. This type of tax could possibly provide the U.N. with additional income of up to $1.5 trillion a year. Currently its budget is about $15 billion per year. In response to a question posed at the 1995 Social Summit to Dr. Inga Kaul about why the U.N. should be allowed to tax international currency, she stuttered out a response that the U.N. "deserved" it. The international tax question is very serious and will not go away until it is passed in some form.

Transfer of Wealth

Another goal of the U.N. is the transfer of wealth. Article 55 of the Charter referring to international economic and social cooperation, calls on the U.N. to promote higher standards of living, full employment, and conditions of economic and social progress and development. The U.N.'s preoccupation with development is rooted in the sharp division of its membership between rich and poor na-

Chart 3-3

Overview of
U.N. Organizations, Agencies, and Commissions

Source: Worldmark Encyclopedia of the Nations—United Nations—Seventh Edition

Organ/Agency/Commission	Year	Purposes and Comments
Food and Agriculture (FAO)	1941	FAO was created as a result of the U.S. Nutrition Conference for Defense in 1941, in which it was resolved that it should be a goal of the democracies to conquer hunger, "not only the obvious hunger that man has always known, but the hidden hunger revealed by modern knowledge of nutrition." It also conformed to President Roosevelt's call for Four Freedoms. In 1983, FAO's Committee on World Food Security adopted a broader concept of world food security with the ultimate objective of ensuring that all people at all times have both physical and economic access to the food they need. FAO works in the area of emergency assistance, fisheries, crops, livestock, forestry, water management, fertilizer supply, commodities and trade, and aid to small farmers.
The World Bank and International Monetary Fund	1944	These two organzations were birthed at the "Bretton Woods" Monetary Conference held in 1944. This conference was called to determine the global monetary structure of the world after WWII. The World Bank was to make loans to help rebuild war-torn countries. The IMF was to determine and monitor world monetary affairs. Since 1944, they have each expanded significantly. Currently there are calls to empower the IMF as a "world central bank" or a lender of last resort and to merge the Interim Committees of each body into one.

United Nations Educational, Scientific, and Cultural Organization— UNESCO	1945	UNESCO is involved in the transmission of existing and pursuit of new knowledge. Its function includes maintaining, increasing and diffusing knowledge by ensuring the conservation and protection of the world's heritage of books, works of art, monuments of history and science. This includes the "preservation and protection of the world heritage of works of art and monuments of historic or scientific interest." UNESCO adopted the International Convention Concerning the Protection of the World Cultural and National Heritage in 1972 which provides a permanent, legal, and financial framework for international cooperations of the world heritage sites which transcends all political or geographical boundaries. It should be noted that the, counterpart for this Convention is the U.S. Man and Biosphere which is located at the U.S. State Department.
International Court of Justice	1945	Successor to and resembles the Permanent Court of International Justice under the League of Nations. Countries who join bind themselves to its decisions.
Economic and Social Development	1945	Promotes a higher standard of living, full employment, and conditions of economic and social development. In 1974, the General Assembly adopted the New International Economic Order which called for a fundamental change in the international order in an effort to reduce the gap between the rich and poor nations. Members stated their desire to work urgently for "the establishment of a new international economic order based on equity, sovereign equality, and interdependence and cooperation among all states."
Commission on Human Rights	1945	At the U.N. Founding Conference in San Francisco, a proposal to embody an international bill of rights was put forth. The Universal Declaration of Human Rights was adopted by the General Assembly on December 10, 1948. Article 1 says all human beings are born free and equal in dignity and rights and that in Article 2, everyone is entitled to all the rights and freedoms set forth in the Declaration. Since then, there have been many other declarations of rights such as the Declaration of the Rights of the Child, Declaration on the Rights of Mentally Retarded Persons, and Rights of Disabled Persons, etc.

International Labor Organization	1919/ 1946	Created by the Peace Conference following WWI, it became the first specialized agency created by the U.N. in 1946. The ILO holds labor conferences in Geneva. Each country sends a four-member team consisting of two governmental representatives and one representing the country's employers and the other, the country's workers. The governing body has 56 members with ten countries having permanent representatives (U.S.S.R., U.S., China, Italy, U.K., Brazil, India, Japan, France, and Germany). The ILO is a promotor of human rights.
Disarmament	1/24/46	General Assembly's first resolution adopted addressed disarmament and established the Atomic Energy Commission—Purpose is Disarmament—elimination of all weapons—nuclear, biological, mass destruction, chemical.
Economic and Social Council	1946	Under Article 55—higher standard of living, full employment, economic/social development, human rights, solutions of economic, social, health, and related problems, and international cultural and educational cooperation.
World Health Organization (WHO)	1948	WHO has developed a "global health for all" strategy. Prevention is the key word. WHO believes immunization, which prevents the six major communicable diseases of childhood, should be available to all. They have several worldwide campaigns and have a provision of safe drinking water for all and education to prevent health problems.
Law of the Sea	1958	The Law of the Sea convention was voted on in 1982 by the General Assembly. It creates for the first time a profit-making venture called "Enterprise" to mine the seabed.
Peaceful Uses of Outer Space	1959	Deals with scientific and technical cooperation and with evolving international law on outer space.

		Report from Iron Mountain.
	1963	
World Food Program	1963	The U.N. and FAO sponsor this program. WFP uses food commodities, cash and services contributed by U.N. member states to back programs of social and economic development and emergency relief. WFP supplies "food-for-work" projects in which food is provided as part-payment for planting trees, digging irrigation canals, building roads, houses, schools, or bridges or working on a variety of other community improvement programs.
United Nations Conference on Trade and Development (UNCTAD)	1964	UNCTAD promotes international trade with a view to accelerate economic development, to formulate principles and policies on international trade, to initiate action of the adoption of multilateral trade agreements, and to act as a center for harmonizing trade and development policies of government and regional groups.
United Nations Development Program (UNDP)	1966	Grew out of several agencies which were begun in 1945. UNDP supports the vigorous drive of the world's developing countries to provide their own people with essentials of a decent life—adequate nutrition, housing, employment, education, healthcare, consumer goods and public services. Secondary goal is to help these countries increase their output of commodities, raw materials, and manufactured items. UNDP is the world's largest channel for international technical cooperation in these fields and on site.
U.N. Population Fund (UNFPA)	1966	The U.N. has been concerned with population questions since its founding. At the first World Population Conference in 1974, the U.N. adopted a plan of action that stressed the relationship between population and overall economic and social development. The followup meeting in Mexico in 1984 reaffirmed 1974 and its plan of action. UNFPA worked (1) family planning, (2) communication and education, population education in schools, (3) basic data collection, (4)

		population dynamics and analyses of demographic data, (5) formation and implementation of population policies and programs, and (6) special programs for women, children, and youth.
U.N. Environment Program (UNEP)	1972	As a result of the first environmental conference in 1972, UNEP was formed. The governing council is comprised of 58 states elected by the General Assembly and it is to promote international cooperation in the field of environment and keep the world environmental situation under review so as to ensure that emerging problems requiring international assistance receive adequate considerations by governments. UNEP has led efforts against marine pollution, environmental law, and has pushed for the Convention on the Protection of the Ozone.
Aging and the Elderly	1973	The General Assembly considered a comprehensive report on the elderly which noted the relative size of older populations of the world. It recommended guidelines to governments in formulating policies of the elderly, including development of programs for the welfare, health, and protection of older people, and for their retraining in accordance with their needs, in order to maximize their economic independence and their social integration with other segments of the population.
World Food Council	1973	The General Assembly decided to convene a conference dealing with global food problems. The 1974 U.N. World Food Conference called for the creation of a ministerial-level world food council to review annually major problems and policy issues affecting the world food situation and to bring its political influence to bear on government and U.N. bodies.
U.N. Center for Human Settlements (Habitat) UNCHS	1976	UNCHS looks to link urban and regional development programs with national development plans. The first conference was held in 1976. The plan of action contained recommendations for national action such as provisions of shelter, infrastructure, services, land use, and land tenure. UNCHS provides technical cooperation in developing countries such as national settlement

| | 1994 | The United States Senate voted between sessions for the General Agreement on Trade and Tariffs which became the World Trade Organization on January 1, 1995. This 28,000-page treaty basically opens all of the borders of the world so that we are integrated from a business and agricultural point of view. |
| World Trade Organization (WTO) | | |

policies, urban and regional planning, rural and urban housing and infrastructure development, slum upgrading and site and services, low-cost building technology.

tions, a division that the secretary-general has frequently characterized as a leading long-term threat to world peace and security. In addition, Article 2 (1) states: "The Organization is based on the principle of the sovereign equality of all its Members." This is evident in the dues the United States pays as compared to other members. We basically pay for twenty-five percent of the U.N. budget, which does not include all of the other fees for the IMF/World Bank, World Trade Organization, World Health Organization, and so forth.

At the Social Summit in Copenhagen in March 1995, The World Social Charter was presented. The following clause is an excerpt:

> We collectively believe that our world cannot survive one-fourth rich and three-quarters poor, half democratic, half authoritarian, with oases of human development surrounded by deserts of human deprivation. We pledge to take all necessary actions, nationally and globally, to reverse the present trend of widening disparities within and between nations.

The Programme of Action from the United Nation's Fourth Women's Conference held in 1995 states:

> The major cause of the continued deterioration of the global environment is the unsustainable patterns of consumption and production, particularly in industrialized countries. . . . Macroeconomic policies need rethinking and reformulation to address these trends.

In the *Gaia Peace Atlas,* which is an important work complementing the United Nations goals and objectives, "greater wealth distribution" (Barnaby, 213) is seen as one of the means to attain economic security. Furthermore, it states, "Before any other changes can be wrought, deprivation must be tackled. This will require decentralized control of the means of wealth creation" (Barnaby, 217). The global reform of the international financial system is called for.

Collectivism (Communitarianism)
The concept of "collectivism," which negates the individual and

individualist thinking and action, is prevalent in all of the actions and goals of the United Nations. Collectivism is:

> The theory that the group [the collective] has primacy over the individual. Collectivism holds that, in human affairs, the collective—society, the community, the nation . . . the race, etc.—is the unit of reality and the standard of value. On this view, the individual has reality only as part of the group, and value only insofar as he serves it; on his own he has no political rights; he is to be sacrificed for the group whenever it—or its representative, the state—deems this desirable
>
> —Piekoff, 17

When you merge the individualistic philosophy of self-preservation and communism (the whole) you arrive at communitarianism which says the community has primacy over the individual. In other words, communitarianism is "reinvented collectivism" or "reinvented communism" which is being espoused on all levels and in every governmental agency, commission, and authority. In addition, our troops are being taught collectivism—the reduction of the individual, and the importance of the team. In an interview conducted by Dr. James Dobson of Focus on the Family with General Charles Krulack, (then) Marine Corp Commandant, General Krulack discussed the new Marine Corp boot camp exercises which are one hundred hours longer. This is part of the transcript from the general's interview, which is tape No. CT117/20600.

Krulack: We added at the end of recruit training something we call "The Crucible"—the defining moment. The term *crucible* was used with special meaning. It's fifty-four hours long, food and sleep deprivation, twenty-nine separate challenges that young Marines must go through. They go through as a team, they do not and cannot accomplish this on their own. The whole idea is to do it as a team. Those challenges are both physical, mental, and moral so that all through the last week of this recruit training, the twelfth week, they bring to culmination all of the values, the disciplines, and selflessness we have tried to inculcate in them the first eleven weeks. If they do not complete the training, they do not become a Marine.

Dobson: You said they cannot make it on their own, it requires teamwork. Explain how that works.

Krulack: It is all oriented toward the military environment to move across a two hundred-yard open area [which requires you] to claw your way through. . . . Unless the Marines do it together, they won't make it.

Dobson: Didn't you tell me when I was there in Washington that you try to keep units together after boot camp to carry through?

Krulack: You are not going to change the values of an eighteen-year-old in twelve weeks. . . . What you can do is give them a new set of values. . . . We are going to hold you accountable. They proceed with the same team in boot camp for the four years they are in the military.

Dobson: That's innovative.

Krulack: That's correct. The key is the peer pressure that is at work and is a positive one.

In order to put Krulack's program in perspective, I interviewed Colonel Ron Ray (retired), one of the most highly decorated veterans who has served in combat in the Vietnam War (two Silver Stars, a Bronze Star, and a Purple Heart). Please see Appendix C.

The Hegelian dialectic is seen in this marriage between the individual and communism (the whole). Our Constitution is based on the freedoms which an individual has. By using collectivist/communitarian principles, the individual has ceded his rights for the "common good" of the whole or the community.

This "team" approach is also used in schools. No longer does the work of an individual mean anything; it is the group. My husband is almost through a master's program. The first thing we noticed when he took his very first course is that he was assigned to a group and the group had a group project which they were graded on. We saw immediately that the individual no longer counted. Most of his classes have all had group projects! Recently I spoke with a junior high school teacher who expressed concern over the emphasis group activities have on the ability of students to think and act as an individual. She commented that they just cannot think as an individual.

In Istanbul at the Habitat II Conference, independent journalist Linda Liotta interviewed Dr. Ismail Serageldin, vice president of the World Bank's Environmentally and Socially Sustainable Development Division, who said:

> We cannot accept . . . that our concern for others stop when we cross an indivisible line that we call a political frontier—that we all are citizens of Planet Earth and that we cannot foresee a situation where the richest twenty percent are getting eighty-four percent of the world's income and the bottom twenty percent are getting 1.4 percent.

In addition, the Group of Seven, the top seven industrialized countries of the world, have made many comments about our "interdependence and interconnectedness," as well as the need to work together as one. In their final report from their 1996 annual meeting in Lyon, France, they state:

> We reaffirm our commitment to the Charter of the United Nations. . . . We continue to regard the United Nations as the cornerstone of an international system whose success or failure is increasingly significant for human security, including the development within countries. . . .

President Clinton, in his January 28, 1998, State of the Union address said:

> We must exercise responsibility not just at home, but around the world. . . . America must stand against the poisoned appeals of extreme nationalism. . . . To meet these challenges we are help-

ing to write international rules of the road of the twenty-first century, protecting those who join the family of nations and isolating those who do not.

The United Nations—The Answer to the World's Problems
In 1995, when the United Nations celebrated its fiftieth anniversary, world leaders came to congratulate the organization. Since words have meaning and are powerful when spoken, it is important to consider what was said and who said it.

> We are in favor of a world order where the role of the U.N. is increasing as an instrument for achieving peace, conflict settlement, and providing development assistance. The U.N. can and should become the main instrument of building new international relations.
>
> —Former Primer Minister Boris Yeltsin, U.S.S.R.

> Interdependence cannot be a meaningful concept if states insist on clinging to selfish national interest. We must be all prepared for the sake of the common good to sacrifice some of our particular concerns and if necessary, some of our sovereignty.
>
> —Prime Minister Dr. Cheddi Jagan (now deceased), Guyana

> The Chinese people are advancing with confident strides on the road of building socialism with Chinese characteristics. We must create a secure and reliable international environment of lasting peace and stability.
>
> —Prime Minister Jiang Zemin, China

> I have a vision of the U.N. General Assembly resembling one day a parliament of the world. I have a vision of the U.N. Security Council assuming additional tasks. One day it might become the focal point for the operational decision-making of this world organization. I have a vision of the U.N. one day establishing a permanent strike force capable of stopping aggressors, as well as

a permanent peacekeeping force with more of a policing role. Mine is a vision of a U.N. consisting not of divided nations but of united people.

—President Vaclav Havel, Czech Republic

Peace

The whole purpose of the U.N. is peace. But what is actually meant by use of this word? While some of the men in this "peace" movement want peace for the sake of real, true peace, many have blinders on, because true peace will never be in a fallen world. It is only when Jesus returns to this earth that we will have true peace.

Then there are those who use the quest for peace as a front for their agenda, which is world domination. Within the early organizations coming out of the Paris Peace Conference of 1919 were several of these such groups, including the World Peace Foundation, and the National Study Conferences on the Churches and a Just and Durable Peace, organized by a commission of the Federal Council of the Churches of Christ in America under the chairmanship of John Foster Dulles, leading international lawyer and statesman.

Then there were a number of small but influential circles, which included the League of Nations Union and the RIIA, as well as political, business, labor, and other interests. Another group, the Commission to Study the Organization of Peace, was established at the end of 1939 under the direction of Prof. James T. Shotwell, who played a prominent role in world affairs since the Paris Peace Conference. Members included Frank Aydelotte, John Foster Dulles, Clark M. Eichelberger, Frank Graham, Philip Jessup, Charles P. Taft, and Quincy Wright—many of whom were members of other groups, such as the Council on Foreign Policy Association and the League of Nations Association (Cheever and Haviland, 54–57).

I think it is evident that the United Nations is a vehicle for purposes other than true world peace. It is a vehicle for control of the people, land and resources of the world. In short, the only peace the United Nations really wants is no opposition to what they want! Hence, the real battle is spiritual.

Chapter 4

The Report
from Iron Mountain

CHAPTER SUMMARY

And the LORD said unto me, A conspiracy is found among the
men of Judah, and among the inhabitants of Jerusalem.

—Jeremiah 11:9

In 1963, fifteen men were asked in secrecy to serve on a commission which also would work in secrecy. The goal they were given
was to "determine accurately, and realistically, the nature of the
problems that would confront the United States if and when a condition of 'permanent peace' should arrive, and to draft a program
for dealing with that contingency." They were told that the "idea
for this kind of study, dated back to 1961 . . . with some of the new
people who came in the Kennedy administration . . . McNamara,
Bundy, and Rusk."

Their report, known as the *Report from Iron Mountain,* was made
public by someone on the commission who, while agreeing with its
conclusions, determined that the American people had a right to
know. The report covered the economic, political, social, ecological, scientific, and cultural aspects of life. Their conclusions are
very, very disturbing to anyone who espouses Christian values and
truths. They conclude that the "elimination of war implies the inevitable elimination of national sovereignty and the traditional nation-state." Therefore, if there is no war and we are one, then that
means a whole new type of society will have to be put in place.

In the report, the commission determined that although war is expensive for the country waging it, war also creates an economic boom. In other words war is a money maker. Therefore, if the world is going to replace war with peace, there needs to be an expense that equals that of war to maintain a certain level of economic growth. The report states that it would be necessary given our complex economy to waste not less than ten percent of our Gross National Product. The following are substitute forms of spending:

1. *Health*—Drastic expansion of medical research, education, and training facilities, hospitals and clinic construction—the objective is government-guaranteed health care for all.
2. *Education*—What needs to be done in health also has to be done for education—drastic upgrading of standards with the objective of making available for all a goal of what now is considered a professional degree.
3. *Housing*—Clean, comfortable, safe and spacious living for all, at the level now enjoyed by twenty-five percent of our population.
4. *Transportation*—The establishment of a system of mass public transportation making it possible for all to travel to and from areas of work and recreation, quickly, comfortably, and conveniently.
5. *Physical environment*—The development and protection of water supplies, forests, parks, and other natural resources, the elimination of chemical and bacterial contaminants from the air, water, and soil.
6. *Poverty*—welfare.

Interestingly, all of the conclusions of the *Report from Iron Mountain* just happen to be the same goals and objectives of the United Nations!

> **Note:** This report has been refuted by the United States government. It is up to the reader to determine if all of their objectives are "coincidences" with reality.

[The King of Assyria said], And my hand hath found as a nest the riches of the people: and as one gathereth eggs that are left, have I gathered all the earth; and there was none that moved the wing, or opened the mouth, or peeped.

—Isaiah 10:14

INTRODUCTION

We must understand the philosophy of world control behind the United Nations—control of not only the leaders of the individual countries who participate at the U.N., but the world's resources: coal, diamonds, gold, titanium, uranium, copper, manganese, agriculture, forests, parks, water—oceans, lakes, rivers, streams, aquifers—and its people.

The United Nations has adopted a number of environmental philosophies for the very purpose of gaining complete control. In Appendix D you will find a chronology of events, laws, and books which are key to understanding the evolution of this evil global agenda. These philosophies are: sustainable development, family dependency ratio, biological diversity (known as "biodiversity"), and the transfer of wealth from the rich countries to the poor so that the resources of the world can be equalized. (While this sounds nice, it basically allows money to be transferred, yet most funds never get applied to the poor at all. Look at Russian communism. They still have the poor while the rulers live like kings.) I would imagine that if all the money which the U.S. and other countries have given in foreign aid went directly to the people, it would be doubtful that the poor would be still poor.

A number of U.N. concepts are being discussed on television, at school, in the government, and even in churches. They include taking care of the environment (the worship of the earth, or Gaia worship, is part of "taking care of the environment"), reducing the population through family planning and condoms because they say the Earth cannot provide for all of the people, getting everyone to participate in community (volunteerism), and reducing what we consume to protect the earth. **Interestingly enough, a planned ca-**

tastrophe will ensure that everyone participates in the community, volunteers, and reduces their consumption. This action will be because the price is too high or because of shortages.

While most Americans think our government would never participate in these kinds of programs, the fact is, the United States has been a world leader in instituting sustainable development, biodiversity, population reduction (sex education, condoms, family planning, etc.), and even the transfer of wealth through foreign aid and grants. The United States has led in strengthening the United Nations, the World Bank, and other global agencies.

My understanding of this very evil, Orwellian global agenda has evolved over the last five years. I first became acquainted with the environment, sustainable development, and population reduction when I attended my first United Nations conference in Cairo in 1994. As I continued to read U.N. material, I was overwhelmed with how pervasive these philosophies are. The mental picture I pieced together as I read from the Cairo documents (newspapers, brochures, and magazines) which talked openly and freely about reducing the population and providing U.N. fertility rates of men and women and other personal statistics about every country, is Orwellian.

REPORT FROM IRON MOUNTAIN
ON THE POSSIBILITY AND DESIRABILITY OF PEACE
Introduction

About a year into attending U.N. conferences, I started to hear about a rare report, *Report from Iron Mountain*. I sat down to read the report, *only to realize that the whole United Nations agenda is based on the report* (or perhaps we could say that there is an amazing coincidence in which the goals and agenda of the U.N. happen to fulfill many of the goals outlined in the report). The world has been evolving toward "peace," which means "no opposition" to what the U.N. is proposing. The U.N.'s goals for the 1990s and beyond mirror the march toward peace as identified in the *Report from Iron Mountain*. It should be noted that when this report was made public, it was highly refuted. When you read it, you will know why.

The report is a summary of the analysis and conclusions of fifteen men who were asked to serve on a commission of "the highest importance" in 1963. (When you refer to Appendix D, observe the environmental laws and U.N. activity which came after that year.) The goal they were given was to "determine, accurately and realistically, the nature of the problems that would confront the United States if and when a condition of 'permanent peace' should arrive, and to draft a program for dealing with this contingency" (Lewin, viii).

Their report was to be kept secret, as they were sworn to secrecy for life. They were told that the "idea for this *kind* of study, dated back to 1961 . . . with some of the new people who came in with the Kennedy administration . . . McNamara, Bundy, and Rusk," people who were concerned that no real serious work had been done about planning for peace—a long-range peace with long-range planning. According to Lewin, the exact details of the Special Study Group were worked out in 1963 after the Cuban missile crisis (xvii).

Interestingly enough, McGeorge Bundy who became Kennedy's National Security Adviser, and Dean Rusk, Kennedy's Secretary of State, came from the Rockefeller Foundation, which has funded both right and left causes, Christian and agnostic organizations, and many pro-world government groups. Nineteen others affiliated with the Rockefeller Foundation who became Kennedy administration appointees included: Col. William R. Kinter, Joint Chiefs of Staff; C. Douglas Dillon, Secretary of the Treasury; Harland Cleveland, State Department Assistant Secretary for International Organization Affairs; Richard Gardner, State Department Deputy Assistant Secretary for International Organization Affairs; Walt W. Rostow, Deputy National Security Adviser; and Henry Kissinger, who served as a consultant (Colby and Dennett, 337–38). In William J. Gill's very fine account of *The Ordeal of Otto Otepka*, he shows how Harlan Cleveland and Walt W. Rostow, and others, could not pass high security clearance as a result of their very close communistic affiliations. Kennedy ended up appointing them to office rather than have them face Senate approval. The changes John Kennedy introduced certainly will not lead to the kind of fairy tale "Camelot" most people envision.

"John Doe," the Special Study Group member who made the report public, did not know who in the White House selected the men who would serve in the Group, but guessed it was an ad hoc committee at the cabinet level or near to it. The Group included an historian, an international law professor, an economist, a sociologist, a cultural anthropologist, a psychiatrist, a literary critic, a physical chemist, a biochemist, a mathematician, an astronomer, a systems analyst and war planner, and an industrialist. (Shortly after this book was published John Kenneth Galbraith, the economist from Harvard, made public that he served on the Special Study Group. He knew that very few people were aware of the Group.) The purpose of the Group was to use a kind of thinking that would free them from cultural, moral, religious, political, and emotional constraints. In the process, the Group developed a computerized "forecasting technique" that they felt would "revolutionize the study of social problems. This new model of 'Peace Games' became a by-product of their study" (Lewin, xxviii) and enabled them to achieve their conclusions in less time.

The letter of transmittal (dated September 30, 1966), that accompanied the final report included six hundred four exhibits as well as a preliminary manual of the Peace Games, and was not part of the published report. The Group was unanimous in its conclusions. Since peace was to be the goal of their deliberations, members had to deal with the "real functions of war in modern societies beyond defending and advancing the 'national interests' of nations. **In the absence of war, what other institutions exist or might be devised to fulfill these functions?"** (emphasis added). Their report considered disarmament and its affect on the economy, various disarmament scenarios, war and peace as social systems, the function of war, and substitutes for the functions of war.

In the foreword by Leonard C. Lewin, who was chosen by John Doe to have the report published, he warns that the general reader may be unprepared for its conclusions:

> He may not be prepared for some of its assumptions—that most medical advances are viewed more as problems than as progress; or that poverty is necessary and desirable, public postures by politicians to the contrary notwithstanding; or that standing armies are, among other things, social welfare institutions in exactly the same sense as are old people's homes and mental hospitals. It may strike him as odd to find the probable explanation of "flying saucer" incidents disposed of *en passant* in less than a sentence. He may be less surprised to find that the space program and the "controversial" antimissile missile and fallout shelter programs are understood to have the spending of vast sums of money, not the advance of science or national defense, as their principal goals, and to learn that military draft policies are only remotely concerned with defense. He may be offended to find the organized repression of minority groups and even the reestablishment of slavery, seriously discussed as possible aspects of a world at peace. He is not likely to take kindly to the notion of deliberate intensification of air and water pollution (as a part of a program leading to peace). That a world without war will have to turn sooner rather than later to universal test-tube procreation will be less disturbing, if not more appealing. But few readers will not be taken aback ... in the report's conclusions . . . that suggest that the long-range planning—and *"budgeting"— of the "optimum" number of lives to be destroyed annually in overt warfare is high on the Group's list of priorities for government action.* I cite these few examples to warn the general reader, the statesmen and strategist for whose eyes the report was intended obviously need no such protective admonition.
>
> —Lewin, xi–xii (emphasis mine)

The following is an outline of the report.

The Nature of War

According to the report:

The nature of war is not to extend or defend a nation's expressed political values or their economic interests but is the principal basis of organization on which all modern societies are constructed. Readiness for war characterizes contemporary social systems more broadly than their economic and political structures, which it subsumes. Economic analyses of the anticipated problems of transition to peace have not recognized the broad preeminence of war in the definition of social systems.

—pp. 79–80

Disarmament and the Economy

In looking at the world, the report states that the "world war industry" accounts for one-tenth of the output of the world's total economy, which means *general disarmament would require a structural change*. In shifting men and materials from war to peace, the men would have to be retrained, but the problem is "to what"? Because war requires vast amounts of money, *a country would have to find an alternative way to spend the monies now being reappropriated for peace time*. The report states there would have to be "increased consumption" in the public sector in the form of national spending for health, education, mass transportation, low-cost housing, water, control of the physical environment, and poverty. In addition, to go to an "arms-free" economy, there would have to be substantial changes in both sides of the federal budget. Basically *the spending for space research would have to equal the amount spent for armament expenditures*.

In addition, in order to disarm there would have to be a *dependence on bilateral/multilateral agreements* between the great powers, which would call for a progressive phasing out of gross armaments, military forces, weapons, and weapons of technology, coordinated with elaborate procedures of verification, inspection, and machinery for the settlement of international disputes. Disarmament would require a twelve-year, three-stage phaseout consisting of (1) a reduction of armed forces; (2) cutbacks in weapons production, inventories, and foreign military bases; and (3) the development of international inspection procedures and control conventions. With each phase, there would have to be an economic conversion plan.

War and Peace as Social Systems

The report points out that

> although war is "used" as an instrument of national and social policy, the fact that a society is organized for any degree of readiness for war supersedes its political and economic structure. War itself is the basic social system within which other secondary modes of social organization conflict or conspire. It is the system which has governed most human societies.

—p. 29

The report states:

> Wars are not "caused" by international conflicts of interest, but the capacity of a nation to make war expresses the greatest social power it can exercise: war-making, active or contemplated, is a matter of life and death on the greatest scale subject to social control.

They state that there are many myths of war which include defending a nation from military attack by another, or deferring such an attack, or defending or advancing a "national interest"—economic, political, ideological—to maintain or increase a nation's military power for its own sake (30–31).

The Functions of War

According to the report, war has provided both ancient and modern societies with a dependable system for stabilizing and controlling national economies. No alternate method of control has yet been tested in a complex modern economy that has shown itself remotely comparable in scope or effectiveness. A healthy military apparatus requires regular "exercise" by whatever rationale seems expedient, to prevent its atrophy. When war is eliminated, the need for the military will end, which will require new institutions to replace the military.

1. *Economic:* First, the production of weapons of mass destruction are produced outside of the economic framework of supply and demand.

> War creates an artificial demand and only war solves the problem of inventory. The economics of war provides additional protection against depressions. Without a long-established war economy, and without its frequent eruption into a large-scale shooting war, most of the major industrial advances known to history, beginning with the development of iron, could never have taken place.
>
> —p. 36

Weapons technology structures the economy . . . war production is progressive because it is production that would not otherwise have taken place. For example, as a result of WWII, the civilian standard of living rose.

War production stimulates the economy and has been consistently a positive factor in the rise of the GNP and of individual productivity.

Although we do not imply that a substitute for war in the economy cannot be devised, no combination of techniques for controlling employment, production, and consumption has yet been tested that can remotely compare to its effectiveness.

2. *Political:* The report stated that war has not only been essential to the existence of nations as independent political entities, but it has been equally indispensable to their stable international political structure. Without war *no government has ever been able to obtain the "right to rule its society."* The basic au-

thority of a modern state over its people resides in its war powers, which define the most significant aspect of the relationship between the state and the citizen. The political functions of war are even more critical to social stability. War includes all national activities that recognize the possibility of armed conflict which in itself is the defining element of any nation's existence *vis-a-vis* any other nation. It is historically axiomatic that the existence of any form of weaponry insures its use. The report uses the word "peace" as virtually synonymous with disarmament and the word "war" as virtually synonymous with nationhood. **"The elimination of war implies the inevitable elimination of national sovereignty and the traditional nation-state"** (39, emphasis mine).

War also serves as a safeguard

> against the elimination of necessary social classes. The younger and more dangerous of hostile social groupings come under the control by the Selective Service System. . . . The armed forces in every civilization have provided the principal state-supported haven for what we now call the "unemployables."
>
> —p. 42–43

3. *Social:* War, through the medium of military institutions, has uniquely served societies, throughout the course of known history, as an indispensable controller of dangerous social dissidence and destructive antisocial tendencies. The war system has provided the machinery through which the motivational forces governing human behavior have been translated into binding social allegiance. It has thus ensured the degree of social cohesion necessary to the viability of nations. No other institution has successfully served these functions.

In war, it is the strong who fight and fall which is the natural selection in reverse. When an animal faces a crisis of insufficiency, it is the "inferior" members of the species that normally disappear. "A new quasi-eugenic function of war is now in the process of formation that will have to be taken into account in any transition plan" (p. 51).

War is the principal motivational force for the development of science at every level from the abstractly conceptional to the narrowly technological. Modern society places a high value on "pure" science but it is historically inescapable that all the significant discoveries that have been made about the natural world have been inspired by the real or imaginary military necessities to the epochs.

4. *Ecological:* War has been the principal evolutionary device for maintaining a satisfactory ecological balance between gross human population and supplies available for its survival. It is unique to the human species (81–82).

5. *Cultural and Scientific:* War orientation has determined the basic standards of value in the creative arts and provided the fundamental motivational source of scientific and technological progress.

Substitutes for the Functions of War

According to the report, "The most detailed and comprehensive master plan for a transition to world peace will remain academic if it fails to deal with the problem of the critical non-military functions." The report was divided up into four sections: economic, political, sociological, and ecological.

1. Economic: Under economic considerations, the writers state that the "economic surrogates for war must meet two principle criteria: they must be *wasteful in the common sense of the word* and *operate outside the normal supply-demand system."* The report projected that our complex economy would require *the planned average annual destruction of not less than ten percent of gross national product* if it was to fulfill its stabilizing function. We are not talking about feeding the poor, because it states in the report that the poor as a social class are needed (58).

Furthermore, the following areas were recommended for the destruction of ten percent of the GNP:

a. *Health*—Drastic expansion of medical research, education, and training facilities; hospital and clinic construction. The objective is government-guaranteed health care for all.

b. *Education*—Drastic upgrading of standards, with the objective of making a professional degree available for all.

c. *Housing*—Clean, comfortable, safe, and spacious living for all, at the level now enjoyed by only twenty-five percent of our population.

d. *Transportation*—The establishment of a mass public transportation system, making it possible for all to travel quickly, comfortably, and conveniently to and from areas of work and recreation.

e. *Physical environment*—The development and protection of water supplies, forests, parks, and other natural resources; the elimination of chemical and bacterial contaminants from the air, water, and soil.

f. *Poverty*—The genuine elimination of poverty defined by a standard consistent with economic productivity.

It should be noted that the U.N. Habitat II Conference in June 1996 had all of the above as goals for the nation-states of the world. The report stated that on a short-term basis, the above recommendations could replace normal military spending provided it was designed like a military model and subject to arbitrary control.

Another way to help "blow" money which was not discussed in the report is through legal fraud. Consider someone in a key place of authority such as a department or agency head. Think how easy it would be in a huge budget to hide "extraordinary" expenses. We read about things like this almost every day in the newspapers.

Another very important economic surrogate for spending money is "space research." The report specifically mentioned "the development of a long-range sequence of space-research projects with largely unattainable goals. For example if colonization of the moon proceeds on schedule, it could then become 'necessary' to establish a beachhead on Mars or Jupiter and so on" (62).

2. Political

The report proposes "the end of war means the end of national sovereignty, and thus the end of nationhood as we know it today" (65). Therefore, the governing of nations after total disarmament would be juridical, suggesting the following:

a. *The United Nations*—vested with real authority
b. *Supranational Court*—supreme court of the world
c. Omnipotent international police force
d. An established and recognized extraterrestrial menace

The report went on to lament that "credibility lies at the heart of the problem of developing a political substitute for war. This is where the space-race proposals fall short." However, the writers suggest the need to find a way to

> unite mankind against the danger of destruction by "creatures" from other planets or from outer space. Experiments have been proposed to test the credibility of an out-of-our-world invasion threat; it is possible that a few of the more difficult-to-explain "flying saucer" incidents of recent years were in fact early experiments of this kind.
>
> —p. 66

Perhaps that is where movies like *Alien* and *Armageddon* come into play, not to mention *The X-Files*.

3. Sociological

The report calls for an effective substitute for military institutions to neutralize destabilizing social elements. Suggestions include some variant of the Peace Corps or Job Corps, or possibly "unarmed forces" (68).

Slavery: The report states, "another possible surrogate for control of potential enemies of society is the reintroduction in some form, consistent with modern technology and political processes of slavery." They state: "It is entirely possible that the development of a sophisticated form of slavery may be an absolute prerequisite for social control in a world at peace" (70). Perhaps we should consider the "school-to-grave" (there is now a strong push for retirees to volunteer in the community, and some have no choice as the rising cost of living makes it necessary for sixty- and seventy-year-olds to work; see sustained development in this chapter) programs as part of this as well as the private prisons which are popping up as a result of "reinventing government." For example, in the state of Maryland, all twenty-six state prisons are part of the State Use Industries (SUI) which is a "sprawling network of thirty shops and manufacturing plants scattered among Maryland's twenty-six prison facilities, generating more than $430 million in sales annually and putting thirteen hundred prisoners in a variety of skilled and unskilled jobs" (Valentine, B1). Inmates are typically paid $1.00 to $2.50 a day plus small "production bonuses" every month. They manufacture office desks and chairs, uniforms, mattresses, plaques, name tags, file folders, street signs, driver's license renewal forms for the Motor Vehicle Administration, grow fish, apples, and corn, and process meats including beef patties, stew meat, roasts, sausage and turkey loaf (Valentine, B1 and B4).

Another way to control individual aggressive impulses the report cited would be through the development of "blood games." They wrote: "If a ritualized manhunt were to be used along the lines of the movie *The Tenth Victim* it might be socialized in the manner of the Spanish Inquisition" (71). Could Ruby Ridge and Waco be considered as examples?

4. Environmental

In 1992, twenty years after its first environmental conference, the United Nations unveiled plans for the environment at a major conference in Rio de Janeiro, which was dubbed "Earth Summit." There the people of the world were told that the environment had precedence over man, who was now relegated to the status of an animal. This is a fundamental inversion/perversion of Genesis 1. Anyone studying the progression of environment issues will see that this agenda has taken on great momentum since that first meeting. In 1987 a key philosophical component called "sustainable development" had been birthed. This concept conceded that the population of the world would have to be reduced considerably in order for the world to have enough resources for "future generations." (Please note there is a whole other philosophy behind "future generations." The World Court is looking to establish another body of law for this concept.) Interestingly enough, the heinous idea of using the environment as a mechanism for reducing the world population as a substitute for war came from *The Report from Iron Mountain*, which hinted that perhaps the environmental pollution model could "eventually replace the possibility of mass destruction by nuclear weapons as the principal apparent threat to the survival of the species" (67).

The report lamented that war was a mechanism of selective population control and that a substitute was needed. They wrote: "War has been the principal evolutionary device for maintaining a satisfactory ecological balance between gross human population and supplies available for its survival" (81–82).

Group members indicated that the problem with making the environment a substitute for war would be difficult to bring about because of the politics. (Let me note here that the radical environmental agenda which was unveiled in Rio de Janeiro in June 1992 at the Earth Summit was consented to by the delegates from the countries of the world as a result of a secret meeting Prince Charles held fourteen months before. At that meeting Senator Al Gore, as well as representatives from other parts of the world, agreed to help get consensus on the Programme of Action, Agenda 21 [a viable non-war substitute]. It should be noted that the International Chamber of Commerce which represents businesses from all over the world, including your community, also was instrumental in lobbying for passage.) Group members also recognized that peace could not be established **while the war system still is in effect because excess population is war material** (74). Perhaps this is why the world has seen a plethora of regional or contained wars and mass starvation by ruthless dictators in Uganda, Ethiopia, China, and elsewhere.

They wrote that the intermediate step for total control of conception would be with a variant of the ubiquitous "pill," via water supplies or certain essential foodstuffs, that could be offset by a controlled "antidote" already under development (73). As a community activist, I could not understand the reasoning behind our school's sex education programs until I went to Cairo and learned the United Nation's agenda to reduce the population of the earth. It was then that I realized the local agenda I was fighting was a global agenda being implemented in the local school system.

Lastly, with regard to population,

> there was no question but that a universal requirement for procreation be limited to the products of artificial insemination [which] would provide a fully adequate substitute control for population levels. Such a reproductive system would have the added advantage of being susceptible of direct eugenic management.
>
> —p. 73

Birth control and birth selection are examples on one side of the life spectrum, with Kevorkian eugenics gaining momentum on the other side of life.

CONCLUSIONS

The report concluded that:

> It is apparent from the foregoing that no program or combination of programs yet proposed for a transition to peace has remotely approached meeting the comprehensive functional requirements of a world without war. While the projected system for filling the economic function of wars seems promising, . . . that is not true with the political and sociological areas. The other nonmilitary functions of war—ecological, cultural, scientific—raise very dif-

ferent problems, but it is at least possible that detailed programming substitutes in these areas is not prerequisite to transition.

When asked how best to prepare for the advent of peace, we must first reply that the war system cannot responsibly be allowed to disappear until 1) we know exactly what it is we plan to put in its place, and 2) we are certain, beyond reasonable doubt, that these substitute institutions will serve their purposes in terms of the survival and stability of society.

Such solutions, if they indeed exist, will not be arrived at without a revolutionary revision of the modes of thought heretofore considered appropriate to peace research. Our final conclusion, therefore, is that it will be necessary for our government to plan indepth for two general contingencies. The first, and lesser, is the possibility of a viable general peace; the second is the successful continuation of the war system. In our view, careful preparation for the possibility of peace should be extended, not because we take the position that the end of war would necessarily be desirable, if it is in fact possible, but because it may be thrust upon us in some form whether we are ready for it or not (emphasis mine).

—p. 94

Interestingly enough, some of the possibilities of attacks we face include terrorism—cyber hackers, extremists, financial fraud, and information wars in cyberspace.

ROBERT S. McNAMARA

Before we take a look at each of the recommendations from the *Report from Iron Mountain* and how they have been fulfilled by the United Nations, let us consider one key individual, Robert S. McNamara.

The Report from Iron Mountain becomes extremely important when you look at the career of one individual who was named a number of times in the report as being in a key position in the Kennedy administration. That particular man is Robert McNamara, who was Secretary of Defense under Kennedy and Johnson, and then was president of the World Bank for thirteen years.

> As a result of our superiority over the Russians, Walt Whitman Rostow, who served in the Kennedy administration and as chief of the State Department's Policy Planning Council, and Jerome B. Weisner, then director of MIT's electronics research laboratory, agreed that it was time to help Russia catch up to our weapons superiority. It was McNamara who in June 1964 eliminate[d] or shelve[d] a whole array of America's most effective or promising weapons [such as] . . . the Skybolt and Pluto missiles; the X-20 Dynasoar; B-70 bomber; 195 Bomarc-A missiles; Nike-Zeus ABM defense system; and the Navy's Typhoon frigates and weapons systems, and 129 Atlas missiles which alone had cost $5.4 billion.
>
> —Gill, 157

As Secretary of Defense, McNamara issued "rules of engagement" that put our soldiers in Vietnam at a disadvantage because they

> were not permitted to fire until their situation became desperate. This kind of suicidal warfare was an everyday occurrence in Vietnam. Yet McNamara's Rules of Engagement were themselves covered up and it was not until 1985—ten years after the fall of Vietnam—that the Defense Department declassified them at the behest of Senator Goldwater [who] then inserted them into the *Congressional Record*. Barry Goldwater remarked that "these layers of restrictions, which were constantly changing and were almost impossible to memorize or understand, although it was required of our pilots, . . . granted huge sanctuary areas to the enemy. Although we lost hundreds of our pilots over North Vietnam, they were never permitted to bomb really strategic targets. Airmen contended that one bomb could have knocked out a huge hydroelectric dam, cutting off most of the communist country's power, flooding its food supply, and probably forcing an end to the war. But that single bomb was never dropped on that critical target.
>
> —Gill, 176–77

Lastly, it was McNamara who covered up the

> Soviet's heavy involvement in supplying the communist forces that were taking an ever rising toll on American casualties. The late Mendel Rivers, chairman of the House Armed Services Committee, told me in a 1966 interview that he repeatedly urged the Secretary of Defense to remove the "classified" label he had imposed for several years on the reports of Russian ships offloading weapons and material at Haiphong. But McNamara, with the cooperation of the media, continued to keep this important information from the American people.
>
> —Gill, 178

According to Bruce Rich, author of *Mortgaging the Earth: The World Bank, Environmental Impoverishment, and the Crisis of Development,* it was Robert S. McNamara who actually turned the World Bank into a "Faustian paradox." Rich spends almost eight percent of his book exposing McNamara's evil management tactics and how his dream of eliminating poverty through World Bank development projects drove countries into social, economic, and environmental chaos.

From the Defense Department, McNamara went to the World Bank, where he served as president from 1968 to 1981. During those years

> he increased bank lending from $953 million to $12.4 billion (sixfold), and the Bank staff from 1,574 to 5,201. The Bank's mission would be for the "sake of the poorest of the poor." McNamara created an environmental office at the bank and declared in Stockholm at the 1972 U.N. Conference on the Human Environment, "The question is not whether there should be continued economic growth. There must be. Nor is the question whether the impact on the environment must be respected. It has to be. . . . These two considerations are interlocked."
>
> —Rich, 81

The Bank, under McNamara's direction, prepared five-year master country lending plans, which set targets and priorities for all Bank lending in a given nation. These reports were confidential; even ministers of a nation's cabinet could not obtain access to these documents. These reports became the "master planning documents" for the Bank's entire lending portfolio. Accountable to no one, not even the board of directors,

> the Bank prepared a development plan for "every relevant aspect" of a "nation's social framework." The Bank would go on to lead scores of governments in formulating these plans, which, it goes without saying would attempt to regulate "every relevant aspect" of society. Based on the Bank's gathering, filtering, and organizing of information, other international agencies would help to finance the elements of the development blueprints formulated under the Bank's aegis. The Bank would guide the generation of such knowledge in order to plan; implicit in the planning is control, and in control domination—over the evolution of human beings and nature on a planetary scale. It is no exaggeration to call such a project Faustian.
>
> —Rich 85–86

The bottom line, according to Rich is that

> bank poverty-oriented agricultural lending actually promoted the destruction of smaller local farms and the displacement of hundreds of millions of peasants around the world. McNamara's poverty strategy in practice only accelerated a process of agricultural modernization and integration into the global market that in the view of many researchers *increased* inequality and *produced* poverty and underdevelopment by displacing rural people formerly rooted in traditional subsistence-farming communities.
>
> —p. 91

In summary, Robert McNamara's middle name is Strange. This

indeed appears to be an appropriate middle name if his real objectives were to reduce population through starvation, which indeed comes when a farmer is displaced from his way of life, and through the elimination of victory when troops are placed at a disadvantage. Having served in the Kennedy administration during the time *The Report from Iron Mountain* was written, and then at the World Bank, where he could "fashion and guide" its environmental and development programs, it appears that he has done much to further the goals of the report.

IMPLEMENTATION OF THE REPORT

The following takes the recommendations from the report and shows with actual examples how the recommendations have or are being implemented.

1. Disarmament

John Kennedy said, "Mankind must put an end to war, or war will put an end to mankind." In 1963, the Moscow Treaty Banning Nuclear Weapons Tests in the Atmosphere, in Outer Space, and Under Water was followed by the telephone Hot Line Agreement. Other early bilateral and multilateral agreements followed, such as the No Nuclear Arms in Space (January 1967) signed by the United States, Russia, and the United Kingdom, the Non-Proliferation Treaty (July 1968), and SALT I (November 1969). In the 1970s, there was the Sea Bed Treaty in 1971, the Biological Weapons Convention in 1972, SALT 1 Interim and the ABM Treaty (SALT 1) and Protocol in 1972. In the 1980s, President Reagan met with Russian leader Mikhail Gorbachev for the 1987 INF Treaty. There continues to be a series of additional non-proliferation types of agreements that continue to this day.

On September 26, 1961, Public Law 87-297, which is the State Department's Publication 7277 entitled "Freedom from War," sets out a major change in the ability of America to defend herself. This publication calls for U.S. troops to be deployed overseas and for foreign troops to be used in America, should and when the need ever arise. Will Americans be ready for the day when foreign troops are deployed here? Will it be sold to Americans as a "friendly invasion"? It states:

An ultimate goal of the United States is a world which is free from the scourge of war and the dangers and burdens of armaments; in which the use of force has been subordinated to the rule of law; and in which international adjustments to a changing world are achieved peacefully.

In 1983 this public law was elevated to treaty status.

In 1995 a nongovernmental panel recommended privatizing many noncombat support activities, merging redundant Pentagon staff members, and eliminating about fifty thousand Army National Guard positions (*Washington Post*, May 24, 1995, A23). That same year, the military started closing bases. Interestingly enough, the U.S. government continued to improve a number of the bases that were going to eventually be closed. For example, San Diego's Naval Training Center opened a new $5.1 million chapel just in time to hold graduation for the facility's last recruit class; it closed in 1997. The Air Force spent $7.1 million in 1995 to renovate a gym destroyed by Hurricane Andrew, even though the base was closed in 1994. The facilities will be used by reserve units (*Washington Times*, October 10, 1996, A13).

In a recent interview with a highly placed naval officer stationed in the Pacific, he said that it is now routine to train military for humanitarian assistance which may be needed in case of natural disaster. We are seeing a complete change in the mission of our military. No longer are they prepared to protect America against a first attack, but they have become exotic peacekeepers.

Furthermore the Pentagon agreed to reduce ballistic submarines from 34 to 18, strategic bombers from 268 to 171, active military personnel to 1,653,000 by 1995, and our active Army divisions from 18 to 12, Navy ships from 545 to 451, and active tactical fighter wings from 24 to 15 by 1995.

The U.N. has long advocated peace. It has called for a reduction in armed forces, military bases, and weapons. It was Costa Rican president Oscar Arias who came up with a "peace plan" to reduce military spending worldwide by three percent a year for ten years. Yet, most recently the Joint Chiefs of Staff testified that America today is woefully unprepared for any kind of attack should one be lodged against us (summer 1998). And it should be mentioned that the Chinese and Russians have strong military might. The October 1998 Omnibus Spending Bill (HR4328) approves the Chemical Weapons Convention Implementation Act.

2. Economic

Wasting ten percent of GNP per year—Johnson's "Great Society" and Vietnam: President Johnson carried on with Kennedy's platform. At a speech at Ann Arbor, Michigan, he called for "an end to poverty and racial injustice" and launched the Great Society which created welfare and many of the massive social spending programs aimed at providing housing for the poor, food stamps, Medicaid and Medicare, and other benefits. President Johnson ran into economic trouble when he escalated the war in Vietnam while funding his social welfare programs because the government had never financed a war and launched an expensive social spending program at the same time. As a result, the deficit in 1968 came to $25 billion, which was twice as large as any other deficit since World War II.

So Lyndon Johnson began deficit spending in earnest and the rest of the presidents have followed. While Ronald Reagan made me feel warm and secure, he was spending the rest of our inheritance. By administering a combination of tax cuts and increased spending, federal deficits totalled $1.34 trillion in eight years. In its report published in 1995, the Grace Commission estimated that our federal deficits would total $3.17 trillion by 1996. We far surpassed that amount in 1997, with a total of $5.7 trillion. In June 1999, President Clinton endorsed the 4,800-page Omnibus spending bill which included: $22.6 billion for food stamps; $9.2 billion for children's nutrition programs; $1.7 billion for the National Park Service; $98.5 million for the National Endowment for the Arts; $1.2 billion for one hundred thousand new teachers; $168.2 billion for the tax administration of Medicare and Medicaid; $47 billion for the Department of Transportation; and $1.9 billion for Bosnia-Herzegovina operations, to name a few of its appropriations. In October 1999 Clinton announced that he had added to his spending budget for 2000, the amount of $1 billion for debt-forgiveness of poor countries.

With the nineteen-member NATO invasion of Kosovo, a sovereign country, it now appears that the original mission of NATO has changed to that of becoming the army of the United Nations. Most of the costs of this war will be borne by the United States since most of the cruise missiles and two-thirds of the aircraft were American. This cost does not take into consideration ground troops, lost or destroyed aircraft (the Stealth bomber costs $43 million), transportation for equipment and troops, aircraft refueling and maintenance, and humanitarian assistance. This expense could be substantially increased depending upon how long the war goes on since it would increase the number of destroyed aircraft and munitions fired. Precision bombs cost about $40,000 each, and Navy tomahawk and Air Force cruise missiles can average $1 million apiece. The cost for Iraq was $102 billion. The Pentagon budget is currently stretched and all of these expenses will require congressionally approved funds (combined reports from the *Financial Times* dated April 9, 1999, and the *Washington Times* dated April 2, 1999). All of this at a time when the stock market crosses ten thousand!

In 1994 President Clinton committed U.S. troops to Haiti to "give democracy a second chance." Congress has spent $2.2 billion of U.S. taxpayers' money with chaos continuing. The per capita income has fallen to $225 per year from $560 five years ago (*Washington Times*, March 23, 1999).

As shown in Chart 4-1, "Overview of Key Economic Indicators 1990-1998," we have been inundated with new tax laws and deficit spending for all of the 1990s.

Chart 4-1
Overview of Key Economic Indicators 1990–1998

Occurrence	1990	1991	1992	1993	1994	1995	1996	1997	1998
Dominant Occurrence	Kuwait War; U.S. banking system in worst shape since 30s.	45 Cn. Unions close in RI; Bank New England fail	Clinton elected; U.S. dollar bailed out by 13 central banks	National healthcare not passed	Dollar crisis—dollar had to be rescued; Bailed out by 15 central banks	Barings Bank goes under—no bailouts given	Banking Modern. Bill introduced	Asian crisis; Hong Kong reverts to China	Extreme marked volatility
Dominant Occurrence	Drexel Burnham Lambert fails; Japan's stock mkt. falls 50% to 20,000	BCCI—$10B bilked	LA riots; NAFTA passed; Japan's stock market falls 50%; Europe devalues	Foreigners bought $45.3B Treasuries	GATT passed—26,000+ pages	Foreigners buy $134B Treasuries		Banking Modern. Bill introduced	Debt problem Russia, Asia, Brazil
Dow	High was 3,000; Market dropped 540 points-recovered bec. Kuwait War	Continuous new highs to 3168.83	Reached historic highs because of low interest —3413; up 4.17%	Continued to reach new highs as result M&A; low int.; 3,700; up $12.54%	Market reached historic highs at 3978; up 2.14%	Reaches historic highs 4000—Feb; 5000—October; up 33.45%	Market reaches historic highs 6560.91 up 26%	Mark up 27%	From high 9334, drop to low of 7539, up 8300; no gain
Foreign Owners of Treasuries	$57,285M	$49,819M	$77,988M	$126,347M	$101,792M	$240,700M	$380,417M		
Federal Reserve	Lowered discount rate to 27-year low @ 3.5%	Tried to "jump start" economy by cutting funds 14 times to 4.5%	Cont. to ease many policy-funds to 3.25%; prime rate 6.25%	Fed funds @ 3%; discount rate @ 3%; prime rate 6.00%	Prime rate began to rise; Fed raises rates six times to 4.25%	Fed cuts discount .25%—first in 3 years to .5%	No rate cuts	No rate cuts	Fed lowers discount rate to stimulate economy
Taxes	Passed largest deficit in history—Budget Reconciliation Act	Emergency Unemployment Compensation Act	Tax Fairness & Economic Growth Act	Rev. Recon. Act of 1993—biggest tax bill since 1930s	Uruguay Round contained many pension provisions		Health Ins. Portability & Acct. Act; Sm. Business Job Prot.	Taxpay Relief Act—had 36 retroactive provisions	Omnibus spending—40 lbs/4800pp.; $500B
U.S. Debt		Total U.S.: $14T			National: $3.4T	National: $3.75T		National: $5.7T	
IMF Funding			$12B approved for Russia						$19B IMF funding for Russia/Latin Am.
Trade Deficits	$92.73B	$7.48B	$61.5B	$99.9B	$151.2B	$152.9B	$166.5B	$1.87B	$142B
Dollar to Yen/DMark	1.48Y 1.62DM (1)	1.24Y 151.70DM	1.25Y 1.62DM	1.12Y 1.78DM	.9975Y 1.540DM (2)	1.431DM	1.07Y 1.504DM	1.30Y 1.77DM	
Mergers/Acquisitions	$180B	$115B	$120B	$220B	$347B	$502B	$1.15T	$926B	$931B—6 mo.
Personal Bankruptcy					80 million	80 million	100 million	125 million	142 million

(1) Dollar dropped to post WWII low of 1.62 DM because of U.S. trade deficit
(2) In April 1998 dollar hits low of 80.63 yen due to U.S. trade deficit

Compiled by Veon Financial Services, Inc.

Space Research: While we cannot provide exact amounts that have been spent on space research and exploration, the fact that John Glenn's 1998 trip in space cost $400 million is an example of what we have paid in this endeavor to waste ten pecent of our GNP per year. America has sent Russia $742 million for the International Space Station, with the understanding they will need another $660 million. The space station is a sixteen-nation venture that will serve as a stepping stone for future missions to Mars and beyond.

3. Political

The United Nations: Birthed in 1945, the United Nations has been given, little by little, great power and resources. Many of its agencies and committees are separate from the main U.N. body and, therefore, have their own budgets and nation-assessed fees. Its agenda is one of world domination where the sovereignty of its member-states will be eliminated. Interestingly enough, it was not until 1972, six years after the writing of *The Report from Iron Mountain,* that this global body began holding "mega-conferences" at which world delegates were invited to participate in an agenda that originated at the United Nations and would ultimately affect the policies and laws of participating countries.

The first major conference, the U.N. Conference on the Human Environment (Stockholm), concentrated on the environment. Interestingly, The *Report from Iron Mountain* stated that it would take a generation to a generation and a half to bring up the environment as a viable alternative. To start the ball rolling, the 1972 Programme of Action highlighted a number of groups, organizations, and agreements with the environment as their priority. What the Stockholm conference did was bring the environment to the forefront by establishing the United Nations Environment Programme (UNEP), which then became the catalyst for developing the agenda that was birthed at that time.

To understand the importance of UNEP, the Group of Seven gave attention to UNEP in their 1998 Final Communique, "look forward to a revitalized role for UNEP as the leading global environment authority." While it is not possible to enumerate everything that has been put in place, we will concentrate on the conferences of the 1990s that mirror the agenda put in place in the 1970s. The following are the conferences in both decades:

Environment
    1972—U.N. Conference on the Human Environment
    1992—U.N. Conference on Environment and Development
Population
    1974—World Population Conference
    1994—U.N. Conference on Population and Development
Unemployment
    1974—Second General Conference of the U.N. Industrial
            Development Organization
    1995—The World Social Summit
Habitat
    1976—The U.N. Conference on Human Settlements
    1996—The U.N. Conference on Human Settlements (II)
Food
    1974—The United Nations World Food Conference
    1996—The United Nations World Food Summit

Each of the above conferences addressed a number of the nonmilitary economic substitutes for war, strengthened the power and control of the United Nations, and enforced the environmental agenda to reduce the population which they say will reduce poverty, and include provisions for low-income housing, education, and health care for all. Lastly, by implementing them, sovereignty is eroded.

    International Law and the International Criminal Court: International law is now the recognized law of the United Nations, foreign policy, and international trade. It is the glue for the United Nations actions with regard to world government. International law will determine your rights and my rights, as most of our state and federal laws are being integrated into and becoming subject to international law. Although the International Court of Justice has been active since the 1940s in dealing with commercial disputes, in July 1998 the nations of the world created the International Criminal Court. This court has the authority, for the first time in history, to transcend sovereign borders and try individuals who are accused of committing crimes against humanity, war crimes, crimes of aggression, and genocide.

International Police Force: While this concept is not new, there are many who are working toward a *permanent* international police force. Please refer to chapter eight. It should be noted that we already have a *de facto* international police force. This police force is the result of memorandums of understanding, agreements, and treaties whereby all law enforcement personnel within a country interact with each other, and all levels of law enforcement in a country interact internationally with other countries. In 1996 the Group of Seven issued what they called the "Forty Points" to counteract terrorism. The recommendations included establishing a

> Central Authority that would be structured to provide coordination of requests, provide control and prioritize incoming and outgoing requests, direct exchange of information between law enforcement agencies, place law enforcement liaison officers in other countries to combat organized crime and terrorism, share forensic law enforcement expertise, and launch joint enforcement operations against criminal and terrorist operations.

As has been proven by the investigation of the bombings of the embassies in South Africa, the FBI/CIA and other agencies cooperated internationally with their counterparts to find the perpetrators.

On a national level, the Department of Justice has been trying to obtain massive new enforcement powers. One proposal is "the establishment of a permanent 'FBI police force'" (Internet, September 29, 1998). Recently Attorney General Janet Reno announced

[the] creation of an office to prepare U.S. cities for terrorist attacks by nuclear, chemical, and biological weapons. Called the National Domestic Preparedness Office, it would be housed inside the FBI and staffed by officials from a variety of federal agencies. [T]he program will begin with two initiatives: an effort to coordinate the establishment of training standards to meet the needs of those who first respond and standardization of equipment to best serve local and state needs. The new program has been in the planning stages for nearly a year. The effort will include FEMA, which is supported by 27 agencies, and the American Red Cross.

—*Washington Times,* October 17, 1998, A2

This fits in very well with the Group of Seven's Forty Points. Most recently the president announced another new initiative which will expand the National Infrastructure Protection Center housed at the FBI and created in 1986.

New Threats to Mankind—Invasion from Outer Space: While I have not concentrated on this area, for years there have been rumors about invaders from space. Recently, a number of movies have been made on this subject with the idea that the people of the world had to unite against an invasion from space.

4. Environmental
Rio "Earth Summit"—Agenda 21: In 1992, ten thousand diplomats from one hundred seventy-eight countries assembled in Rio de Janeiro to commit themselves to a global agenda for the **environment which just happens to be one of the key Iron Mountain ways to waste money.** Agenda 21 contained three global pacts:

1. The Convention on Biological Diversity which designates where man can live, which states that fifty percent of the land mass of the U.S. should be put back to wilderness—as it was before man came to live there;
2. The Convention on Desertification; and

3. The Convention on Climate Change.

Chart 4-2 and Appendix E show what the U.S. has done in contributing to sustainable development. It established the United Nations Commission on Sustainable Development. Today all countries, including the United States, have established their own commissions on sustainable development which report to the U.N. Commission.

The move to use the environment as the common denominator to integrate the economic and social areas with the environment began with the OAS Convention on Nature Protection and Wild Life Preservation in the Western Hemispheres which was agreed to on October 12, 1940. The radical environmental infrastructure, which began at the first Earth Summit in 1972 was completed twenty years later in June 1992 with the adoption of Agenda 21 at the Rio Earth Summit. Agenda 21 is radical because it requires that many of the freedoms in our Constitution be altered in order to conform to the philosophy of the "greater good of mankind" versus individual rights (this is communitarianism or the third way). Agenda 21 says the belief that man has dominance over the earth is outdated and that the preservation of the environment necessitates that life be based on holism and nature. Since this change requires "reinventing" life as we have known it, most people are perplexed at what is going on around them.

The two hundred ninety-four pages of Agenda 21 are written in ambiguous "code" language. Unless you know the U.N.'s definitions, which are not provided, you cannot accurately guess what the document means and how it affects you. In reading various U.N. documents in addition to Agenda 21 it becomes quite apparent that the United Nations not only assumes a new form of governance (government) over the world but advances the following:

1. The empowerment of its own agencies and a system;
2. Control of the world's resources so that they become "sustainable";

Chart 4-2
The U.N. Conference on Environment and Development
Rio Earth Summit, June 1992

Adopted	Established	Outcome	Global Pacts
Non-legally binding Authoritative Statement of Principles for a Global Consensus on Management, Conservation and Sustainable Development of All Types of Forests	U.N. Commission on Sustainable Development (President Clinton has established a "President's Commission on Sustainable Development" to enact Rio)	An agreed programme of cooperative international work for the sustained and responsible development of the planet for the 21st century. "A bold mandate for change . . . a call to modify the norms of our economic behavior . . . based on a new awareness of the destructive impact of human activity on the environment."	Convention on: BIOLOGICAL DIVERSITY Desertification Climate Change

BIOLOGICAL DIVERSITY

Reorganize Western Civilization Around Nature
(Earth and preservation thereof over people—Usurps Gen. 1)

Purpose:

—Property rights granted only to those who would not harm "biodiversity"

"Biodiversity is a phrase coined to describe the variety of the genes, species and ecosystems found on our planet. It embraces all life forms, from plant and animal life to micro-organisms and the water, land and air in which they live and interact. . . . They are found in the ecosystems of forests, pastures, rangelands, deserts, tundra, rivers, lakes and lease. Human impact on biodiversity include: Human Social Organization, Global Trade. Economic systems that fail to value the environment and inequity in the ownership, management, and benefits . . . of biological resources."

Al Gore wrote in *Earth in the Balance*, "We must make the rescue of the environment the central organizing principle for civilization. . . . Use every policy and program, every law and institution, every treaty and alliance, every tactic and strategy, every plan and course of action . . . to halt the destruction of the environment and to preserve and nurture our ecological system." Bill Clinton, by presidential directives, has directed the President's Council on Sustainable Development to affect the Rio Earth Summit Programme of Action and all of the pacts and treaties.

Wetlands Project
—Would set aside about 50 percent of America and Canada as reserve wilderness areas with interconnected corridors and human buffer zones. Complete cities would be moved into "human islands" in which the movement of people would be restricted.

Biosphere Reserve Plan
—Calls for protected areas such as wilderness areas or nature reserves, for conservation and monitoring . . . ecosystems; calls for managed use areas which would surround protected areas.
—Currently 324 Biosphere Reserves in 82 countries, 47 of which occupy, 43,560,254 acres in the United States and include

Parks/Preserves in the U.S. and millions of acres

Aleutian Islands 2.70M	Glacier Bay-Admiralty Isl. 8.25M	Glacier National Park 1.01M
Central California Coast 1.06M	Mojave and Colorado Desert 3.19M	Denali National Park 1.92M
Champlain-Adirondack 9.98M	Noatak Nat'l Preserve 8.20M	YELLOWSTONE NATIONAL PARK 2.20M

Sources: Eco-logic and other U.N. publications
Copyright © 1999 TWG, Inc

3. A philosophical shift from man having dominance over the earth to holism;
4. A change in personal property rights so that the environment takes precedence;
5. A transfer of wealth; and
6. The financial empowerment of transnational corporations that already have designed new equipment to conform to the environmental agenda and which countries of the world will be required to buy in order to reduce their ozone problems, etc.

For example, in trying to understand how all of life is being "reinvented," in 1994 retired California professor Roderick Nash in a speech delivered at the Federal Role in Ecosystem Management Conference convened by the Congressional Research Service, discussed the shift to holism and ecosystem management as "holism—a way of thinking about nature as interrelated and a way of thinking about humans as members and not as master of an ecosystem." Nash went on to say that under "dualism" (the traditional Christian/Cartesian perspective), man was in control of earth/nature, whereas under holism, man is equal to the earth and therefore, "we are at a crossroads in the history of life on this planet." All of this is reflected in Agenda 21 and has been adopted by our federal government as well as the federal agencies. The U.S. Fish and Wildlife Commission, the Bureau of Land Management, the Environmental Protection Agency, the National Park Service, etc. have already implemented ecosystem management. This change in philosophy is seen in the actions of the 103rd Congress to appropriate more and more land around national parks, national landmarks, protected landscapes and seascapes, and protected areas.

The Convention on Biological Diversity: Biodiversity and ecosystem management are interrelated and neither can be understood without the other. Part and parcel of Agenda 21 is the *U.N. Global Biodiversity Assessment,* which is an eleven hundred thirty-five–page study of how to protect the plants and animals. In short, in order to protect the plants and animals, man will have to be restricted as to where he can farm and live, since any human activity impacts the natural land and animal kingdoms. This is already being done through restricted areas such as: strict nature reserves for science purposes, wilderness areas for wilderness protection, national parks for ecosystem protection and recreation, natural monuments for natural features, habitat/species management areas for conservation through management intervention, protected landscapes and seascapes and managed resource protected areas to protect and conserve all these areas. All this is accomplished through county and state zoning and land-use planning legislation.

The next time you drive past or through a national or state park, remember that it is part of ecosystem management. Also understand that if the state or federal government chooses, they can expand the national and state park to encompass more land in order to "protect" it.

While there is discussion as to how much of the land in America should be set aside for the protection and management of natural habitats, the Global Biodiversity Assessment recommends "thirty percent of the U.S. land area." However, the magazine *Wild Earth* recommends "at least half of the land area of the forty-eight conterminous states." While our Senate refused to ratify the U.N. Convention on Biological Diversity, the state of Maryland was one of the first states to pass it in 1997 under the slick title of Smart Growth and Rural Legacy legislation. Basically this legislation will designate where people can and cannot live in the state of Maryland. In January 1999, Vice President Gore proposed that $100 million be given to communities to develop smarter growth years to reduce congestion, improve urban planning, and stem uncontrolled development. Gore stated, "With this . . . we intend to help you build what we hear you asking for . . . livable communities, comfortable suburbs, vibrant cities." The monies will be raised from "green bonds" whose proceeds will be used to create greenways and community parks and to preserve farmland and other open spaces (CNN Internet, January 11, 1997).

It should also be noted that President Clinton announced in his 1998 State of the Union address that he was going to take measures to ensure Americans have "clean water" as well as protect our rivers. From that speech came the American Heritage Rivers Initiative to control the major waterways in America by transferring ownership from the state to the federal government and the "River Navigator," which is a public-private partnership. This is international policy when both Congress and state governments are being bypassed.

Sustainable Development: Another key philosophical tenant of Agenda 21 is "sustainable development." Sustainable development is a new concept which was unveiled in Rio and is the environmental equivalent of the blood running through a person's body. For the complete history of sustainable development, please read *Prince Charles: The Sustainable Prince.* A paraphrased definition of what it is and means is one which I have used:

> The world has too many people and not enough resources to feed and clothe them. If we do not reduce the population they will eat up and use all of the earth's resources and future generations will be left without any resources. The United Nations is the best global body to monitor, manage, and preserve the resources of the planet.

Population Reduction Is Part of Sustainable Development: The call for a reduction in the earth's population has been evolving since 1927 when the first population conference was organized by Margaret Sanger, with the assistance of the League of Nations, the International Union of the Scientific Study of Population, and the International Labor Organization. Margaret Sanger cofounded International Planned Parenthood Federation, which with its affiliates and counterparts today, distributes condoms worldwide and supports population reduction through sex education programs.

In 1954 a conference was held in Rome in collaboration with a number of United Nations agencies in which there were linkages drawn between economic development and fertility. The decision of parents as to the size of their family was viewed as a basic human right.

In 1965 the United Nations convened a conference along with the Economical and Social Council of the U.N. (ECOSOC) to include related fields and policy issues such as demography. The decision of parents with regard to the size of their family was considered within a social and international context.

In 1974 U.N. Secretary-General U Thant authorized the establishment of the U.N. Population Fund (UNFPA) which signalled a philosophical shift within the U.N. as to its decision to focus on policy and family planning. There in Bucharest, the U.N. called for "a new economic order by eradicating the cause of world poverty by ensuring the equitable distribution of the world's resources."

In 1984 another population conference was held in Mexico which reviewed the World Population Plan of Action adopted in 1974. At that conference, the stabilization of world population with specific time perspectives was suggested by the conference's secretary-general.

In 1994 the theme of the Cairo population conference was, "population, sustained economic growth and sustainable development." The goal is to hold the world's population to 7.27 billion in 2015 and 7.8 billion in 2050, which is called "zero population growth." At that conference, the World Bank made public that, in the future, all developmental loans from the Bank would be tied to a country's population reduction.

Family Dependency Ratio: When I was analyzing the Programme of Action for the Fourth Women's Conference held in Beijing, China, in September 1995, I came across the phrase "family dependency ratio." Because the United Nations never defines their words or the meaning to their words, I came up with my own definition after reading the document. While it was very "Orwellian," it appeared to be in line with U.N. aspirations. In order to confirm my understanding, I asked Maurice Strong, secretary-general of the first environmental conference held in 1974 in Stockholm and the

Chart 4-3

FAMILY DEPENDENCY RATIO

A PHILOSOPHY OF PRODUCTION/CONSUMPTION

**Any House/Apartment/Farm
in the U.S.A. or world**

102 SOUTH MAIN STREET
<u>Producers</u>
Mom   Dad
<u>Non-producers</u>
Baby   Grandparent

1. How much was produced at home and work?

Work

+ Home   =   AAAAA

2. How much consumed (energy, water, food, etc.)

– Consumed   =   BBBBB

3. Are you a net consumer or producer?

CCCCC

PRODUCERS

1992 Rio Earth Summit, when I was at the first Gorbachev State of the World Forum in October 1995, if I was correct. Chart 4-3 shows a diagram of this concept.

I asked Mr. Strong this question:

> There are four people who live at 102 South Main Street. The mother and father work and are producers. The baby and grandparent do not and are nonproducers, which means they are consuming and not producing. What the IMF/WB wishes to do is find a way to measure the total production of mom and dad at work and at home and then deduct from that figure the total consumption of the household to determine if that household is adding to the earth's resources or subtracting from them.

This was his response:

> You are correct and much more. I will not attempt a definitional discussion on sustainable development. We want to put it in business terms. We have Earth, Inc., with depreciation, amortization, and maintenance accounts so that we are not living off of capital. If we continue to equate wealth creation with the liquidation of our natural capital, we will be headed for bankruptcy, and that is the direction we are going now. We need all of the elements you mentioned and more to bring the ecological systems and behavior toward them in line with our economic and social aspiration. Those things have to be brought into a new balance if we are going to enjoy a sustainable way of life on our planet.

Now that I understand sustainable development, I see it all around me in the business world. Since I am not a full-time employee where I earn a paycheck, but am in a commission industry where I am paid based on my sales, I have seen over and over again that a person's worth is now attributed to his or her production! The bigger the producer you are, which means the more toys you can buy, the greater your value. Not much attention is paid to the morals by which the sales are made.

The above is in direct conflict with God's plan of creation and basically is an excuse to take control of all of the earth's resources so as to preserve them!!! Those who have orchestrated the control are the ones who enjoy the "fruits of their labor" while you and I starve.

In addition, the World Bank has divided up the assets of the world into the following categories as part of an expanded definition of sustainable development:

1. Natural capital—the minerals of the earth, water, forests, anything natural.
2. Manufactured capital—anything built, such as roads, buildings, homes, etc.
3. Human capital—every living person on the earth, including their age, health experience, education, and ability to work.
4. Social capital—how people think, that is, politically correct thinking.

What we are now comprehending is that the population of the world has to be reduced drastically. It was Jacques Costeau who said something to the effect that three hundred fifty thousand people would have to die each day in order to get population figures down. Prince Philip is reported to have said that if he were reincarnated he would come back as a virus to reduce the population. In a speech he gave in 1983 he said:

> The population explosion is the single most important cause of the degradation of the human environment and quality of life as well as the major cause of the destruction of the natural environment and extinction of species. I think it is the realization of this fact that has brought family planners and those concerned with human and natural environments together. How to persuade the hundreds of millions of actual potential, rich and poor parents all over the world to limit the size of their families.

> —Philip, 126–28

In researching where sustainable development originated, I found it in the 1977 U.S.S.R. Constitution, chapter 2, article 18.

> Article 18. In the interests of the present and future generations, the necessary steps are taken in the U.S.S.R. to protect and make scientific, rational use of the land and its mineral and water resources, and the plant and animal kingdoms, to preserve the purity of the air and water, ensure reproduction of natural wealth, and improve the human environment.
>
> —Finer, 153

However, since that constitution has been superseded by a newer one, in an interview with Jeb Bruggman, Secretary-General of International Council for Local Environmental Initiatives (ICLEI), he said this about sustainable development:

> I like to say, in a historical context that we spent most of the twentieth century arguing over two doctrines of development. There is the socialist doctrine of development and the capitalist doctrine of development and we spent all our resources battling between these two doctrines. We had the Cold War, we had real wars. I mean, hundreds of billions of dollars. And, it wasn't until the Cold War came to an end, 1987 the World Commission on Environment Development put forward a third doctrine called sustainable development which is about balancing between social equity, the long time socialist concern, economic vitality, the capitalist concern and then this new concern that neither paid any attention to which is environmental sustainability. So, we have a new concept for how to develop now and we're just beginning to learn how to put it into the President's Commission on Sustainable Development (PCSD) practice."

Chart 4-4 shows this merger.

Even Prince Charles has said that we must find "common ground" between communism and capitalism. Sustainable devel-

Chart 4-4

THE BRUNDTLAND COMMISION
MERGED SOCIALISM WITH CAPITALISM

Our Common Future, 1987

SOCIALIST
CONCERN FOR
DEVELOPMENT

SUSTAINABLE
DEVELOPMENT

CAPITALIST
CONCERN FOR
DEVELOPMENT

GLOBALIZATION=ONE WORLD—NO BORDERS

opment has been embraced by state, local, and county governments. The president has the President's Commission on Sustainable Development. Their activities are outlined in Appendix E. At the 1999 World Economic Forum in Davos, Switzerland, Vice President Al Gore was introduced as being a proponent to sustainable development.

On the same day in which I found the definition of sustainable development in the 1977 U.S.S.R. Constitution, I sat down that evening to watch a ten-year-old television epic called *Amerika* with Kris Kristofferson, Sam Neill, and Mariel Hemingway (someone had sent me a copy). This twelve-hour story is about the state of America ten years after it has been invaded by Russia. The symbol used in the film for the merger between the United States and Russia was the U.N. logo surrounded by the pre-1990 Russian flag on one side, and the American flag on the other. As I watched this video, my mind went back to the first and only time it played on television in 1987, and my bewilderment at seeing the United Nations logo with the two flags! At the time Mikhail Gorbachev was prime minister of the U.S.S.R. and raised great opposition at the film's airing. All of this now makes sense in light of sustainable development!! What does this say for our congressional, senatorial, and presidential leaders who are enforcing the global agenda?

The concept of sustainable development has been embraced by all of the United Nations and its member-states, the Clinton administration, the Guttmacher Institute, American Association for the Advance of Science, the American Humanist Association, the Center for Population Options, the Population Council, the Rockefeller Foundation, the Ford Foundation, Council on Foreign Relations, Planned Parenthood Federation of America and its counterpart, International Planned Parenthood, and all of the radical feminist groups like the National Organization for Women (NOW) and the Women's Environment and Development Organization (WEDO). Needless to say, our First Lady is a leader not only in the radical feminist movement, but in the environmental and world government movement. Lastly, it should be noted that the church, through neglect, ignorance, and complacency, has agreed to the above goals and agenda.

Other U.N. Conferences: In Appendix F you will find "The United Nations: The Four Pillars of the U.N. Agenda for Implementing World Government" which highlights the environment, economic, social, and military goals.

I would be hard pressed to explain or list all of the other U.N. conferences which have been held, but a few of their names will tell you how they fit in with the objectives of *The Report from Iron Mountain:* 1990—World Summit for Children, in which universal access to basic education was highlighted; 1990—World Conference on Education for All, whose goal was to foster social cohesion, provide universal access to basic education, reduce adult illiteracy by half, and promote health, productivity, and employment; and 1996—Habitat II, which unveiled the goal of all of the environmental agendas and how we would live in the twenty-first century. Boutros Boutros-Ghali said:

> The Habitat II conference addresses the future of humankind in a very comprehensive and integrated way. It is bringing together the different strands of development: the issues of population, movement and urbanization, employment generation, environmental infrastructure and living conditions, participation and governance, legislation and finance, and sustainable use of resources.

It is interesting to note that emergency management is now taking on a "sustainable" dimension.

A GLOBAL ECONOMIC CRISIS AND THE GOALS AND OBJECTIVES OF THE UNITED NATIONS

I believe that in a world where the global stock market is controlled and where many of the most brilliant minds on the face of the earth have been called upon to help the global powers accomplish any objective they want, that an economic meltdown is also part of their agenda. Consider the following:

1. Depending on an individual country's ability to prepare, the disruption caused by an economic meltdown will determine how many people survive. Most third world countries don't have an adequate infrastructure now. Without adequate food supplies on hand there could be mass starvation, which would conveniently fit their plans.

2. The president has already issued all of the executive orders needed to seize control of **all** resources. On May 22, 1998, the Policy on Critical Infrastructure Protection program was released, which sets up a "National Infrastructure Protection Center (NIPC), which includes the FBI, the Secret Service, other federal law enforcement agencies, the Department of Defense and the intelligence agencies, which are all ordered to cooperate with the NIPC." We will live in a totally controlled society where everyone cooperates for the sake of one another.

3. Many world leaders and key global analysts are calling for global cooperation. The U.N., World Bank, and IMF have disaster departments. These are being coordinated with disaster departments at the nation-state level. In addition, the U.N. Office for the Coordination of Humanitarian Affairs-OCHA has printed "Guidelines for the Use of Military and Civil Defence Assets in Disaster Relief" which coordinate disaster relief from the global to the local (see chapter eight).

4. People will be at the mercy of government for food. Our societal structure will change as the government takes center stage in providing people with the very necessities they currently provide for themselves.

5. The high levels of consumption by the developed countries will vanish, while the impoverished countries are obliterated. No more cars—the alleged ozone problem will vanish. We will get back to basics and as close to nature as can be once all of industry is eliminated. Furthermore, people will be herded into specified areas to live, urban settlements, so the government can take care and protect them.

6. If the economy is ruined, we can start over again with electron-

ic money when the country is ready to establish a new monetary system or perhaps the new money system will "rise" like a phoenix out of the ashes of the old.

7. For the sake of the world, we will act as one and not as individual nation-states. Our interdependence will take on new meaning as we will have to "pool" our resources in order to make it. Reinvented government is a global effort to "standardize" the political structure of all of the countries of the world. The new "community" or communitarian structure will go into effect.

8. A worldwide economic crisis is a sacrifice to Gaia. Gaia or "Mother Earth" demands that the earth reduce its population so as to protect its resources. To my knowledge, the earth has never told us what it wants. However, the Bible has clearly said that the earth has an abundance of resources to feed man who has dominance over the earth. If a planned economic catastrophe occurs and brings countries who are not prepared into starvation, then it is a sacrifice to this pagan religion. It also is a "cleansing" of the earth since a population reduction will reduce the consumption of the earth's resources.

Economic Crisis Considerations

I believe that a whole "new world order" is in the making as a result of a coming economic crisis, which may very well be used as the catalyst to change the world. This is not a preparedness handbook. The purpose is to help you stand in the gap and to understand the true philosophical agenda which is "coming down." There are things which each individual can do to protect himself:

1. You need to take the information in this report and determine if it is truth. Ask the Lord. He will show you. Purchase some of the books in the bibliography and see if they say what I have stated.

2. Determine which level of seriousness you need be prepared for? Your preparation level will reflect how serious you feel the threat is. Should you make some minor but reasonable contin-

gency plans like converting to propane gas or adding a wood burning stove or not? Or should you make major contingency plans like selling your present home and buying one with the proceeds which would be free and clear? Should you sell all of your investments and buy gold and silver, or should you purchase some versus none? Should you buy dehydrated or freeze dried food for a "just in case" scenario? Should you stock up on barter goods?

3. If you have IRAs or tax deferred investments, should you cash them out and pay the tax? How long should you stay in the market?

4. Should you move from your present location to a smaller house with more land or a house which has well water and a septic system?

While I am qualified to give financial advice and recommendations, that is not the purpose of this book. The purpose, as I stated in the introduction, is to alert the Remnant and all those who want to be the Remnant, that there is more to a world economic crisis than just "the return of Jesus Christ." I believe that it will be "our finest hour." In order to make it your finest hour, you must understand the real agenda behind any catastrophic event which can change the way our country operates.

The Economic
Structure

Chapter 5

Economic Globalization and the Loss of Sovereignty

CHAPTER SUMMARY

Globalization is the color which the world is being painted. I have defined it as "the blending together of economies, people, laws, politics, monies, and social ethics into one." The passage of the 1980 Depository Institution Deregulation and Monetary Control Act not only lifted any restrictions on interest which banks had to pay on deposits, but eliminated rules prohibiting Americans from international investments. According to Lord Meghan Desai, a professor at the London School of Economics, it was deregulation which birthed globalism and the Group of Seven who fostered and set in motion all of the forces, plans, strategies, and global institutions to accomplish the Herculean task of taking autonomous countries as well as banks, businesses, manufactures, etc., and blending them into one through mergers and acquisitions, and standardization.

To foster this new era of economic openness, a number of new structural changes have been set in place: a global accounting system, global stock exchange, global custody, global settlements system, and global customs agreement.

Facilitating the globalization process are the world's central banks. Most people think the Federal Reserve is part of the United States government. It is not. It is a private corporation which was given the right to control our economy in 1913 with the passage of the Federal Reserve Act. The Fed is not federal and it has no reserves. If you take a dollar bill or any bill out of your wallet, you will see that it is a "Federal Reserve Note." It is not currency authorized by the U.S. Treasury! Every single country in the world has a central bank which controls their monetary system. Therefore, if a country is not doing the will of the international bankers— the owners of these private corporations, all they have to do is sell that country's currency at the same time in order to bring the renegade country to its knees!!! The real reason for the problems in Asia, particularly with Malaysia, Thailand, and Korea is that they wanted to keep their own economic sovereignty. The bank which oversees all of the world's central banks is the Bank for International Settlements. According to Bill Clinton's mentor, Dr. Carroll Quigley, who wrote *Tragedy and Hope:*

> The powers of financial capitalism had another far–reaching aim, nothing less than to create a world system of financial control in private hands able to dominate the political system of each country and the economy of the world as a whole. . . . The apex of the system was to be the Bank for International Settlements in Basle, Switzerland, a private bank owned and controlled by the worlds' central banks which were themselves private corporations.

Then there are other global groups and organizations, some more powerful than others but all working for the same goal—world government! The first is the Group of Seven/Group of Ten which is comprised of the world's largest, most industrialized countries (with the exception of Russia, which was made a full partner in 1998): Canada, U.S., Japan, Italy, France, Germany, and Great Britain. The G-7/G-8 is known as the "Global Board of Directors" since they basically set the tone for where the world is going, while the rest of the world has no option but to follow.

Some of the world's most powerful organizations include the International Chamber of Commerce, the International Organization for Security Commissions, the Prince of Wales Business Leaders Forum, and the World Economic Forum.

Lastly, in order to bring the United States into compliance and conformance with the rest of the world, there is one law which must be dismantled, the Glass-Steagall Act. Once this is eliminated, then the way is clear for **one** currency—a global electronic currency.

INTRODUCTION

It was Pontius Pilate who asked, "What is truth?" Since then, those words have been echoing throughout history. Is what we see and hear on television and radio, and read in the newspapers truth or fable?

Since 1995, I have been piecing together a gigantic global puzzle—one with enormous reach and power. My ability to understand the various pieces has been enhanced by my personal attendance at numerous very major and high-level economic conferences, which include meetings of the IMF/World Bank, the Group of Seven, the World Economic Forum, and the Bank for International Settlements, to name a few. Globalization and all that it entails is at the heart of this puzzle.

In order to come to grips with the subject of global economics, which can be considered a giant octopus with many tentacles, we need to look at the infrastructure, the players, and the agenda.

If you have no background in economics, you may need to read this section twice. The information provided here is derived from my economic newsletters, which include in-depth research from four years of daily newspapers and financial magazines as well as attendance at the international economic conferences mentioned above. A number of charts are provided for you to formulate a picture of what has been set up internationally and how it affects your pocket and mine.

Lastly, if this were a football game with one team representing national economic sovereignty and the other representing world government, world government would be winning. The projected score would be 90–10.

THE INFRASTRUCTURE—GLOBALIZATION

Whenever a painter begins a new painting, he "washes" the canvas with a background color. When we talk about the global economic structure, we want to wash the canvas with the "color" called globalization. I have defined globalization as "the blending together of economies, people, laws, politics, monies, and social ethics into one." The word "one" is key. The Bible tells us that when two come together into marriage, they become one. They function as one and not two separate people as they start to blend together for the sake of family, unity, and harmony.

As a result of globalization, the finances and economy of the United States have been married—merged—with the other countries of the world to become *one*. **This blending together includes our country with socialist, Marxist, and communist countries. When you look at globalization in this way, it becomes an economic merger between capitalism and socialism which parallels the reinventing government/communitarian/third way political merger and the environmental merger as seen in sustainable development!**

How did this happen? Where was our Congress? First of all, none of this could have happened if our Congress had not approved, fostered, and written the laws for it to take place. There are three governmental actions that fostered the globalization process: deregulation, mergers and acquisitions, and standardization.

Deregulation
According to Lord Meghan Desai, a professor at the London School of Economics, it was deregulation which birthed globalism, and the Group of Seven who fostered and set in motion all of the forces, plans, strategies, and global institutions to accomplish the Herculean task of taking autonomous countries, as well as business banking, finance, manufacturing, communications, travel, consumer products, computers, technology, etc. and blending them into one—through mergers and acquisitions, and standardization. Up until 1979, the economic and financial laws of America were written for the furtherance and good of our country. In 1980 all of that began to change with the passage of the Depositary Institution Deregulation and Monetary Control Act (1980 Deregulation Act),

which basically lifted any restrictions on U.S. banks as to the amount of interest they could pay or charge. At the time this was heralded as being "good" for America, since banks would have to pay the market rate. For a little while, money market funds paid up to sixteen and seventeen percent because prime rate had risen to twenty-two percent. Many, including myself, were ecstatic at how much interest we earned! However, what was not advertised was the fact that this bill also erased any laws prohibiting Americans from investing outside of the United States, thus allowing foreigners to invest in America. It basically erased our national investment borders. Significantly, many of the other Group of Seven countries— including Britain, Italy, France, Canada, Japan, and Germany— were passing similar laws at the same time.

It should be mentioned here that the real agenda of the 1980 Deregulation Act was to make it look like the saver was going to be paid current market interest. It sounded good until you consider that banks dictate the kind of interest they will pay. If they all pay the same amount, they have just set "current market rates." Consider current interest rates, in which savings accounts are paying anywhere from two to four percent, while interest rates charged on credit cards are eighteen to twenty-one percent! This law was written for the banks and not for the saver!!

Mergers and Acquisitions

At one time most of the companies in America were "national," that is, they only operated and sold their products in America. Then with the development of world trade and commerce, many companies became "international," i.e., they sold their products overseas. Little by little they expanded and needed to have manufacturing plants in other countries. When they started building corporate headquarters in other parts of the world, they became transnational, i.e. they had a corporate office in more than one country. It is the multinational and transnational corporations that are helping to run the world. In many cases, the net worth or the sales income of these corporations surpasses that of many small countries!

As a result of the deregulation laws and the elimination of many trade, tariff, and other national laws, corporate buyouts are now transnational—they supersede national borders. It has become "survival of the fittest," as only the big and powerful corporations are able to survive. In 1991, the Bush administration pushed bank reform very hard, looking to allow banks to diversify so they could "improve their profitability and compete in the global marketplace." Until then, banks could only do business with adjoining states. One of the changes was to phase out interstate banking, giving banks with a large capital base the ability to cross **any** state boundary. This created a wave of mergers among smaller banks so they could take advantage of the opportunities created for the large banks. Mergers included BankAmerica buying Security Pacific for $84.7 billion, Chemical Bank buying Manufacturers Hanover Trust for $61.3 billion, NCNB Corporation buying C&S/Sovern Corporation, and the Bank of New York buying Irving Bank Corporation (*Washington Times*, August 13, 1991, C1).

In 1995 there was an unprecedented $502 billion in mergers and acquisitions, growing to $1.15 trillion in 1996 worldwide. Cross-border acquisitions in pharmaceutical, telecommunications, financial services, and entertainment industries spurred the big increase. David Mulford, chairman of CS First Boston said, "What's emerging is truly a global economy" (*Wall Street Journal,* September 9, 1996, A2). Other key mergers included Boeing buying McDonnell-Douglas, which created the world's largest aircraft manufacturer, and the merger of Grand Metropolitan PLC (British owner of Burger King and Pillsbury) with Bailey's Irish Cream to form the sixth largest food and beverage company (*Washington Times,* May 13, 1997, B1). In 1997 mergers and acquisitions had reached $926 billion, which was matched in the first six months of 1998!

There has been a method to the merger and acquisition madness. In 1933 there was a banking act passed called the Glass-Steagall Act. This was passed by two congressmen (whom the bill is named for) as a result of the 1929 stock market crash. They sponsored the bill in order to put a wall of separation between investment banks and commercial banks. As a result of the global trend which is prevalent in Europe to combine the functions of banks, insurance companies, and brokerage firms into one large conglomerate, there is a concerted effort underway to eliminate Glass-Steagall, which prohibits this type of conglomerate. Those pushing to break down the walls put in place by the 1933 law say it is an "outdated law."

While this law may not be replaced by a new one soon, the mergers and acquisitions which have been taking place for the past several years have already broken down the Glass-Steagall walls just by the fact that the mergers have occurred. For example, the financial merger between NationsBank and BankAmerica Corporation which took place in April 1998 created the fifth largest bank across twenty-one states—effectively from coast to coast (*Washington Post,* April 14, 1998, 1) In addition, Deutsche Bank, Germany's largest bank, is looking to buy Bankers Trust, which would be the largest cross-border acquisition of a U.S. financial institution.

The largest merger in 1998 was between Citicorp and Travelers Group, for $82 billion. This merger created the world's largest financial services company and changed the face of banking in the United States and abroad (see chapter five). Travelers Group had already purchased Salomon Inc. in 1997, combining under one umbrella the brokerage firm Smith Barney, Travelers Life and Annuity, Primerica Financial Services, and Travelers Property and Casualty. The 1998 merger between Travelers Group and Citicorp merged the nation's second-largest bank with Travelers. The new company, Citicorp, Inc., will have one hundred million customers in one hundred countries and allow Travelers to sell its insurance and brokerage to Citicorp's sixty million credit card customers while Citicorp would be able to boost its asset management and securities brokerage business around the world. It was this merger that effectively dismantled the Glass-Steagall Act, which is key to worldwide banking, insurance, and brokerage industries (*Washington Post,* April 7, 1998, A13).

On the global level, two Bavarian banks merged to create the

188—United Nations: A Global Straitjacket

second biggest bank in Germany. Bayerische Berinsbank and Bayerische Hypotheken-und Wechsel-Bank merged in July 1977. The
new bank, Bayerische Hypo-und-Vereinsbank, is second only to
Deutsche Bank in Germany (*Financial Times,* July 22, 1997, 15).
Speaking of Deutsche Bank, it is preparing to offer mutual funds in
America. In 1999, with the consolidation of Europe, many more
bank mergers are taking place.

Overseas where many banks are state owned, privatization is
an important part of globalization because it takes a state-owned
enterprise and brings it public by incorporating the bank as a public company and then sells shares on the stock exchange.

This process is being done all over the world. Once a state-
owned enterprise is brought public and shares are sold on a stock
exchange, that then makes it a candidate for a buy-out or merger
and acquisition. In Finland, the government approved the merger
of Postipankki, the country's third largest bank, with Finnish Export Credit, the state-controlled commercial lender. The new group
will be the second largest banking consortium in Finland. Industry
analysts suggest this could pave the way to the privatization of state-
owned banks (*Financial Times,* October 8, 1997, 18). On October
13 Finland's largest bank, Merita, announced a plan to create the
largest financial services group in the Nordic region by merging
with Norbanken, Sweden's fourth-largest lender. In what is considered the first cross-border merger between retail banks, it marks
the latest stage in the rapid consolidation of the region's financial
services industry (*Financial Times,* October 14, 1997, 17).

In Latin America, Spain's Santander Banking Group purchased
the Brazilian bank Banco Noroeste. Earlier in the year, HSBC Holdings, which owns the HongkongBank Group in China and Midland Bank in the United Kingdom, purchased Brazil's Bamerindus
Group. This purchase is part of a concerted effort to have a pres-
ence in Latin America (*Financial Times,* August 16–17, 1997, 1). In
Venezuela, overseas groups now control forty-seven percent of all
bank assets, compared to one-half of one percent three years ago.
Banco Bilbao Vizcaya of Spain now controls Venezuela's largest

bank, Banco Provincial. In addition, American Express Bank joined with Banc SRL to form Banco InterAmerican Express in Sao Paulo. The U.S. insurer American International Group recently purchased fifty-one percent of Banco Fenicia (*Financial Times*, September 4, 1997, 15).

Credit Suisse, Switzerland's oldest bank, and Winterhur, its oldest insurance company, merged to create the country's largest financial conglomerate. This merger will put the Credit Suisse Group, which owns America's First Boston, ahead of its two rivals, Union Bank of Switzerland and Swiss Bank Corporation. In addition, Union Bank of Switzerland purchased Germany's Schroder Munchmeyer Hengst, a Frankfurt-based bank owned by Lloyds TSB of the U.K. (*Financial Times*, August 27, 1997, 11).

Other cross-border mergers include the sale of PacificCorp, which provides electricity to 1.4 million people in Oregon, Utah, and Wyoming, to ScottishPower PLC, one of Britain's largest power companies (*Washington Times*, December 8, 1998, B7). In August 1998 British Petroleum purchased Amoco. In March 1999 they announced the purchase of ARCO. These combined mergers now make British Petroleum the largest oil company in the world. **Instead of an army with guns and bullets, the twenty-first century uses mergers and acquisitions to take control!**

In January 1999 Exxon and Mobil Oil merged for $74 billion, the largest deal in the history of America. This created the world's largest oil company and the largest publicly traded company, surpassing General Motors with an annual revenue of more than $200 billion. Exxon-Mobil will control about fourteen percent of America's retail gas pumps, about the same as the Shell-Texaco joint venture. This deal reunites the biggest chunks of John D. Rockefeller's Standard Oil monopoly broken up eighty-seven years ago on antitrust grounds (*USA Today*, B1).

Should we mention here that scores of mom-and-pop gas stations have been forced to close recently, unable to buy the new gasoline storage tanks mandated under unreasonable federal government environmental regulations? Do you get the picture of what is happening here? Where is the independent store operator—the little guy? Just as Sam's Club and Walmart, not to mention Lowes and Home Depot, have run the independent businessman out of business, so, too, all of this has greater meaning and deeper implications in world government. Do you want a job? You will dance to the tune of world government if you want to keep it. That new tune may conflict with your personal beliefs and values.

Standardization

Standardization is the process of bringing the various laws of all of the countries of the world into conformity with global goals. In other words, national laws will be obsolete once the globalization process is finished. They will have been superseded by new international laws.

The necessary global infrastructure is only possible through standardization, i.e. all countries pass the same laws in the areas of accounting, banking, stock exchanges, delivery and settlement of investments, manufacturing, trade, etc. When this process is completed, and it almost is, the respective industries worldwide will adhere to the same rules on a global basis. The cross-border merger and acquisition process seen above already testifies to how far advanced this whole process is. Following are some specific examples.

Global Accounting: In order to keep track of a global financial marketplace, a new global accounting system is in the process of being created. The International Accounting Standards Committee (IASC) is spearheading new standards to be put into place by 1999 so that the companies listed on the world's leading stock markets will all use the same accounting methods. Part of the change in accounting rules will specify how derivatives will be reported. It is on this international stage that the world's leading (securities) regulators are also trying to find a solution to the second derivatives problem—their measurement. Sir Brian Carsberg, the secretary-general of the IASC and former U.K. regulatory chairman, is spearheading this new accord, which will be presented to the International Organization of Security Commissions (IOSCO). With IOSCO approval, the accord, in theory, will be accepted in all of the world's leading markets (*Financial Times,* June 27, 1997, 2). Please see the International Organization of Security Commissions (IOSCO) for further information (*page 217*).

In preparation for a global set of accounting methods, a number of foreign companies are switching to U.S. accounting standards. In order to be in a global position to be of service, megamergers are taking place between many of the world's largest accounting firms. Price Waterhouse and Coopers & Lybrand have merged to form the world's largest accounting firm in order to be in position for the twenty-first century. They are targeting a number of emerging countries and regions, such as Russia, China, Southeast Asia, India, and Latin America (*Washington Times,* September 19, 1997, B10).

Global Stock Exchanges: I was told by a key individual whom I interviewed at the 1996 annual meeting of the International Organization of Security Commissions (IOSCO) that the bottom line of globalization would be one stock exchange for the entire world. He said that this would come about as smaller stock exchanges merged and the resulting exchanges then merged with others. For example, he said that all of the stock exchanges in the Caribbean would merge and those in Central America would merge. Then these two areas would merge and so forth worldwide.

My first confirmation of that prediction came in the September 29, 1997, edition of *Financial Times,* which reported "efforts to integrate Central America's six tiny stock exchanges are taking hold, although the underdevelopment of national markets is slowing the pace." It goes on to describe the development of each exchange in Central America and then comments: "The promotion of public ownership faces deep-rooted suspicion from Central America's business community, which is dominated by close-knit family groups reluctant to venture into uncharted territory or give up full control of their companies." Lastly, the article says that "the Inter-Ameri-

Chart 5-1

The Emerging Global Stock Exchange

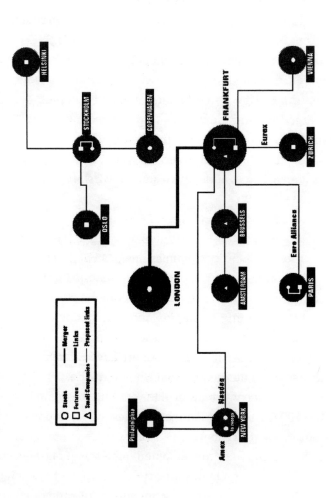

can Development Bank [World Bank] is supporting efforts to modernise these markets."

In June 1997 "the Swedish and Danish stock exchanges announced their plans to merge their dealing systems to create an integrated equities trading market, the first cross-border link of its kind among European borders." Furthermore, it is anticipated that this could be "the first step toward the creation of a pan-Nordic market, embracing Oslo and Helsinki" (*Financial Times,* June 12, 1997, 15). There has continued to be great merger activity in Europe because of the EMU. Chart 5-1 has been adopted from the *Financial Times* to show the activity between stock exchanges and how they are merging around the London Stock Exchange, which is located in the "City of London" (as opposed to the city of London itself, which is where the Bank of England, their courts, the Tower of London, and the London Stock Exchange are), considered the "financial capital of Europe" (*Washington Post,* December 31, 1998, A1).

Global Custody: As a result of American investors and companies buying shares of stock or bonds in foreign countries and companies, there is an investment intermediary that facilitates the cross-border stock and bond trade, called "global custody." This encompasses two operations: the safekeeping of pension monies, and the purchase/sale and settlement of stocks, bonds, and mutual funds in the account. The whole process becomes pretty complicated when you consider all of the American-based mutual funds and pension investors that purchase international stocks and bonds which use global custody companies to buy, sell, and hold investments. As a result, there are a number of global financial laws covering the purchase and settlement part of the transaction. This multi-trillion-dollar industry ($40 trillion) is dominated by companies like Morgan Stanley, Chase Manhattan (the biggest U.S. bank and largest global custodian as a result of its merger with Chemical Bank), Northern Trust and Citibank in the U.S.; Midland Securities Services, London; Royal Trust, Canada; and Cedel Bank, Luxembourg (*Financial Times,* July 11, 1997, i-iv).

Global Settlements System: In June 1997 the world's largest banks approved "the creation of a global settlements system to handle the $2,400 billion of payments that flow through the foreign exchange markets" daily. The Group of Twenty, a consortium of leading banks from Europe, North America, and Japan (the three major regions of the world) will set up a new company, CLS Services, to be located in Great Britain, which will develop a real-time system for settling foreign exchange transactions. Other participants in the foreign exchange market will be invited to become shareholders. This is in anticipation of the global stock exchange, which will trade twenty-four hours a day. In addition, CLS will take over two rival institutions. The Group of Twenty includes: Bank of America, Citibank, J. P. Morgan, Bankers Trust, and Chase Manhattan in the United States; Bank of Tokyo-Mitsubishi and Fuji Bank, Japan; Societe Generale, France; Deutsche Bank and Dresdner Bank, Germany; and Barclays Banks and National Westminster Bank, United Kingdom. The G-20 is responding to a demand by central banks that the private sector find a solution to problems posed by settlement risk in the foreign exchange markets. A global stock exchange needs a global settlements system. Here it is.

Interestingly enough, on my way home from the Group of Seven meeting in Lyon in July 1996, I met a businessman named Pierre Francotte, who is managing director and resident counsel for Euroclear. He works with a group out of London called the Capital Markets Forum, which is part of the International Bar Association. The Capital Markets Forum is a group of international attorneys looking to "modernize national securities ownership, transfer and pledging laws," which are aspects of the global settlements system (Capital Markets Forum, 1). The forum is changing U.S. laws in order to set up a system of "legal harmonization in the field of conflicts of laws, which determine the legal systems that apply to transfers of ownership and pledges of securities held . . . through a web of intermediaries [to facilitate global financial transactions]" (letter from Francotte dated July 26, 1996). In addition, Francotte wrote me that the forum is seeking to pass a "new version of Article 8 of the [U.S.] Uniform Commercial Code . . . which is in line with the recommendations of the group of experts, [and] is in the process of being incorporated in the legal systems of the fifty states in the U.S. It has already been adopted by about twenty-five states, including Illinois, Pennsylvania, and Maryland" (Francotte, July 26, 1996).

By introducing model legislation directly to each state, the group could then facilitate the necessary change in U.S. law in just several years instead of the ten to fifteen years necessary to go through federal channels. Do you like the idea of an international group writing model legislation to be used in all of our state assemblies? This should be viewed as a loss of national and state sovereignty, as our laws are now conforming to international law. If it surprises you that an international organization would be writing model legislation to change the landscape of America, read on.

Global Customs Agreement: The World Customs Organization (WCO), the World Trade Organization (WTO), and the United Nations Conference on Trade and Development (UNCTAD) are looking to abolish border inspections. These reforms are scheduled to be in place by 2000. These radical reforms are part of the massive twenty-five thousand-page World Trade Organization document approved by the United States Senate in December 1994. According to Peter Frohler, head of UNCTAD's trade infrastructure branch, companies worldwide will save tens of billions of dollars a year. Maria Livanos Cattaui, secretary general of the International Chamber of Commerce (ICC), hailed the changes as a "major breakthrough for world business." Again, no borders, a loss of sovereignty, and no control over what is coming into a country—it could be drugs, body parts, guns, illegal aliens—anything! No one is looking! Do you think this will provide a field day for the various mafias?

THE PLAYERS

In the movie *Anne of Avonlea,* the young Canadian teacher, Anne Shirley, has been given a rough time at a private girls school. Those who run the school also own the town and they want this orphan out. To fight back, Anne's mentor presents her with an old diary which was kept by the founder of the town many years ago. Anne reads, "In order to play the game, you must know the players."

There are many players in the economic globalization game. Some are known, while others operate in anonymity—which suits their purposes. On chart 5-2 you will find a diagram to help you place the players and identify them. They are: the Federal Reserve Bank (FRB), the Group of Seven (G7) and the Group of Ten (G-10), the Bank for International Settlements (BIS), and the International Organization of Security Commissions (IOSCO). We considered the GATT/World Trade Organization, the World Bank/International Monetary Fund, and the United Nations in an earlier chapter. There are secondary players extremely important in making the above agenda meld together.

The Federal Reserve, A Central Bank

If you take a piece of paper money out of your wallet—any denomination—you will see these words: "Federal Reserve Note—This note is legal tender for all debts, public and private." You might ask yourself why the paper money does not state that it is a note from the Treasury of the United States. After all, the Federal Reserve is not the Treasury. So what is it? The Federal Reserve is a "central bank." To put it in everyday terms, it is a private corporation that claims to provide a service to the people of the United States by furnishing the money that is used in our banking system.

Another way to look at it is that the monetary system of the United States is in the hands of a few very wealthy and powerful individuals who control virtually *every* aspect of our economy. What this means is that the power of the Federal Reserve exceeds and supersedes that of our president and Congress. The Federal Reserve is not accountable to them; it has never published an annual report and its meetings are not reported to the press until six months after a monetary decision, and they pay no taxes!

Have you ever considered why Americans cannot forgive them-

Chart 5-2

IOSCO (Security Commissioners)	Bank for Int'l Settlements (BIS) Tripartite	IAIS (Insurance Supervisors)

| PWBLF | Group of Ten Central Banks | World Economic Forum |

CENTRAL BANKS OF THE WORLD
UNITED NATIONS
WORLD BANK/INTERNATIONAL MONETARY FUND
IMF being changed to a World Central Bank

GROUP OF SEVEN
has their own government structure—
appears to guide the U.N.

MULTINATIONAL CORPORATIONS—MNCs (ICC)
through MNCs, laws changed to accommodate world trade

Deregulation	Merger and Acquisitions

Key to world globalization—ONE

GATT/WORLD TRADE ORGANIZATION

(North America Free Trade)   (European Common Market Agreement)   (Asian Free Trade Agreement)

selves the interest on the federal debt? It is because they do not owe it to themselves, they owe it to a private corporation who demands interest. The next question is: "How did we get a central bank?" Please refer to three very fine books: *The Secrets of the Federal Reserve* by Eustace Mullins, Bankers Research Institute, 1993; *The Federal Reserve—An International Mystery* by Thibaut deSaint Phalle, Praeger Press, 1984; and *Tragedy and Hope* by Carroll Quigley, originally published by MacMillian, 1965. Dr. Carroll Quigley was Bill Clinton's mentor from Georgetown University and the one to whom Clinton paid special tribute at his first inaugural address.

The Federal Reserve has been amended over one hundred and ninety-five times since its founding, with another new amendment introduced in March 1999 which is currently being considered in Congress. One of those amendments, Section 25 (a), set up the Edge Act. It is this bill that allowed national banks to establish foreign branches in order to conduct "international or foreign banking" activities. Those who passed the original act in 1913 would not recognize it today as its power and domain far surpass what was ever realized or intended. The Fed is a very important member of the Bank for International Settlements.

To help understand how the Federal Reserve has evolved and the magnitude of the impact of our whole monetary system being outside of the control of the U.S. Treasury, Congressman Charles A. Lindberg, Sr., made this statement on the floor of the House of Representatives on December 22, 1913.

> This Act establishes the most gigantic trust on earth. When the President signs this bill, the invisible government by the Monetary Power will be legalized. . . . The worst legislative crime of the ages is perpetrated by this banking bill.
>
> —Mullins,28

Who Owns the Fed?: The Federal Reserve is a private corporation and, as such, works for the benefit of the owners, which include Rothschild Bank of England, Rothschild Bank of Berlin, Lazard

Brothers Banks of Paris, Israel Moses Seiff Banks of Italy, Warburg Banks of Hamburg and Amsterdam, Lehman Brothers Bank of New York, Kuhn, Loeb Bank of New York, Chase Manhattan Bank, and Goldman, Sachs Bank (see Chart 5-3). Whenever the Federal Reserve raises interest rates, the owners benefit, not the people of the United States. Higher interest rates become a burden to those who owe money, as well as to those who would like to borrow money.

> In this long overdue study of the Federal Reserve System in the United States, the author carefully traces the historical development of the U.S. central banking system. . . . He points out the recurring efforts to substitute monetary policy for fiscal policy, which has resulted in inflation not only in the United States but throughout the world. . . .
>
> —statement made by Dr. Fritz Leutwiler, chairman of the governing board of the Swiss National Bank and former president of the Bank for International Settlements, *The Federal Reserve: An International Mystery*, deSaint Phalle,. xi

In looking to define central banks, Dr. Quigley says:

> Notes were issued by . . . "banks of issue" and were secured by reserves of gold or certificates held in their own coffers or in some central reserve. . . . There were formerly many banks of issue, but this function is now generally restricted to a few or even to a single "central bank" in each country. Such banks, even central banks, were private institutions, owned by the shareholders who profited by their operations.
>
> —Quigley, 54–55

With regard to the evolution of central banks, the following were founded long before the Federal Reserve: Bank of Sweden, the oldest, in 1668; the Bank of England in 1694; the Bank of France in 1803; the Bank of Italy in 1861; and the German Bundesbank in 1870.

Chart 5-3

The Monetary System of the U.S.

The Federal Reserve—Created in 1913
Privately Owned Bank
by

Rothschild Bank of England	Israel Moses Seiff Banks of Italy	Kuhn, Loeb Bank of New York
Rothschild Bank of Berlin	Warburg Banks of Hamburg and Amsterdam	Chase Manhattan Bank of New York
Lazard Brothers Banks of Paris	Lehman Brothers Bank of New York	Goldman, Sachs Bank of New York

The Government of the United States
The Treasury of the United States

They no longer control the monetary system of the country.
We pay interest on the debt to the Federal Reserve, not the Treasury.
Because of that, we are beholden to a global organization
which is ultimately the Bank for International Settlements.

The Ability of Central Banks to Bring a Country to Its Knees

If every country has a central bank, i.e. private corporation which is controlled by the same group of banks and individuals who own the Banks of England, France, Italy, Germany, Canada, Japan, Russia, etc., and they all own some of every country's currency, then if someone wanted to bring a country's currency down, all it would take is for all the central banks to sell that country's currency at the same time. If you consider Chart 5-4, you can see how easy it would be to bring a country to its knees! After doing extensive research on the Asian crisis, I found that is what happened. Malaysia, Thailand, and South Korea did not want to join the World Trade Organization's Financial Services Agreement. In order to help them make a decision, their currencies were devalued!

Central Bank Chairmen Are More Powerful Than Presidents

In light of the above and the fact that the world monetary system is dependent on private corporations, i.e. central banks, it is important to go back and take a look at what the central banks are doing.

In an article on December 2, 1996, about Hans Teitmeyer, chairman of Germany's central bank, the Bundesbank, the *Washington Post* wrote:

> Hans Teitmeyer may wield greater power than any president or prime minister in Europe. He has never been elected to public office, yet he can make or break the fortunes of governments as well as investors. In this era of global markets and instant communications, the clout of central bankers has become awesome. Their word can affect the trillion dollars a day that churn through foreign exchanges. As chairman of Germany's Bundesbank, Teitmeyer holds special influence because the market affects the fate of other currencies.

What does this reveal?

1. Teitmeyer (or any other central bank chairman) *has more power* than presidents or prime ministers.

Chart 5-4

The Central Banks of the World

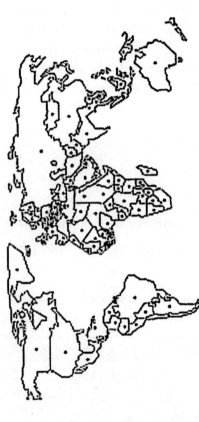

Every country has a central bank. To devalue the currency of the country which is out of favor, all you have to do is have the central banks sell its currency at the same time. All central banks report to the Bank for International Settlements

2. Central bank governors and chairmen are *unelected* since they are appointed.
3. Because all of the world's countries have borrowed money from these private corporations called central banks, they are beholden to them.

The *Washington Post* article further states, "Politicians . . . must take political deaccession." In defining what this means, *de* means "away, down, reverse"; *accession* means "the attainment of or the succession to an office." In other words, politicians rank under the central bank chairman in power!!

When Alan Greenspan Talks, World Markets Listen: With regard to the power of the Federal Reserve and specifically its chairman, Alan Greenspan, the *Washington Post* wrote:

> Second to the president, Alan Greenspan is arguably the nation's most powerful person. As chairman of the Federal Reserve, he guides U.S. monetary policy, adjusting short-term interest rates to change the cost of borrowing . . . and with a couple of choice words, he can momentarily send the stock market to heaven or hell. Tomorrow, Greenspan will preside over the mysterious ritual that is at the heart of his power, the Federal Open Market Committee, the Fed's top policy making group will gather here to debate whether to raise short-term interest rates for the first time in two years. . . . The most careful Fed watchers can't be sure what the wizard of monetary policy will ultimately opine.

Should America's financial system be governed by a private corporation that is described as "mysterious" and in which the unelected chairman is called a "wizard" (*Washington Post,* March 24, 1997, A1)? Now, if you are the unelected chairman of one of the world's largest central banks and you control the monetary policy for the entire country, who has more power? In America, who has more power—Alan Greenspan or Bill Clinton?

Who Is Alan Greenspan? Perhaps we had better reconsider the kind of power unelected people have in our government and ask, "Who is Alan Greenspan?" According to a human interest story, he played for a year with the Henry Jerome swing band. The manager of that band went on to become Richard Nixon's law partner. Greenspan is a fan of Ayn Rand and "was swept away by *Atlas Shrugged, The Fountainhead,* and her philosophy of objectivism or enlightened selfishness." At seventy-one, he recently married TV reporter Andrea Mitchell after being divorced for a long period of time. He earned both his masters degree and doctorate from New York University. James Wolfensohn, president of the World Bank, is a close friend of his, and he has served under Nixon, Ford, Reagan, Bush, and Clinton. In summary, Greenspan is a "man for all seasons" who does the bidding of the BIS, as he is a key player on their team. This should say something to Americans who are concerned about the economy and our sovereignty.

Central Banks Consolidating Power: (See "The Empowerment of Central Banks," chapter seven.) Currently central banks, corporations, and financial markets are in the process of *consolidating power.* This was first seen with the amalgamation in Europe as individual central banks took steps to be folded into one new united central bank of Europe (ECB). The European Investment Bank (EIB), its predecessor, paved the way for a united Europe by helping to standardize the currencies between countries joining the EMU. The new united currency, the euro, was traded as early as May 1998 in the bond markets.

Bank of England—A Central Bank: The actions of the Banks of England and Japan demonstrate this consolidation process. On May 6, 1997, the Bank of England received a number of new powers, which include the power to set interest rates without permission from the government, as well as have a separate pool of foreign exchange reserves be given them from the Treasury, which they can use at their discretion to intervene in the currency markets. These powers are viewed as the "most radical internal reform to the Bank of England since it was established in 1694—over three hundred years ago," according to Gordon Brown, the chancellor of the exchequer (*Washington Times,* May 7, 1997, 1). The article went on to say that Brown is "modeling the Bank of England much more closely after the U.S. Federal Reserve, which can adjust rates even if that causes short-term political discomfort for the White House." He said this new independence will provide strong political say on the makeup of a nine-member committee that will set interest rates and will function like the U.S. Federal Reserve Open Markets Committee and the Bundesbank Council (*Financial Times,* May 7, 1997, 8). In addition, the Bank of England's monetary policy committee would be monitored by a reformed court, which is part of the bank's governing body. This court will consist of no more than nineteen members—the governor, two deputy governors, and sixteen non-executives, which will be representative of industry, commerce, and finance (*Financial Times,* May 7, 1997, 8). The Bank of England is a major force in the world's gold market, buying and selling for both its own account and clients' accounts.

Bank of Japan: Then in February 1997, Japan's central bank was given more power to determine monetary policy under new proposals that would abolish the official role of the central bank's finance ministry. Under these reforms, the bank's seven-member policy-making body would be restructured and strengthened so as to have the same number of members as the U.S. Federal Reserve and the Bank of England—nine. This new policy-making board would draw six of its members from business and academia in addition to the central bank's governor and two vice governors. The stated purpose for this move is to provide more autonomy in line with international standards and the government's plans for the deregulation of financial markets by 2001, a topic that the G-7 discussed in Denver in 1997.

Harmonization of Powers: As yet, the Bank of England (BOE) and the Bank of Japan (BOJ) do not have the authority to intervene in foreign exchange markets or inflation or monetary targets. However, the Bank of Japan, the Bank of England, the Bundesbank, the EIB, and the Federal Reserve Bank, do have the same freedom to set interest rates apart from government opinion. Lord Acton said something along the lines of, "Power tends to corrupt; absolute power corrupts absolutely."

The Bank for International Settlements (BIS)

Until recently, the name Bank for International Settlements seldom made the newspapers. Operating in great obscurity in Basle, Switzerland, this institution wields even greater power than the Federal Reserve, as it is considered the "central banks' bank." The BIS, operating on the global level, coordinates with the local central bank in each country the material changes in domestic law necessary to bring the world monetary system into harmony. Over the years it has, like the Federal Reserve, amassed greater and greater control over more aspects of the global monetary system.

According to Dr. Quigley:

> The powers of financial capitalism had another far-reaching aim, nothing less than to create a world system of financial control in private hands able to dominate the political system of each country and the economy of the world as a whole. . . . The apex of the system was to be the Bank for International Settlements in Basle, Switzerland, a private bank owned and controlled by the worlds' central banks, which were themselves private corporations. Each central bank in the hands of men like Montagu Norman of the Bank of England, Benjamin Strong of the New York Federal Reserve Bank, Charles Rist of the Bank of France, and Hjalmar Schacht of the Reichsbanks (Bundesbank-Germany) sought to dominate its government by its ability to control. . . . The BIS is generally regarded as the apex of the structure of financial capitalism whose remote origins go back to the creation of the Bank of England in 1694 and the Bank of France in 1803. . . . It was set up rather to remedy the decline in London as the worlds' financial center by providing a mechanism by which a world with three chief financial centers in London, New York, and Paris could still operate as one.

—Quigley, 324

Ten times a year, the heads of the world's major central banks—the G-10 countries—meet "at their supranational second home, the BIS at Basel. . . . They [are] 'international freemasons,' possessing a natural second allegiance to the often lonely interest of international monetary order . . ." (Solomon, 28).

It was the Bank for International Settlements that designed the present borderless flow of monies between countries when it pushed for the deregulation of monetary laws of the major North American, European, and Asian countries around the world, thereby creating the monetary flow of more than $1.2 trillion on a daily basis. The BIS also designed a number of very sophisticated investment instruments being used today, such as derivatives, futures, and options. It also paved the way for trading treasury bonds on a global basis.

Remember the stock market crash of 1987? That event empowered the BIS to find support for its "Basle Capital Accord," which extended the "Basle guidelines into comprehensive harmonized global rules and oversight for *all* financial firms" (Solomon, 437). Solomon writes that this accord includes foreign exchanges, securities, derivatives trading, and interest rate fluctuations.

According to the BIS report "Changes in the Organization and Regulation of Capital Markets," published in March 1987, many of the needed changes in national laws have been affected in most countries to facilitate the BIS agenda. Since every country is different, the final completion date for each country will vary.

In the United States, these changes have come in the form of deregulation and the reversal of any national law that would prohibit the free flow of money in or out of the country. The 1980 Monetary Control Act is the chief cornerstone of this movement. It removed all of the restraints in the U.S. banking system, such as the interest rate ceiling or Regulation Q—the amount of interest a bank could pay on deposits. It also created NOW accounts for all depository institutions and hence changed the definition of money, which in turn changed the definition of a bank, i.e. Merrill Lynch, a brokerage firm could now offer money market fund accounts (de-

Saint Phalle, 138). Do you see how all of the money is being concentrated in the hands of the big banks which are now multinational and transnational?

The 1980 Monetary Control Act also erased Regulation D, which set a minimum required amount of reserves to be held by commercial banks. Because of how laws such as this one are applied to foreign branches of U.S. banks, the way has been opened for capital to leave the United States, thus, opening up the door to the globalized economy we see today.

The BIS—The Basle Committee on Banking Supervision(BofBS): This important and powerful committee consists of representatives from the central banks of the G-10 countries (see Chart 5-5). This committee also works very closely with the International Organization for Security Commissions in *harmonizing world security exchange regulations.* It has been said of the work of the Basle Committee that "although the Committee focus is on supervision of internationally active banks within the G-10 countries, its conclusions are generally applicable for all banks no matter where they are . . ." (*1995 IOSCO Annual Report*). It might be noted that the G-10 represents the highest concentration of money, power, and wealth that there is in the world.

The International Monetary Fund/World Bank

One year before the United Nations Charter was signed, over seven hundred delegates from forty-four countries met to construct a world monetary system which would be used to govern the world after the war. Sponsored by the United Nations, the Monetary and Financial Conference, now known as "Bretton Woods" (because of where it met in New Hampshire) had two objectives: (1) "to reduce obstacles of international trade," and (2) "to bring about the harmonization of national policies of member states" (see Chart 5-6).

Two key players at that historic conference were John Maynard Keynes, the British socialist who boasted that what was set up in Bretton Woods was "the exact opposite of the gold standard," and Harry Dexter White, who was Assistant Secretary of the Trea-

Chart 5-5

Bank for International Settlements

BIS=Committee on Banking Supervision

Established in 1975 by the G-10.   Secretariat is in Basle, Switzerland.

>

IOSCO TECHNICAL COMMITTEE

shares the common goal of improving the quality of supervision worldwide with BIS CoBS

^

INTERNATIONAL ASSOCIATION OF INSURANCE SUPERVISORS (IAIS)

>

>

GROUP OF TEN CENTRAL BANK GOVERNORS

Source: 1995 IOSCO Annual Report

Chart 5-6

The United Nations and the Commission on Global Governance

"New Opportunities for Global Cooperation in a Post-Cold War Era"

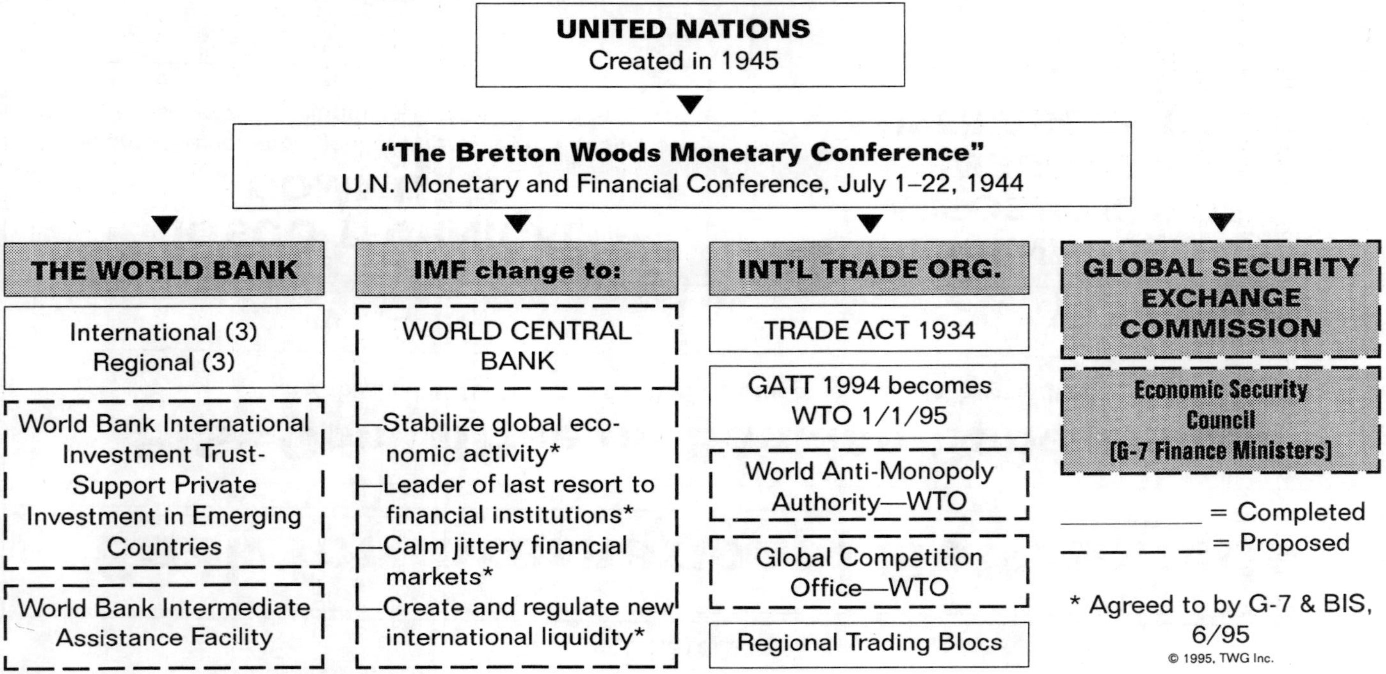

UNITED NATIONS
Created in 1945

"The Bretton Woods Monetary Conference"
U.N. Monetary and Financial Conference, July 1–22, 1944

THE WORLD BANK	IMF change to:	INT'L TRADE ORG.	GLOBAL SECURITY EXCHANGE COMMISSION
International (3) Regional (3)	WORLD CENTRAL BANK	TRADE ACT 1934	Economic Security Council [G-7 Finance Ministers]
World Bank International Investment Trust-Support Private Investment in Emerging Countries	Stabilize global economic activity*	GATT 1994 becomes WTO 1/1/95	
	Leader of last resort to financial institutions*	World Anti-Monopoly Authority—WTO	
World Bank Intermediate Assistance Facility	Calm jittery financial markets*	Global Competition Office—WTO	
	Create and regulate new international liquidity*	Regional Trading Blocs	

——— = Completed

- - - = Proposed

* Agreed to by G-7 & BIS, 6/95

© 1995. TWG Inc.

Note: Changes Proposed from Human Development Report 1994.

sury. White was later named by Whittaker Chambers and Helen Bentley as a covert agent for the Soviets.

Harry Dexter White drew up the plans for the International Bank for Reconstruction and Development, now known as the World Bank. Its purpose was to help Europe and other war-torn countries rebuild after the war. In 1947, the World Bank turned to "developmental" loans to help countries build economically, or so they said.

The World Bank is today comprised of a number of organizations which have expanded their power and might. Chart 5-7 showing these organizations. It is interesting to note that for a bank, they are involved in the environment through the Environment Development Institute in which they control water policy reform, agriculture and forestry, urban and industrial management as well as social issues. They are more than just a bank.

At a number of the conferences which I have attended, there are usually protests against the oppressive policies of the World Bank. Many third world countries, which are deeply indebted to the bank, are unable to build schools, roads, hospitals, and other needed infrastructure as a result. In the book *Mortgaging the Earth* by Bruce Rich, he lays out a number of "white elephant" projects which have been instrumental in creating this indebtedness.

The International Monetary Fund was also the brain child of Harry Dexter White. In 1944 the American Bankers Association published a report on the IMF in which it recommended that Congress not approve it, as the fund was too big, too elaborate, too complicated, and too difficult for the public to understand. Just as the World Bank has expanded, so too, has the IMF. In the 1960s, a liquid form of money was created by the IMF called "Special Drawing Rights" or SDRs. This form of money is basically printed out of "thin air" whenever money is needed and is inflationary in nature because it adds money to the system without accountability. In the 1980s, the fund took on two new roles—that of managing and financing the international debt rescheduling between third world countries and private international banks; and that of granting loans

Chart 5-7

THE WORLD BANK AND ITS GLOBAL ACTIVITIES

INTERNATIONAL BANK FOR RECONSTRUCTION & DEVELOPMENT (IBRD)	INTERNATIONAL DEVELOPMENT ASSOCIATION (IDA)	INTERNATIONAL FINANCE CORPORATION (IFC)	MULTILATERAL INVESTMENT GUARANTEE AGENCY (MIGA)
IBRD—Countries have to be a member of the IMF in order to join the IBRD. Obtains its financing from medium to long-term borrowings in the U.S. and Europe as well as central banks and other government institutions. Its purpose is to promote economic and social progress in developing nations, the same as IDA.	Purpose is to promote economic and social progess in developing nations by helping raise their productivity. The country has to have a per capita GNP of less than $865. Loans are at a lower interest rate than IBRD.	Established in 1956, IFCs purpose is to assist the economic development of developing countries by promoting growth in their countries. This is done through development of capital markets, the promotion of private sector infrastructure, privatization, the exploration of new markets for investment finance and advisory services and the direct mobilization of funds. IFC has: —Driven globalization —Originated of "country" funds, like Korea Fund —Worked with 150 country funds —Invests up to 25% of capital in new companies —Leveraged $19B or 2,000 companies in 125 countries	MIGA has 134 members and was established in 1988. It has as its principle responsibility the promotion of investment for economic development in member countries through guarantees to foreign investors against losses caused by noncommercial risks to encourage the flow of capital. In 1996, MIGA issued 68 contracts for $862 million covering $2.3B. Guarantees have been issued to Kuwait, Kyrgyz Republic, Mali, Nepal, and Papua New Guinea.

SOME OF THE MAJOR WORLD BANK PROGRAMS

HUMAN RESOURCES DEVELOPMENT	Environmentally Sustainable Development
Several areas: —Poverty-reduction activities—43% of total IDA directly targeted to the poor to increase productivity —Population, health and nutrition—produced 2 reports for Cairo —Education—invested $21.5B through 500 projects in 100 countries —Participatory Development—with NGOs, 41% projected approved by bank involved NGOs.	Established in 1993. Development could be achieved and sustained only through the integration of economic, social, technical, and ecological dimensions. Working on natural resources and ecosystem management, food security, urbanization, and infrastructure. —THE GLOBAL ENVIRONMENT FACILITY (GEF) This is a financial mechanism that provides funds to developing countries for projects/activities to protect the global environment: climate change, biological diversity, international waters, and depletion of ozone. The GEF has its own structure.

OTHER WORLD BANK ACTIVITIES

Environment Development Institute	Int'l Centre for Settlement Investment Disputes
Through the Environment and Natural Resources Division, works to advance sustainable development: —Water Policy Reform—two programs —Agriculture and forestry—the global process of structural adjustment, reform and transition in addition to the changing role of the state as a result of privatization —Urban and Industrial Management—Urban Management/Industrial Pollution Management —Social Issues—Social fund promotes decentralization —Mainstreaming the Environment—promotes understanding of parliamentarians, journalists/NGOs between economic and the environment. Biodiversity conservation.	This was established under the Convention of the Settlement of Investment Disputes between states and nationals of other states in 1965. ICSID seeks to encourage greater flows of international investment by providing facilities for the conciliation and arbitration of disputes between governments and foreign investors. ICSID publishes a semiannual international investment law journal. Source: 1996 World Bank Annual Report

to third world countries. The monies which the fund uses are comprised of contributions from member-states and is based on the Lenin-Marxist concept of redistribution of wealth. Today there is great discussion going on in international financial circles to further expand the power of the IMF to that of a world central bank.

Group of Seven/Group of Ten

The Group of Seven: Who are the Group of Seven (G-7)? For a number of years I asked that question. I felt like there was never a satisfactory answer, so in 1996 I determined to attend one of their meetings. I was absolutely astounded to find out that the Group of Seven have their own global structure. On the following pages you will discover this structure as you learn how the G-7 review and oversee the areas of finance, trade, justice, labor, housing, the environment, and transportation on a worldwide basis. They act essentially as a "global board of directors." This is as scary as it sounds when you realize the power these countries have and the course of world government toward which they have steered the world.

The Group of Seven today consists of the top seven industrialized countries of the world: the United States, Canada, France, Germany, England, Italy, and Japan, and represents sixty-five percent of the world's gross domestic product and the majority of votes in the United Nations Security Council. In 1998 Russia officially became a member of the G-7, making it the G-8. Pretty funny when you consider Italy has more money than Russia! In 1971 Richard Nixon took the dollar off of the gold standard. As a result of the world's strongest country severing its currency from gold, most of the countries of the world had no choice (we are told) but to follow. For the first time in history—since the book of Genesis—man traded in paper, which had no value behind it except whatever he thought it was worth! By 1973, the world experienced a currency crisis. Currency markets were forced to shut down twice in order for the world powers to come up with a solution. That year President Nixon called a number of world leaders (Britain, France, Germany, and Japan—Canada and Italy were added several years lat-

Chart 5-8

THE GROUP OF SEVEN GLOBAL STRUCTURE

PRESIDENTS/PRIME MINISTERS AS OF JUNE 1998

USA	Bill Clinton
Canada	Jean Cretien
England	Tony Blair
France	J. Chirac
Germany	Gerhard Schroder
Italy	Hassimo d'Alana
Japan	Keizo Obuchi
E.U.	Romareo Prado
Russia	Boris Yeltsin

Our secretaries meet with their G-7 counterparts

ENERGY B. Richardson

LABOR A. Herman

TRADE Barchesfsky

FINANCE L. Summers

TRANSPORTATION R. Slater

FOREIGN M. Albright

JUSTICE J. Reno

COMMERCE R. Daley

er) together to help manage the international monetary affairs of the world. They have been meeting since that time. When you consider the article from the *Anaheim Bulletin,* which said the United States Senate acknowledged the United Nations to be a world government, you can see that a new governmental body was being set in place. The U.N. agenda is driven by the G-8 countries as a result of their economic strength and power in the Security Council.

The Information Superhighway was created and fostered by the G-7. It is the G-7 who are also structuring the world police system to combat terrorism. At the G-7 meeting in Lyon, France, the G-7 renewed their determination to work together in partnership with leaders of other countries in our "increasingly interdependent and interactive world with rapid globalization" (*G-7 Final Communique from Lyon,* June 1996).

The Group of Ten (G-10) is an expansion of the Group of Seven (without Russia) and includes Switzerland, Holland, Sweden, and Belgium, the countries where the major money centers of the world are located. The countries of Holland, Belgium, and Luxembourg, are counted as one and are known as the Bendelux countries. The Basle Committee on Banking Supervision, which is part of the Bank for International Settlements, is composed of representatives of the central banks from the Group of Ten countries. You can see how cozy all of the relationships are.

For several years Russia has wanted to become a full partner of the Group of Seven. In 1990 Mikhail Gorbachev "crashed" the G-7 meeting. In 1996 Russia observed the political discussions of the G-7 and even had their own press briefing room in which to hold one of the shortest press briefings in G-7 history. In 1997 Russia was allowed to participate in every area with the exception of finance, and held a pretty intensive press briefing, which was packed.

After each G-7 meeting, the countries issue a "communique" outlining items they have covered and agreed to. From the 1973 communique, which was two pages long, to more recent communiques, which have been as long as sixty pages, I think it is fair to say that their agenda has expanded to the point where they are now considering domestic problems as collective domestic problems, i.e. we are all integrated and must work together. Consider some of the following excerpts from previous communiques (the emphasis is mine):

> The **interdependence** of our destinies makes it necessary for us to approach **common** economic problems with a sense of **common** purpose and to work toward mutually consistent economic strategies through better **cooperation**. . . .
>
> —Group of Seven 1988 Joint Declaration
> from San Juan, Puerto Rico

> Over the past fourteen years, the world economy and economic policy have undergone profound changes. In particular, the information technology revolution and the globalization of markets have **increased economic interdependence,** making it essential that governments consider fully the international dimensions of their deliberations.
>
> We agree that the protection and enhancement of the environment is essential. The report of the World Commission on Environment and Development has stressed that **environmental considerations must be integrated into all areas of economic policy-making if the globe is to continue to support mankind** [sustainable development]. We endorse the concept of sustainable development. Global climate change, air, sea, and fresh water pollution, acid rain, hazardous substances, deforestation, and endangered species require priority attention.
>
> —Group of Seven 1988 Economic
> Declaration, Toronto, Canada

> We the Participants in the Lyon Summit . . . discussed how we could build a **better international system** to secure **security** and **stability**. . . . In an increasingly interdependent and interactive world with rapid globalization in progress, we renewed our de-

termination to **work together** amongst us and in **partnership** with leaders of other countries. . . .

—Group of Seven 1996 Joint Declaration, Lyon, France

The Denver Summit of the 8 as major industrialized democracies, have discussed the steps necessary, both internationally and domestically, to shape the forces of integration to ensure prosperity and peace for **our** citizens and the entire world as we approach the twenty-first century (emphasis mine).

—Final communique, 1997 Denver, Colorado

The agreements made and implemented are far too many to even enumerate here. However, they have continuously strengthened a number of United Nations organizations and agencies, giving the IMF "very broad powers to 'meet the new challenges in global capital markets'." The G-7 welcomed the "World Bank's Strategic Compact to reduce poverty and forge new partnerships with the private sector," and they "reaffirmed the crucial role of the United Nations in maintaining international peace and security and in fostering global partnership and sustainable development." They have strengthened and reinforced the environment as being dominant, put together a global police infrastructure that reaches down to the local level (and your police department), and worked in all areas— transportation, education, housing, etc.—to integrate global policy. For more information, please see the website: *http:// www.library.utoronto.ca/www/g7,* and refer to chapter eight.

International Organization of Security Commissions (IOSCO)

This international group of security commissioners has been meeting in obscurity since 1975. The only place a person will hear of IOSCO is in global economic power circles and in industry publications, such as the *World Securities Law Report.*

In an interview this writer had with the assistant secretary-general of IOSCO, he called his organization "the U.N. of securities regulators." SEC commissioner Arthur Levitt calls IOSCO "the single organization that brings securities regulators from around the world." He further states:

There has never been a greater need for us to work together. We regulate one of the most innovative industries on the face of the earth, whose main commodity—capital—has little regard for national borders. We must expand our cooperation to cover regulatory issues beyond enforcement [emphasis mine].

The activities of IOSCO basically make it a "global security and exchange commission," i.e. a global regulatory body that is bringing together national laws to conform to an international jurisdiction over the whole global marketplace.

In describing itself, IOSCO writes that its members are the

securities and futures regulators, responsible to ensure in their own jurisdictions high standards of transparency, integrity, and investor protection, need to continuously adapt their regulatory framework and procedures to this changing environment. The IOSCO is at the heart of this global cooperative effort. IOSCO is today the most relevant technical cooperative forum for securities and future regulators and self-regulatory organizations worldwide.

—*1995 IOSCO Annual Report,* p. 2

It works very, very closely with a number of BIS-related groups. Its technical committee deals with (1) standardizing accounting methods on a global level (the global accounting discussed earlier); (2) the regulation of secondary (stock) markets and derivatives; (3) the regulation of market intermediaries such as the Tripartite Group (the tearing down of the Glass-Steagall Act); and (4) the enforcement and exchange of information between all its one hundred and eighty-seven members.

IOSCO—Not A Cure for Economic Meltdown: Regulatory authorities and conference participants totaling five, and sixty-eight persons from sixty-nine countries took part in the October 1996

IOSCO conference with security regulators from China and Russia participating for the first time. Attendees made it clear that if they put enough rules and regulations in place, they could prevent a global economic meltdown. I was able to have an interview with a commissioner from the executive committee who pointed out that, on one hand, they (the BIS/IOSCO) had created derivatives, futures, and options for which they could not predict market reaction on any given day, while on the other hand, the emerging market countries of the world are basically leaping from the "dark ages" to the computer age, creating stock markets and sophisticated trading tools without appropriate experience. How then can IOSCO prevent an economic meltdown when it cannot predict *all* the different combinations of human action it is trying to regulate? This very gracious man nodded his head in agreement.

Secondary Associations and Business Groups

The decrees and policies of the international organizations and commissions affiliated with the United Nations would fall on deaf ears if it were not for groups and organizations that are set up to facilitate change.

International Chamber of Commerce (ICC): Founded in 1919 by a group of international businessmen, the ICC represents seventy-five hundred businesses and associations in one hundred and thirty countries around the world. As a group they supported the creation of the United Nations in 1945, and currently advocate regional government or the "New Federalism," Medicare, the voucher system for education, federal land use planning, the Equal Rights Amendment, and sustainable development. Many of their policies have furthered world government through the United Nations. They have consultative status with the Economic and Social Council of the United Nations (ECOSOC). Unfortunately, many people are unaware that their local Chamber of Commerce, which they think only is concerned about local business, supports and reports to the International Chamber of Commerce. Please refer to Chart 5-9. Their website is: *www.iccwbo.org.*

Chart 5-9

The International Chamber of Commerce Structure
"World Peace Through World Trade"

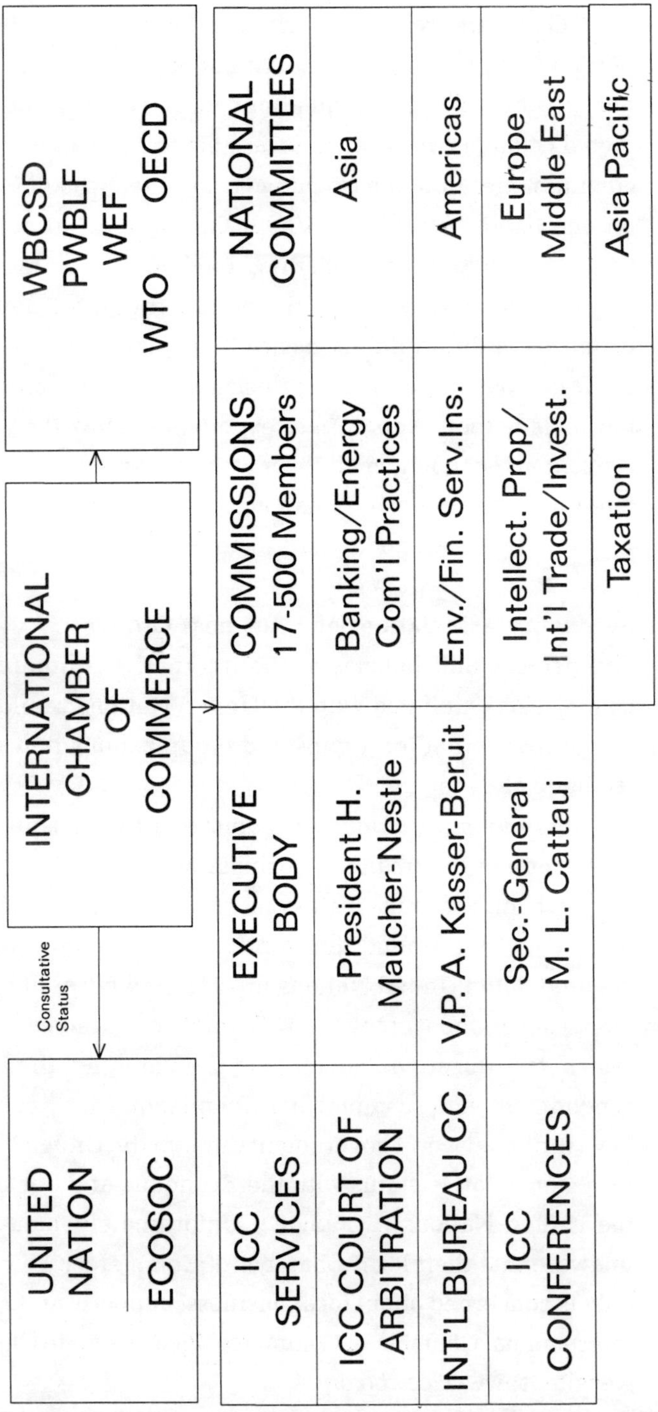

UNITED NATION		INTERNATIONAL CHAMBER OF COMMERCE		WBCSD PWBLF WEF WTO OECD
ECOSOC	Consultative Status →			

ICC SERVICES	EXECUTIVE BODY	COMMISSIONS 17-500 Members	NATIONAL COMMITTEES
ICC COURT OF ARBITRATION	President H. Maucher-Nestle	Banking/Energy Com'l Practices	Asia
INT'L BUREAU CC	V.P. A. Kasser-Beruit	Env./Fin. Serv.Ins.	Americas
ICC CONFERENCES	Sec.-General M. L. Cattaui	Intellect. Prop/ Int'l Trade/Invest.	Europe Middle East
		Taxation	Asia Pacific

The World Economic Forum (WEF): The WEF is a not-for-profit foundation that acts as a "bridge builder between business and government." Since 1971 it has brought together one thousand corporate chief executive officers from around the world with the key leaders of the United Nations, the World Trade Organization, the International Monetary Fund, the World Bank, the Organization for Economic Cooperation and Development, and the World Health Organization, along with leading scientists and world leaders, for a week of workshops, discussions, and networking that has as one of its purposes the strengthening of a one-world global agenda. Of all of the U.N. and U.N.-related conferences which I have attended, this is by far the most powerful and prestigious. In 1998 their theme was "Priorities for the Twenty-First Century" and its agenda dealt specifically with the empowerment of the IMF/World Bank to reduce global currency volatility. Interestingly enough, global currency volatility was exactly what happened in 1998 and the soon-to-be-completed empowerment of the International Monetary Fund as a world central bank is still part of their agenda.

The 1999 meeting had as its theme "Responsible Globality: Managing the Impact of Globalization." At that meeting they continued to discuss the empowerment of the IMF as a world central bank and the linking of the regional currencies—the dollar, yen, and euro—as one! It should also be noted that along with an appearance and speech by Vice President Al Gore, Britain's Princess Anne was a speaker. What this conveys is the power of the meetings and the interest of the British royal family in them. Previous years' themes have included: "The New Direction for Global Leadership" (1991), "Rallying All the Forces for Global Recovery" (1993), and "Sustaining Globalization" (1996).

As I have analyzed the mix of governments and businesses, I believe it is reasonable to conclude that the World Economic Forum acts as a **"People's Parliament"** for the United Nations. When you bring together multinational and transnational corporations with balance sheets in the billions and trillions of dollars—far exceeding the net worth of many small countries—and these CEOs interact with the world's international governmental structure, the United Nations, along with other governments, they have the power to literally "move mountains" and that is what they are doing—facilitating the global agenda which is "global corporate fascism"! Their website is: *www.weforum.org.*

World Business Council for Sustainable Development (WBCSD): This is a coalition of one hundred and twenty international companies from thirty-four countries and more than twenty major business sectors who are concerned about the environment. They have adopted the United Nations view and policies on the environment which basically says that the world has dominance over man. They promote business leadership, policy development, and the best practices to accomplish their global goals, which are to "develop closer cooperation between business, government, and all other organizations concerned about the environment and sustainable development." Member companies include: AT&T, British Petroleum (who purchased Amoco), DAN Hotels, Dow Chemical, DuPont, Eastman Kodak, Fiat, Hitachi, Itochu, S. C. Johnson & Son, Shell International, Texaco, 3M, Volkswagen, Waste Management International, and Xerox, to name a few.

Prince of Wales Business Leaders Forum (PWBLF): As seen in chapter two, Prince Charles is a very, very powerful world leader who works behind the scenes. He and his organization, the Prince of Wales Business Leaders Forum, are mentioned here again because of their prominence and the role they play politically and environmentally. At the conclusion of the 1990 organizational meeting of the Prince of Wales Business Leaders Forum, one hundred multinational and transnational chief executive officers agreed that:

1. CEOs have a critical lead role to play in setting company values and ensuring that local managers are briefed, encouraged, and prepared to listen to local community leaders;
2. Companies must strive to adopt total processes and products based on principles of "sustainable development"; and
3. Business executives should assist community leaders in inner

cities and isolated rural areas to regenerate their neighborhoods by developing business skills (Prince of Wales Business Leaders Forum, "Stakeholders: The Challenge in a Global Market, Conclusions and Follow-up Action," Charleston, South Carolina, 20–21 February 1990, 5–6).

The mission of the PWBLF is to

promote continuous improvement in the practice of good *corporate citizenship* and *sustainable development* internationally, as a natural part of successful business operations. It aims to work with members and partners to: (1) Demonstrate that business has an essential and creative role to play in the prosperity of *local communities as partners in development*, (2) Raise awareness of the value of corporate responsibility in international business practice, (3) Encourage *partnership action between business and communities* as an effective means of *promoting sustainable economic development* [emphasis mine].

The italics emphasize the goals and agenda which Prince Charles shares with the United Nations, which is economic, political, and environmental control and dominance.

The PWBLF operates in twenty-six countries, concentrating on post-communist countries and developing economies. Corporations with which the prince works very closely include both foreign and American companies: 3M, American Express, TRW, Coca-Cola, SmithKline Beecham, ARCO, CIGNA, DHL Worldwide Express, Levi Strauss & Company, the Perot Group, the Office of Ronald Reagan, and U.S. West International, to name a few.

It is the prince who has worked behind the scenes in setting up the radical United Nations environmental agenda. In his book *Business as Partners in Development,* the Prince states, ". . . the debate is no longer about extreme alternatives—about communism versus capitalism, the free market versus state control, democracy versus dictatorship—but about finding common ground."

Again, we must understand that Prince Charles is basically establishing a **global political policy** and setting up a "reinvented form of government" worldwide!! This form of government—a marriage between business and government—fits in very well with the **aristocratic form of governance which is feudalism.** You see, under a feudalistic form of government, the king owned everything and the peasants worked at the pleasure of the king. If you did not agree with the king, you did not work or have a way to earn a living. When our form of government is being replaced with public-private partnerships, the checks and balances in the Constitution are obliterated and we have no protection or rights—perhaps we could call this **"reinvented feudalism."**

THE GLASS-STEAGALL ACT

This act is virtually unknown to most people, even those who work in the banking field. While I had studied it in a banking class I took years ago, as well as in a class to obtain my securities license, most people do not think about this bill. However, it was a very important law enacted in 1933 as a result of the 1929 banking crash. This bill, along with the McFadden Act of 1927 (which prevented interstate banking: the ability of banks to do business in states in which they are not located), were instrumental in setting up "fire walls" to protect consumers from the world of stock, bond, and bank monopolies.

As a result of attending my first Group of Seven meeting in Lyon, France, in 1996 and then the annual meeting of IOSCO that October, I became aware of a financial entity in Europe where they did not have these two laws. Called "financial conglomerates," these are your true "one-stop-shopping," as they are banks that own insurance companies and brokerage firms. Individuals can bank at one of these financial conglomerates and purchase a certificate of deposit, life and disability insurance, commercial insurance if they have a business, and stocks and bonds if they want investments.

Glass-Steagall adopted five key changes to the Federal Reserve Act:

1. It created the Federal Deposit Insurance Corporation (FDIC) to protect bank depositors through insurance;
2. Restricted investment banking activities to acting only for its own account;
3. Prohibited the affiliation of any bank to engage principally in investment banking activities (bringing stocks and bonds to market);
4. Made it illegal for any depository institution to engage in investment banking and receive deposits at the same time and; and
5. Prohibited interlocking directorates and certain other links between member banks and firms or individuals primarily engaged in investment banking.

In short, it separated the functions of a bank from that of an investment firm that brings (underwrites) stocks and bonds to market and has a sales force to sell them (stock brokers). Financial conglomerates today are everything that our Congress in 1933 said was bad for the country. So whom do we believe? The lawmakers of 1933 or the ones today?

Congressman Jim Leach, chairman of the Committee on Banking and Financial Services, considers "the reform of the Glass-Steagall Act the most exciting comprehensive banking bill of the century and more consequential than any prior legislation excepting perhaps the Federal Reserve Act in 1913" (speech at a conference sponsored by the American Bar Association, May 1997). Is he correct? What in the world does this mean? What are the repercussions of this action? What will be the impact on Americans?

The statement by Congressman Jim Leach, who is a member of the World Federalists, a one-world government organization, and who has been vice president of the Parliamentarians for Global Action, testifies to the concerted drive by a number of globalists in Congress to break the Glass-Steagall Act. This action would in essence bring U.S. banking institutions into conformity with other banks around the world. The BIS defines mega-banks—banks who can offer insurance and underwrite and sell securities and other services—as "financial conglomerates." *In essence, breaking Glass-Steagall would standardize our banking system with the global banking system that is emerging as a result of the BIS-orchestrated changes in the national laws of all countries.* For example, all banks could sell insurance, own stock brokerage firms, and syndicate stocks and bonds. Lastly, it would open the door to the "cashless society" or "E-money." Many other countries are further along in the conversion of paper money to E-money than is the United States. The American banking system would be in a position to facilitate this global changeover. Without the repeal of the Glass-Steagall Act, this cannot happen. In America, the FDIC is spearheading the E-money conversion.

In answer to a question I raised, Mr. Leach replied that the repeal "would make banks more meaningful . . . and they would not be crippled by a regulatory environment in terms of their powers." He also called for a national insurance commission, as other countries around the world have. Currently each state, as protection against too much central power, has its own state insurance commission.

This may be part of the reason for the Federal Reserve approving Mitsubishi Bank's plan to buy the U.S. units of the Bank of Tokyo, which will create the world's largest bank with $826 billion in assets (*Washington Times*, March 9, 1996, A11).

Lastly, there is an old rule that says if you want to know who controls what, "follow the money." According to the BIS, the world's banking assets are valued at more than $20 trillion, insurance premiums at $2 trillion, stock market capitalization at over $10 trillion, and the market value of listed bonds at $10 trillion. In light of the growth in the wealth of the world, which lawmakers do you trust?

In a press briefing given by Secretary of the Treasury Robert Rubin at the 1998 Group of Seven meeting in Denver, Colorado, I asked him the following questions on the repeal of the Glass-Steagall Act:

Veon: In light of the globalization process and your participation as a G-7 finance minister and with the Bank for International Settlements, what steps remain to bring the United States into full harmonization with regard to financial conglomerates in the U.S.? Has Glass-Steagall been effectively repealed with the merger and acquisition activity in the banks and insurance markets?

Rubin: The answer is that over the last decade, I suppose, at an ever-increasing rate, the regulators—the Office of the Controllers of the Currency and the Federal Reserve Board—have . . . allowed more and more non-bank activity by financial institutions—non-bank financial institutions. And the result is that the Steagall walls have eroded. Having said that, Glass-Steagall is still in effect. And so there is something very substantially short of a complete elimination of the walls between banking, insurance, brokerage, investment banking, and other financial services. Legislation is now working its way through Congress to repeal Glass-Steagall to deal with the bank holding company act.

Veon: Will that then complete financial harmony or globalization for the U.S. with regard to the other countries of the world?

Rubin: Well, for one thing, the financial modernization legislation has a long way to go. Secondly, even if this passes sometime this year or next year, there are a lot of other issues that exist if we're going to get a World Trade Organization Financial Services Agreement.

In 1997, even before my questions to Robert Rubin, there was much orchestration to dismantle the Glass-Steagall Act step-by-step. Consider the following, which primarily occurred during 1997 and set the stage for similar activity during 1998. The first few stones were verbal; the last several were really boulders being hurled at Glass-Steagall as the mergers and acquisitions heated up and expanded.

Stone 1: Proposed Law Is End Run Around Glass-Steagall
In December 1996, the Fed increased the amount of revenue that a

bank can earn from a financial subsidiary from ten percent to twenty-five percent. Congressman Jim Leach, a key supporter of financial conglomerates, introduced the Financial Services Competitiveness Act, which would repeal Section 20 (separating banking from securities) of the Glass-Steagall Act. This law would create a new category of investment bank holding companies that would be permitted to work in a wider range of activities than currently allowed. In addition, the Fed announced it was looking to remove some of the "firewalls" that banks must keep between their main operations and non-bank subsidiaries that deal in securities (*Financial Times,* January 14, 1997, 7). While this bill has not yet passed in several previous years, you can be sure that it will be reintroduced until it passes.

Stone 2: Proposal to Allow Banks to Own Commercial Firms

Secretary of the Treasury Robert Rubin is reviewing a proposal forwarded to him by Undersecretary John D. Hawke to let banks own and be owned by commercial companies, breaching the longstanding wall between banking and commerce. The treasury is leaning toward a proposal that would allow nonfinancial companies to own banks and permit mergers between banks, insurers, and securities firms. Obviously removing the barrier between banking and commerce would reshape the financial services industry. Some of the nation's largest banks could find themselves as takeover candidates by multinational corporations, such as Amoco or IBM (*Wall Street Journal,* January 24, 1997, A2).

Stone 3: Testimony by Interested Parties

In February 1997 while testifying before Congress, both bank and securities regulators called for the overhaul of federal banking laws to suit the changing global financial landscape. Comptroller of the Currency Eugene A. Ludwig said:

> Banks are facing competition not only from *non-bank* financial
> service companies such as GE Capital, Merrill-Lynch, and GMC,

to name but a few, but also from firms that traditionally have not offered financial services such as telecommunications and computer companies.

Alan Greenspan said Congress should allow banks to get into new businesses, such as insurance or securities underwriting, as long as the activities do not create new risks for the financial system or taxpayers (*Washington Post,* February 14, 1997, G1). Interestingly enough, those who testified just happen to represent the areas of the tripartite, having a vested interest in banks, financial services, and insurance, and representing the Bank for International Settlements through the Federal Reserve!!

Stone 4: Non-Financial Banks and Non-Financial Companies Getting Positive Vibes to Merger

In commenting on the above activity, the *Wall Street Journal* on May 23, 1997, reported: "The momentum to restructure U.S. banking law appears to be growing, even as an array of regulators warn against letting banks merge with manufacturers and other non-financial companies" (A2).

In May 1997 Treasury Secretary Robert Rubin went on record with his approval of banks merging with commercial entities. *There are concerns that this type of merger could concentrate financial power in too few hands and any crises in banks could then spread to the corporate parent* (*Wall Street Journal,* May 23, 1997, A2) (emphasis mine).

Stone 5: Without Law Passed, Banks/Financial Services Merge

In order to enhance the need for the repeal, the market has been very busy with mergers and acquisitions beginning with the alliance of Salomon Brothers and Fidelity Investments, which will enable Salomon to distribute some of the equities they underwrite through Fidelity's discount brokerage network. Fidelity has one and a half million customers and is the largest mutual fund company in the U.S., and is now the second largest discount brokerage firm (*Financial Times,* January 20, 1997, 19).

In 1995 ABN Amro, Holland's largest bank, agreed to buy Standard Federal Bankcorp, a Troy, Michigan, thrift for $1.9 billion, making this acquisition the largest in ABN Amro's history, giving it control of one of the biggest thrifts in America. ABN already has an extensive U.S. banking empire concentrated mostly in Chicago. ABN has been buying up American banks for about fifteen years, has fifteen North American offices, and employs eleven thousand people, with $75 billion in assets. Its holdings include LaSalle National Corp, LaSalle Bank FSB, LaSalle Home Mortgage (the largest single-family mortgage lender in Chicago), ABN Amro Capital Markets Holding Company, and a number of other branches and banks in Michigan, Indiana, Illinois, and northwest Ohio. The ABN acquisition of Standard Federal could lead to other non-U.S. banks, such as Hong Kong and Shanghai Banking Corp, Royal Bank of Scotland, and Allied Irish Bank acquiring U.S. banks (*Wall Street Journal,* January 25, 1995, A3).

In other news, Morgan Stanley and Dean Witter, Discover & Company agreed to merge into the world's biggest securities company in a transaction valued at $10.2 billion. Morgan Stanley has offices in nineteen countries, while Dean Witter has mutual funds and credit cards that serve more than forty million Americans. This merger would move Merrill Lynch out of the number-one spot and move Morgan Stanley/Dean Witter in (*New York Times,* January 26, 1997, A1). Morgan Stanley was formed during the 1935 breakup of the J. P. Morgan empire.

In April 1997 it was announced that Bankers Trust would buy the nation's oldest stock brokerage firm, Alex Brown, Inc. for $1.7 billion. This action by Frank N. Newman, chairman, CEO, and president of Bankers Trust, erases the barriers between commercial and investment banking before Glass-Steagall is repealed. Newman targeted Alex Brown before the Fed changed its rules to twenty-five percent in December. By acquiring Alex Brown, total income generated would be around twenty percent. It is apparent, due to the obvious desire to eliminate Glass-Steagall, that the Federal Reserve will approve this purchase since it facilitates the erosion of the fifty-year-old barrier between the banking and brokerage industries (*Washington Times,* April 8, 1997, B7, and *Washington Post,* April 20, 1997, H1).

Stone 6: Insurance Companies Buying Brokerage—the Final Step in Erasing the Glass-Steagall Wall of Separation

The deal of the year for 1997 was the purchase by Travelers Group of Salomon, Inc. for $9.3 billion, moving Travelers closer to its goal of becoming a financial supermarket, handling everything from health insurance to retirement plans. Called "Wall Street's Big Bang," Travelers Group becomes the third-largest securities firm after Morgan Stanley Dean Witter Discover & Company and Merrill Lynch & Company. Andrew Fraser, reporting for the *Washington Times,* commented: "It raises the stakes in the consolidation game being played out across the financial services industry as relaxed regulations and global competition cause an urgent rearranging of the landscape." Salomon will be merged with Smith Barney, also owned by Travelers, to create Salomon Smith Barney Holdings Inc. Commenting further on the merger, Linda Chase, a financial services analyst at Towers Perrin (a New York-based business consulting firm) said: *"This is the beginning of the creation of the financial supermarket of the future, which is why it is so cutting edge. Nobody is in a position to do this"* (*Washington Times,* September 25, 1997, B9). It should be noted that Warren Buffet is the largest stockholder of Salomon Inc. (*Washington Time,* September 25, 1997, B9, emphasis mine). **This was the second-to-last step in erasing the Glass-Steagall Act. The final step occurred in 1998 when Citibank and Travelers merged, thus fulfilling the definiion of a financial conglomerate.**

The bottom line

Only crooks, in this case crooks with a global world view, throw stones at glass. When Glass-Steagall is gone, *the new world economic order will begin.* Glass-Steagall has, in reality, come down without legislation being enacted since actions speak louder than words. It will crumble as a result of precedence. This paves the way for a whole new world order as a cashless society is now possible—no dollars, yen, or marks, only computer units. Just think what could happen if the computer lost your account! Also, it underscores the fact that central banks, not the Congress, are in control. To prepare for the cashless society, the number of days in which a stock trade settles has been reduced to one. The securities industry used to allow five days for a transaction—a buy or sell—to settle (a match between the purchase of the stock and the money needed to purchase or visa versa).

Chapter 6

The Economic Structure
Economic Regionalism—
the EMU and the Free Trade
Areas of the Americas

CHAPTER SUMMARY

The Economic and Monetary Union—EMU

The world has been divided up into regions. The five regions are (and coming): the Americas (the thirty-four countries of our hemisphere, excluding Cuba because it is a dictatorship), the eleven countries of the European Common Market (the new name is the Economic and Monetary Union or "EMU," which is pronounced "M-U"), the Asian Free Trade Association, Africa, and the Middle East. The most developed of these regions is the European Common Market, which began trading with a combined currency, the euro, on January 1, 1999. The newest region-to-be is Africa, which the Group of Seven highlighted in Denver of 1997, and to which the World Economic Forum gave its blessing in January-February, 1998. The most volatile is the Asian region and the newly birthed region.

In January 1999 the Economic and Monetary Union (EMU) of Europe was birthed. The goal of a united Europe is not new. The history of the struggle for a united Europe has given spice to history—there have been many kings and popes who have fought to become emperor of Europe. Included in the quest were Caesar, Charlemagne, who was crowned in A.D. 800 by Pope Leo III; the

Hapsburg Charles V; Napoleon Bonaparte, who crowned himself at Notre Dame Cathedral; Prince Otto von Bismarck; Adolph Hitler; and now the European Monetary Union–EMU.

With the EMU comes a new currency. Very simply, the euro is a new, visual symbol of a new way of life. It symbolizes the passing of a former way of life under individual nation-states to a new, integrated empire, a sort of "revived Roman Empire." The euro will change how corporations and countries do business. It will have a profound effect on the strategy and operations of businesses—pricing policy, corporate and country finance, legal contracts, international systems, country borders, and sovereignty.

The new and rising European Common Market will fulfill the dream of Napoleon who said, "I wanted to found a European system, a European code of laws, a European judiciary. There would have been but one people throughout Europe." The next step for the European Parliament will be to choose a president. In view of European history, could we consider this person the "emperor" of the "revived Roman Empire"?

The Free Trade Areas of the Americas

Most people are not aware that America has been integrated economically (and politically) into a new free trade area dubbed "the Americas." The formal document was signed in April 1998 in Santiago, Chile. Because this new arrangement is a public-private partnership, it does not have to be voted on by Congress, as it is being implemented by federal executive agencies—the departments of Housing, Transportation, Treasury, Justice, Labor, etc.

The State Department publication No. 10536, *Words Into Deeds —Process Since the Miami Summit,* will show the significant progress toward the total integration of our hemisphere. Ministers representing labor, transportation, finance, justice, energy, telecommunications, science and technology, education, anti-crime initiatives, trade and commerce, and health and human services have been working together since 1994 to implement the initiatives listed in this rather thick report. Interestingly enough, the Declaration of Principles supporting the summit of the Americas states in the opening two paragraphs:

> The elected Heads of State and Government of the Americas are committed to advance the prosperity, democratic values, and institutions, and security of our Hemisphere. **We reiterate our firm adherence to the principles of international law and the purposes of principles enshrined in the United Nations Charter. . . .**

INTRODUCTION

We are confronted on every side with projections about the future. Movies like *Independence Day* and *Armageddon* give us an interesting, though unrealistic, view of what may be ahead. The future should be seen from the international level and not the local level. In 1998, two very important and historic events took place. One has been written about for over twenty-six hundred years, but more specifically in the last forty years, while the other has gone unreported and unheralded. The truth is that the world is being divided up into economic "regions" in order for it to be managed from an international perspective.

Regional Chart

The five economic regions are: the Americas (the thirty-four countries of our hemisphere, excluding Cuba because they are a dictatorship), the European Common Market (eleven to fourteen countries), the Asian Free Trade Association, Africa, and the Middle East. The most developed of these regions is the European Common Market, which began trading with a combined currency, the euro, on January 1, 1999. The newest region-to-be is Africa, which the Group of Seven highlighted in Denver in 1997, and to which the World Economic Forum gave its blessing in January-February 1998. The most volatile is the Asian region. The newly birthed region, the Americas, will be discussed here along with what was formerly called the European Common Market and is now the Economic and Monetary Union or "EMU" (pronounced "M-U").

Chart 6-1

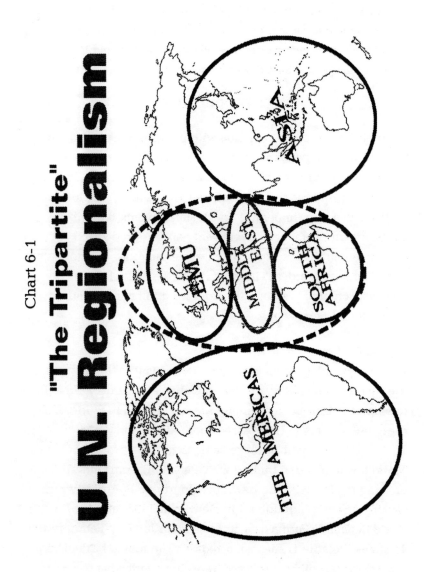

"The Tripartite"
U.N. Regionalism

WORLD CURRENCY

I remember hearing somewhere that there would be a world currency at some time in the future. In 1990 I read a book called *Euroquake* in which the author claimed that by the end of the 1990s the dollar, yen, and Deutsche mark would all be equal in value. Our dollar has been on a roller coaster ride down since President Nixon severed any connection between the dollar and gold in 1971. In April 1994 the dollar reached one of many historic lows against the yen when the dollar dropped to less than one yen in value—to .80 yen from a 1971 high of 3.55—or a 77.7 percent loss in value. The dollar had also dropped from a 1971 high of 3.65 against the German Deutsche mark to 1.35, or a 68 percent loss in value. Since that time the dollar has rebounded to two-year highs. This is not because of our economic strength, but because the dollar appears to be used as a "bouncing currency" in order to make imports cheaper and provide an opportunity for countries outside of America to benefit from a strong dollar, which in turn has made our exports more expensive.

For a number of years I have been writing about what happens when the dollar, yen, and Deutsche mark (now euro) are equal to one. In March 1998 I wrote:

> Based on the newly emerging economic regions, I believe the future world currency will come about when the predominant regional currencies are fixed against one another. For example, the value of the euro will be fixed at 1.16 to the dollar. In the Americas, the other currencies of the hemisphere will be fixed against the dollar. Currently we can see only a sixteen-point difference in value between the euro and the dollar. And at this point, we don't know the future value of the dollar to the euro after integration with the other countries and currencies in our hemisphere. Therefore, I believe that it is safe to say that at some point, the euro, the dollar, the yen, and the other two dominant regional currencies will be fixed against one another so that they all have the same value. What is this? A world currency.

Interestingly enough, in the January 25, 1999, edition of *Business Week,* an editorial entitled "Let the Dollar Go Its Own Way" reported the following:

> Here's a scenario for you. If the new euro drops fifteen percent in value against the dollar, and the yen rises ten percent, all three currencies could easily reach parity. So if euro=dollar=yen, what then? There will be talk of linking the three currencies at the upcoming World Economic Forum meeting in Davos, Switzerland, as part of the effort to improve the international financial architecture.
>
> —*Business Week,* January 25, 1999, p.126

You may be wondering what all of this has to do with your finances. **Everything!!!!** You see, there are winners and losers with a regional currency and with a world currency. The stronger currencies will have to be devalued and the weaker currencies will have to be strengthened in order to reach a new equal value. The stronger currencies will have to give up economic power and strength in order to "transfer" value to the weaker currencies. **This will impact our current style and standard of living.** In order to understand how this could come about, we need to consider the impact of the euro (Economic and Monetary Union—EMU) and the dollar (the Americas).

THE ECONOMIC AND MONETARY UNION (EMU) OF THE EUROPEAN COMMON MARKET

Michael Camdessus, managing director of the International Monetary Fund, said this about the integration of Europe:

> European monetary union will be the most important decision for the international monetary system since the breakdown of Bretton Woods [1973] and it will make a constructive contribution to the emergence of an international economic order.
>
> —*The European,* January 10, 1997, 19

At the most recent Group of Eight meeting in England, the participating world leaders applauded the integration of the currencies that will comprise the euro.

Introduction

On January 1, 1999, the economies of Austria, Belgium, Finland, France, Germany, Ireland, Italy, Luxembourg, the Netherlands, Portugal, and Spain formed a new economic powerhouse that now accounts for almost one-fifth of the world's economic output and trade. The Economic and Monetary Union of Europe (EMU) was birthed. While there was great speculation about this historic occasion, it happened "without a hitch." The birth was made easier with $350 billion in reserves—seven times those of the dollar. It combines eleven economies with a total gross domestic product of $6.8 trillion—not far behind the United States' $7.25 trillion (*Washington Times*, December 31, 1998, A12, "Euro to challenge dollar to be leading currency").

In 2002 when the euro banknotes and coins hit the streets, 290 million Europeans, with a GDP of $5.1 trillion, will be using the same currency. On that day, the German mark, the French franc, and the Italian lira will die. A formidable rival to the U.S. dollar will appear. The euro will revolutionize the way Europe does business and create a global currency that could rival the American dollar as a reserve holding in the vaults of the banks of the world (*Washington Times*, March 26, 1998, 1). For various economic reasons, the governments of Britain, Sweden, and Denmark have chosen to remain out for the time being, and Greece was not able to meet the financial and economic criteria.

Today the EMU and the United States are each other's largest trading partners, with a combined trade worth more than $230 billion and with about three million U.S. workers employed by European-owned companies, and with fifty-one percent of foreign direct investment in the United States coming from the European Union, while more than forty-two percent of foreign investment in the EMU comes from the United States.

History

The goal of a united Europe is not new. The history of the struggle for a united Europe has given spice to history—there have been many kings and popes who have fought to become emperor of Europe. Included in the quest were Germanic Charlemagne, who was crowned in A.D. 800 by Pope Leo III; the Hapsburg lineage with Charles V; Napoleon Bonaparte, who crowned himself at Notre Dame Cathedral; Prince Otto von Bismarck; Adolph Hitler; and now the European Monetary Union–EMU (Hilton, 21–31).

It was the 1951 Treaty of Paris, signed by France and Germany, that created the European Coal and Steel Community as a way to obtain greater economic strength. This pool of iron, coal, and steel resources was later enlarged to include Italy, Belgium, the Netherlands, and Luxembourg. In 1957 the Treaty of Rome brought the European Economic Community (EEC) into being, with the initial goal of removing trade and economic barriers between member states and unifying their economic policies.

In 1969 the heads of state and government of the European Community decided they would create an economic and monetary union (EMU). Those joining the EMU have done so at three different times. In 1973 the above six members were joined by the United Kingdom, Ireland, and Denmark. In 1985 Spain, Portugal, and Greece entered, followed by Sweden, Austria, and Finland in 1995 (*The European,* 4–5).

The Euro

In December 1991 the Treaty of European Union was established in Maastricht (the Netherlands), which set provisions for economic and monetary union, to be followed eventually by political union, including joint foreign and security policies. It was through the European Rate Mechanism (ERM) established in Maastricht that the values of individual countries' currencies were to be pegged against one another. In January 1993 the European single market became a reality for three hundred forty-five million people in twelve EMU countries.

In order to bring the different countries into one economic entity, it was important that their economies were in a position to converge by means of similar economic status. The following requirements for membership were established:

1. National governments should not have budget deficits above three percent of GDP on January 1, 1999;
2. National governments should not have more than sixty percent of GDP as public debt;
3. Inflation should not be more than one and a half percent above the average rate of inflation of the three best performing countries;
4. Interest rates should not be more than two percent higher than those of the three countries with the lowest inflation; and
5. Countries were to be members in the Exchange Rate Mechanism.

In addition, the path to the euro also targets the continent's extensive job protection, social benefits, and tax policies. It will require the **standardization** of each of these areas into common law.

The euro began trading electronically on May 4, 1998. All credit and paper transactions by businesses and individuals will be conducted in the euro for the public from January 1, 1999. The euro will exist only in credit (plastic, mortgage, and IOUs) form until 2002, when it will also take on the form of coin and currency. Between January 1, 1999, and January 1, 2002, national paper currencies will exist alongside the credit form of the euro. (If you go to Europe and charge your purchases, your credit card will not reflect national currency, but the euro instead.) By June 2002 national currencies will cease to exist as the euro will become the sole currency. The euro started trading at 1.17 and fell to 1.00 on the dollar. Not since the Roman Empire has 65% of world currencies equalled.

European Central Bank

On July 1, 1998, the European Central Bank (ECB) was officially born. Headquartered in Frankfurt, the ECB appointed a president and an executive board. The ECB is the successor to the European Monetary Institute, which was formed four years ago in anticipation of the EMU.

The effect of the ECB is seen in the newly created European System of Central Banks (ESCB). The ECB will make the major decisions that affect the Economic and Monetary Union, while the "old" central banks will execute money market operations at the local level. They will act as intermediaries between local transactions and the European Central Bank (*The European* July 3–9, 1997, 22). In short, the ECB will be the European equivalent of the Federal Reserve for the European region.

There was great discord over who would head up the European Central Bank, obviously a plum position. After eleven hours of debate, the European Union leaders agreed to a compromise, which calls for Wim Duisenberg (Germany) to be nominated for a full eight-year term. While he agreed to step down at the time of the compromise, he recently has said he will not. The French were to have their chance at being the leader of the ECB and are rather irate that the Germans have not kept their word. The executive board is comprised of Christian Nor (France), Ottmar Issing (Germany), Sirkka Hamalainen (Finland), Eugenio Domingo Solans (Spain), and Tommasso Padoa-Schioppa (Italy), who served a term as the managing director of the Bank for International Settlements, the most powerful central bank in the world.

Effect on the Dollar

While it is hoped the euro will lead Europe to a new age of prosperity and competitiveness, the euro will affect Americans as well as Europeans. Business contracts are currently written in U.S. dollars, but with the advent of the euro, those contracts will be switched to euros.

A massive shift from dollars to euros will fundamentally change the balance of the world's financial system. The euro may be where the buck stops. A strong euro means European exports to the United States will be more expensive and U.S. exports to Europe will be cheaper. This is good for U.S. manufacturers, but it also means higher inflation in the United States because of the higher cost of European goods. Currently, the dollar comprises sixty percent of the world's central bank reserves. The dollar is used in at least eighty percent of the world's financial transactions, and accounts for twenty-seven percent of the world's production (*Washington Post,* April 1, 1998, 1).

As a result of the new giant financial market that will be birthed by the euro (the European stock market is expected to grow from $2.5 trillion to $7.5 trillion), investment banks such as Morgan Stanley, Goldman Sachs, and Merrill Lynch are shifting people from New York to London in order to exploit EMU's possibilities. The euro government bond market is valued at $1.9 trillion, almost as big as the U.S. Treasury market. It is anticipated that the euro will speed deregulation (*Business Week,* April 27, 1998, 96–97).

In May 1998 China signaled its intention to gradually convert a portion of its huge foreign currency reserves into euros once it has judged the strength and stability of the new European currency. The EMU is China's fourth largest trading partner. And about sixty percent of China's $140 billion foreign exchange reserves are currently denominated in dollars (*Financial Times,* May 6, 1998, 4). In October 1998 it was reported that the Japanese purchase of U.S. Treasuries had fallen in the last twelve months from eighty-two percent as a proportion of all bond purchases to forty-five percent, and that they expected it to fall below thirty percent. According to Avinash Persaud, head of currency research at J. P. Morgan, "What we are seeing is a clear long-term reweighting of Japanese portfolio investments from the dollar into the eurozone. This is happening at quite a fast pace." Another interpreted the Japanese actions as "realiz[ing] that EMU will bring liquidity" (*Financial Times,* October 29, 1998, 17).

Higher Cost of Living for Americans

The euro has been called a "Trojan horse" by David Bowers, European equity strategist for Merrill Lynch and Company (*Business*

Week, April 27, 1998, 92). While no one can predict exactly how the dollar will be impacted, it is a safe bet that **there will be a change from its current value.** As Europe changes from the use of the dollar to the euro, as central banks exchange their dollar reserves for euros, and as American and foreign corporations switch to the euro to do business in Europe, it is reasonable to say that it will impact the value of the dollar in a considerable way. Recent research shows that at the same time the euro is gaining strength, that the switch by many Latin American countries to the dollar is beginning. See the next section.

What this means for you and me is that it will take more dollars to live. The Federal Reserve, in order to attract and keep foreign investments in U.S. Treasury bills, notes, and bonds, will have to raise interest rates higher than other countries in order for the dollar to remain attractive. This will increase our cost of living.

Other Effects of the Euro

Also, we need to consider that the fifteen countries in Africa whose currencies are linked to the French franc will be switching to the euro. With that many African countries tied to the euro, perhaps their new economic trade area will use the euro. In addition, many countries in eastern and central Europe that use the dollar might also adopt the euro, as may other "non-euro" countries, such as Sweden, Denmark, Norway, and Switzerland (*Washington Post,* April 16, 1998, 1).

Let me point out that U.S. Treasury Secretary Robert Rubin at the Group of Eight Finance Ministers meeting in London in 1998, which I attended, said that he did not expect any change on the dollar. He

> expects the dollar to continue to play a central role in the international system . . . [based on] the size and strength of the U.S. economy. [As a result of] the extensive ties between the U.S. economy and the rest of the world, none of this will change with the creation of a successful euro.

What Does the Euro Symbolize?

Very simply, the euro is a new, visual symbol of **a new way of life** (*The European,* January 18–24, 1996, 7). It symbolizes the passing of a former way of life under individual nation-states to a new, integrated empire—a sort of "revived Roman Empire." The euro will change how corporations and countries do business. It will have a profound effect on the strategy and operations of businesses—pricing policy, corporate and country finance, legal contracts, and international systems.

In addition, corporations in the past have relied on commercial bank financing. With the euro, corporations will have to be more dependent on a liquid capital market in corporate bonds. In addition, it currently takes five days for money to be transferred from one EMU bank to another. With the European Central Bank, settlement will be immediate (*Financial Times,* November 21, 1997, Special Section, EMU-II).

The euro also symbolizes the fact that governments will lose influence and that the national frame of reference will fade in light of the European Common Market. While national governments will set tax rates and establish labor regulations, they will not make policy for the whole. Their function will basically equal that of the eroded function of the states here in the United States. They will be paper-pushers.

Conclusion to the Euro

In my opinion, the euro will "fly" and it will become a strong currency. I cannot believe that, after forty years of preparation, the countries, governments, international investors, and international organizations like the United Nations and Group of Eight will allow it to "go down the tubes." It was the Marshall Plan, the North Atlantic Treaty Organization (NATO) alliance, the Organization for Economic Cooperation and Development (OECD), and the Fulbright student exchange programs which were the institutions that built bridges across the Atlantic and led to reconciliation among former European adversaries.

246—United Nations: A Global Straitjacket

During a September 1996 meeting at Dublin Castle, European finance ministers and central bankers *convinced skeptical international investors* that the euro will be a serious rival to the dollar as a global currency in the early years of the twenty-first century (*Europe Special Report,* November 1996, 6–7). To quote Martin Huefner, chief economist at Germany's Bayerische Vereinsbank:

> The dollar is now the overwhelming world currency and it will get some competition. If a mouse is sleeping with an elephant and the elephant turns over, the mouse jumps out of bed. If it's two elephants and one turns over, the other doesn't care.
>
> —*Washington Post,* January 12, 1997, A1, A26).

The new and rising European Common Market will fulfill the dream of Napoleon, who said: "I wanted to found a European system, a European code of laws, a European judiciary. There would have been but one people throughout Europe." The next step for the European Parliament will be to choose a president. In view of European history, could we consider this person the "emperor" of the "revived Roman Empire"?

THE FREE TRADE AREAS OF THE AMERICAS (FTAA)

As a result of long-term planning and considerable press, most people know of the coming change to the euro. However, the unification of the thirty-four countries of the Western Hemisphere in April 1998 is not known to most North Americans. Everything about the Free Trade Areas of the Americas (FTAA) is different from the European Monetary Union. The "Americas" is a public-private partnership; it does not need the consent of Congress. In addition, the Clinton administration has been working for the past five years to **integrate** key U.S. federal agencies with corresponding agencies in the other thirty-three countries (finance, transportation, education, etc.).

On April 19, 1998, I witnessed, via a television monitor in the press room of the Summit of the Americas conference in Santiago,

Chile, the thirty-four presidents of the Western Hemisphere countries sign a document that integrated our countries into this entity called the Free Trade Areas of the Americas. As I analyzed what I was witnessing, I realized that it was, in essence, a "new constitution for the twenty-first century." While it is true that Bill Clinton stated in his 1998 State of the Union address that "we [America] will forge new partnerships with Latin America, Asia, and Europe," I had not anticipated that it would mean the America we know would change as we integrate our government responsibilities with those of the other countries in our hemisphere! When you consider that we, the FTAA, will form a partnership with Europe, this makes us one—another form of world government.

The following history and analysis are based on my trip to Santiago, Chile, documents taken from the Internet, and the State Department report entitled *Words into Deeds,* which outlines the progress toward this integration since 1994.

Background

In 1994 the first Summit of the Americas was held in Miami, Florida, with the presidents and prime ministers of the other thirty-three countries of the Western Hemisphere in attendance. Cuba was not a participant because it does not hold democratic elections. At that meeting, participants agreed to form the "Free Trade Areas of the Americas," which would be completed by 2005. According to a 1998 publication by the State Department, entitled *Words into Deeds: Progress Since the Miami Summit* (publication number 10536), significant progress toward the total integration of our hemisphere has been made by these countries. On the opening page, Bill Clinton comments:

> For the first time ever, we established an architecture for hemispheric relations from the Arctic Circle in the north to Argentina in the south. We created a work plan from which the democratic governments of the Americas could be judged by their people. We established a follow-up process to ensure that the decisions

we reached at the Summit would be carried out. And we built a framework for further discussion at this year's summit in Santiago, Chile, based on our shared values, common interests, and joint mission to pursue a true partnership for hemispheric peace and prosperity.

The infrastructure that has been put in place in the last three and one-half years is quite extensive. There are twenty-three separate initiatives gathered into four main areas:

1. Preserving and strengthening the community of democracies in the Americas;
2. Promoting prosperity through economic integration and free trade;
3. Eradicating poverty and discrimination in our hemisphere; and
4. Guaranteeing sustainable development and conserving our natural environment for future generations.

The report shows the progress that has been made under each of the initiatives. Interestingly enough, all of these initiatives are concerned with the same issues discussed in many United Nations conventions, and treaties and action items of the mega–conferences, such as the 1992 Earth Summit in Rio, the 1994 U.N. Conference on Population and Development in Cairo, the 1995 Social Summit in Copenhagen, the 1995 Fourth Women's Conference in Beijing, the 1996 Habitat II Conference in Istanbul, and the 1996 World Food Summit in Rome.

In order to implement these initiatives, ministers representing labor, transportation, finance, justice, energy, telecommunications, science and technology, education, anticrime initiatives, trade and commerce, and health and human services have been working together since 1994. What this means is that the new infrastructure now includes the thirty-four ministers representing each of these areas, and that those ministers are integrating their organizations with each other, creating new laws and the legal infrastructure necessary to integrate the thirty-four countries into one—a hemispheric example of standardization.

As a result of the Summit of the Americas, the United Nations Convention on Climate Warming (which the U.S. Senate refused to ratify) is automatically subject to the rules and regulations of the Free Trade Areas of the Americas, along with sustainable development and a number of other U.N. treaties that the U.S. Senate has not ratified. Adherence to international law is a given, as many national laws will be eliminated in order to integrate the thirty-four countries into one economic unit.

The integration will be done on several levels through:

1. The actions by the various ministers—trade, education, finance, etc.;
2. The signing of separate bilateral agreements between the U.S. and the rest of the thirty-four countries in which they agree to work together to open markets and the other processes of government between countries; and
3. The signing of the Free Trade Areas of the Americas agreement, which is a public-private partnership.

It should be noted that just as America will sign bilateral accords with the other thirty-three countries, so too will each of the thirty-three countries sign bilateral accords with the other thirty-three countries, so that by the time they are finished, one thousand eighty-nine bilateral accords will have been signed to integrate the countries into one.

In contrast to the EMU, the new Free Trade Areas of the Americas is set up completely differently, since it is a public-private partnership, which I will explain more fully a little further on in the book.

The Summit of the Americas Declaration of Principles
The Declaration of Principles supporting the Summit of the Americas states in the first two paragraphs:

The elected Heads of State and Government of the Americas are committed to advance the prosperity, democratic values and institutions, and security of our Hemisphere. **We reiterate our firm adherence to the principles of an international law and the purposes and principles enshrined in the United Nations Charter** and the Charter of the Organization of America States (OAS), including the principles of the sovereign equality of states . . . by building strong partnerships. . . . Our Declaration constitutes a comprehensive and mutually reinforcing set of commitments for concrete results [emphasis mine].

The document then calls on the Organization for American States (OAS), the World Bank Inter-American Development Bank (IDB), which is part of the World Bank, the Pan-American Health Organization (PAHO), and the United Nations Economic Commission for Latin America and the Caribbean (ECLAC) for integration. *This Declaration does not call on the Congress of the United States or the Constitution!! It must be remembered that the Constitution states our rights (freedom of speech, etc.) come from God and cannot be altered, amended, or taken away. Under the United Nations Charter, our rights come from government and can be taken away based on our behavior, actions, and speech.*

During an interview in Santiago, I asked Attorney General Janet Reno about America's new dependence on international law. She answered that international law is necessary to get the terrorists and computer hackers. When I countered with, "Do you see an integration as we become more combined to international law on the national level?", she said:

I don't think we are becoming more combined. . . . I think what is vital is that we develop processes and procedures that help us ensure justice, protect human rights, and avoid arguments, fusses, and discussions about processes and rules as opposed to the basic issues, which are when somebody commits a crime that they should be held accountable promptly, swiftly, and according to constitutional standards.

Interestingly enough, at the Group of Eight meeting in England in May 1998, international crime was one of the key issues, with numerous agreements made for national police departments to work together to combat international crime. Whenever or wherever jurisdictions overlap, sovereignty is eroded.

Common Currency

With regard to a common currency, former Federal Reserve chairman Paul Volcker predicted in 1991, "In five years, you will find a fixed exchange rate among the peso, the U.S. dollar, and the Canadian dollar" (*New York Times,* December 18, 1991, D2). Former Congressman and Housing Secretary Jack Kemp said in October 1997 that he wants a single currency for the United States and the other thirty-three nations in the Western Hemisphere. Kemp, who is considering a presidential bid in 2000, said: "They would have a common currency linked to the U.S. dollar, and you'd have stable exchange rates as a result" (*Washington Times,* October 27, 1997, A4). Since December 1994, our U.S. Treasury Secretary has been meeting with the finance ministers from the other thirty-two countries. In December 1998 in Santiago, Chile, Rubin said:

> The United States, Chile, and the whole of the hemisphere have tremendous opportunities in today's economy—if we all meet our challenges. Prosperity in each of our markets provides better opportunities for our trading partners, and instability in any one of our economies creates uncertainty with respect to all of the other economies. In an interdependent world, each country helps itself by getting its own economic house in order and in helping other countries to do the same. That's the key to sustaining global growth and to facilitating the integration of our economies. And that is the path to prosperity into the next century.

Up until April 1999 there had been no open discussion about a common currency or a currency in which all of the South American countries would link their currencies to the U.S. dollar. As a result of the Brazilian crisis in December 1998, there arose discussion about using the dollar for all of the Americas. In testimony before the Joint Economic Committee on the subject of turning the Western Hemisphere into a dollar zone (surprise, surprise), Deputy Treasury Secretary (now Treasury Sec.) Lawrence H. Summers said:

> In no sense can dollarization be seen as a panacea if other things are going wrong, [but] if dollarization helped to achieve greater economic stability and growth in countries in our hemisphere which have suffered so much instability in the past, it would be clearly in the economic and broader national interest of the United States. [Note: "Dollarization" is their term for backing the currencies of the individual sovereign countries of our hemisphere with the dollar.]
>
> —Hill, B8

At the same time, there has been much hype by the leaders of Argentina, Mexico, and other Latin American countries about the possibility of adopting the dollar. Currently the only Latin countries which use the dollar is Panama and El Salvador. This approach so far has the blessings of many in the Clinton administration, as well as Alan Greenspan, chairman of the Federal Reserve. Let's think about this. **Do you realize that the whole structure of our country and Constitution has been changed, and that without a vote by the people of the United States this merger of country and finances is taking place? This is another fine example of tyranny!**

Lastly, the Free Trade Areas of the Americas, like the European Common Market, will require a common currency and a common central bank. The U.S. dollar and Federal Reserve will fulfill each of those.

Congress Bypassed Through Public-Private Partnerships

A portion of a summary taken from the Summit of the Americas Internet site (*http://www.americasnet.net*) entitled "The Road to the Summit: From Miami to Santiago" states:

In the closing remarks of the Summit [Miami 1994] President Clinton stated, "Our goal is to create a **whole new architecture** for the relationship of the nations and the peoples of the Americas to ensure that *dichqs* become *hechos*, that words are turned into deeds." This **"new architecture" was a new system of cooperation between the countries of the Americas** [emphasis mine].

What is this new architecture? It is a public-private partnership. Refer to chapter two. According to the summit documents, the partners in this public-private partnership are as follows:

Public—Governments and International Organizations
- Organization for American States (OAS)
- Inter-American Development Bank (IDB)
- (U.N.) Economic Commission on Latin America and the Caribbean (ECLAC).

  These three form what is known as the "Tripartite" Cooperation Committee to coordinate activities. The partnership also includes the thirty-four governments of the Western Hemisphere at the ministerial level.

Private—Nongovernmental Organizations
- Nonprofit organizations and private businesses (corporations). No names were provided

  Remember this is a partnership—a business arrangement—and because it is not a treaty or a convention, it does not have to go through Congress. **This bypasses Congress (just as executive orders bypass Congress)!!**

Clinton said in his closing speech:

Here in Santiago, we embrace our responsibility to make these **historic forces** to lift the lives of all our people. That is the future we can forge together. It is a future worthy of a new Americas in a new Millennium [emphasis mine].

In a May 11, 1998, speech then by Deputy Secretary of the Treasury Lawrence H. Summers to the Council of the Americas, he said, "The FTAA will be important not just for the future of this region but also because it will in many ways be the *template* for the major global challenge at the dawn of a new century" (emphasis mine).

At the Group of Eight meeting in June 1998 in England, I asked Canadian prime minister Jean Chretien if he, as the new chairman for the Summit of the Americas, was concerned about the effect of the euro on the Canadian dollar and then the forthcoming integration of the thirty-four currencies of the Western Hemisphere. He responded:

> No. It is a development that will take some time before [we know if] the euro will be really effective and how it will operate. The question will be how many countries will use the euro as their monies of reserve. We don't know yet. As you know, most of the countries of the world use the American dollar for their reserves.

It appears as we look at the integration of the euro and the switch by those countries out of the dollar, that with all of the additional dollars floating around the world which would be inflationary to our economy that by "dollarizing" the Latin American countries, it would soak up the excess dollars and thereby "save" our economy and promote the "growth" which Summers, Greenspan, and others say is a reason for making this drastic change.

CONCLUSION

America may feel a double whammy. The integration of the euro is expected to impact the value of the dollar; the subsequent impact of the integration of the dollar with the other thirty-three currencies of the Western Hemisphere will also impact its value. I think Prime Minister Chretian's response was simplistic, given the complexity of what is being tried for the first time in history. When America was born, the states agreed that they would be one under the Constitution and therefore have a common currency. The rulers of the world are taking historically individual nation-states and combining them into one, a completely different situation.

I believe it has been made clear that we are at the mercy of the international system and those in key positions who are "calling the shots." *I believe that the most important conclusion for you to reach is the fact that the cost of living will increase.* The change by both corporations and countries from the dollar to the euro will affect how you and I live. The integration of the thirty-four countries of the Western Hemisphere into one new unit called "The Americas" will also impact how we live. We in America will be forced to reduce our standard of living so that third world countries like Bolivia, Guatemala, Argentina, Columbia, and other Latin American countries, can improve theirs. This specifically is called a transfer of wealth. The United Nations and other global bodies have incessantly called for a transfer of wealth so those from the south (poorer countries) can improve their standard of living and those from the north (richer countries) can reduce theirs. This is happening in Europe. The rich countries of Germany, Italy, France, Belgium, and Holland, will have their economies merged with a number of the post-communist countries in an effort to equalize all economies. Again, a transfer of wealth.

How all of this will work out is very uncertain. As an investment professional, I cannot believe that the large multinational and transnational corporations and banks will be adversely affected since they are seekers of gold at any cost. I cannot believe, however, that the strong economic infrastructure that is in place will be diminished to a point where we are beggars. However, I do believe that our burden to make a living and keep more of what we make will be made heavier. This will be exacerbated by the economic effects and restructuring brought about by Y2K.

Chapter 7

The Manipulation of the World's Stock and Currency Markets

CHAPTER SUMMARY

I believe that the market volatility during the summer and fall of 1998 was created for the sole purpose of providing greater power to the International Monetary Fund to intervene in currency markets, extend lines of credit to troubled countries, supervise the national banks, brokerage firms, and insurance companies of the world, and create a world bankruptcy court. In addition, the October 20, 1998, Omnibus Spending Bill sets up a special commission made up of five former U.S. Treasury secretaries to study the possibility of merging the IMF/World Bank and the World Trade Organization. These actions comprise the "final thrust" for global economic sovereignty. What Americans should be asking themselves is, "Why is our Congress doing all this to facilitate a global economic infrastructure above our national infrastructure?" We are at a turning point in all of history. Our economic sovereignty is being extinguished before our very eyes.

However, that is not to say that our economy is without worries as the dollar has dropped against the Japanese yen during the fall of 1998. While newspapers say it is because of our rising deficits, other news articles reveal that the Japanese have stopped buying our Treasury bills and are redirecting their monies to Europe. This loss of Japanese investment is exacerbating the liquidity problems which we are having. The Federal Reserve has reduced interest rates to increase consumer spending. However, as Japanese investments in our Treasury bills decreases and as other foreign investors redirect their monies to Europe, the Fed will have to raise interest rates as an incentive to keep those monies here. Perhaps we could say that the Fed, and our economy, is between a rock and a hard place.

The funding of the International Monetary Fund was on the lips of Bill Clinton, Alan Greenspan, and Robert Rubin for 1998 as they stressed most vigorously the need for U.S. taxpayer dollars to fund the expansion of the IMF. In his speech at the opening of the annual meeting of the IMF/World Bank on October 6, 1998, Clinton said:

> The world faces perhaps its most serious financial crisis in half a century. **The U.S. must fulfill IMF obligations.** We must modernize and reform the international financial system to make it ready for the twenty-first century. The institutions built at Bretton Woods must be updated for 24-hour global markets [emphasis added].

On October 20, 1998, Congress approved $18 billion in new monies for the IMF. The stock markets opened October at 7843, only to close up fifteen percent at 8592. This has not happened since 1987. Is it a coincidence? For 1998 the markets were up thirty-two percent!

Lastly, the October 31, 1998, Halloween headlines read, "G-7 Leaders Hint Worst Is Over in Global Crisis" (*Washington Post,* October 31, 1998, G1). The article said that "the heads of the Group of Seven countries hailed 'significant steps taken over recent weeks to strengthen confidence in the world economy.'" It went on to say that a "new approach, proposed by Clinton a month ago would provide large international lines of credit to countries threatened by financial contagion." Really. Clinton made this same proposal on October 6. Why did it take a month to make headlines? What changed the tune of the G-7? Nothing less than $18 billion of taxpayer money! The G-7 now says the worst is over. Not really. When a country loses economic sovereignty, its troubles have only just begun.

INTRODUCTION

At a number of the high level economic meetings which I have attended, the rulers of the world have discussed the apparent market volatility in great detail. Their solution is to strengthen the International Monetary Fund so that it has the power to intervene in currency markets and to punish countries who do not allow them to monitor their finances. It is apparent that the new global infrastructure for the twenty-first century which the international bankers are setting up is a "final thrust" for power, since it will give the international bankers complete control over a nation's banking system, brokerage firms, and insurance companies. Accompanying this is a loss of national sovereignty.

1997—Leading Up to the Final Thrust

Amid the Asian crisis in July, our stock market reached historic highs. In 1997 the mergers and acquisitions continued—between banks, brokerage firms, and insurance companies. There was a push for consolidation of power worldwide through bank mergers and acquisitions and the repeal of the Glass-Steagall Act. Mergers were not only by country, but were also cross-global mergers, like Spain and Brazil. Our trade deficit grew to $187.7 billion. The dollar rose to a thirty-one–month high—a fifty percent increase against the yen and twenty percent increase against the Dmark—since its low in April 1995 when the dollar dropped to .80 yen and 1.35 Dmarks. A strong dollar provides foreign manufacturers with significant advantages over American manufacturers and products. In order to join the euro, countries had to qualify, and the number of countries eligible to join was realized. As a result, many countries and corporations will, in order to do business in Europe, switch business contracts from the dollar to the euro. There have also been discussions to switch oil contracts to euros from dollars. On the global level, a total global support system was beginning to be realized through a global accounting system, a global custody operation, a global settlement system, and a global customs agreement. Finally, a number of global exchanges were consolidated to pave the way for the global stock exchange to be located (probably) in London.

1998—The Final Thrust

This year was one of great surprise. Surprise with regard to the stock market and the unanticipated loss of up to $3 trillion in paper gains, Bill Clinton's level of honesty and integrity, and reckless-ness of a Congress that would allow a president to commandeer the passage of a $500 billion spending bill, which is forty-eight hundred pages long, under duress in order to keep the govern-ment funded!!!!

The stock market reached a historic high on July 17 when it climbed to 9337. Due to a number of situations that the market determined to be dangerous, the market dropped back to 7539, the low for the year. Mergers and acquisitions continued at a fury and were on hold during the volatile summer months. They are now back in full force. As of June, mergers had already exceeded the volume for 1997!

On October 20 our Congress, which ran two weeks over, passed a forty-pound Omnibus Spending Bill that took forty-eight pages to list where taxpayer monies were being spent! The $18 billion for the IMF, which was requested by Alan Greenspan, Robert Rubin, and President Clinton, is included. These monies were to be used as leverage for contributions from other countries to raise an addi-tional $100 billion for the IMF to lend to countries in distress, which in turn makes them more attractive to transnational corporations. This constitutes part of the "final thrust," as the IMF will now have control over which country "qualifies" for additional help through lines of credit. The question should be asked if the IMF needed more monies from U.S. taxpayers. It was shown by Rep. James Saxton that the IMF already had $98 billion to lend, which includ-ed quota reserves of $43 billion, $32 billion in gold, and lines of credit of $32 billion.

This spending bill also sets up the International Financial In-stitution Advisory Commission, which will consist of five former

U.S. Treasury secretaries who help determine the future role and responsibilities of the IMF and the merits and costs related to the consolidation of the organization, management, and activities of the IMF, World Bank, and World Trade Organization (WTO). Within six months of their report, President Clinton will call for another "Bretton Woods conference." All of this continues to set the stage for the "final thrust."

I think one of the most telling speeches that I have heard from the House floor was on the night of October 20 by Representative David McIntosh, who said:

> Eleven years ago, in 1987, a Democratic Congress sent President Reagan a massive omnibus spending bill that weighed about twenty-four pounds and had twenty-one hundred pages. In his State of Union address, Reagan took the bill, slammed it on the table, and said, "Congress shouldn't send these bills and if you do I will not sign it." A Democratic president is forcing this Congress to pass a massive omnibus bill on a veto threat that if we spend anything less, he will veto it and shut down the government. Ten years ago that omnibus bill cost the tax payers $604 billion. This year's bill cost them $577 billion. Ten years ago it was twenty-one hundred pages. This year it's forty-eight hundred pages. The bottom line is that Clinton has effectively denied a tax cut for the families. For two weeks Clinton sent up one demand after another for a billion here and a billion there, all to be spent in Washington. We need a balanced budget, spend more on a strong national defense to protect our shores and help small business survive by cutting the red tape rather than the rules/regulations that go with it.

The Changing Picture

To the unsuspecting American, the changes taking place in America are more than structural, they are philosophical—a fight for total control through deficit spending. For example, while our country has undergone severe banking problems in the early 1990s, and several dollar crises, we are also in the process of "going global." In 1990, when the United States went to war in Kuwait, Bush had to ask the permission of the United Nations. When he did, he referred to the changes taking place in the world as "the new world order." Several years later, in 1992, the United States entered into a very extensive agreement with the North American Free Trade Association (NAFTA) and we also signed the General Agreement on Trade and Tariffs (GATT) in 1994, which is more than twenty-six thousand pages and designed to tear down our borders for "free trade." At the same time, we have had some of the most oppressive tax bills passed, while our trade deficits have skyrocketed and the Federal Reserve has fiddled with interest rates to jump start the economy (1990–1993), only to change its mind and increase interest rates in 1994 when the dollar had a crisis and dropped to historic lows against the Japanese yen. Now under the guise of "modernizing banking laws" by repealing the Glass-Steagall Act, banks, brokerage firms, and insurance companies will now be able to do business in each other's industry, thus becoming one. As such, the proposed law to modernize banking laws will bring all three under the control of the Federal Reserve, a private corporation, and out of the supervision of the U.S. government!

The "Pretty" Picture
In studying the above, the picture you see is not pretty. All too often we whitewash the truth. Let's take an example of what appears to be a very successful businessman. He has what appears to be a very thriving operation. His personal gift is his sales ability. He really knows how to "pitch" his product and/or service and get the sale. As a result, he is very busy as he has a lot of back orders. From all appearances it would look as if everything is okay, but it is not because he does not know how to manage money. Suppliers are knocking on his door for the money he just spent on the new corporate jet, the bonus he deserved, and the expansion of the plant to meet the new orders. He knows that if he cannot keep up the flow of orders, his inability to handle money will catch up with him.

What kind of lies and manipulation will he resort to? If he and his corporation don't make it, only those doing business with him will be affected. But if the government does not make it, what happens to our society?

The Real Picture

The real picture is that we are standing on a global economic precipice. It appears Asia is having a severe economic problem while the transnational corporations and banks are buying its assets for a song. The slowdown from Asia is being felt globally, the U.S. trade deficit is going up, the dollar is dropping against the yen and Deutsche mark, and the consumer is being told to continue spending so that the recession doesn't worsen. The answer to all these woes, we are told, is a *"new international economic architecture"* for the twenty-first century, which will solve all these problems. All of the current clamoring and orchestrations are leading to the "final thrust."

The BIG Picture

Interestingly enough it is Bill Clinton who started many of the changes to the international infrastructure. At the 1995 Group of Seven meeting in Naples, Italy, Clinton said, "Mexico taught us that the world clearly needs better tools to identify problems like this so they can be prevented." On January 30, 1998, the *Washington Post* reported: "Now in the midst of the Asian Financial Crisis, this famed speculator George Soros and the U.S. Treasury Secretary have concluded that the system is broken and needs fixing." Lawrence Summers identified in February 1998 that the "Clinton Administration has been working . . . to build a global economic system ready for the twenty-first century—a system in which trade, capital and know-how can flow freely. The shape of this new system . . . is not yet fixed." (Note: When you haven't figured out what you are doing, it is never fixed.)

The bottom line: The apparent market volatility is masking the final loss of economic sovereignty for both the United States and the other countries of the world. To help you make wise choices, the BIG picture is presented here.

THE NATIONAL LEVEL

History

The idea of world government goes back to the Tower of Babel. Other than the tower, there have been many great empires—Babylon, Assyria, Egypt, Greece, and Rome. In this century, there have been concerted efforts to unify the world through the United Nations. Currently the balance of world power is being shifted *from* the United States as the dominant economic force *to* Europe. How could this happen? While America still has a very strong and powerful economy, it is our debt that is pulling us down. If you refer back to the "Overview of Key Economic Indicators 1990-1998" chart (Chart 4-1), you will see how the massive national debt has grown, the number of tax bills repressing growth, the bankruptcies, and how the orchestrations of the Federal Reserve to stimulate the economy and encourage consumers to spend, have all contributed to today's situation. Compounding this is America's lack of liquidity.

When the market first became volatile, investors moved from stocks to bonds. As a result of the hedge fund bailout, they then moved again from bonds to cash. The move to cash has exacerbated the amount of funds available for lending. The liquidity crisis in Asia, however, is far worse than ours. It is and has been the American economy that has always been used to jump start the world economy when there has been a problem. Today it is extremely important that Americans continue to spend. If we stop spending, the music stops—for the world! In order to keep that from happening, the Federal Reserve has recently reduced interest rates so that the American consumer will continue to be enticed to spend.

Lastly, the American economy has a history of being sacrificed for the sake of other economies. By making the dollar stronger, our exports become more expensive so that other countries can sell their products because they are cheaper. By weakening the dollar, imports are cheaper and cheap labor competes with American-made products, which are higher priced as a result of our standard of living. For the last two years, the dollar has been strong, putting our exports at a disadvantage. Now with a substantially weakened dollar, cheaper imports will be even cheaper.

We are a debtor nation not only to ourselves but to our creditors (the Federal Reserve, the Japanese government, and other foreign governments)!!!! Where will this lead? At a minimum, to recession and to a weakened position in world dominance. While all of the above is transpiring, the "final thrust" for financial and economic control of the world is being orchestrated on the global level.

The U.S. Stock Market
In light of the market volatility, what are the experts saying?

This is volatility with a capital 'V.'
—Jeremy Hawkins chief economist, Bank of America, London

This has been the most disquieting and risky set of circumstances I have seen in my professional career.
—John Lipsky, chief economist at Chase Manhattan Bank

Investors have really been in denial. It's a bear market. The only question is how long it lasts.
—Ed Yardeni, Deutsche Bank

A form of debt liquidation is now in progress—in the harshest terms—in Russia, Japan, and Asia. It would be foolish to believe this chaotic process will be over quickly.
—Henry Kaufman

People are having problems with liquidity and are running scared from anything they can't turn into cash quickly.
—Steve Slifer, economist with Lehman Brothers Holdings, Inc.

What is failing the world is not capitalism but globalism. We are reaping the harvest of having tried to weld the world's na-

tional economies, in disparate stages of development into one global economy.

—Pat Buchanan

The Effect of Global Market Volatility: On July 17, 1998, the United States stock market reached an all-time high of 9337, the highest ever in the history of the Dow Jones. What followed in the three months afterward has been more than astonishing. Suddenly, like a cyclone, the Asian crisis created three months of global market volatility. If you study the response of the market from July 17 to October 31, you will see that there is no coherent rhyme or reason for its movements.

In Chart 7-1 you will find a "Chronology of Political and Economic News and the Market's Response for Summer/Fall 1998," which reflects the market's response to political and economic happenings. My observations are:

1. In 1997 the world stock market, we are told, had a near meltdown. The Dow dropped 554 points to 7161, which was a seven percent correction.
2. From April 1998 to July 17, 1998, the market continued to climb to new highs, crossing 9000 for the first time in April, and 9300 on July 17. During that time, mergers and acquisitions continued. The world appeared to be fine, even though Asia had been going though a crisis.
3. Greenspan's word determines market direction. See June 15, July 22–23, September 24, October 2, and October 8. (Just who is Greenspan that global markets shake?)
4. The week of July 22 world markets tumbled on Greenspan's remarks about IMF funding and by the end of the week, dropped 401 points to 8937. A correction? Yes. An adjustment? Yes. Indication of seriousness? No.
5. The week of August 4 the market dropped 396 points as a result of weak economic indicators. A correction? Yes. An adjustment? Yes. Indication of seriousness? No.

Chart 7-1

Chronology of Political and Economic News and the Market's Response for Summer/Fall 1998

Date	Incident	Economics	Gain/Loss Dow
10/24/97	World market near meltdown—Hong Kong down 1211; London down 157; New York down 187; Asian woes hit Wall Street		(187)=7848
10/28/97	Nuclear sales to China too "chancy", foes insist; queries on sexual past irk Clinton	Dow takes a 554-pt. plunge, Asian crisis triggers 7% correction; trading halted first time since Kennedy was assassinated in 1963	(554)=7164
4/10/98	Tornadoes swept the South, killing 38	Mutual funds fattened by biggest month ever—investors put $1.7B a day into mutual funds during March=$37.5B	103=9000 (first time)
5/27/98	U.S. heads for $39B surplus on soaring tax revenues	NationsBank to dominate merger (with BankAmerica)	(151)=8964
6/4/98 (week)		Intel sell-off sparks sharp fall in Dow; 14,000 managers apply for early retirement at ATT	(87)=8803
6/10/98 (week)	Clinton defends visit to Tiananmen; made-over Monica makes her debut in glossy fashion	American and Philadelphia stock exchange agree to merge	(20)=9050
6/15/98 (week)	Clinton to raise abortion, arrest issues in China; Selective Service could easily begin calling up women	Greenspan predicts more bad news in Asia, urges Congress to pass IMF, markets fell worldwide, foreign investor bought bonds, said U.S. economy has largely overwhelmed the drag from Asia	
6/25/98	Clinton to address censorship in China. U.S. businesses push renewal of MFN trade status	ATT & TCI merge; IMF ready to throw Russia lifeline; Mobile system rivals join forces (Psion, Motorola, Nokia, and Ericsson in consortium to lead new communications generation)	95=8924
6/27/98 (week)	China welcomes Clinton in Chernomyrdin in Tiananmen	Dow Jones waffle; record high S&P stock keeps selling like hotcakes—S&P finishes at 1132	11=8935
6/29/98 (week)	Pakistan is defiant as N-tests are condemned	ATT chief says he can defend deal	3=8944

Date		Japanese hopes lift markets	+97=9049
7/2/98 (week)	Suharto rebuilds political base to shield fortune		
7/8/98	Russians say loan by IMF may fall short of need	Investors' confidence in Russia fades further, Brazil's pension system is potential time bomb	(7)=9085
7/10/98 (week)	Senators back sale of wheat to Pakistanis	Japanese banks cut back on U.S. presence, GM strikes	(85)=9089
7/15/98	Starr targets chief guard	Wall Street lifted by strong profits, subdued inflation	149=9245
7/17/98 (week)	Lockheed Martin ends $11B buy of Northrup	Nasdaq tops 2000, Dow closes over 9300.	94=9337
7/22/98	China conducts test as Clinton visits—rocket-motor firing	Fed is ready to tighten if necessary	(106)=9190
7/23/98	Greenspan raises prospect of market's fall again (triggers a sharper reaction in Europe with bigger falls on exchanges in Paris, Frankfurt, and Madrid)	Market tumbles again—Greenspan warns market ready for fall; IMF funding measure shelved and Republican infighting	(61)=9128
7/24/98		Stocks plunge 195 points—earning woes seen as impetus; finishes below 9000	(195)=8933
7/25/98 (week)	Gunman shoots his way into Capitol, 2 officers killed; injured suspect held—in the hallowed halls, tranquility vanished	Dow up slightly; ends week off 401; up 13% for year	4=8937 Week down 40
7/29/98	Lewinsky gets immunity, will say Clinton lied	Consumers grow edgy, confidence high	(93)=8934
7/31/98 (week)	Lewinsky's dress to get DNA test		(7)=9085
8/4/98	Court [shrouded] in secrecy—much under wraps in 2 Clinton cases	Index signals manufacture slide, reflects Asia crisis; GM strike	(97)=8787
8/5/98	Dow dives 299 points	GM shutdown causes drop in indicators	(299)=8487
8/6/98	After wild swing Dow closes up	Asian woes apply brakes	59=8547
8/8/98 (week)	Clinton vows to find and punish bombers (the bombing of U.S. embassies occurs on Friday—no market response)	Jobless rate holds steady at 4.5%	20=8598
8/11/98	As rescue teams work, $2 million reward is set	Bell Atlantic strikes	(23)=8575

Date	Description	Value
8/12/98	BP to acquire Amoco; Bell deal ends strike	Industrials lose 112 pts on troubles abroad; global stocks slide on fears over econ.; 770.9 million shares trade—5th highest	(112)=8462
8/13/98	Kenya has two suspects in bombing	Dow rallies as techs set strong pace	+90=8553
8/14/98	Bodies return to US soil; Clinton weighs nuance of "sex"	Fears over devaluation send Russian markets into dive	(94)=8459
8/15/98(end wk)	Clinton may admit sex with Lewinsky	Stock markets stage recovery after week of falls worldwide	(35)=8425
8/22/98 (week)	Afghan damage moderate to heavy; across area, security is stepped up	Stock markets shaken by currency devaluation fears; stocks fall in world markets; fear turmoil Asia/Russia; market dives 283, closes dn 78	(78)=8533
8/26/98	Ruble falls 9% on economy fears	Indicators give mixed signals on economy	+36=8602
8/27/98	Investors face $33B losses from Russian bond default; Chernomyrdin in urgent talks with IMF	Dollar to yen: 1.44; durable goods sales surge, easing fears in U.S. over Asian woes: GM strikes	(120)=8602
8/28/98	Global effort nets suspect in bombing embassy; Yeltsin ouster sought in financial mess—Dow plunges	Corporate profits hit by Hong Kong recession; Russian crisis hits world markets; jobs still readily avail. despite econ. cooling	(357)=8166 (Feb level)
8/29/98 (week)	Defiant Yeltsin won't step down—Dow tumbles again amid global fear; Clinton speaks of forgiveness, but doesn't ask it	3M to close plants and shed 4,500 jobs	(114)-8051
9/1/98	Dow plunges 512.61 pts, 6% drop erases year's gains as global economic woes continue	As stocks drop, local investors keep chins up; second worst day ever	(513)=7539 LOW FOR YEAR
9/2/98	Investors ignore bears' snarls	Billionaires are battered, top managers take a bath; in August $1.9B flowed out of stock funds vs. the 1998 average monthly inflow of $20.8B	288=7827
9/15/98	Clinton fights back with rebuttal of Starr charges. "sinner" is repentant at breakfast; Duma backs Soviet-era chiefs—Primakov	Starr charges fail to hurt U.S. stocks; Nikkei tumbles after U.S. slide; dollar to yen: 1.33	180=7795
9/18/98 (week)	House Republicans balk at full funding for IMF	Asian woes help push U.S. exports to low level	(216)=7874
9/22/98	Clinton tells U.S. terrorism is at top of world's agenda; impeachment bid is renewed by panel members	U.S. markets not spooked by Clinton testimony; battle for skies broadens with "one-world" alliance	38=7933

Date	Event	Value
9/24/98	Pakistan will sign nuclear test ban, even if India does not	Greenspan warns of effects of global crisis on economy; markets surge on interest rate cut; Fed moves to help hedge fund	138=8036
9/25/98 (week)	Long-Term Capital Management has market exposure of $200B, EPA tells 22 states: cut emissions	Dow-Jones lower after near collapse of hedge fund; World Bank sounds alarm over risky emergency loans	(152)=8002
10/1/98	U.S. rate reduction fails to excite investors	Dow tumbles 230 points as bonds soar	(230)=7843
10/2/98 (week)	U.S. is poised to lead strike over Kosovo; Jordan contradicts Clinton on Lewinsky; mounting gloom for investors as stocks fall, Rubin offers global plan	Greenspan: Fed aided fund bailout to shield global economy; Day of decline roils world stock markets, Dow falls 2.7%, Nasdaq drops 4.8%; dollar to yen: 1.35	(210)=7633
10/8/98	Scores of Democrats likely to back impeachment probe; Russians protest economic woes	Fed chief signals bigger rate cut, Greenspan cites weaker economy; banking reform remains in doubt	(1.5)=7740
10/9/98 (week)	Impeachment inquiry opened; military tells plan for attack on Serbs	Global crisis hits declining dollar, dollar drops 8%, worst one-day drop in 25 years to 118.30 on yen for third day in row; dollar down against yen 20% from August high; IMF agrees on Brazil funds	(10)=7731 YEAR LOW 7539
10/14/98	Tentative accord reached on IMF funds; conditions; NATO approves air strikes on Yugoslavia; Hyde may narrow impeachment charges	Reforms ok'd for IMF seen as ineffective; Japanese plan gives world markets a lift; Monsanto & AHP call off marriage	101=8001
10/15/98	Panel split on calling Lewinsky: Hill, Clinton "wrapping up" details of huge spending bill; doctor succeeds in fertilizing egg with 2 mothers	House IMF bill makes few gains; legislation to reform bankruptcy goes belly-up in Senate	30=7968
10/16/98	Negotiators reach accord on spending; worried Fed cuts interest rate again in an effort to prevent the slowing economy and nosedive financial markets from tripping the U.S. into a recession	Rate cuts buoy markets and consumers; banks lower cost of money; stocks surge 330 pts.; market up highest for week in history	330=8299
10/31/98	Economy appears healthy as consumers keep spending	Dow spurt brings rebound to 15%; Dow has biggest one month gain since 1987; Dow up 1100 pts. from October 8 low drop	97=8592

Sources: Baltimore Sun, Washington Post, Washington Times, and Financial Times
The bold line on the right represents a change in trading patterns of the stock market. The shading denotes days of unusual activity.
There is about $5 trillion invested in mutual funds. For years, investors have been investing as much as $20 billion a month.
The Federal Reserve announced on September 1 that they would make $50B in cash available to the system in light of Y2K.

6. The week of August 11 was one of surprise as British Petroleum announced it was buying Amoco, Clinton was ready to admit the truth about Lewinsky, stocks globally were getting nervous, and fears about Russia gained awareness. The market closed down 150 points. A correction? Nothing really showed that. An adjustment? Yes. Indication of seriousness? No, because what happens in Russia really has no real bearing on America, as Germany has far more loans extended to them than America.

7. The week of August 26 the stock market rose thirty-six points, but turned ugly as a crisis in Russia took shape with Yeltsin refusing to step down amid the turmoil. Our markets dropped almost five hundred points to a low of 8051.

8. That following Monday, September 1, the global economic woes over Russia continued with a further drop of another 513 points to 7539. All gains for the year were wiped out. Again, what happens in Russia does not affect us. Why now?

9. On September 25 the hedge fund, Long-Term Capital Management, went belly up and was saved only after the Federal Reserve Bank intervened (first in history) with a bailout. The market dropped almost six hundred points and the dollar started to drop against the yen.

10. The week of October 1 the Feds one-quarter–point rate cut failed to lift the markets as the Dow plunged. This is because one-quarter point really has no effect. It is not enough to make a difference. Investors sold bonds and fled to cash. A correction? Yes. An adjustment? Yes. Indication of seriousness? Mixed.

11. The week of October 8 an impeachment inquiry opened for the first time since Richard Nixon, and for the third time in our history. The dollar dropped eight percent against the yen in the worst one-day drop in twenty-five years, for a total drop of twenty percent since August. The stock market reacted by going down ten points. **This makes no sense when you consider the stock market dropped almost five hundred points for the problems in Russia and says the weak dollar and impeach-**

ment mean nothing!!!!! A correction? Yes. An adjustment? Yes. Indication of seriousness? Should have been.

12. Congress passed the $500 billion Omnibus Spending Bill (October 20, 1998), which included $18 billion for the IMF. In response, the Fed reduced interest rates one-quarter of one percent in a surprise move. The market rose 330 points to 8299. (If you compare the market response to Greenspan in Nos. 3 and 10 with 12, there appears to be a "wobble effect" with various responses that don't add up. Who has the power?)

13. *The last week of October topped off the previous three months' market volatility by closing up fifteen percent from the September low. This was in spite of Yeltsin being confined to a sanitorium (Nos. 6–8) while a communist hardliner replaced him. Perhaps we should ask if the market was celebrating the return of communism to Russia or the empowerment of the IMF, which is part of the "final thrust?"*

Market Patterns: Up until October 1998, the market had traded in a five hundred-point trading ban. It then recovered eleven hundred points in the same month that the Congress passed one of its largest spending bills. Was the real reason for the sudden volatility the restructuring of the global economic architecture?

It should be remembered that in order to "fix" something the way someone *wants it*, it needs to be "broken" first. This is what is occurring now. While nothing is really broken, it currently *appears* to be, so that more power can be transferred from the national level to the global level, which is the "final thrust."

Recession=Debt, Loss of Liquidity, and a Weak Dollar

While it appears that the market volatility may have been orchestrated in order to have sufficient reason to change and empower the global level, there are some long-standing *real* problems that are possibly exacerbating the plan to "fix" the system. They are debt, loss of liquidity (federal and corporate), the value of the dollar (trade deficits), and a switch to the euro. Any of these could put the economy into a deep, long-term *recession* (debt, liquidity, and a weak dollar lead to recession, or an economic loss of power and position). This is all part of the decline of America in world power and position. It should be noted that one of the indicators of recession is a drop in commodity prices. In mid-August 1998 the Chicago-based Commodity Research Bureau Index of seventeen leading commodity prices fell to its lowest level since 1977. From mid-1997 to mid-1998, international prices of nickel and copper have fallen about forty percent. Prices for timber, rice, rubber, and vegetable oils also dropped, in some cases dramatically (*Financial Times,* August 31, 1998, 13).

Debt

Debt Owed to the Federal Reserve: In England's past, when someone borrowed money and could not pay it back, they were tossed into debtor's prison. In America, our debtor's prison is called the Federal Reserve. In 1913 Congress passed the Federal Reserve Act, which created a new system of money management in the United States by using a private corporation, the Federal Reserve. Unfortunately, the Fed is not federal and it has no reserves. The Treasury and the Congress gave up all responsibility for our monetary system to a private corporation comprised of international bankers. If the Fed wants to create growth in America, they increase the amount of money available to borrow. If the Fed wants to create recession, they withdraw money from the system, which forces interest rates to go up and slows the economy. How do Americans borrow from the Fed? Our government issues Treasury bills, notes, and bonds.

Consumer Debt: **Whenever the Fed needs money, it creates it out of thin air and charges America interest on the money it has borrowed.** Why is it that the American people cannot forgive ourselves the interest on the federal debt? Because we do not owe it to ourselves, but to a private corporation. In 1995 the interest on the national debt comprised fourteen percent of the federal budget. In 1999 our federal deficit was over $5 trillion. In 1980 it was less than $1 trillion. The interest is not paid to the Treasury, but to the Federal Reserve, a private corporation!

Back in the 1940s and '50s, it was almost a shame for people to go to the bank for a loan. It was not done unless a person was in dire straights with no other options. Today, credit is extended on the spot with very few questions asked. Lines of credit and credit cards are mailed to consumers on a regular basis. In the 1980s, bankruptcy was streamlined, making it less difficult to file. The result has been a large increase since that time in bankruptcy filings. Today we face a situation where household debt is $5.7 trillion, and the amount of household income equals that amount. As a result of corporate downsizing, delinquencies are up. Most Americans are living on the edge financially as they have bought the "big house," the yuppie automobile, and all of the accessories. A slump in the U.S. economy would compound everyone else's problems. Even though the Fed has reduced rates by one-half of one percent, mortgage rates are rising.

On October 19, 1998 Alan Greenspan voiced his concern over the economy: "As dislocations abroad mount feeding back into our financial markets, restraint is likely to intensify." Clearly a spending reduction will not have a positive effect, as spending is needed to stimulate the economy. With regard to the market and volatility, Greenspan said, "In fifty years of looking at the American economy on a day-to-day basis, I have never seen anything like this" (*Washington Times,* October 19, 1998, A18). When people have too much debt, they stop spending. When Americans stop spending, the "party is over." In order for the world to avoid a serious recession, it is vitally important that Americans continue to spend. However, they can only spend if they feel they have the ability to spend. If they think they will lose their job or have any other concerns, they will not buy. It appears that the Fed is trying to prevent a full-blown liquidity crisis by lowering the interest rates. As you can see from the 1990–1998 economic review, the Fed has been trying to stimulate consumer spending for quite some time. One of these days it just won't work because consumers will say, "I can't spend anymore no matter how attractive the prices or interest rates!"

Loss of Liquidity

Liquidity is the ability of a country, government, business, or consumer to spend. It is the ability to spend and the ability to have credit, if there is no cash. A loss of liquidity can happen on all three levels. The two levels we will discuss here are the federal level and the corporate level.

Federal: As mentioned above, when Americans buy U.S. Treasury bills, notes, and bonds, they are supporting our federal deficit. The Federal Reserve buys and sells U.S. Treasuries to determine how much liquidity is in the system. The fact that Japan has been one of the largest purchasers of our Treasury notes over the years says that they have been banking with us because we are reliable. However, they are in trouble and have had a number of problems. What happens when someone needs money? They go to their bank. I started to question the unusual volatility in late July and August of 1998. It appeared that there was one major problem in the stock market per week and that the market was being taken down, little by little. As I analyzed this action, it appeared that the action was enough to get the fainthearted (or smart) out of the market. If America is broke, then what was happening is that the only place to free up any kind of money would be the stock market. And what did you hear last summer? You should invest in Treasuries!! It appears that our government has no money.

Japan Switches to Eurobonds from Dollars: In April 1998, there was a very large sale of our Treasury bills by the New York Federal Reserve for an unnamed seller, who traders strongly felt was Japan, since their currency was under siege at the time. For a second time in 1998 it was announced that Japan sold another large block of Treasury bills.

In my March 1998 newsletter, I pointed out that as the euro comes on line there would be a shift in global monies from the dollar to the euro. It was reported on October 29, 1998, that the Japanese purchase of U.S. Treasuries has fallen in the last twelve months from eighty-two percent as a proportion of all bond purchases to forty-five percent, and that it is expected to fall below thirty percent. According to Avinash Persaud, head of currency research at J. P. Morgan, "What we are seeing is a clear long-term reweighting of Japanese portfolio investments from the dollar into the eurozone. This is happening at quite a fast pace." More importantly, according to Tim Bond, an economist at Barclays Capital, "the Japanese have realized that EMU will bring liquidity" (*Financial Times,* October 29, 1998, 17).

Corporate: Liquidity is the availability of investor monies for corporations to borrow. Corporations only have two ways to raise monies. One way is to float bonds in the market place and the other is to borrow from banks, which is more expensive. However, bonds are only useful when investors are willing to purchase them. As a result of the 1998 market volatility, investors have decided to sell bonds and move to cash, which has created a vacuum and a loss of liquidity. This action reflects a loss of investor confidence. When investors buy bonds, they are providing the funds for corporations to continue with their operations. When there is no source of money for them to borrow, the system dries up and corporations have to curtail operations. In order to keep the whole system moving, the grease needed to keep the system moving is people investing in bonds. A share, bond, or currency, is worth what someone is willing to pay for it. When the balance of buyers and sellers is upset, it can lead to very sharp movements in prices, such as those that bargain hunters find at the January sales (*Financial Times,* October 10–11, 1998, 6).

Debt and loss of liquidity are two key reasons why the U.S. could very well be on the verge of recession. The third is the switch from the dollar to the euro as a reserve currency for the world.

The Dollar

The Floating Dollar: Up until 1971, the monetary system of the world was always backed by some type of tangible good or currency. Going back to biblical days and the ancient Asian and Middle Eastern trading routes, gold, silver, clothing, animals, and food, were the currency of the day and medium of exchange. In August 1971 when Richard Nixon officially severed all connections the United States dollar had to gold, he changed forever how the countries of the world would effect commerce. No longer would any of the world's currencies, with the exception of the Swiss franc, be backed by gold. Currencies would now float against one another. As such, if any central bank or group of central banks, hedge funds, or speculators wish to bring a country to its knees, all they have to do is sell a country's currency all at the same time. Whenever you manipulate (mess) with the value of a country's currency, you are manipulating with their economic strength, which is as vital as the blood in our veins. All one has to do is look at what has occurred in Thailand, Malaysia, and Korea. In 1971 the dollar was the strongest currency in the world, as one dollar bought 3.66 Deutsche marks and 3.57 yen. In 1985 the Group of Seven determined the dollar was too strong and agreed to devalue it by a third. Our dollar has continued to drop. By April 1995 the dollar had sunk seventy-seven percent against both major currencies from its 1971–1973 high.

Interestingly enough, this flotation of value is used by corporations to play the currency of every country they manufacture or do business in according to what will benefit them. The volatility of the currency is seen in our newspapers and magazines on a daily basis. The headlines of the March 20, 1995, issue of *BusinessWeek* read: "Hot Money. The dollar is crashing. Mexico is in a meltdown. The European currency system is collapsing, but for traders and investors, by instantly moving trillions of dollars around the globe, they fan the flames." The dollar was at .92 on the yen and 1.40 on the Deutsche mark. Meanwhile, on May 5, 1997, *BusinessWeek* changed their tune and wrote: "Alarm bells have been going off in Detroit, and some in Washington, over the rise of the dollar—up fifty percent against the yen and twenty percent against the German mark over the past two years." In October 1998 headlines said, "Global crisis hits declining dollar, deteriorating Dow as the greenback suffered its worst one-day loss in twenty-five years" (*Washington Times*, October 9, 1998, B11). Consider the following:

The Dollar to Be Replaced by the Euro: In 1991, Daniel Burstein wrote:

> A seismic shift is occurring in the composition of global wealth. It is *convulsing the structure of international power relationships and changing the rules of international business competition.* It is the Euroquake. . . . [The challenge facing Europe is to] restore Europe [to the Europe] of 1914 when [it] was the biggest economic power in the world and had the best educated population, one that [will have] twice the population of the United States and four times the population of Japan.

(Note: In June 1998 I interviewed Jean-Claude Trichett, Central Bank Minister from the Bank of France and the future "Alan Greenspan of the European Central Bank," he said the same things!) Burstein says that the three spheres comprised of the United States, Europe, and Japan (the Triad) will "hold the balance of military power, economic strength and political pull." *He also saw America as the "odd man out in the Triad."* Furthermore, he wrote that "the euro will become the common currency of the European Community by 1997. It will be backed by a 'EuroFed' central banking system." Furthermore, he wrote that "the first-ever election for the 'president of Europe' will be held in the year 2000." He also wrote:

> A new global currency agreement will be hammered out between 1995 and 1997. This agreement will be the "New Bretton Woods." Precipitated by the rise of the euro and the *shift to nondollar pricing* of raw materials, a global monetary realignment will also be influenced by a variety of factors (the EuroFed, strength of the yen, weakness of the dollar, ongoing U.S. deficits). The new exchange rates will reflect the economic strength achieved by Europe and Japan . . . yen to dollar: 105, the DM to the dollar 1.2.
>
> —Burstein, 347

Burstein provided the following comparison.

The Decline of America in Power and Position

The bold type signifies America at the beginning of the 1980s and Roman type indicates America at the end of the 1980s:

- **The United States was the world's largest creditor.**
- The United States became the largest debtor nation in history. Japan, meanwhile, replaced the U.S. as the world's leading creditor with West Germany second.
- **Japan and the United States both suffered modest trade deficits while West Germany's traditional trade surplus was reduced nearly to zero as a result of the oil crisis that followed the Iranian revolution.**
- Japan and Germany were neck and neck in the race to enjoy the world's biggest trade surplus. Their positive annual trade balances have ranged from $70 billion to nearly $100 billion in recent years—far, far ahead of other nations. The U.S. has consistently posted staggering annual trade deficits in the $100-$170 billion range.
- **Despite a growing appetite for imported foreign goods, the U.S. was still the world's largest exporting nation.**
- West Germany, with a work force less than one-fourth the size of America's, caught up to the U.S. as the world's leading exporting nation in absolute terms.
- **Americans invested twice as much abroad as foreigners invested in the United States.**
- Foreign investors—principally European and Japanese—invested almost exactly twice as much in the United States as Americans invested abroad in 1989.
- **The two largest banks in the world were American banks, Citicorp and Chase Manhattan.**
- The world's ten largest banks were all Japanese, while the biggest non-Japanese banks were French and German. Citibank teetered on insolvency.
- **The U.S. dollar was worth over 260 Japanese yen and 3.1 Deutsche marks at times in the first half of this decade.**

- The dollar had fallen as low as 1.23 yen and 1.6 Deutsche marks.
- **The American economy was seen as the global "locomotive." American economic trends set the agenda for the world economy—sometimes causing "shocks" in Japan and Europe.**
- Japan and Germany were increasingly acknowledged to be the leading stimulator of the rest of the world's economy. The U.S. government became reliant on Japanese and European investors to finance a third or more of Washington's annual budget deficit.

You can see that much of what Burstein wrote has happened or is in the process of happening. While his time frame appears to be off by about three years, it is apparent *that the economic power of the United States will be reduced in order to bring Europe up in power and position.* This shift has been facilitated domestically through deficit spending, taxation, debt, bankruptcies, and now globally as the countries and companies of the world shift from the dollar as a reserve currency to the euro.

European Federation

For a moment, let's analyze the philosophy behind a strong Europe. There have been many proponents of a "European Federation," which include Dante, William Penn, Jean Jacques Rousseau, and Giuseppe Mazzini. Winston Churchill, another strong proponent, said:

> Our constant aim must be to build and fortify the strength of the United Nations. Under and within that world concept we must recreate the European family in a regional structure called, it may be, the United States of Europe. France and Germany must take the lead together. Great Britain, the British Commonwealth of Nations, mighty America, and I trust Soviet Russia—for then indeed all would be well—must be the friends and sponsors of the new Europe and must champion its right to live and shine.
>
> —Cheever, 767

(I interviewed Daniel Cheever in 1995. He was special assistant to Alger Hiss at the U.N. organizational meetings in 1945.)

However, they were not the first. The prophet Daniel wrote about a ten-nation confederacy inside the Holy Roman Empire at the end of the age. Perhaps what we are seeing is the fulfillment of what was written in the book of Daniel. It should be obvious that the above did not just happen.

Conclusion

Part and parcel of the "final thrust" is a massive consolidation of power on the international economic level in which the International Monetary Fund is being given very broad and deep powers to have the final say as to how a country handles their finances. (How would you like it if the federal government decided to tell you what you could and could not buy and how to spend your money?) There are also plans to consolidate the IMF, WTO, and World Bank. All of this is with the blessings of our Congress, which plans to give control of our insurance companies and brokerage firms to the Federal Reserve when they pass a banking modernization law in 1999. And the final step in the consolidation of the currencies of the world will be a global currency, the beginning of which can be seen in the current price of the euro to the dollar of 1.07. With only a seven cent difference between the two, we are there!!

THE INTERNATIONAL LEVEL
Introduction

It is not enough to understand our economy at the national level. We must look up to the international level. Unfortunately Americans are being "dumbed down" when it comes to understanding anything higher than the local level. Over the years, there have been many calls for a "new international monetary system." Bill Clinton is credited with having started the ball rolling at the 1994 Group of Seven meeting in Naples, Italy. Today, the Group of Seven has adopted the need for a new global architecture as its mantra. The IMF, which is poised to become a world central bank, obviously approves. Other non-G–7 world leaders approve. Most "imminent" economists and thinkers approve. Everyone seems to approve, except the American people—who don't know or understand!

At the 1998 annual meeting of the IMF/World Bank, Michael Camdessus, managing director of the IMF said:

> To extend the enormous progress of the last fifty years into the next half century, we need **a new architecture for the international monetary system.** . . . To face [the new challenges and new crises], we need to move to a *higher* level of international cooperation . . . as we face simultaneously the difficult tasks of renovating the system while managing crisis. . . . This new architecture must rest on five underlying principles: *transparency, soundness of financial systems, involvement of the private sector, orderly liberalization of capital flows, and modernization of international markets harnessed with standards of best practices and means for enforcing them* [emphasis mine].

The new architecture has been evolving since its inception in 1944. I have identified four stages in its evolution. We are currently in the fourth.

The Steps Leading Up to the "Final Thrust"

Zbigniew Brzezinski said at the Gorbachev State of the World Forum in 1995 that the "New World Order would come step by step and stone by stone." The following are the steps which have already been taken:

Phase I—1940s: The creation of the Bretton Woods Monetary System (1944), which includes the World Bank (WB) and the International Monetary Fund. A year later, in 1945, the United Nations was formed, and in October of that year our Senate ratified the U.N. Charter. The purpose of the World Bank was to make loans to war-torn countries for the purpose of rebuilding. The stated purpose of the IMF was to make loans and to monitor the global economy with regard to monetary stability. As a result of America's post-war strength, the dollar was deemed the reserve currency of the world. Both the World Bank and the International Monetary Fund have evolved substantially since the 1940s and perform a very wide and broad array of economic, financial, and market functions. As stated, part of the new architecture will be the replacement of the dollar as the world's reserve currency.

Phase II—1970s: As a result of the amount of dollars floating around overseas and their stated convertibility to gold, Richard Nixon, in August 1971, had no choice but to sever any remaining ties the United States dollar had to gold in order to protect what was left of our gold reserves. It was General Charles deGaulle who realized, as a result of the Vietnam War, that America's gold reserves were being depleted. He was the last leader to convert his United States dollars into gold. As a result of this drastic, never-been-done-before move, the monetary systems of the world began to "float" against one another in order to determine its new value. For the first time since biblical days when gold, cattle, clothing, and food were the mediums of exchange, the countries of the world found that their money would only be worth what someone else was willing to pay for it.

Phase III—1980s: In 1980 Congress passed the Monetary Control Act of 1980, which tore down financial borders between countries. At the same time, similar legislation was passed in the other Group of Seven countries—Canada, Germany, Japan, Italy, Great Britain, and France. As a result of these laws, the process of "globalization" began. I have defined globalization to mean, "through constant change, the blending together of economies, people, laws, politics, monies, and social ethics into one; the convergence or harmonization, i.e. homogenization of the world from individual nation-states to one world, 'a world without borders.'"

The Monetary Deregulation Act of 1980 is remembered by most Americans when you explain that they were paid up to fifteen percent interest on their money market funds for a short period of time. Today that same law, by taking away the interest rate ceilings banks paid, allows banks to pay only two to three percent on savings accounts and charge up to fifteen to twenty-one percent interest on credit cards! Under the guise of floating interest rates, the legislation was passed to create a level playing field on a global basis for money to seek the highest yield or fastest play to be found worldwide without any legal or economic barriers! Today more than $1.3 trillion moves around the world on a daily basis looking for the highest/quickest profit and play. Some of these players, like George Soros, are called "rough traders" and are partly responsible for causing havoc in a lesser developed country by buying its currency with or without loans, using it for hedging and ultimately devaluating it when the country takes action to curb the investment to protect itself. Countries that have experienced the downside of this sophisticated form of financial rape are Indonesia, Malaysia, and Thailand.

Phase IV—Today, The Final Thrust: The 1990s constitute the final thrust for *control of the world's monetary system by giving the International Monetary Fund greater powers over the market and surveillance in the marketplace.* These powers could make it a "global federal reserve." There are many other recommendations to empower the IMF as an international credit corporation, provide international bankruptcy protection, and enforce the Basle Core Principles on all countries. Eventually if a country does not comply, it will be fined or penalized in some way.

Economic Regionalism—The Foundation for Global Currency

In order to prepare for this new system, the regions of this world are being divided up into economic trading zones. They are: the Americas (Canada, U.S., Mexico, Central and South America, called the Free Trade Areas of the Americas)*, the EMU (Economic and Monetary Union of Europe—eleven countries became one on January 4, 1999), and APEC (Asian-Pacific Economic Council—in the

---

* In order for the dollar to have the same value as the Colombian, Mexican, or Peruvian peso, the dollar has to drop in value while those currencies have to increase. In order for the euro to "fly," there will have to be a mass exit from the dollar to support this new currency. A double-whammy for the United States and Americans.

process of being formulated). Robert Rubin is heading up the Finance Ministers of the Americas, who desire to fix the currencies of the Americas to the dollar. Obviously the euro will be a consolidation of eleven currencies into one. There is no doubt that a lead currency will arise out of Asia and it will be the Japanese yen. Regions not discussed but part of the EMU "regions" are the Middle East and Africa.

Recently Michael Howell, managing director of Crossborder Capital, an investment advisory group, said that the division of the world into three currency blocs would be the best way of preventing hedge funds from causing chaos. Furthermore he said that "the problem is that there are too many currencies in the world" and that regional currencies would remove volatility (*Financial Times,* October 22, 1998, 22).

Also, there is no doubt in my mind that once the regional currencies are set so that they are compatible with one another, they will be "harmonized" so that they will trade within five to ten percent of each other, making them, in essence, a **global currency.** Even now, going into the 1999 G-7 meeting, this is being discussed.

Consolidation of Power and Power Players

The following will explain the shifts in power and the empowerment of key players on the international level.

The Treasury Departments and Central Banks: In a speech before the Council on Foreign Relations* in September, Bill Clinton requested that G-7 finance ministers and central bankers meet to discuss the current international architecture. The treasury departments of the world have effectively become part of each country's central bank. For example, here in the United States, the Federal Reserve is a private corporation with the power to control and op-

---

* Since actions speak louder than words, I believe that it is possible to deduce that this "final thrust" is already in the implementation stage because the Council on Foreign Relations is the American branch of the British Royal Institute for International Affairs (RIIA). The objective of both of these groups is to bring America back under the control of the British. In America, this control will be finalized when the banking modernization act, known in the 1998 session as "HR10," is passed sometime in early 1999.

erate our monetary system, something they have been doing since 1913 when our Senate passed this evil legislation through deceptive orchestration. What Clinton in effect called for is a merger between the Department of the Treasury and the Federal Reserve. If you have noticed, you always see Robert Rubin and Alan Greenspan together. They testify together, they hold joint press briefings together, and they participated in the IMF/World Bank meeting together. This is a *coup de grace,* as the private banking corporations of the world now have complete control over all aspects of a country's money.

The Empowerment of Central Banks

For years the central banks only dealt with the monetary systems of their countries. They did not deal in commercial paper or bail out hedge funds. However, the central banks have been aiding the markets by buying commercial paper to increase the liquidity of their countries. For example, in September 1998 the Bank of Japan emerged as the biggest investor of their commercial paper. By the end of September they held about forty percent of the amount outstanding in a market dominated by commercial banks as a result of the inability of those banks to extend credit to buyers (*Financial Times,* October 16, 1998, 1).

In the fall of 1998 the Bank of England began accepting bond issues by governments and companies from outside the United Kingdom as securities during its daily operations to provide liquidity to London's money markets, as opposed to only accepting securities issued by the U.K. government. On October 26, 1998, it began accepting sterling denominated bonds issued by such institutions as the World Bank and the European Central Bank (ECB). The bailout of the hedge fund Long Term Capital Management was orchestrated by the Federal Reserve Bank of New York and is an American example.

In 1998, at the Group of Eight meeting in London, England, the G-8 central bank ministers met with the G-8 finance ministers for the first time to hammer out world economic policy. What this action shows is the new merger between a country's central bank-er and treasury secretary in "becoming one." It also shows the consolidation of national economic sovereignty with that of the central bank.

New Financial Architecture for the 21st Century

Over the past four or five years, there have been a number of recommendations with regard to the "financial architecture for the twenty-first century." Until the Asian crisis, there was not a *need* to "fix" the architecture. However, the crisis conveniently gives the framers of the world economic infrastructure the "real" excuse to now integrate (combine, consolidate, blend) the economic (and political) systems of the world into *one*. It was ex-German chancellor Helmut Schmidt who said, "The proper role of a central bank depends upon the monetary system of the world" (Solomon, 497).

Surveillance: At this time the IMF is in the process of taking on a number of new responsibilities, which include "surveillance" of the world's banking systems and the flow of monies worldwide. As a result of new "accords" from the central bank's bank, the Bank for International Settlements in Basle, Switzerland, in the future there will be a supervisory inspection of all banks in the world by the World Bank and IMF. Any bank that is not compliant will be merged or shut down. In short, this is another takeover of our national banks via the Federal Reserve and IMF. The pending bank modernization bill, HR10, contains this measure.

World Bankruptcy Court: In order to "protect" countries from bankruptcy, the global powers are looking to set up a World Bankruptcy Court through the IMF. One only wonders who will receive a bankrupt country's natural assets!

Lines of Credit: It is thought that extending lines of credit to countries in jeopardy the same way a credit corporation does would help save afflicted countries from bankruptcy. This function would be an IMF responsibility. And such empowerment would basically make the IMF a "global federal reserve" with the powers of global banking supervision. The reason why Greenspan, Rubin, and Clinton demanded the $18 billion from Congress is to fund the IMF credit corporation.

Create a Stabilization Intervention Fund: In order to keep currencies in balance, there is a recommendation for a "stabilization fund" to be set up in order to keep the exchange rates between countries (regions) within agreed-upon bounds. According to John Grieve Smith (*Financial Times,* October 7, 1998, 10), the need for a stabilization fund would go further than a "new Bretton Woods." The way to get to this point would be for each region to develop regional arrangements and manage the rates between them (see *Economic Regionalism*). Global management would then start by managing the relations between the dollar, the yen, and the euro/pound, perhaps aided by the IMF or the Bank for International Settlements. This fund could be looked at like a "mutual fund" in that all countries would pool their resources. It would provide liquidity to or take it away from the currency markets, depending on the international capital flows to a country. It could buy emerging market currency when a panic outflow occurs and sell the currency when foreign capital inflows are strong. It would also be in a position to deter speculation and dampen currency market volatility (*Financial Times,* October 7, 1998, 10).

The Merger of the IMF/World Bank/World Trade Organization: There are moves to merge these organizations into one so that they can better carry out their mandates. As mentioned earlier, the recent Omnibus Spending Bill sets up a special commission comprised of five former U.S. Treasury secretaries who will study this merger. Within six months of the study's completion, Clinton will call for a "new Bretton Woods" Conference.

A similar recommendation on the table is to make the IMF Interim Committee a permanent working committee comprised of members from the World Bank and the World Trade Organization. This idea was supposedly the sole idea of Britain's finance minister, Gordon Brown, at the recent IMF/World Bank meeting. It appears that this recommendation fits in very nicely with the special commission to be established.

Emergency Trade Insurance Pool: Back in February 1998, the Group of Seven discussed the creation of an emergency trade insurance pool to help cash-strapped Asian companies continue their manufacturing businesses. At the October 1998 IMF/World Bank meeting, Clinton unveiled the newest measures that our government is going to put in place. The United States has taken the lead to make funds available to the Overseas Private Investors Corporation (OPIC) in order to create an insurance pool of monies so that third world countries can have trade insurance on their exports. This will be backed up by the Export-Import Bank of the United States (Ex-Im Bank). The most recent Omnibus Spending Bill provided $785,000,000 to Ex-Im Bank and $32,000,000 to the Overseas Private Investment Corporation. Furthermore, the other G-7 countries will combine their export credit agencies to work together on this insurance pool—another level of integration on the global level.

All of these are additional steps in changing the economic sovereignty of the world's countries as duties and responsibilities that belonged to individual states are now going to be taken away and given to a global authority.

Interestingly enough, it was "rough speculators" who, we are told, caused the Asian collapse. None of the above addresses their part in the volatility of the world's currency markets!

Conclusion

The fact that all currencies float against one another and that there is a large pool of speculative money that moves electronically around the world is evidence of the volatility that this kind of floating exchange system metes out to its participants. It is, in essence, a very sophisticated game of financial rape.

Alan Greenspan has admitted that the West is experiencing the first serious financial crunch in fifty years. As shown, we have to look at both the national and international levels. On the national level there are problems—America's debt and trade deficits, loss of Japanese investments, and loss of liquidity. All of this will impact our markets and our economy.

On the international level, we must look at what is being set in place. There is no doubt that the market volatility was caused for the sole purpose of empowering the International Monetary Fund, the World Bank, and the Bank for International Settlements to take a greater lead in international currency markets. This will constitute the final loss of national economic sovereignty. Once gone, it is gone forever.

What we have just shown is that there is more to the crisis than meets the eye. The real game of ball is not being played in a stadium, but on the international level!

God is our refuge and strength, a very present help in trouble. Therefore will not we fear, though the earth be removed, and though the mountains be carried into the midst of the sea. . . . Be still, and know that I am God: I will be exalted among the heathen, I will be exalted in the earth.

—Psalm 46:1,2,10

Chapter 8

The Political Structure: The Global Emergency Preparedness Infrastructure

CHAPTER SUMMARY

In doing research, I have found that we are indeed integrated from the police/fire/rescue/emergency on the local level to the global level, which would include all types of terrorism. In chapter four we mentioned an international police force. Just think, with all the natural disasters, the world automatically needs to be integrated from the local police/fire/rescue/emergency to the global level which would also include terrorism. Natural disaster preparedness provides a wonderful opportunity to integrate these agencies which could then be considered an "international police force." Take note of all the different countries in which we send aid and rescue teams when a natural disaster occurs. Also take note of the kind of police and FBI programs on television. In particular, Tom Clancy's *NetForce* which aired in early February. Consider the following:

The Group of Seven in 1978 started to address the topic of terrorism and other acts of violence such as aircraft hijacking, hostage taking, and attacks against diplomatic and consular personnel and premises.

In addition to the above and transnational crime which is taking place in every country of the world, the U.S. is now sending our law enforcement officials overseas to train, act as consultants, and lend technical support to their foreign counterparts. The FBI and DEA are opening new offices around the world, acting as consultants, training their counterparts, and working on U.S. investigations with international links.

In April 1994 the State Department and the FBI jointly opened an International Law Enforcement Academy in Budapest that trains police officers from former Eastern bloc nations and other countries emerging from the former Soviet Union. In 1998 another law enforcement academy was opened in Santiago, Chile.

In 1987, the U.N. General Assembly voted to designate the 1990s as a decade in which the international community, under U.N. auspices, would pay special attention to fostering international cooperation in the areas of natural disaster reduction. Proclaiming 1989 the International Decade for Natural Disaster Reduction, it adopted an International Framework of Action for the Decade (U.N. General Assembly Resolution 44/236 of December 22, 1987).

The U.S. State Department and the Bureau of International Organizational Affairs are looking to set up a new network—the Global Disaster Information Network—which would operate as a broad global partnership involving governments, international organizations, NGOs, academic and research institutions, the media, and other entities to include businesses and citizen groups, engaged in disaster preparedness, response, recovery, and mitigation at all levels.

The Federal Emergency Management Agency (FEMA) is an independent agency reporting to the president with the task of responding to, planning for, recovering from, and mitigating against disaster. Begun in 1803, FEMA has evolved in the last one hundred and ninety-seven years as a result of a number of natural disasters. FEMA works on the global level.

Where is all this leading? It was not until I connected the International Criminal Court (ICC) with the preparedness infrastructure to guard against terrorists of all kinds, that I realized the ICC was the final legal step in prosecuting individuals who are accused of being a terrorist.

INTRODUCTION

In a world in which the Queen of England and Hillary Clinton use the phrase "global village," I have been trying to figure out since the 1996 Group of Seven meeting in Lyon if the world is integrated with regard to police/fire/rescue/emergency preparedness from the local level to the global level. I have questioned if the increased number of terrorist events are real or planned in much the same way the stock market is managed—are they set up in order to change laws and further integrate the world? I would imagine so.

In his speech, "Investing in a Secure Millennium," given on October 3, 1998, Deputy Treasury Secretary Lawrence H. Summers said:

> ... Two seismic events have helped set off a tide of global integration with enormous potential. But it is not enough to watch that tide wash away the remnants of the **old order.** As the President said last week in his address to the United Nations General Assembly, we have to decide *what will be left in its wake.* As he said then, to seize the opportunities, and defeat the threats of this **new global era,** we need a **new strategy** of security—one aimed at forging a **new network of policies and institutional arrangements.** ... The United States has a vital interest in helping to build this **new foundation.** ... And we believe that **proactive, internationalist economic policies** can play an integral role in bringing it about [emphasis mine].

In the summer of 1998 when several of our foreign embassies were bombed in Africa, Secretary of State Madeleine Albright said: "This is a different kind of warfare. We have never fought this before. We are not prepared for this. This is the war of the future. This is a long, sustained war." Interestingly enough, in a time in which the threat of "communism" is not considered a threat and the world is told we are in peace, the countries of the world are all concerned about terrorism due to nuclear and/or biological attacks, or cyber terrorism. A non-war related threat is that of natural disasters.

In 1998, I attended a separate Group of Eight-related conference in London in which one of the speakers featured was Ms.
Valerie Strachan, head of the British Customs Office. Following her
presentation, I asked her if police/FBI/Secret Service agencies
are connected from the local up to the global level. Ms. Strachan
told me that they are not integrated in that way. When I countered
with memorandums of understanding and the legal framework the
Group of Eight (G-8) was establishing, she still could not figure out
what I was asking. In doing some research, I found that such integration exists, and deals with all types of terrorism. In chapter four
we mentioned an international police force. Just think, with all the
natural disasters, the world automatically needs to be integrated
from the local police/fire/rescue/emergency to the global level which
would also include terrorism. Natural disaster preparedness provides a wonderful opportunity to integrate these agencies which
could then be considered an "international police force." Consider
the following:

GROUP OF SEVEN/GROUP OF EIGHT

In 1978 the Group of Seven started to address the topic of terrorism
and other acts of violence, such as aircraft hijacking, hostage taking, and attacks against diplomatic and consular personnel and
premises. In 1981 they agreed to exchange information on terrorist
threats and activities, and to explore cooperative measures for dealing with and countering acts of terrorism, for promoting more effective implementation of existing antiterrorist conventions, and
for securing wider adherence to them. In 1984 they agreed to further actions, which included each country closing gaps in its national legislation that might be exploited by terrorists and reviewing the sale of weapons to states supporting terrorism.

At their 1986 summit in Tokyo, G-7 leaders

> recogniz[ed] that the continuing fight against terrorism is a task
> which the international community as a whole has to undertake,
> . . . urge[d] all like-minded nations to collaborate with us, partic-

ularly in such international fora as the United Nations, the International Civil Aviation Organization and the International Maritime Organization.

In addition, they called on all states to improve extradition procedures, establish stricter immigration and visa requirements, and have the closest "possible bilateral and multilateral cooperation between policy and security organization and other relevant authorities in the fight against terrorism." By 1987 there was an annual statement on terrorism. Each time, the statement was made stronger, encouraging improvement in airport and maritime security. Their statements also included pledges to make the United Nations system stronger in order to meet the challenges of the future: economic, human rights, protection from terrorists, and the reduction of nuclear arms and weapons.

In their 1991 "Political Declaration: Strengthening the International Order," the G-7 stated they felt that a revitalized U.N. would strengthen the international order. As a result of the tragedies in Bangladesh, Iraq, and the Horn of Africa, they saw the need to

reinforce U.N. relief in coping with emergencies . . . to strengthen the coordination, and to accelerate the effective delivery, of all U.N. relief for major disaster . . . improvement in the arrangements and support from donor countries and NGOs . . . to meet urgent humanitarian needs in time of crisis.

The statement went on to reaffirm "taking collective measures against threats to the peace and to suppress aggression: settling disputes peacefully, upholding the rule of law and protecting human rights."

By 1994 G-7 final declarations included taking a stand against transnational crime and money-laundering. Stating that it was a worldwide problem, they determined to strengthen international cooperation and in 1995 welcomed the U.N. Conference on Organized Transnational Crime. That same year, their statement said that as a result of increased terrorist acts, which included the Tokyo subway attacks, the bombing in Oklahoma City, hostage taking in Budennovsk, and the bombing in France, "these and other events point to a number of trends including an upsurge in domestic terrorism, an increase in hostage and indiscriminate violence by religious extremists and apocalyptic groups which practice terrorism." As a result, they called for an international and domestic legal framework, an exchange of expertise and information to prevent terrorist acts, the prevention of the movement of terrorists, and an increase in the safety at airport, maritime, and other public facilities.

THE UNITED STATES

Then in Lyon, France, in June of 1996, the G-7 issued "Forty Points" to counteract terrorism, some of which are outlined in the following chapter. As a result of the forty points and "Twenty-five Recommendations from a 1996 Paris Terrorism Ministerial Meeting," the United States has cooperated extensively with the United Nations, the Organization for Economic Cooperation and Development, NATO, and a host of other multilateral and bilateral agencies. According to a list of actions taken, the United States has:

1. Strengthened its team approach to counter terrorism, which combines diplomacy, law enforcement, intelligence, and other U.S. assets.
2. Set aside $12 million for counter- and antiterrorism training programs worldwide.
3. Hosted a number of symposiums on security for ground transportation, explosive detection, chemical/biological terrorism, and other related topics.
4. In 1988 created the National Infrastructure Protection Center, housed at the FBI, to protect the integrity of the nation's public and private electronic and digital infrastructure in finance, communications, transportation, etc.
5. Enacted the Anti-Terrorism and Effective Death Penalty Act,

which increases the sentences for terrorist crimes and enhances U.S. authority to penalize funding for terrorist groups.

6. Passed executive orders and federal statutes that bar financial assistance to designated terrorist organizations.

7. Revised the Immigration and Nationality Act in 1996 to strengthen the ability of U.S. immigration officials to exclude and deport individuals suspected of terrorist activities.

8. Ratified all ten counterterrorism conventions in force at the end of 1997 and signed the International Convention for the Suppression of Terrorist Bombings on January 12, 1998.

9. Entered into extradition treaties with more than one hundred nations.

10. Negotiated new mutual legal assistance treaties to expand the scope and quality of counterterrorism information exchanged with cooperating law enforcement agencies in the Group of Eight countries and elsewhere.

11. Began exploring ways to accelerate information exchanges and has established an FBI database for forensic information on terrorism. The FBI is offering the G-8 partners the opportunity to participate in the database project.

The Development of the United States Emergency Response Infrastructure

Since 1995 the United States has been setting up an emergency response infrastructure to counteract any kind of disaster as a result of biological, nuclear, or cyber attacks. As a result of the Antiterrorism and Effective Death Penalty Act of 1996. The Office of Justice Protection (OJP) is the department's principal link to state and local jurisdictions in the areas of criminal and juvenile justice and victims services. They are now bringing that expertise to the state and local level with the establishment of the Office of State and Local Domestic Preparedness Support within the OJP. The following is an outline of steps taken as enumerated by Attorney General Janet Reno before the Senate Appropriations Committee on February 4, 1999.

America's Terrorism Czar

Working in Oliver North's old office at the National Security Council, Richard A. Clark is the White House terrorism czar.

> As chairman of the governments' chief counterterrorism group for the last seven years, he has become what John le Carre calls an "intello-crat"—a gray baron who seems to command nothing more than his desk, yet waves a wand and sends soldiers, guns, money and spies around the world.
>
> —*New York Times*, February 1, 1999

He has a reserved seat at the cabinet level and his vote carries the same weight as those cast by the chairman of the Joint Chiefs of Staff and the director of Central Intelligence. Clark has written four classified presidential directives on terrorism which have expanded the government's counterterrorism operations to $11 billion a year.

Federal Bureau of Investigation (FBI)

The FBI has been designated the lead agency for domestic terrorism through its counterterrorism section. It is to identify, prevent, deter, and defeat terrorist operations before they occur. The FBI works with the Federal Emergency Management Agency (FEMA) which has been designated the lead agency for consequence management (after the attack). In a terrorist attack, FBI personnel will be supplemented with employees of the Federal Emergency Management Agency, the Environmental Protection Agency, the Department of Energy, the National Domestic Preparedness Office (to be established), and the Department of Defense.

The FBI has established eighteen joint terrorism task forces which operate in major cities. Two hundred members of state and local law enforcement have participated with the FBI and others to investigate terrorism incidents along with representatives from the Bureau of Alcohol, Tobacco and Firearms, the Customs Service, the Secret Service, and the Immigration and Naturalization Service. The FBI is developing a comprehensive approach to all states which will help to prevent, deter, and respond to terrorist threats. They will coordinate crisis response activities with the Counter-terrorism Center or the International Terrorism Section. In 1989 they expanded the Terrorist Threat Warning System to reach all aspects of the law enforcement and intelligence communities.

Federal Emergency Management Agency (FEMA)

The Federal Emergency Management Agency is an independent agency reporting to the president, with the task of responding to, planning for, recovering from, and mitigating against disaster. Begun in 1803, FEMA has evolved in the last one hundred and ninety-seven years as a result of Hurricane Carla in 1962, Hurricane Betsy in 1965, Hurricane Camille in 1969, the Alaskan earthquake in 1964, and the San Fernando earthquake in 1971. In 1979 President Carter issued an executive order that merged many of the separate disaster-related agencies such as the National Fire Prevention and Control Administration, the National Weather Service Community Preparedness Program, the Federal Disaster Assistance Administration, etc., into FEMA. At that time, FEMA began the development of an Integrated Emergency Management System with an all-hazards approach that includes direction, control, and warning systems that are common to the full range of emergencies from small isolated events to the ultimate emergency—war. FEMA employs twenty-five hundred people and is supplemented in its endeavors by over five thousand stand-by disaster reservists. It has ten regional offices across America and a FEMA training center at Emmitsburg, Maryland, which trains local county and city officials from across the United States to prepare their communities. As a result, crisis exercises are being tried across the country. For example, in my hometown of Racine, Wisconsin, FEMA is working with local officials to analyze a "variety of scenarios and talk about how they would respond" (*Racine Journal Times,* November 12, 1998, A1). One task will be to coordinate volunteers. It works in partnership with other organizations, which include state and local emergency management agencies, twenty-seven federal agencies, and the American Red Cross.

The Office of National Security Affairs coordinates activities in support of FEMA's roles and responsibilities in terrorism preparedness, planning, exercises, and response. In 1989 the National Urban Search and Research Response System was added to create a framework for structuring local emergency services personnel into integrated disaster response task forces. Each emergency support function is led by a primary agency that has been selected based on its authorities, resources, and capabilities in a particular functional area. After a request for federal assistance from a governor is received and approved by the president, task forces may be activated or placed on alert when a major disaster threatens or strikes a community. Today there are twenty-seven FEMA Urban Search and Response Task Forces throughout the United States. Two of these task forces operate under the auspices of the U.S. Agency for International Development and respond to international disasters. The key to triggering FEMA's entry into any state is their governors' declaring a state of emergency. By doing that, the jurisdictional barriers are broken. The federal government may send FEMA or the National Guard in, and other states may send various kinds of assistance—electrical workers, fire fighters, etc.

FEMA works on the global level through the Global Emergency Management System, which is an online, searchable database containing links to websites in a variety of categories.

Cooperation Between Russia and America

In 1996 a partnership between the Federal Emergency Management System (FEMA) and the Ministry of Civil Defense, Emergencies, and the Elimination of the Consequences of Natural Disaster (EMERCOM) of Russia began. Called the United States-Russian Federation Cooperation on Natural and Technological Disaster Prevention and Response, it began as a result of their common objectives to save lives and protect property from the effects of natural and technological disasters (Internet report, FEMA home page, dated March 1, 1998).

Other federal departments and agencies which are active participants in this partnership include U.S. Agency for International Development's Office of Foreign Disaster Assistance, the Department of Agriculture's Forest Service and Farm and Foreign Agriculture Services, the Department of Defense's Office of Emergency Preparedness Planning, the National Guard, the Department of Energy's Office of Non-Proliferation and National Security, the Department of Health and Human Services Public Health Service, the Department of State's Office of Russian Affairs, and the Department of Transportation's Coast Guard. In addition, many state and local governments have participated in these bilateral cooperative disaster management activities including Alaska, Arkansas, Arizona, Iowa, Nebraska, New York, Massachusetts, Oregon, Virginia, Washington, and others.

In 1997 the priorities established for their joint work plan included: region to region collaboration, exchange of training courses, exchange of exercise observers and participants, exchange of scientific and technical information, and coordination of assistance in complex humanitarian emergencies.

While there have been many exchanges between Russia and American officials with participation in training exercises in both countries since 1996, by 1998 their joint exercises which were between FEMA's Region X and EMERCOM's Far East Region, and included the National Guard and Civil Defense of Russia, were designed to build "disaster resistant communities by engaging State [U.S.] and Oblast [Russian] governments, the business communities and non-profit organizations in the process of building local disaster preparedness, response, and mitigation capabilities" (Internet report, FEMA home page, dated March 1, 1998).

Another program of exchange between Russia and America is the Soviet-American Police Exchange program. In 1990, ten high-ranking Soviet militiamen from Leningrad and Moscow spent twelve days visiting in Bakersfield, California, with their American counterparts. The Soviet policemen participated in group activities and with host police officers as they went about their daily routines. Several of the Russian policemen participated in a previous exercise of this nature several years ago while numerous American policemen visited Russia (Walters, A8). In 1994, two Soviet policemen attended the California Highway Patrol Academy in Sacramento for a five and a half month program (Walters, B2). Earlier in 1999, a retiring Calfornia policeman joined the American firm DynCorp Aerospace Corporation, an international firm which contracts with the State Department to provide contract police coverage. As part of his new job, Richard Duthler will be part of a training and peacekeeping mission with the United Nations International Police Monitoring Force in Bosnia, where he will train for the new Bosnian police force and monitor their daily activities. There are twenty countries that have police assigned to Bosnia (combined reports from Bonesteel and Bailey).

The National Infrastructure Protection Center (NIPC)

Established in 1998, the NIPC plays a major role in the national plan for cyber protection according to Presidential Domestic Directive 63 (PDD 63) which is to deter, detect, analyze, investigate, and provide warnings of cyber threats and attacks on the critical infrastructures of the United States. They are to evaluate, acquire, and deploy computer equipment and cyber tools to support investigations and infrastructure protection efforts. The FBI partners with the Office of Justice Programs (OJP) to provide a national level coordinating office and single point of contact for the state and local responder community. The NIPC has personnel from the FBI, the Department of Defense, Department of Energy, the CIA, the National Security Agency, Secret Service, Postal and Inspection Service, as well as state law enforcement. They train five hundred state and local law enforcement personnel at a one week hands-on course. NIPC plans to train investigators from the municipalities represented in the Major Cities Police Chiefs' and the Major Sheriffs' Association, and has been consulting with the International

Association of Chiefs of Police and the National Sheriffs' Association. See First Responder Local Level.

The FBI Counterterrorism Center

Established in 1995, it encompasses the operations of the FBI's International Terrorism Operations Section and the Domestic Terrorism Operations Section. There are nineteen other federal agencies which assign personnel to the FBI Counterterrorism Center. Those agencies include the Air Force Office of Special Investigations, the Bureau of Alcohol, Tobacco and Firearms, the Federal Bureau of Prisons, the Central Intelligence Agency, the Defense Intelligence Agency, the Department of Commerce, the Department of Defense, the Department of Energy, the Department of Transportation, the Environmental Protection Agency, the Federal Aviation Administration, the Federal Emergency Management Agency, the Immigration and Naturalization Service, the IRS, the National Security Agency, the Naval Criminal Investigative Service, the U.S. Customs Service, the U.S. Marshals Service and the U.S. Secret Service.

The National Domestic Preparedness Office (NDPO)

At this writing, this is a serious thought which appears to be all but official in its implementation. The NDPO will be led by the FBI working in partnership with the Office of Justice Programs and all federal agencies engaged in weapons of mass destruction preparedness efforts. It is to be an advisory committee of state and local authorities which will be the bridge between the federal domestic preparedness program planning for the needs of the state/local emergency response and healthcare community. The NDPO will be an interagency effort to enhance government-wide coordination among federal programs offering terrorism preparedness assistance to state and local communities. It will serve state and local authorities as the single federal point of contact. It will be a partner with the Counterterrorism Center to ensure domestic preparedness programs and will prepare special bulletins and related information on weapons of mass destruction issues to a much broader base of state and local agencies consisting of law enforcement, fire fighter, emergency medical services, public health, and emergency management through law enforcement on the Internet.

The Local Level: The First Responder

The first responders are those in the local community who pick up the pieces, locate, extricate, and treat the victims. They are the ones who restore order out of chaos. They need to be taught and to have the right equipment to deal with a range of unconventional weapons. The proposed Office of State and Local Domestic Preparedness Support will coordinate the delivery of training, equipment, and technical assistance to the state and local first responders. The National Infrastructure Protection Center, along with the National Domestic Preparedness Office, plans to conduct outreach and training efforts for the local first responders and state and local law enforcement. The NIPC will train investigators.

NATO Fiftieth Anniversary

April '99, the fiftieth anniversary of NATO was held in Washington, D.C. The plans and security for it were exceptional. An article in the *Washington Post* opened this way: "With war raging in Kosovo and at least forty world leaders set to gather in Washington at once, the nation's capitol will resemble a police state." They went on to say that sharpshooters in SWAT gear will stand on downtown rooftops and helicopters will swirl overhead; bomb-sniffing dogs and robots will be ready to detect whether suspicious packages contain explosives; federal decontamination sites will assist emergency workers in case of a chemical or biological assault; giant, concrete barriers will prevent pedestrians and traffic from entering downtown Washington; thousands of law enforcement officers will cover the streets; and fire trucks and ambulances will be in constant motion throughout the city. In addition, officers from fifty law enforcement agencies, as well as the city's enforcement agencies and emergency fire and rescue personnel have trained for seven months to deal with potential bombings, chemical and biological assaults, and threats against officials (Fernandez and Horwitz, A4). Is this a picture of things to come?

In contrast, when I attended the fiftieth anniversary of the United Nations in New York City, where over one hundred and eighty heads of state gathered, the only precautions were to line the United Nations building wth police. The only time helicopters flew overhead was when Bill Clinton was present.

U.S. LAW ENFORCEMENT OVERSEAS

In response to transnational crime occurring in every country of the world, the United States, in addition to the list above, is now sending our law enforcement officials overseas to train, act as consultants, and lend technical support to their foreign counterparts. The FBI and Drug Enforcement Administration (DEA) are opening new offices around the world, acting as consultants, training their counterparts, and working on U.S. investigations with international links.

In April 1994 the State Department and the FBI jointly opened an International Law Enforcement Academy in Budapest that trains police officers from former Eastern bloc nations and other countries emerging from the former Soviet Union. In 1998 another law enforcement academy was opened in Santiago, Chile.

In Haiti, the United States established the first-ever Haitian civilian police academy and is working with the U.N. to develop a civilian police force with international monitors to ensure the safety and security of all ethnic groups there.

There are two hundred U.S. law enforcement personnel in Bosnia. In addition, the State Department, along with the law enforcement community, is training police, prosecutors, court reporters, and judges from around the world.

The State Department is working bilaterally with countries to establish treaties that will enable our law enforcement officials to work freely with their foreign counterparts, exchanging information, extraditing wanted criminals, seizing assets, freezing bank accounts, and retrieving stolen cars.

With all of the partnerships being formed today at every level, we are seeing our FBI being used as experts in other countries, our police force being exchanged with that of other countries, the emergency management system working together on common problems, and a host of other interconnected and interrelated projects. In addition, our Marines, Navy, and Air Force are using cities such as Pittsburgh, Oakland, California, the Eastern Shore in Maryland, Chicago, Dallas, and other cities across America to practice "war games." What does this all really mean?

The State Department's Bureau for International Narcotics and Law Enforcement Affairs (INL)

In 1978 this department only handled narcotics. In 1994 international crime was added to its portfolio and the name was changed to the Bureau for International Narcotics and Law Enforcement Affairs (INL). It exists to: (1) combat international crime, (2) help emerging democracies strengthen their national judicial and law enforcement institutions, and (3) strengthen efforts by the United Nations and other international organizations to assist member states in combating international criminal activity.

The State Department is working with other concerned governments through extradition treaties, mutual legal assistance agreements, information exchanges, and law enforcement training and technical assistance. Specialized training addresses money-laundering and related financial frauds, illegal trafficking in persons, vehicle and aircraft theft, small arms trafficking, tax fraud, and public corruption.

There are extensive partnerships among the FBI, the Drug Enforcement Administration (DEA), the Bureau of Alcohol, Tobacco and Firearms (ATF), the International Criminal Investigative Training Assistance Program (ICITAP), and the Department of State's Bureau of Diplomatic Security.

The INL supports the Department of Justice in providing training for criminal justice officials in the Newly Independent States and Central Europe (Azerbijan, Kazakhstan, Kyrgyzstan, Poland, Hungary, etc). They have resident legal advisors in Russia, Ukraine, Poland, and Latvia, and in addition, provide funding to state and local universities and NGOs there to develop training in the areas of community policing.

In addition, the INL programs deal with:

1. Money-laundering and financial aid fraud, in which the Department of Justice, the IRS, the Office of the Comptroller of the Currency, Secret Service, and others work with their counterparts to develop new laws, regulations, and investigative capabilities that will enhance banking safety and soundness;
2. Firearms trafficking, where the INL is actively participating in several multilateral and bilateral fora to address the growing threat of illegal firearms trafficking; and
3. Alien smuggling, where the INL is responsible for promoting international cooperation to halt illegal trafficking in human lives.

The Global Disaster Information Network (GDIN)

In January 1999 I attended a conference on Y2K conducted by the World Federalists. While they painted Y2K to be as bad as what everyone had been saying, I was able to interview a fascinating gentlemen who is involved in many high-level happenings. He specifically told me he has worked for seventeen years with Al Gore who, as a young representative, was interested in emergency management and disasters. This gentleman told me of GDIN.

In 1987 the U.N. General Assembly voted to designate the 1990s as a decade in which the international community, under U.N. auspices, would pay special attention to fostering international cooperation in the areas of natural disaster reduction. Proclaiming the 1990s the International Decade for Natural Disaster Reduction, it adopted an International Framework of Action for the Decade (resolution 44/236 of 12/22/87).

The State Department and the Bureau of International Organizational Affairs are looking to set up a new network—the Global Disaster Information Network—which would operate

> as a broad global partnership involving governments, international organizations, NGOs, academic and research institutions, the media, and other entities to include businesses and citizen groups, engaged in disaster preparedness, response, recovery, and mitigation at all levels.

The establishment of GDIN on an international basis is seen as essential to U.S. foreign policy and national security. And because the United States has vital commercial, humanitarian, and political interests in disaster-prone countries, GDIN must be effective and link existing **national, commercial, multilateral, and bilateral systems, as well as be an incentive for improvements in such systems.**

On the global level, GDIN is already working with the Department of State, the Department of Defense, FEMA, and USAID to form an interagency team to plan implementation of the global phase, which would include:

1. An effective interoperable network of early warning, mitigation, and response systems of value to all nations;
2. A quick response system linking the United States and foreign commercial and government satellites and other remote sensing tools, which will assist in natural and technological disasters as well as complex humanitarian emergencies;
3. Increased information sharing between governments, NGOs, and international organizations and the development of methods of handling sensitive information;
4. The uses, enhancement, and support of current disaster relief efforts and international public-private partnerships to reduce loss of life and property;
5. Fostering global information standards; and
6. The encouragement of governments, NGOs, international or-

ganizations, and educational institutions to require that disaster managers comply with international standards.

In the future, GDIN is looking to set up a worldwide network of operations centers. As of October 1997 GDIN was in preliminary discussions with the International Federation of Red Cross and Red Crescent Societies (IFRC), European Union (EU), United Kingdom (U.K.), the World Meteorological Organization, and others that might take advantage of this system.

Since GDIN is in the preliminary stages of being set up, there are discussions as to where it should be lodged. The options are:

1. Making GDIN a U.N. project, which would plug it into an organization with offices in every country and existing emergency systems (in this scenario, the U.S. would lose control);

2. The International Federation of Red Cross and Red Crescent Societies—a worldwide organization with a reputation for neutrality (again the U.S. would lose control and have to fund it); and

3. Keep GDIN as a separate system, creating a separate international organization that would be a nonprofit, public-private partnership.

According to *World NetDaily*, January 6, 1999, the National Guard is planning in May 1999 its first national mobilization of its 480,000 troops since 1940 in preparation for civil unrest resulting from the Y2K millennium bug in conjunction with FEMA.

Pentagon to Seek Military Leader Over Civilians

It was recently reported that the Pentagon has decided to ask President Clinton for the power to appoint a military leader for the continental United States because of what it sees as a growing threat of major terrorist strikes on American soil. The plan calls for the military leader to have the power to order thousands of doctors, stretchers, and emergency personnel to be sent to afflicted areas according to the Defense Department. Although the White House has responded favorably to this request, civil libertarians fear that such military power could slowly expand to threaten the privacy, liberty, and lives of private citizens. They state that the FBI already has the powers necessary to handle such a crisis if it arises.

At stake is the possible repeal of the Posse Comitatus Act which was passed after the Civil War to rein in the military. It bars federal troops from doing police work within the borders of the United States. However, former Senator Sam Nunn of Georgia said that in the event of nuclear terrorism or in the event of chemical and germ attacks, the Pentagon has the power to step in domestically. A senior Pentagon official who spoke on the condition of anonymity, warned that a major terrorist attack had the potential to be "the most threatening event to civil liberties since Pearl Harbor." His reference was to how, after Japan's attack on the United States in World War II, the American military locked up some 120,000 Americans of Japanese ancestry (*New York Times*, January 28, 1999).

Definition of Terrorist

We should be asking, "Where is all of this leading?" Besides the Y2K concerns and the possible or probable attacks from weapons of mass destruction or cyber terrorism, I think there may be another reason for all of this preparation. Louis J. Freeh, director of the Federal Bureau of Investigation, testified along with Janet Reno before the Senate Committee on Appropriations on February 4. In discussing terrorism, he had to explain what a terrorist is. His speech is available from the Senate Committee on Appropriations and is yours for the asking. His testimony described those which the government considers a domestic terrorist threat by singling out several of the following:

The threat from right-wing extremist groups includes militias, white-separatist groups, and anti-government groups. All right-wing extremist groups tend to encourage massing weapons, ammunition, and supplies in preparation for a confrontation with federal law enforcement, as well as local law enforcement who are often perceived as agents for the state/federal government. The goal of the militia movement is to defend and protect the United States Constitution from those who want to take away the rights of Americans. The militia movement believes that the United States Constitution gives Americans the right to live their lives without government interference. The FBI focuses on the radical elements of the militia movement capable and willing to commit violence against government, law enforcement, civilian, military, and international targets (U.N., visiting foreign military personnel). The American militia movement has grown over the last decade. Factors contributing to growth include:

- *Guns*—the right to bear arms is an issue which almost all militia members agree and most militia members believe a conspiracy exists to take away their guns.
- *Mistrust of federal law enforcement* is frequently mentioned in militia literature and overall militia mythology. FBI and ATF actions such as Ruby Ridge, the Branch Davidians, and the Freeman standoff, are cited.
- *The United Nations* is perceived as an organization bent on taking over the world and destroying American democracy and establishing "the New World Order."

In light of the above, the International Association of Undercover Officers will sponsor two conferences during the summer of 1999 to discuss the "enemy," "conspiracy theories," and "extremists' communications." They cite the "pro-life movement, churches—the cult mentality, New World Order, God-given laws, theocracy v.s. democracy, and sovereignty" as topics of discussion.

It was not until I connected the International Criminal Court with the preparedness infrastructure to guard against **terrorists of all kinds** that I realized the International Criminal Court was the final legal step in prosecuting individuals who are accused of being a terrorist.

Chapter 9

The Legal Structure: The International Criminal Court— Armageddon Set in Utopia

CHAPTER SUMMARY

It was the U.S. which called for an unrecorded vote on July 17, 1998, that led to the passage of the "Final Draft" document establishing the United Nations International Criminal Court. For the first time in history since the Roman Empire, whose legal jurisdiction was over most of the known world at that time, a world court is being established on a global basis to try individuals for the four "core" crimes which the court is empowered to rule on: genocide, crimes against humanity, war crimes, and aggression (undefined).

A key figure at the International Criminal Court proceedings was Dr. Benjamin Ferencz, a man who has worked tirelessly for over fifty years to get an international criminal court established. Dr. Ferencz has written over half a dozen books on the subjects of aggression, an international criminal court, international law, and planethood. A graduate of the Harvard Law School, he was designated the chief prosecutor for the U.S. in the Nuremberg trial against SS extermination squads responsible for the genodical murder of over a million people. It should be noted that those who served at Nuremberg, at the express wish of Winston Churchill, ignored the fact that Hitler and his Nazi Party "were all drawn from the most powerful occult society in Germany, the Thule Gesellschaft, whose inner core was involved with seances and black magic rituals" and "that the black magic not be revealed to the general public after the war. The Allied prosecution and judges at Nuremberg consciously ignored the occult aspects of the Nazis' tremendous power and cruelty." In an interview with Dr. Benjamin Ferencz, when asked if the court would try additional crimes in the future, he replied:

> In the future we will add many crimes. As I indicated before, everything is global—economic, finance, crimes, terrorism, narcotics, or environment—these are all the problems which can only be dealt with in a global way. We have not yet adapted to that reality—we will, step by step. Here we are limiting our focus to those which have already been universally condemned—aggression, war crimes against humanity, and genocide. From here we will move on to things like narcotics, terrorism, and environmental deprivations and economic privation—it is really something unjust about having a billion people in the world living in poverty while a football player makes millions of dollars a year. So this irrationality has got to be dealt with in some way and I have no doubt that it will come.

In summary, the head of the Indian delegation, Mr. Dilip Lahiri, said this about why his country voted no to the ICC. Perhaps it really sums up the Frankenstein monster that has been birthed.

> We have always had in mind a Court that would deal with truly exceptional situations, where the State machinery had collapsed or where the Judicial system was either so flawed, inadequate, or nonexistent that justice had to be meted out through an International Court, because redress was not available within the country. If this is our common understanding, and we have always been told that it is, it must follow that the **Statute should have been drafted so that it was clear that the ICC was being established to deal with truly exceptional situations. That, however, has not happened.** Instead of legislating for the exception, the

scope of the Statute has been broadened so much that it could be misused for political purposes or through misplaced zeal, to address situations and cases for which the ICC was not intended, and where, as a matter of principles, it should not intrude. What the zealots have achieved, therefore, is a contradiction in terms: a Court framed with Armageddon in mind is set in Utopia [emphasis added].

You can see the "open door" which has been set up at the international criminal court level. The arrest of former Chilean dictator Augusto Pinochet is a prime example of what India was talking about.

INTRODUCTION

On July 17, 1998, the United States called for an unrecorded U.N. vote that led to the passage of the document establishing the United Nations International Criminal Court (ICC). For the first time since the Roman Empire (whose legal jurisdiction was over most of the known world at that time), a world court is being established to try individuals for the four "core" crimes on which the court is empowered to rule: genocide, crimes against humanity, war crimes, and aggression. Like all U.N. agendas, the ICC not only empowers the international system, but supposedly fills a major void in the original United Nations Charter. The road to creating the ICC is most interesting. A number of factors need to be discussed in order to understand what the court is, how it will function, and what it means to Americans. These factors are international law, the role of Dr. Benjamin Ferencz, the movement toward an ICC, the World Conference on Human Rights, the Group of Seven/Group of Eight, and the role of nongovernmental organizations.

INTERNATIONAL LAW

International law is the glue for the U.N.'s actions with regard to world government. Just as each country has its own set of laws—civil, criminal, penal, family, commercial, etc., so, too, does the U.N.

jurist, historian, theologian, and diplomat Hugo Grotius who guided the transition of modern international law from the law of nature (the law of God) to natural law based on universal reason. His writings are considered the foundation for modern international law (Henkin *et. al.,* xxiv). The term "international law" is credited to the English jurist Jeremy Bentham. Contemporaries of Bentham were Jean Jacques Rousseau and Immanuel Kant, who also wrote about ways to maintain peace among nations (Ferencz [a], 17–18).

In 1899 the "First International Peace Conference" in history was held, with a follow-up conference in 1907. In 1910 when President Theodore Roosevelt accepted the Nobel Peace Prize, he deplored the failure of the previous international conferences to create an executive or international police power to enforce the decisions of arbitration courts and to prevent violence between nations (Ferencz [a], 3).

The next major legal instrument in the evolution of international law was the League of Nations, which the United States did *not* ratify. This was followed by the United Nations Charter, which *was* ratified by our Senate in 1945. According to Edison W. Dick, a member of the UNA/USA (United Nations Association/USA) who spoke at a workshop at the September 1995 United Nations Fiftieth Anniversary Conference in Washington, D. C.:

> More international law has been developed through the U.N. system during the past fifty years than in the entire previous history of mankind. The U.N. has been directly responsible for the conclusion of more than 465 multilateral agreements covering virtually every area of state interaction and human endeavor from the Law of the Sea to narcotic drug control, from the environment to international trade and copyright law, from arms control to the advancement in women's rights. . . . The development of international law to the extent we know it today would not have been possible outside the framework of the U.N.

He further cited the International Law Commission, "which has played a more pronounced role in the General Assembly's efforts to foster the codification of international law."

The sources for international law are treaties, customs, general practices of law, judicial decisions, and academic writing. Interestingly enough, the whole body of academic writing is very large. The number of books coming out with regard to the United Nations and what it should do are almost as numerous as the sands of the sea. The whole theory behind academic writing is that if enough people like the ideas and concepts put forth in a book and if enough people write on the same topic, then the ideas and philosophies proposed will end up becoming a custom, and then over time, established law. So what is international law? Any rule that the "one-worlders" want it to be. International law is basically rules and regulations that are brought into being according to what specific situations need. It should be noted that every agreement coming out of the U.N. General Assembly further establishes and expands international law.

In 1987 the United Nations began to consider "A Comprehensive System of International Peace and Security," which was put on the agenda by the Soviet Union after Mikhail Gorbachev wrote a widely-publicized article calling for "a system for a universal legal order which will ensure the primacy of international law in politics." In addressing the United Nations in 1988, Gorbachev said, "Our ideal is a world community of States which are based on the rule of law and which subordinates their foreign policy to activities to law." In 1990 French president Francois Mitterand said, "The time has come for international law to reign. We are faced with a choice between the law of the jungle and the rule of law." President George Bush addressed the General Assembly several days after Mitterand and said, "It is in our hands . . . to cap a historic movement toward a new world order and a long era of peace. We have a vision of a new partnership of nations that transcends the Cold War." Four months later, on January 16, 1991, Bush declared to the American people in his State of the Union address, "We now have before us the opportunity to forge for ourselves and for future generations a new world order, a world where the rule of law, not the law of the jungle governs the conduct of nations." International law was increasingly being recognized as a vital component for a peaceful world (Ferencz [a], 7–18).

DR. BENJAMIN FERENCZ

A key figure at the International Criminal Court proceedings was Dr. Benjamin Ferencz, a man who has worked tirelessly for over fifty years to get an international criminal court established. He has been active in many peace and international law organizations, and is an accredited nongovernmental observer at the United Nations. As such, he was allowed to address the ICC Plenary during the first week of the proceedings. Dr. Ferencz has written over half a dozen books on the subjects of aggression, an international criminal court, international law, and planethood. A graduate of the Harvard Law School, he served in the Army where he helped liberate several German concentration camps and served as a war crimes investigator. At the age of twenty-seven he was designated the chief prosecutor for the United States at the Nuremberg war crimes trial. It should be noted that those who served at Nuremberg, at the express wish of Winston Churchill, ignored the fact that Hitler and his Nazi Party "were all drawn from the most powerful occult society in Germany, the Thule Gesellschaft, whose inner core was involved with seances and black magic rituals" and were instructed "that the black magic not be revealed to the general public after the war. The Allied prosecution and judges at Nuremberg consciously ignored the occult aspects of the Nazis' tremendous power and cruelty" (McLaughlin and Davidson, 160–161). [Note: Spiritual warfare at its finest!]

In his book *New Legal Foundations for Global Survival*, Dr. Ferencz suggested that the way to add to the United Nations structure without having to amend the U.N. Charter, which he said would be a very difficult thing, would be to establish independent agencies. When I asked him if the ICC was being established as a result of his suggestion, he gave an absolute "Yes." In 1971 Joseph Clark, a former president of the World Federalist Association, wrote about the same idea:

> Still another approach is to advance step by step toward global governance [JV: government], using the U.N. but without trying to amend the Charter [by letting] the U.N. establish new agencies such as an International Criminal Court. By means of these voluntarily funded functional agencies, national sovereignty would be gradually eroded until it is no longer an issue. Eventually a world federation [JV: government] can be formally adopted with little resistance.
>
> —Clark, 14

I asked Dr. Ferencz to describe the kind of position and importance that the International Criminal Court has in international law. Calling the court a "missing link" in international law, he said it is a "foundational cornerstone." Other stones leading up to the ICC, he said, were the Nuremberg trials, the creation of the International Criminal Tribunal for the former Yugoslavia in 1992, and the International Criminal Tribunal for Rwanda in 1994. When questioned about the importance of the ICC and the advancement of global governance, he said:

> We are moving into another century and it's going to be different from the century we are going out of, which was the bloodiest in human century. . . . We have not yet adopted our ideas to the twenty-first century. . . . We are thinking in terms of sovereignty, . . . which should be regarded as ridiculous today, which are, in fact, obsolete today.

While Dr. Ferencz can provide all of the rhetoric he wants about the need to try criminals who have committed heinous crimes, it should be noted that he is a "one-worlder." The following should be considered when analyzing his ICC stance:

1. During the Nuremberg trials, "Winston Churchill reportedly insisted that the black magic of the Nazi Party not be revealed to the general public after the war and the Allied prosecution and judges at Nuremberg consciously ignored the occult aspects of the Nazis' tremendous power and cruelty" (McLaughlin and Davidson, 261).

2. On the back of a two-page article that Dr. Ferencz handed out at the ICC was an advertisement for the magazine The World Today, which is published by the Royal Institute for International Affairs (RIIA). The RIIA is the successor group to the seven trusts of Cecil John Rhodes, which were endowed upon his death. The sole purpose of these trusts was and is to return the "lost colony" of America back to Britain. The RIIA was responsible for its American counterpart, the Council on Foreign Relations, being established by David Rockefeller.

The facts put a new "spin" on Ferencz's desire to have an international criminal court. Is he, out of the evil of WWII, trying to protect the world from genocide, crimes against humanity, and war crimes? Or does he, as a one-worlder, foster occult practices and have the same vision as Rhodes—to return America back to Britain through international law and the United Nations?

THE MOVE TOWARD AN INTERNATIONAL CRIMINAL COURT

The move for an international criminal court started after World War I when Elihu Root, founder of the American Society of International Law, and his assistant, U.S. Army Judge Advocate John Scott Brown, championed the cause (Ferencz, 73).

It was Zbigniew Bzrezinski who, at the 1995 Gorbachev State of the World Forum, said that the "new world order would come step by step and stone by stone." He stated a truth very well as the new world order has not and will not come all at once, but it will come as subtle as weight gain. It will come and, for the most part, has come; it is a matter of a person's perspective as to whether or not he recognizes it. As part of the stepping stone process, there have been many U.N.-commissioned studies and reports completed to establish additional powers, treaties, commissions, agencies, and systems, the addition of which the U.N. justifies by its mandate to serve the world's people.

In one 1994 study entitled *Renewing the United Nations System*, Erskine Childers and Sir Brian Urquhart call for a strengthened United Nations through various kinds of international taxation, a U.N. Parliamentary Assembly, a reconstituted (empowered) International Monetary Fund (currently there are a number of recommendations that are being implemented to give the IMF the powers of a "world central bank"), the consolidation of a number of U.N. functions, and U.N. Humanitarian Security Police to protect emergency relief operations (Childers and Urquhart, 186). Another study by the Commission on Global Governance published in 1995 entitled *Our Global Neighborhood* builds on a number of previous studies and proposes a new concept called "global governance," which members say is

> part of the evolution of human efforts to organize life on the planet. . . . The challenge is to strike the balance in such a way that the management of global affairs is responsible to the interests of all people in a sustainable future, that is guided by basic human values, and that it makes global organization conform to the reality of global diversity.
>
> —Carlsson and Ramphal, xvii

Furthermore, the commission states that when the U.N. Charter was signed, "a new era in international behavior and governance [began]" (Ramphal and Carlsson, 1). The recommendations put forth in this four hundred-page book are extensive and include a call for an international criminal court.

In 1994 as well, the United Nations Development Programme published its *Human Development Report*. In it, Jan Tinbergen, who won the 1969 Nobel Prize for Economics, proposed:

Mankind's problems can no longer be solved by national governments. What is needed is a world government. This can best be
achieved by strengthening the United Nations system. . . . Completely new institutions would be needed. These could include,
for example, a permanent World Police which would have the
power to subpoena nations to appear before the International
Court of Justice or before other specially created courts.

—p. 88

Also published in 1994 was a book by Dr. Ferencz, in which he
wrote that the United Nations needs:

1. **A Disarmament Enforcement Agency,** which would conduct
an arms census and halt the production of new weapons and
the establishment of new military installations, etc.;
2. **A U.N. Sanctions Agency,** which would ensure that sanctions
against a transgressor are comprehensive and interrupt all economic and diplomatic relations and all means of transport and
communications;
3. **A Police Agency,** which would carry out all measures by using
peacekeeping forces and other forces placed at the disposal of
the Security Council or recruited directly by the U.N. for a particular situation; and
4. **A U.N. Social Justice Agency,** which would deal with viola-
tions of fundamental human rights that pose a threat to peace.
It would monitor the global human rights situation and alert
the Security Council to dangerous social injustices and oppres-
sion that might rise to levels that threaten peace (Ferencz [a],
309-342).

Note that all of these ideas pose progressive steps, if not under
their specific names, then at least in concept. For example, at a
number of workshops that I have attended over the years, the concept of a "rapid deployment force" has been mentioned as a way to
prevent any aggression from happening within a country. Even

President Clinton supports this idea. Just think what it would entail by way of the additional law enforcement required to track people who may be considered dangerous or who are "obstructing the peace," which might be defined as "extreme nationalism."

Other International Courts

The ICC is not the first international court. There are several that have preceded it: the World Court, which arbitrates disputes between countries, the International Centre for Settlement of Investment Disputes, which arbitrates financial disputes between countries, corporations, and individuals, and the Law of the Sea Tribunal, which hears disputes concerning the seas, fishing, and territorial rights.

The World Court

The International Court of Justice was established at the San Francisco Conference in 1945. It is a successor to and resembles the Permanent Court of International Justice created in the 1920s, which was part of the League of Nations. As a principal organ of the U.N., the International Court or "World Court" as it is called, is located at The Hague in the Netherlands. It is housed in the Peace Palace, which was donated by Andrew Carnegie. Each ornate room inside the impressive palace is decorated by a different country. The fifteen independent judges are known as "members" of the court (Sachs, 31).

The purpose of the court is the rule in cases involving states. Proceedings may not be instituted by or against an individual, corporation, or other entity that is not a state under international law; however, where an individual, corporation, or other entity is involved with a country, that case would have automatic access to the court. The court rules on legal disputes which involve differences in interpretations of specific bilateral or multilateral treaties or other legal instruments. It also provides advisory opinions requested by the General Assembly, Security Council, or authorized specialized agencies. It rules on disputes over territorial claims and territorial possessions, disputes relating to the Law of the Sea, and disputes involving commercial interests or property rights (Sachs, 32–33).

According to Edward Bok, the World Court is an American idea. In referring to the Permanent Court of International Justice created after World War I, he wrote:

> We proclaimed it for years: we argued for it: we labored for it and finally it was worked out, very largely, by the best American brains. It is of American origination: it came into the world consciousness because of American initiative: it is American in its conception and American in its reflection of our strong national belief in courts of justice.
>
> —de Bustamente, 6

The International Centre for Settlement of Investment Disputes (ICSID)

The International Centre for Settlement of Investment Disputes, established in 1966, has one hundred and thirty-nine signatory states and is divided up by regions of the world. There are now over one thousand investment treaties, and most of them provide for the settlement by ICSID arbitration of disputes arising out of investments covered by the treaties. What this means is that various country laws now provide for the ICSID to arbitrate investment disputes. Some of the laws and treaties also provide for the submission of disputes to ad hoc arbitration under the Arbitration Rules of the United Nations Commission on International Trade Law. The Organization for Economic Cooperation and Development (OECD) continues to work toward that goal as well.

The Centre also prepares publications and carries out research and advisory work in the fields of arbitration and investment law, and is working on the multivolume *Investment Laws of the World* and *Investment Treaties*. Some of the cases heard in 1987 included: *American Manufacturing & Trading, Inc.* v. *Republic of Zaire; Phil-*

ippe Gruslin v. *The Government of Malaysia*; and *Tradex Hellas S.A.* v. *The Republic of Albania.*

The arbitration process includes a panel of conciliators and a panel of arbitrators. Each contracting state may designate up to four persons to each panel and the chairman of the administrative council may designate up to ten persons.

The administrative council has been meeting for twenty-nine years (1996) and convenes before or during each annual World Bank meeting. The activities of the Centre are financed by income received from its arbitration proceedings. It interacts and interfaces with the International Chamber of Commerce and many of the agencies and committees of the United Nations and the World Bank.

The Law of the Sea

The Law of the Sea was negotiated over a period of seventeen years and placed into effect on December 10, 1982. This gigantic and complex law, which consists of seventeen parts, nine annexes, and over four hundred and thirty-five articles, created an international governmental infrastructure over all ocean space and the territory above to the heavens.

The organizational structure of the Law of the Sea itself looks much like a "mini-United Nations," with a *Council,* which consists of thirty-six members who have the power to enter into agreements with the U.N. and to oversee two commissions—the Legal and Technical Commission and the Economic Planning Commission, which is involved with the mining and management of mineral resources; the *Assembly,* which elects a Secretary-General, and is the governmental board of the *Enterprise*; and the *Secretariat.* What makes the Law of the Sea different from other U.N. agencies is that it has a profit-making entity. This new profit-making arm, the Enterprise, will provide the United Nations with income from the sale of permits or rights to mine the ocean beds. Debts incurred by the Enterprise in raising the other half of funds shall be guaranteed by all states' parties.

At the time the Final Act was signed, then Secretary-General Javier Perez de Cuellar said: "Efforts begun almost **fourteen** years ago to establish a new legal order for ocean space are now irrevocably transformed." The statute states:

> The Convention itself establishes a *comprehensive framework* for the *regulation* of *all* ocean space. It contains provisions governing, inter alia, the limits of national jurisdiction over ocean space, access to the seas, navigation, protection and preservation of the marine environment, exploitation of living resources and conservation, scientific research, sea-bed mining and other exploitation of non-living resources, and other settlement disputes. In addition, it *establishes new* international bodies to carry out functions for the realization of specific objectives [emphasis mine].

The Tribunal for the Law of the Sea will hear disputes between countries and companies on mining rights for the oceans and seas of the world. Do you wonder why the price of fish has gone up? The United States has not ratified this treaty yet. It will probably be brought up in 1999.

The World Conference on Human Rights

In June 1993, seven thousand participants, which included representatives from more than eight hundred nongovernmental organizations, met in Vienna to consider a Programme of Action to strengthen human rights around the world. The secretary general of the conference, Mr. Ibbrahima Fall, said the Vienna Declaration "provides the international community with a new 'framework of planning, dialogue and cooperation' that will enable a holistic approach to promoting human rights and involve actors at all levels—international, national, and local" (U.N. Department of Public Information [UNDPI], 2).

U.N. Secretary-General Boutros Boutros-Ghali said human rights

brings us face to face with the most challenging dialectical conflict ever: between "identity" and "otherness," between the "myself" and "others." Thus the human rights that we proclaim . . .
can be brought about only if we transcend ourselves . . . to find
our common essence beyond our apparent divisions, our temporary differences, our ideological and cultural barriers.

—UNDPI, 7

The Secretary-General went on to explain that in 1986 the General
Assembly adopted a "Declaration on the Right to Development,"
which states that "the human person is the central subject of development and should be the active participant and beneficiary of the
right to development." He further elaborated by saying, "There can
be no sustainable development without promoting democracy and,
thus, without human rights" (UNDPI, 18).

It should be noted that the Declaration on Human Rights includes one hundred and thirty-nine clauses and spans fifty pages.
These rights "reaffirm their [nation-states] commitment to the purposes and principles contained in the Charter of the United Nations and the Universal Declaration of Human Rights" and emphasizes "the responsibilities of all States, in conformity with the Charter
. . . and international law." It affirms that "human rights and fundamental freedoms are the birthright of all human beings, their
protection and promotion is the first responsibility of Governments"
(UNDPI, 28). Furthermore, it states that

all human rights are universal, indivisible and interdependent
and interrelated. . . . It is the duty of States, regardless of their
political, economic and cultural systems, to promote and protect
all human rights and fundamental freedoms. The processes of
promoting and protecting human rights should be conducted in
conformity with the purpose and principles of the Charter of the
United Nations.

—UNDPI, 30

There is much in this list of human rights, such as the transfer of wealth to "help alleviate the external debt burden of developing countries," the empowerment of nongovernmental organizations "to create favorable conditions at the national, regional, and international levels to ensure the full and effective enjoyment of human rights," and protection against terrorism "in all its forms and manifestations as well as linkage in some countries to drug trafficking . . . aimed at the destruction of human rights, fundamental freedoms and democracy" (UNDPI, 32). Sad to say, the laws of the world are not based on the United States Constitution or our Bill of Rights, which guarantee that we have unalienable rights, which cannot be altered, amended, or taken away, which come from God not government, and which cannot be numbered.

In short, the Vienna Declaration defines human rights to include the right to have access to basic resources, education, health services, food, housing, employment, and the fair distribution of income. In order to provide this for **all** people of the world, there will have to be a transfer of wealth from those who have to those who don't. Perhaps this is the "economic privation" which will become part of future crimes.

Most recently, Bill Clinton issued an executive order to implement the United Nations Declaration on Human Rights.

THE GROUP OF SEVEN/GROUP OF EIGHT

Although I was curious about the actions that the Group of Seven made public in 1996, I did not realize that they were setting up the infrastructure for the International Criminal Court through mutual cooperation between various levels of law enforcement worldwide (e.g., extradition procedures, etc.).

Group of Seven

For most people, the phrase "Group of Seven" has no meaning because of the lack of understanding about who its members are and their roles in international affairs. However, since 1975, the leaders of the most industrialized nations—the United States, Canada, Germany, Japan, Italy, Great Britain, and France—have met to discuss global problems and how the world should approach the twenty-first century. Russia was added in 1998, making it the Group of Eight. While the conventional thinking of most Americans is that each country is responsible for its own fate, the Group of Seven stated early on that the "interdependence of our destinies makes it necessary . . . to work toward mutually consistent economic strategies through better cooperation" (Group of Seven 1998 Joint Declaration, San Juan, Puerto Rico).

Over and over again, as I have attended three G-7/G-8 meetings, I have seen a continuous process designed to integrate our countries in every way conceivable. The title of the final communique or document summarizing the agreements among the Group of Seven leaders in Lyon in 1996 was entitled "Toward Greater Security and Stability in a More Cooperative World." Beginning with that summit and continuing on at the Denver Summit in 1997, the emphasis was for the G-7/G-8 countries to find a way to work together on mutual *international* problems. However in Birmingham, England, in 1998, the emphasis was entirely different. There was a concerted effort to work on "common" national problems together. This shows a definite progression to integrate policies and procedures from the international level to the national level, and is another step toward integrating the countries of the world into one cohesive unit.

Although in the beginning the G-7 only handled economic affairs, in 1981 it issued its first statement on terrorism. While there have been other statements since then, it was not until the 1996 Lyon Summit that the "Forty Points" were issued to fight terrorism. Agreeing to work together as one, the Forty Points encourage G-7 nations to:

1. Enter into mutual legal assistance arrangements in order to exchange information on transnational/terrorist cases.
2. Assist one another in cases that may not be in their jurisdictions.
3. Insure that mutual assistance treaties provide comprehensive assistance.

4. Coordinate prosecutions when crimes involve more than one country.

5. Develop an international network for extradition to insure that criminals and terrorists have nowhere to hide.

6. Establish a Central Authority that would be structured to provide coordination of requests. The Central Authority should provide control and prioritizing for incoming/outgoing requests. Direct exchange of information between law enforcement agencies should be permitted by domestic laws or arrangements.

7. When extradition is impossible, insure that criminals and terrorists are brought to justice and tried through other mechanisms.

8. Intensify mutual education in one another's legal systems and exchange law enforcement/judicial personnel that combat criminals and terrorists.

9. Develop reciprocal arrangements for witness protection.

10. Intensify efforts to use new technologies to obtain testimony and information from witnesses outside the country.

11. Take all lawful steps available to prevent one's national territory from providing safe haven to criminals.

12. Strengthen the work of Interpol to combat transnational crime and terrorism.

13. Enhance the use of law enforcement liaison officers posted to other countries to combat organized crime and terrorism.

14. Combat the spread of international firearms trafficking.

15. Increase sharing of forensic law enforcement expertise.

16. Improve and share electronic surveillance and undercover techniques, taking full account of human rights.

17. Effectively share and protect sensitive information on combatting crime and terrorism.

18. Launch joint enforcement operations against criminal and terrorist operations.

19. Improve national and international training and information sharing on techniques to deter, investigate, and prosecute money laundering.

20. Cooperate to exchange information in money laundering operations.
21. Urge all international organizations to coordinate their work programs to combat international crime and terrorism.

In their statement, G-7 leaders said they "were concerned about the support given to international terrorism through money and arms, sanctuary and training and violent acts such as hijacking." They further resolved to strengthen and broaden action within the international community to prevent and punish such acts. In response to the "Forty Points" from Lyon, the U.S. House passed HR 3953, which enacted many of the G-7's "Forty Points to Combat International Terrorism" and set up a National Commission on Terrorism here in the United States. One wonders if this is the commission that will be used to coordinate requests through the Central Authority.

At the 1997 Group of Eight meeting in Denver, Madeleine Albright announced that the Forty Points had been put in place and that "terrorists would have no place to hide!" In 1998 the final communique issued by the leaders of the G-8 contained stern warnings about drugs and international crime:

> Globalization has been accompanied by a dramatic increase in transnational crime, which takes the form of trafficking in drugs and weapons; smuggling of human beings; the abuse of new technologies to steal, defraud, and evade the law; and the laundering of the proceeds of crime.

Furthermore, such crimes pose a threat to not only "our own citizens and their communities but also [pose] a global threat which can undermine the democratic and economic basis of societies." Please notice the terminology, the integration of countries by way of laws and action. The G-8 leaders announced that they:

1. Supported the efforts to negotiate within the next two years a

United Nations convention against transnational organized crime.

2. Agreed to implement the newly presented ten principles and points of action agreed to by their ministers on high-tech crime. These principles call for close cooperation to reach an agreement on a legal framework for obtaining, presenting, and preserving electronic data as evidence while maintaining privacy protection.

3. Welcomed the FATF decision to continue and enlarge its work to combat money laundering in partnership with regional groups, to establish financial intelligence units (FIUs) where they do not already exist in line with national constitutions and legal systems, and to combat official corruption arising from large flows of criminal money.

5. Committed to developing a multidisciplinary and comprehensive strategy, including principles and an action plan, for future cooperation amongst countries regarding all forms of trafficking of human beings.

6. Endorsed joint law enforcement action against organized crime and welcomed cooperation between competent agencies in tackling criminal networks.

In addition to the above, G-8 leaders asked their ministers to report back by the June 1999 meeting in Germany on the progress of its action plan on high-tech crime, money laundering, and trafficking in human beings, and asked their environment ministers to report back on combatting environmental crime. They also stated the need for states to partner with the international community to combat illicit drugs.

Most recently the White House released a statement commenting that "drug and firearms trafficking, terrorism, money laundering, counterfeiting, illegal alien smuggling, trafficking in women and children, advanced fee scams, credit card fraud, auto theft, economic espionage, intellectual property theft, computer hacking, and public corruption are all linked to international crime activity" and that they are a "serious and potent threat to the American people at home and abroad." As a result, officials outlined ten initiatives to further American efforts to fight international crime. These include:

1. *The International Crime Control Act of 1998,* which will contain significant new law enforcement tools for the fight against international crime;

2. The completion of a Comprehensive Threat Assessment within six months;

3. An international conference on "Upholding Integrity Among Justice and Security Officials" to be held within the next six months and hosted by the vice president;

4. The creation of the U.S. National Infrastructure Protection Center, which will protect interconnected U.S. communications and information systems from attack by international criminals;

5. An increase in border law enforcement through the deployment of advanced detection technology and investment in new resources;

6. A commitment to aggressively deploy new tools so that criminals are denied access to U.S. financial institutions; and

7. Action on a call by the United States for new criminal asset forfeiture regimes worldwide and new asset forfeiture sharing agreements with international partners, and a treaty with the Organization of American States (OAS) partners to fully implement a hemispheric convention to combat the illicit manufacturing of and trafficking in firearms, ammunition, and explosives (this is part of the integration of the United States with the other countries of the Western hemisphere through the Free Trade Areas of the Americas partnership signed in Santiago, Chile, in April 1998).

All of these actions should be rather frightening to the average American, as our whole legal system is being rewritten to include the other countries of the world and our tax dollars used to erect this new legal infrastructure. The new laws will result in a planet that is closely monitored and controlled. The globalists will hunt for the international criminal who might be a terrorist (broad definition), a drug pusher, part of the Mafia, or just a "nationalist."

The end result of all that is being put into place is that the globalists are creating a "sustainable" crime cycle to feed the new court system. Several years ago, *The European* reported on a U.N. conference held in Naples, Italy, convened to counteract international organized crime. A diagram was provided showing the territories of various global crime syndicates and what their specialities were, which included drugs, arms, immigrants, money laundering, cars, nuclear material, body parts, prostitution, baby trafficking, terrorism, rare animals, kidnapping, and piracy. The article further stated that "unhindered by tariffs, quotas, or the long arm of the law, organized crime is booming." It should be noted that under the General Articles of Agreement (GATT) and its commitment to "open borders," trucks can now pass between countries without any bills of lading or inspection. Who knows what is in those trucks or containers? Could be . . . drugs, arms, immigrants, body parts, cars, etc.? Will the ICC try the real criminals? Only time will tell.

NONGOVERNMENTAL ORGANIZATIONS

The empowerment of the United Nations' structure has always been facilitated by nongovernmental organizations. These are groups with a "global peace can only be through a one-world government" philosophy. They are registered as nonprofits and thereby enjoy many exemptions afforded by tax laws. They have consultative status at the United Nations and thereby enjoy power, position, and funding. Nongovernmental organizations could be considered a "civilian army" of the United Nations, as they are lobbying for many U.N. policies at the village, town, city, and state levels across America and around the world. In addition to funding from the U.N., they are also empowered by grants from most of the major foundations, such as Rockefeller, Pew, MacArthur, Mellon, Scaife, Carnegie, and Ford, to name a few. Without the NGOs across America, the U.N. would not have been ratified by our Senate. From an international level, it is the NGOs who have lobbied to expand the radical agenda of the U.N. at various conferences over the last twenty-five years. Lastly, without the support of NGOs, the environmental agenda would be a ridiculous philosophy that no one would even consider.

Under the umbrella of the International Criminal Court Coalition, over eight hundred nongovernmental organizations have lobbied for the ICC both at the United Nations in New York and in Rome. The group's convener was Bill Pace, president of the World Federalist Movement, an organization that has worked to establish world government. Some of the other weightier NGOs include Amnesty International, the European Law Students Association, Human Rights Watch, International Commission of Jurists, Lawyers Committee for Human Rights, Parliamentarians for Global Action, and the Women's Caucus for Gender Justice. All of these organizations are for world government or have no problems with the concept.

Just an aside: My congresswoman, Constance Morella (R–MD), is a member of the Parliamentarians for Global Action. She and Congressman Jim Leach, who chairs the House Banking Committee, have both been long-time members. One should wonder why these individuals are members of an organization that seeks a one-world parliamentary system in every country, when America has a two-party democratic system?

The coalition's demands include:

1. The ICC should have the *broadest possible jurisdiction* over the most serious crimes of international law, such as genocide, war crimes, and crimes against humanity. (This constitutes a loss of sovereignty.)
2. The ICC should have *automatic ("inherent") jurisdiction over genocide, war crimes, and crimes against humanity.* This means that **a state accepts the court's jurisdiction** over these crimes

by ratifying the ICC treaty. (This again constitutes a loss of sovereignty.)

3. The ICC should be able to exercise *universal jurisdiction* over genocide, war crimes, and crimes against humanity in keeping with established rules of international law.

4. The ICC should *complement national criminal justice systems.* The ICC should be able to exercise jurisdiction when it determines that national criminal justice systems fail to carry out their primary responsibility for bringing to justice individuals who commit crimes within the court's jurisdiction. (This means that the step beyond our legal system is the ICC.)

5. The ICC should have an *independent prosecutor* empowered to initiate proceedings of his or her own motion. (This person would have great and vast powers to reach into any country and supersede that country's president/prime minister and court system.)

6. The ICC should be able to perform its tasks free from the interference of any political body, including the U.N. Security Council (S/C) and states. The S/C should not be able to delay or stop ICC investigations or prosecutions. (No check on the actions of the ICC—it would operate without accountability!)

7. All state's parties, including their courts and officials, should be obliged to comply without delay to orders and requests of the ICC at all stages of the proceedings. (This constitutes loss of sovereignty.)

8. The ICC should ensure justice for the victims of international crimes, including women and children, and should ensure that all aspects of its work take gender into account.

To fund their efforts, the ICC Coalition received funds from the governments of Denmark, Norway, Sweden, and the United Kingdom. In addition, they also received monies from the usual pro-U.N./anti-U.S. Constitution foundations which include: the John D. & Catherine T. MacArthur Foundation, the Paul and Daisy Soros Foundation, as well as individual donors and participating NGOs.

I overheard several of the conference's volunteer youth asking about what kind of compensation they were going to receive for their time and energy. The leader responded that there would be something for them and not to worry. I have heard the volunteers discuss this same subject at other conferences. Is it conceivable that today's youth are selling their birthright for a bowl of porridge and a short-term job?

Empowerment of the NGOs

According to *Our Global Neighborhood* (Ramphal, 331), in order for the U.N. system to expand in every way possible to meet their concept of global governance and to enhance the continued expansion of international law, they "look for the emergence of a group of 'good global citizens' states and representatives of civil society organizations [which] should be prepared to work together and provide leadership." They further state that without this group, "the full potential of the international rule of law as a means for peaceful resolution of disputes will remain unrealized."

Several empowerments of the United Nations yet to be fulfilled include a **"people's parliament."** Currently, by the powers given to the NGOs through various treaties, the NGOs are gathering more and more power to enforce their agendas at the local level. Through a number of changes that are taking place, a "people's parliament" is in place. While it may not have a physical chamber from which to operate, it already is operational as a result of NGO empowerment and the key recognition being given to other groups that would be a part of the people's parliament, such as professional groups, foundations, and multinational and transnational corporations.

TRIBUNALS—STEPPING STONES TO THE ICC

The first individual tribunal to be set up since Nuremberg was the International Criminal Tribunal for the former Yugoslavia in 1993. To date, including the budgeted year of 1998, the amount the tribunal has budgeted was $184,609,822. The court has four hundred and two staff members with twenty-nine seconded personnel, twenty-two legal assistants, and two hundred and twenty-one interns from fifty-three countries. They have conducted twenty public indictments against seventy-four individuals, with twenty-six of the accused in custody. The cost to try the seventy-four individuals has been $2,494,727.32 per person (Ferencz [b]).

Most recently, one of its star suspects, Bosnian Serb Milian Kovacevic, died of a heart attack while awaiting trial at The Hague for genocide. A month before, another Serb who had been convicted hung himself in his private cell at the prison in Scheveningen (*Washington Post,* August 8, 1998, A14).

The other tribunal, the International Criminal Tribunal for Rwanda (ICTR), was created at the end of 1994. The ICTR made it explicit that genocide, war crimes, and crimes against humanity would be punishable even if the conflict was national and not international. The cost for Rwanda through 1998 was $56,736,300. So far, thirty-five individuals have had indictments, costing $1,621,037.14 per person. The court employs four hundred and eighty-four persons representing sixty-four nationalities, with six judges and thirteen secondees. Both courts have outlawed the death penalty (Ferencz [b]).

It should be noted that the tribunals are under Security Council control, which hopefully reduces the politics. And the focus of a tribunal is narrow in scope and does not open a door for other types of crimes.

THE COURT

Guidelines for the Court

The following guidelines correspond to the demands of the ICC Coalition listed above:

1-3. The ICC was given automatic ("inherent") jurisdiction for genocide and crimes against humanity for states that ratify the ICC. Non-state parties can accept ICC jurisdiction over a crime. Inherent jurisdiction means that a state accepts the court's jurisdiction over these crimes by ratifying the ICC treaty. The ICC has the same jurisdiction over these crimes as the state. The court will only be able to prosecute where crimes have been committed either by a state that has signed the treaty or on the territory of a signatory. The ICC will be able to exercise jurisdiction over nonstate parties.*

In addition, states can "opt-out" for seven years on war crimes. The United States is against the fact that there is no opt-out for crimes against humanity.

4. Under the principle of "complementarity," the state will take up a case first. The ICC will take over if the state is "unwilling or genuinely unable" to prosecute.

5. The ICC was given an independent prosecutor, which means the prosecutor can refer cases to the ICC *proprio motu*, acting on NGO information.

6. There were limits on the ability of the Security Council to withhold cases from the court. The Security Council can refer cases to the court. Consensus is required among the permanent five members for the council to withhold cases for a year. They will be able to invoke "procedures of national law" when executing a request for cooperation but will have to ensure that national procedures are in place.

7. States will be able to withhold cooperation on grounds of national security.

8. Victims of crimes will be given reparations. Rape, forced pregnancy, and sexual slavery are included as war crimes and crimes against humanity. The definition of gender was defined as "two sexes, male and female, within the context of society."

The Court Is Based on English Law

When individuals are tried at the ICC, **they will not be tried by a**

---

* With regard to the ICC being able to exercise jurisdiction over nonstate parties, U.S. delegate David Scheffer said that it would be a fundamental violation of the principle that states cannot be obligated to a treaty they have not joined. Furthermore, the only way a U.S. citizen could be tried at the ICC is if the state on whose territory the crime is committed does not object. Other inclusions to the ICC include the right to prosecute both sides of an internal armed conflict and the enlistment of soldiers younger than age fifteen.

jury as would be found in the United States, but will be tried by judges. This system of law is patterned after the European form of law. This has grave implications, for if the whole world is to be tried by a system incompatible to ours, then it appears that our system will be modified. Furthermore, the judges will come from all over the world. What could it possibly mean? Do these countries have the same court system? Any person being tried at the ICC could possibly stand before a panel of judges from Russia, Vietnam, Iran, South Africa, Colombia, Thailand, Burma, and North Korea, among others.

Cost of the Court

As mentioned, the ICC is being set up as an independent agency of the United Nations. It is expected that the court will receive funding from the United Nations. The final statute makes it very clear that the court will need to accept voluntary contributions from nongovernmental organizations. We can also assume that it will gladly accept corporate donations and monies from private individuals. We can be assured that, human nature being what it is, those who give will enjoy immunity from prosecution.

How the ICC Will Work

In order for the ICC to work, it will require that all countries lend a helping hand in the form of cooperation. Let us say a foreigner living in Britain is identified as an alleged international criminal. It will be up to the independent prosecutor to issue a warrant for his/her arrest. That warrant will be processed through diplomatic channels, and eventually it will be up to the local or state law enforcement system to process the request, assist with any investigation, serve the warrant, arrest the suspect, and house the suspect in a local or state prison facility until sent to The Hague for trial.

The United Nations has a prison facility inside the Dutch penal compound at Scheveningen. The size of the compound is about to double in order to "accommodate the next wave of anticipated arrests. The facility, which reporters are not permitted to visit" was described recently by inmate Bosanski Samac, currently on medical leave, who was being interviewed. He said he and his fellow suspects "enjoy a common room [that] is equipped with pay TV channels, a dartboard, and ping-pong table, and is supplied with newspapers and the Croatian edition of *Playboy*" (*Washington Post*, August 8, 1998, A 14).

Voting NO

In an October 1997 speech before the United Nations General Assembly, Bill Clinton said this:

> At the dawn of a new century, so full of hope, but not free of peril, more than ever we need a United Nations where people of reason can work through shared problems and take action to combat them, where nations of good will can join in the struggle for freedom and prosperity, where we can shape a future of peace and progress and the preservation of our planet. I applaud the U.N.'s recent resolution calling on its members to join the major international antiterrorism conventions, making clear the emerging international consensus that terrorism is always a crime and never a justifiable political act. And before the century ends, we should establish a permanent international court to prosecute the most serious violations of humanitarian law.
>
> —*Washington Times*, September 23, 1997, 1

At the May 1998 Group of Eight meeting in Birmingham, England, Clinton, along with the other G-8 leaders, again called for an International Criminal Court. However, in Rome the Clinton administration was opposed to the ICC, a stance that was at odds with one of its favorite allies, Britain. The chief reason is that the Department of Defense is concerned about the possibility of American soldiers being tried at the international level.

Voting against the ICC along with the United States were some unlikely bedfellows: China, Libya, India, Qatar, Yemen, Iraq, and Israel. The countries of China with its 1.2 billion people, India with her 800 million people, and America with our 500 million people, comprise the majority of the people of the world. Hopefully this will reduce the power of the court, but only time will tell.

Why would these countries opt out? According to the Final Statute, any country which opts out will not come under the courts jurisdiction. Also it is thought that any country which voted "no" will not be subject to its statutes. However, Jesse Helms says this is not enough. In order for America to be fully protected, we will have to withdraw "from all foreign peacekeeping activities and reopen troop-basing agreements with its allies to protect U.S. forces from prosecution by a new global court." These agreements would include guarantees from foreign countries that they would not extradite any U.S. soldier for trial. In addition, "from the American point of view, the prosecutor will be able to charge citizens of countries that do not sign the treaty." This raises an interesting point since the Final Statute is written in such a way as to lead one to believe that a country voting "no" would not be tried to begin with since the ICC is supposedly only for countries which do not have a developed court system of its own.

Are there other reasons for the U.S. voting no to the ICC? It should be noted that there are those who feel Bill Clinton should be tried for genocide in the war with Iraq, and that Madeleine Albright should be tried for not allowing the U.N. to intervene in the Rwandian war. It again appears that the prosecution process will be "selective."

Future Crimes
There is no doubt that there will be many additional types of crime that will be added in the future. The Final Statute was passed giving the ICC jurisdiction over war crimes, genocide, and crimes against humanity. The crime of aggression was named, but not defined, which means the **Conference of the Parties** will have to meet to provide a definition at a future date. The draft document which the proceedings began with included a clause on **terrorism**. As a result of its vague and contentious verbiage, it was deleted

from the Final Statute. It read:

> Terrorism means undertaking, organizing, sponsoring, ordering, facilitating, financing, encouraging, or tolerating acts of violence against another State directed at persons or property and of such a nature as to create terror, fear or insecurity in the minds of public figures, groups of persons, the general public or populations, for whatever considerations and purposes of a political, philosophical, ideological, racial, ethnic, religious or such other nature that may be invoked to justify them.

During an interview with Dr. Benjamin Ferencz, I asked if the court would try other types of crimes in the future. He replied:

> In the future we will add many crimes. As I indicated before, everything is global—economic, finance, crimes, terrorism, narcotics, or environment—these are all the problems which can only be dealt with in a global way. We have not yet adopted to that reality—we will, step by step. Here we are limiting our focus to those which have already been universally condemned—aggression, war crimes against humanity, and genocide. From here we will move on to things like narcotics, terrorism, and environmental deprivations and economic privation—it is really something unjust about having a billion people in the world living in poverty while a football player makes millions of dollars a year. So this irrationality has got to be dealt with in some way and I have no doubt that it will come.

It is interesting to note that "economic privation" occurs when some people have too much money. Let us consider some candidates: Oprah Winfrey, who made $97 million in 1997; Michael Jordan of the Chicago Bulls, $53 million; and Jordan's teammate, Dennis Rodman, $12.9 million. Three of the one hundred highest-paid CEOs are Casey G. Cowell of U.S. Robotics, who made $33,969,000; James C. Smith of HealthCare Compare Corp., $7,700,00; and

Michael R. Quinlan of McDonalds, $7,700,000 or more (*Chicago Tribune,* May 11, 1997, 2).

Consider that the Group of Seven has been discussing and establishing the infrastructure to combat international financial crime. A possible future crime, which could be construed as obstructing the peace of the world, might be the crime of "aggressive nationalism." In 1996, French president Jacques Chriac affirmed the Group of Seven's commitment to the United Nations Charter as the cornerstone of an international system. In his chairman's statement, he said that "all forms of discrimination and intolerance, including aggressive nationalism" would not be tolerated. Interestingly, President Clinton in his January 28, 1998, State of the Union address said: "America must stand against the poisoned appeals of extreme nationalism. We must combat an unholy axis of new threats from terrorists, international criminals, and drug traffickers."

Sovereignty

For the first time in history, a world body has the right to come into a country and try its citizens if that body believes they are guilty of an international crime. The fact that an international body has the right to extend its reach into a country and prosecute individuals opens the door to further rights "needed" in the future in order for that body to carry out its duties to mankind. In addition, the national laws of every country will have to be altered or amended in order to accommodate the ICC's request for assistance with investigations, the serving of warrants, and the imprisonment of criminals—another breach of national sovereignty. Lastly, the treaty

> violates a fundamental principle of international law by claiming to bind states that are not signatories. It also undermines the U.N. Charter by circumscribing the powers of the Security Council in relation to the Court. In essence, the membership of the U.N. General Assembly, which has never before had binding authority, has assumed the power to indict, prosecute, convict, and jail American or any other nation's citizens. Even proponents of the

treaty concede the danger of the very independent prosecutor mounting some kind of politically motivated vendetta against, say, the president of the United States.

—*Wall Street Journal,* July 20, 1998, 6

Armageddon Set in Utopia

The Wall Street Journal-European said it best in their July 21 editorial entitled "A 'Ken Starr' for the World":

In principle the court should only proceed when national legal systems are unable or unwilling to do the job. But having watched apparently clear documents like the U.S. Constitution perverted for political ends, the intentions of the treaty drafters are of only secondary concern. Ultimately, the law will be what the judges decide it is, and the paramount question therefore becomes the manner of their selection. Disturbingly, both the judges and prosecutor are to be elected by the state parties to the treaty with every country's vote counting equally, and taking into account such politically correct considerations as "the representation of the principal legal systems of the world," "equitable geographical representation," and "a fair representative of female and male judges."

In summary, the head of the Indian delegation, Mr. Dilip Lahiri, said this about why his country voted "No" to the ICC. Perhaps it really sums up the Frankenstein monster that has been birthed.

We have always had in mind a Court that would deal with truly exceptional situations, where the State machinery had collapsed or where the Judicial system was either so flawed, inadequate, or nonexistent that justice had to be meted out through an International Court, because redress was not available within the country. If this is our common understanding, and we have always been told that it is, it must follow that the Statute should have been drafted so that it was clear that the ICC was being estab-

been drafted so that it was clear that the ICC was being established to deal with truly exceptional situations. That, however, has not happened. Instead of legislating for the exception, the scope of the Statute has been broadened so much that it could be misused for political purposes or through misplaced zeal, to address situations and cases for which the ICC was not intended, and where, as a matter of principles, it should not intrude. *What the zealots have achieved, therefore, is a contradiction in terms: a Court framed with Armageddon in mind is set in Utopia* [emphasis mine].

The Aftermath of the ICC

The most blatant use of the new powers of the International Criminal Court has been the arrest of General Augusto Pinochet, the former prime minister of Chile. At the request of the Spanish government, he was arrested by the British government on October 16, 1998, while in a London hospital. The Spanish government, with the help of human rights organizations, compiled a detailed dossier against General Pinochet. He was arrested for crimes against humanity. On December 10, 1998, British Home Secretary Jack Straw approved the request of the Spanish government for Pinochet's extradiction. This action was heralded by human rights groups as the "birth of a new era for human rights, on the very eve of the fiftieth anniversary of the Universal Declaration of Human Rights" and, in particular, Amnesty International, which is involved in the legal battle to extradite the general (*Financial Times*, December 10, 1998, 1). Chilean foreign minister Jose Miguel Insulza responded, "Chile does not recognize the rights of foreign countries to judge crimes committed on Chilean soil" (*Financial Times*, December 10, 1998, 9). This is only the beginning of what is to come—history repeats itself.

As we go to press on December 31, 2000, Bill Clinton signed the ICC Treaty. It will now go to the Senate for full ratification. What this also means is the judicial laws of all countries will be harmonized.

Chapter 10

Conclusion

This book clearly spells out an agenda that goes back to the Garden of Eden—the struggle for control of the heart and soul of the world. I have shown in this book the "teeth" of the modern-day equivalents of the ancient civilizations of the Egyptians (Exodus); the Midianites, Anakims, Emims, Rephaims, and the Horims (Deuteronomy); the Canaanites, Hittites, Amorites, Perizzites, Hivites, and the Jebusites (Joshua); the Amalekites (Judges, 1 & 2 Samuel); the Moabites, Ammonites, and the Edomites (2 Chronicles) in the Old Testament, and the Romans in the New Testament.

The battle is the same now as it was then—spiritual warfare. However, the Israelites in the Old Testament and the apostles and early church in the New Testament understood not only the opposition—where it came from and what it was—but they understood time and seized the moment without counting the cost. Jesus Christ was *born into* world government, Roman law in the first century was universal. It was the equivalent of today's international law through the United Nations. The early Christians certainly understood the rules of Rome and worked around and through it without becoming a part of it or adding to it.

In contrast, the end-time church is *going into* world government **without knowing or understanding its agenda and, therefore, blind as to the approaching hour and how to "stand in the gap."** It is this lack of understanding that makes Christians ripe for compliance. Everyone understands that when an enemy is tangible and out in the open, they will fight in battle to defend motherhood and apple pie. Only those who are committed to serving God in the fullest sense of the term have spiritual eyes to see, ears to hear, and can understand the day and hour in order to seize the moment.

Time

In an article entitled "Kairos Time" by Gwen Shaw, the author discusses the two definitions of "time" as found in the New Testament. She explains:

> The first word is *chronos* (5550 *Strong's Concordance*). This refers to "time as succession, without any moral impact as to the opportunity and accomplishments in that time" (*Lexical Aids to the New Testament* by Spirols Zodhiates). The other Greek word for "time" is *kairos* (2540 *Strong's Concordance*). *Kairos* time is a time of opportunities and accomplishments, and not just the succession of moments. *Chronos* time has no challenge nor accomplishment at all. *Kairos* time implies that which time gives an opportunity to do. It can be better understood as "opportune time"; the necessity of accomplishing the task at hand, whether it is convenient or not, must be grabbed hold of and understood in order for us to fulfill *kairos* time. *Kairos* time is that once-in-a-lifetime opportunity, that second or minute, hour or year, when a golden opportunity is sovereignly given to us by the Almighty. What we do with it can change our lives, the lives of others, a nation, and even the world. It might even save a generation of people from destruction, as it did in the story of Queen Esther who had been made queen "for such a time as this."
>
> *Kairos* time is often related to "crisis time." It is important in these last days that we understand God's timetable and are prepared to play our role in God's plan for our destiny. Sin blinds us and makes us insensitive to *kairos* time. That which could be a *kairos* time in our lives becomes just a *chronos* time, a time of passing moments until life is over, and it's time to die. *The Holy Spirit is calling the Bride of Christ, the church of the Living God, to*

wake up and discern the times. He is anxious for us to understand
that this is kairos *time. This is crisis time. He is urging us to buy up*
every opportunity that God gives us in these passing moments.

—Shaw, 1, 16–19

Eyes to See, Ears to Hear, and a Mind to Understand

For example, consider the wise men who came a great distance to
worship Jesus, the Messiah, the Son of God. They were not only
very learned men who had great wealth, but they studied, searched,
and sought for truth. Out of all the people in the world, only these
three (along with Mary, Joseph, Zechariah, Elizabeth, and their
friends in the local Jewish community—a small remnant) understood world events and discerned the importance of the star in the
east. The wise men acted on their research, which formed their
convictions, and proceeded to follow the star. They seized the moment, which was *kairos* time.

Jesus chose twelve disciples—a remnant—who turned the world
upside down based on what they saw, heard, and understood. You
and I are heirs to a relationship with Jesus Christ, which has been
paid for with His blood and the blood of His disciples or other martyrs (Hebrews 11) throughout all of history who have stood in the
gap. **This is our heritage. Will we forsake it now?**

Today, twenty-one centuries later, the world finds itself again
in world government. This bondage is not as a result of guns and
bullets, but ideology founded and based on "peace." I still find it
amazing that it was the Kennedy administration, not the Eisen-
hower, Johnson, or Nixon administrations, that commissioned the
Report from Iron Mountain to examine how the world would live
"in the absence of war." As explained earlier in this book, there are
too many coincidences between that report and United Nations
goals and objectives.

I have shown how the world, and specifically Americans, have
much to lose, as the last vestiges of our Constitution are in the
process of being replaced by the United Nations Charter and our
form of government is being turned upside-down in order to con-

form to a new type of government based on the United Nations goals and objectives. This new government is called "reinvented government," which is based on communitarianism. Another way to explain it is the "Third Way." It is a merger between capitalism and communism in the same way that sustainable development and globalism are mergers between capitalism and communism.

You and I—as Christians and as Americans—are at a turning point. While I believe a global crisis *may very well be* the catalyst to take us into the "next phase" of world government, I sincerely hope I am wrong. However, the agenda presented here is accurate. I have used the U.N.'s own documents and words of those who espouse and promote this most destructive agenda.

Vision

These are "Noah's days" as well. Days in which those who understand the day and hour will prepare—physically, emotionally, mentally, and spiritually. **If and when a storm of great magnitude hits, will you be anchored deeply enough to "make it"? Or will you bend with the wind of adversity and change?**

How do we put in perspective the day and hour? We must have a vision. The Bible tells us that without a vision the people perish. Without a vision, the apostle Paul who, at his conversion was shown the things he would suffer, would not have established the Christian church. Without a vision, the twelve apostles could not have turned the world upside-down. Without a vision, our forefathers would not have marched in the snow or slept in the cold for a new country that would stand against the tyranny of monarchy. Many gave their lives, fortunes and sacred honor for it.

Formula for Success

There are many ways in which the spiritual battle we face today can be fought and won. In a number of cases in the Old Testament, the Israelites prayed, fasted, and used praise to confound the enemy. In other cases, it was the solid faith of a remnant that went against a multitude. In still other cases, it was a combination of all of the above. In all cases, those choosing to take action understood the strategic importance of the hour—*kairos* time.

What examples do I give you that are similar to the situation we face today? There are many. The two that come to mind are from World War II. The first is the ten Boom family, who risked their possessions, their business, and their lives to protect Jews who came to them from all over Holland. They went against the tyrannical laws of the day to seize the moment and redeem the time—*kairos* time.

The second example is that of the life of Deitrich Bonhoeffer, a German Lutheran theologian, who understood the threat of Hitler and national socialism. As such, Bonhoeffer accepted the Lutheran teaching that there was a distinction between politics and religion. He held this view until Hitler came to power and national socialism grew, destroying the basic values of Christianity, and eventually replacing righteousness with tyranny. He came to view Hitler as an Antichrist, an

arch-destroyer of the world and its basic values, the Antichrist who enjoys destruction, slavery, death, and extinction for their own sake, the Antichrist who wants to pose the negative as positive and creative.

—Bonhoeffer, 34

He felt that

to refrain from taking any part in the attempt to overcome the national socialist regime conflicted too deeply with his view that Christian principles must in some way be translated into human life and that is in the sphere of the material, in state and society, that responsible love had to be manifested.

—Bonhoeffer, 31

Bonhoeffer went on to analyze the state of the church and came up with his "cheap grace/costly grace" concept. He wrote:

Cheap grace is the deadly enemy of the church. Cheap grace means grace as a doctrine, a principle, a system. It means forgiveness of sins proclaimed as a general truth, the love of God taught as the Christian "conception" of God. Cheap grace is the preaching of forgiveness without requiring repentance, baptism without church discipline, communion without confession, absolution without personal confession. Cheap grace is grace without discipleship, grace without the cross, grace without Christ, living and incarnate.

—Bonhoeffer, 30–31, 47

He then contrasted that with costly grace, which he said

is the treasure hidden in the field; for the sake of it a man will gladly go and sell all that he has. It is the pearl of great price which the merchant will sell all his goods to buy. It is the kingly rule of Christ, for whose sake a man will pluck out the eye which causes him to stumble, it is the call of Jesus Christ at which the disciple leaves his nets and follows him. Costly grace is the gospel which must be sought again and again, the gift which must be asked for, the door at which a man must knock. Such grace is costly because it calls us to follow, and it is grace because it costs a man his life, and it is grace because it gives a man the only true life. It is costly because it condemns sin, and grace because it justifies the sinner. Above all, it is costly because it cost God the life of his Son and what has cost God much cannot be cheap for us. Costly grace is the sanctuary of God; it has to be protected from the world, and not thrown to the dogs. It is therefore the living word, the word of God. Costly grace confronts us as a gracious call to follow Jesus; it comes as a word of forgiveness to the broken spirit and contrite heart. The only man who has the right to say that he is justified by grace alone is the man who has left all to follow Christ.

—Bonhoeffer, 47–48, 55

Based on the world government concepts and philosophies as discussed in this book, it would be gravely wrong to tell you "everything is bright and wonderful." You can hear on the news daily how our freedoms are gradually being taken from us. I am told that Chuck Colson recently made the comment that within five years the church would be underground.

The world is looking for both a Redeemer and for men and women, who with uncompromising vision and valor, understand the day and the hour. Every day we are confronted by more reports that America is slipping down a moral abyss that knows no boundaries. Our children have sex shoved down their throats at every turn, the magazines at the checkout counter have articles and pictures on the front cover which should make any person working toward holiness blush. Our schools have become war zones and our kids zombies as their brains, eyes, and ears have been put to sleep and filled with foolishness. We adults, in our quest for material possessions—which signify to the world the level of success that we have achieved—have forgotten our purpose. All of this is in addition to the political and economic sleeves of the global straitjacket.

True leadership means each of us standing as an army of **one** without compromise—understanding the odds and fighting for that which is higher, more pure and noble. To use Peter's words, it is "girding up the loins of your mind" (1 Peter 1:13). These are *kairos* times for end-time servants. Servants are not born, they **become,** through continuous acts of the heart, will, and mind, offering themselves to God for His use. It is the mind that counts the cost and the heart that consents, supported by the will.

I have made the agenda clear, as well as the day and hour which we are living in. Our time in history is God's gift to us. What we do with it is our gift to Him. I leave you with the following scripture and song:

We are troubled on every side, yet not distressed; we are perplexed, but not in despair; persecuted but not forsaken; down cast, but not destroyed; Always bearing about in the body the dying of the Lord Jesus that the life also of Jesus might be made manifest in our body.

—2 Corinthians 4:8–10

Am I a Soldier of the Cross?

Am I a solder of the cross, a Follower of the Lamb? And shall I fear to own his cause, Or blush to speak his name?

Must I be carried to the skies on flowery beds of ease, While others fought to win the prize, And sailed through bloody seas?

Are there no foes for me to face? Must I not stem the flood? Is this vile world a friend to grace, To help me on to God?

Sure I must fight if I would reign; Increase my courage Lord! I'll bear the toil, endure the pain, Supported by the Word.

Jesus told His disciples:

Many prophets and kings have desired to see those things which you see and have not seen them; and to hear those things which you hear, and have not heard them.

—Luke 10:24, *Dake's New Testament,* 71

Are You Being Delphied?

The Rand Corporation in the early 1960s developed the Delphi technique for the purpose of maneuvering segments of the public into accepting predetermined government policies. In the 1970s and '80s, it was ideally used to convince land owners of the merits of accepting joining and general plan maps. Now it is being employed to persuade the public to accept outcome-based education and the licensing of all employees, via endorsements in the Certificate of Initial Mastery (CIM) and Certificate of Advanced Mastery (CAM) programs, a.k.a. school-to-work.

The goal of the Delphi technique is to lead a targeted group of people to a predetermined outcome, while *giving the illusion* of taking public input and *under the pretext* of being accountable to the public. For the Delphi to work, it is critical that the targeted group be kept away from knowledgeable people who could lead them away from the Delphier's *predetermined* outcome.

One variation on the Delphi technique is to use a series of meetings. The attendees are often given a number or a colored card when they enter the room, to determine at which table they are to sit. The purpose of this is to break up the groups of potentially knowledgeable people who arrive together so that they will be sitting with strangers and therefore be subdued.

Typically, at each table is a facilitator, someone who will know which way to help "steer" the group. Usually the people at each table are instructed to answer among themselves some of the questions and arrive at a table *consensus*. Someone is chosen to speak for the table, most of the time it is the person who has been *secretly pre-briefed* about the desired Delphi outcome. The table spokesperson is the only one allowed to address the podium and the others have little opportunity to address the podium or the crowd directly.

Anyone knowledgeable enough, or brave enough, to speak out in opposition will not be welcomed. Often they are told from the podium, "We don't have time to discuss that now," or "We discussed that on another date," or "We can discuss that after the meeting." They will attempt to quiet, isolate, and discredit dissenters. After attending the Delphi meeting, participants may feel uneasy that they are in disagreement with the apparent majority. The Delphi technique is often successful in bluffing people into submission. Don't let them succeed. Call their bluff.

The Delphi technique often uses a series of surveys to bring about "consensus." The surveys are promoted as information gathering regarding the wishes of the targeted public, but in reality they are *designed to manipulate the desired outcome*. The survey will sometimes use a grading like, "agree all of the time," "agree most of the time," "agree some of the time," "agree not much," "agree never." Or, the survey grading will ask the respondents to use ratings like "most important," "moderately important," "least important."

The questions are typically "loaded" questions. An example is the question asked of Oregon teachers on a Delphi technique survey: "Do you agree or disagree that the following elements of H.B. 3565 [Oregon's Education Act for the 21st Century] will lead to improved student learning if implemented?" The survey listed such items for the teachers to agree or disagree with: "site councils," "increased accountability for school site and districts," "full funding for preschool programs to enable all students to enter school ready to learn," "extended school year," "certificate of initial mastery," etc. The question is patently "loaded." For example, site councils are not charged with improving student learning. Their function is to implement the state law, dole out professional development courses and money to selected teachers, and apply for grants from foundations and the federal government. For the teachers to answer "agree" or "disagree" that the site councils will lead to improved student learning is *misdirecting* the respondent.

The Delphi surveys serve to "educate" the people taking the survey. After the first survey is taken, the respondents are given an analysis and told that most people agreed or somewhat agreed on the predetermined outcome. Then usually they are given another survey and asked if they can be *flexible* and try to rethink the "few remaining" areas of disagreement. When the series of surveys are accomplished, the respondents are told that the majority of respondents achieved "consensus" with whatever direction the pollers wanted in the first place.

These techniques were developed decades ago. The Rand Corporation has more recently been developing games that groups of business people, site council members, organizations, etc., can use to help "sell" people on collectivism, consensus vs. majority rule, etc.

Never, ever compromise when it comes to "right and wrong." With the right attitude you shouldn't care what people think, as long as you are standing up for what is right. Accept persecution gratefully.

—*reprinted courtesy of Walters Printing*

The End-Time Servant

by Joan Veon

The servant is not greater than his lord. If they persecuted me, they will also persecute you. . . .

—John 15:20

With the signing of the United Nations Charter in 1945, the type of war fought throughout the ages changed. The battle shifted from the use of force as a strategy for conquering nations, to one of "peace," i.e. no opposition to U.N. agenda. The weapons used would now be in the form of doctrines and philosophies contrary to the Constitution of the United States and the biblical principles contained therein.

As this new war has escalated, Christians looking to keep the *status quo,* which they interpret as peace and quiet, have failed to identify current events with the ageless battle which has been raging since the Garden of Eden. Furthermore, this inability to recognize the call to "stand in the gap"* has rendered them useless for such a time as this.

The End-Time Servant, on the other hand, views the unfolding of current events as a way to anticipate the spiritual and emotional preparation needed for battle. The true End-Time Remnant is comprised of these faithful servants who have a sense of mission.

"The Gap" principal necessitates Christians being in a position to identify the enemy. In order to do so, they must be holy. In order to be holy they must *strive* for inner purity and *crave* truth.

---

* Ezekiel 22:30—Examples: Noah, Abraham, Daniel, David, Rahab, Ruth, Paul, Nicodemus, martyrs, M. Luther, etc.

Discernment comes only as a result of this quest and is a gift from the Lord. It is this process which then leads and guides to the point of "standing in the gap" (John 17:17; 18:37).

End-Time Servants—those choosing to "stand in the gap"—can identify their opponents because they are looking for them. End-Time Servants are on guard as a result of their own spiritual maturity, developed on a daily basis.

Those who "stand in the gap" know automatically, as the level of evil rises, that their lives may be required as a result of their stand. This understanding of the deeper spiritual principles mirrors the sacrifice of Christ for us.

The person who "stands in the gap" must *desire*, above all, to do so. For by the very act, they are separating themselves from the ordinary (complacent, sleepy) Christians who reject their message and who walk by their own power, cloaked with a self-imposed level of righteousness and surface knowledge.

To "stand in the gap" will require vision. To obtain vision, one must *thirst* for it since it only comes with the selfless desire to serve God at any cost. The mind of this ever-ready Christian is constantly analyzing, assessing, weighing, calculating, connecting, and anticipating in order to build, improve, stretch, and determine what is required.

The End-Time Servant will be easily picked out from the rest of humanity by his confidence, joy of the Lord, and overcoming vision. The amount of stature a servant exudes will be etched in the glow of his face and in the refinement of his character. As a result, he will be easily identified by the enemy as he rises above their cowardly form.

The End-Time Servant has control over temptation, knowing that victory is achieved when the flesh is crucified. The armor of the End-Time Servant is steadfastness, boldness, and courage, which are perfected only by fighting the daily skirmishes of the ageless philosophical battle between good and evil. The more the End-Time Servant "stands in the gap," the more prepared he will be to stand fast when it appears that all hell is breaking loose

(2 Corinthians 10:4–5).

As a result of his steadfast vision and battle scars, the End-Time Servant has an unspoken, inaudible relationship with fellow servants as their inner strength—hearing with their hearts and expressing with their eyes—provides that special bond. In quietness and confidence, the End-Time Servant bears the hurts and absorbs the rejection, knowing it is temporary. He recognizes that his efforts may be unknown and unsung in this life (2 Corinthians 11:23–33).

His ability to discern truth from error provides him with the mastery to identify when the next battle will be fought. The lies, deceit, deception, and distortion of the enemy are what summon his inner spirit with justice, truth and boldness. The End-Time Servant craves to be used and prepares daily for the opportunity to serve. It is only through the Remnant's indomitable battle-ready spirit that we will **endure** to the end.

If we fight we will win, if we retreat, we will be destroyed.

—General Douglas MacArthur

Interview with Col. Ron Ray

January 20, 1999

Note: This is the verbal transcript and is in no way to be compared to a written presentation.

JV: Could you comment on the new Marine program?

RR: Let me say that there was a time in the Marine Corps where the recruiting poster said that it was the individual that counted. A phrase which came out of the second Korean war—the one we lost after China came in, the first one we won, was "gung ho" which means to "work together." There is no question that there has always been in the American military subordination. The individual does subordinate himself in taking the oath—he subordinates his personal interests, which may mean family and longevity—for the greater common good, which used to be the commonwealth. That's why we still take an oath which asks God to uphold the principles in the Constitution.

As the true nature of the American military has shifted, Gen. Krulack seems to be trying to create this separate legion with his own value system which is separated and apart. Let me give you some background as to where I am coming from. **What the general is doing is evidence of the problems created for the Marines—and the country—as we departed from the basic principles of what constitutes lawful order, oath of loyalty to the country, the virtues needed in the military, and the use of appeasement as a military policy** (emphasis added).

Lawful Orders and the Oath of Allegiance: As a soldier, you put yourself at risk to defend those principles—once embodied in our way of life—against enemies foreign and domestic. The enlisted oath says, "I will obey the orders of the President of the United States and the officers appointed over me, according to regulations and the Uniform Code of Military Justice, so help me God." In other words only *lawful* orders are obeyed and one cannot be asked to do anything contrary to regulations of the Land and Naval Forces, Article 1, Section 8. The president does not have the authority to make those regulations, only Congress does, and they are elected by "We the People." Thus, the president does not have the authority to send young people to Macedonia under a foreign commander who has taken an oath to the United Nations. Without prior congressional approval the president has been sending American forces to Macedonia since 1993. This constitutes illegal deployments which we've been doing for six years. This problem of illegal deployments was illustrated in the case of the young American soldier who would not wear the U.N. uniform. Yet the president has continued to send troops while many in Congress who have abdicated their rightful power, look the other way. There is a crucial difference between the two.

Now what am I saying? The individual takes an individual oath. To put that in an historical context, the last missed opportunity for Germany to avoid the catastrophe which became World War II was when the oath the officer corp took *to the country* was changed to an oath *to the leader of the country*—Hitler, "the Fuehrer." That was the defining moment when they took an oath of loyalty. Today we are starting to hear more and more about "loyalty" instead of "duty, honor, and country." Loyalty parades are being held all over the country. Veterans are being put together with police and firemen, making for a lot of blurred distinctions. Today America is in **a situation in which Congress' role over the military has been blurred and lost, and the president's authority over the military is totally unconstitutional.**

The blurred distinction between the military and the police

becomes extremely critical when you take into consideration that the policeman assumes a great deal more risk because he uses defensive force, not offensive force which the military uses. The soldiers duty is to make war on enemies, not to make war on Americans. [Please refer to chapter eight and the section on "Military to Seek Military Leader Over Americans."] The police deal with criminal elements within the country as opposed to foreign enemies exterior to the country. At Ruby Ridge and at Waco what you saw with the killing of thirty-some American citizens and children is the blurring of the power lines. There, military assault forces were used against American citizens, an action which used to be just unthinkable. This same thing happened to American citizens in April 1775 in the Boston Commons by the British. Now the idea of the individual being responsible and accountable, including the president, is very important.

Virtue: This was the *esprit de corps* that animated the American Revolution—a spirit of virtue, honor, and patriotism. Virtue is not a religious term; it actually means the simple obedience to truth and reality—being dedicated to reality. The second principle of American military service was that of divine services which was the other *esprit de corps* that animated the War of Independence. Divine services were held originally in our armed services twice a day. Officers were encouraged always to be in attendance as a good example to their men. There was no compulsory Christianity, but they sure gave people an opportunity to come to know the Lord Jesus Christ.

Individual Initiative: Now with regard to individual initiative in our military, every time I've looked at history, as well as my own experience in the Vietnam War, is that individual Marines always have been taught to use initiative. If everybody in the squad was killed and there are two PFCs left, they'd argue over who was senior, and somebody would take command. They were taught assumption of authority, which is initiative, which is individual action. It's not a group thing, which is what they teach in totalitarian countries, and what they taught in Nazi Germany after the loyalty oath was taken in 1937 or 1938. It is what the community countries teach where there's very little initiative below the more senior office level.

You don't see in communist countries what you saw at Normandy—you saw it in lots of battles where an individual soldier not only takes the initiative to attack like Audie Murphy did, but you seen an individual soldier take the initiative to take command because the leaders above him were killed. So there was a balance between individual initiative, integrity, and accountability with teamwork like you see in sports. But we're now starting to see, in my view, something that is approaching initiation. There's a difference between training and initiation. Let me give you an example. In the movie *The Sands of Iwo Jima,* John Wayne left his wife and "married" the corps. We are now starting to get something closer to the foreign legion, with less dedication to the principles of the country, and with a feeling of isolation from the citizenry.

We have been in a state of transition from what we used to be, to what we are in the process of becoming. The change can be marked from the time since the Secretary of War became the Secretary of Defense in the late 1940s. We haven't really won any of the wars that we've had. War has only two possible approaches when the country is threatened. A nation with soldiers committed to "duty, honor, and country" either makes war with victory as the aim, or the nation has "loyal" troops and appeases the enemy by acquiescing in encroachments on liberties and the way of life, and encroachments upon the constitutional or legal protections which soldiers are supposed to defend. There are only those two alternatives.

Appeasement As a Military Policy: To use General MacArthur's words, "Something very new has been introduced." After he was relieved of command during the Korean War, he spent three days testifying before a combined House and Senate Armed Services Committee and Foreign Relations Committee in 1952. In that historic testimony, he said something new had been introduced into the history of arms, and that was the idea of appeasement as a military policy. Appeasement, of course, we saw at Munich as a diplomatic policy, but we'd never seen appeasement as a military policy. That's the first time.

In other words, when diplomacy fails, when men could not agree to settle international disputes diplomatically, and it was because there was already a state of war, you simply declared what was in existence. You declare a state of war—belligerency—in other words, once Pearl Harbor was attacked, a state of war existed and all that Congress had to do was declare *the existence of a state of war,* which changed the nature of the relationship. Most people don't understand what's going on when that happens, because we haven't declared war since after the December 7, 1941, attack. There's no question that the appeasement which was introduced in Korea as military policy had no historical precedent for it. None. *No country or nation ever adopted a military policy of appeasement.* Once military force was used, victory was the goal. Diplomatic appeasement has existed throughout history, *but never military appeasement.* America does not understand, and many in Congress did not understand, what had been said or they would not have permitted what happened in the Vietnam War to follow. MacArthur passed quietly. As he said, "Old soldiers never die, they just fade away." We are now walking on ground which I was never taught. In thirty-four years of Marine Corps service, active, reserve, enlisted, commissioned—from enlisted private to Colonel 06, I was never given a course in the Constitution which I was sworn to defend. These distinctions were not taught to me, and that is no accident.

JV: Would you say that this idea which Krulack was talking about whereby the Marines are kept in the same team for four years, that is the beginning of a new philosophy that is being taught?

RR: I think that's probably true. **We really don't fight wars anymore; we participate in U.N. military missions overtly or co-**

vertly [emphasis added]. We always talk about unit cohesion, *esprit de corps.* The Marine Corps' always talking about *esprit de corps.* Prior to the War Between the States, the Marines didn't play any particularly great role, either on the Conferederate or the Union side. The motto of the Marine Corps was *fortu dide,* which is really kind of an anchor of all virtues. It's more than courage—it's a spiritual quality. It had to do with truth and courage and it was an idea which was inculcated. People who were willing to be under and submit to lawful authority. The centurion in the Bible demonstrated this when he told Jesus, "I train him. I tell him to go, he goes. I tell him to come, he comes. I'm a man under authority. You don't have to go into my house. I'm not worthy, Lord, but I know if you say the word my servant will be healed." He was a man under lawful authority. We had individuals with fortitude and imbued with the spirit of American liberty who were under lawful authority.

The motto of the Marine Corps changed after the Civil War to *semper fidelis,* which means "always faithful." This symbolized a change and I've never found an adequate explanation for the change, nor whether it was always clear what we were being faithful to.

I served in the Marines from 1960 to 1994, and we never heard a lot about God. Now in the Marine Corps that was created on November 10, 1775, divine services were held twice a day and a sermon was required once a week as part of the country's First Principles, which were written by John Adams and passed by the Continental Congress on November 28, 1775. The forty-four principles *include all provisions of the Ten Commandments.* The moral foundations of the country were also the foundations of the American military. By the way, I haven't found an officer or general officer who knew what they were because they are not taught anymore. In fact, the introduction of approved sodomy in the military in 1993 with the "don't ask, don't tell" compromise (which the Republicans and people like Sam Nunn and some so-called conservatives said was a great victory) was a specific surrender of America's first military principle, which required commanding officers and those in authority to show in themselves to be of the highest degree of virtue, honor, and patriotism, and they were specifically charged to do all things necessary and proper to guard against and to suppress immoral and dissolute behavior for the welfare of those under their command. In other words, they were specifically charged to look for and guard against immoral and dissolute behavior because there's nothing that could undermine the American military spirit quicker than immoral and dissolute behavior. In World War I, if a marine or sailor came down with a venereal disease, he was court-martialed. It was a legal and moral issue of the highest regard. During World War II when we began to pass out condoms to our military forces, it was treated as a medical problem. So we've moved a long way from those forty-four principles, and I think Krulack (if he's well-intentioned) is trying to run on the fumes of what was there before, and maybe he's trying to preserve it the best way he knows how. Currently, he still separates men and women in recruit training.

There is something about all of this that has religious connotations. It looks a little bit like some of the homo-eroticism of initiation that you see in some other militaries back through history. Certainly the Greeks had this kind of the idea . . . what do men fight for? Ultimately the question is what are we fighting for? If they only fight for their buddies, which got to be sort of the lexicon . . . the prevailing philosophy after Vietnam was that they fight for each other, they fight for their buddies. If that's true, we've abandoned the important military first principles of duty, honor, and country in fighting to preserve our way of life fighting for liberty, the Constitution, protecting home and family, and perhaps this was summed up as well by one of the greatest generals the Marine Corps produce, who retired in the late 1920s. His name was General Smedley Butler. He had two medals of honor. He was just as distinguised as he could be. At the press conference when he retired, he began to understand that some of the things that we've all identified were happening. They said, "General, sum up your career." He said, "I kept the world safe for United Fruit Company." They said, "What do you mean, General?" He said, "Well, the dollar goes overseas, the flag follows the dollar, and eventually the soldier follows the flag. War is a racket." While that pamphlet was not promoted, it was available through the Marine Corps book service. I don't know any mid-level field grade officer in the Pentagon that doesn't believe that the latest strike in Iraq was politically motivated. They all believe that the timing was politically motivated. But it was carried out. Loyalty.

JV: What you have really explained is sort of like a lady or man who has gained weight over a number of years, and they don't really understand that their body is changing until one day they realize they are not what they used to be. I suppose that is what we are really seeing.

RR: We are. Increasingly we have a military that's willing to do whatever they're told. For example, in the case of the illegal order given to Michael New, the responsible question he asked his superiors, with assistance from me, was: "By what proper authority do you ask me to wear the uniform of another government?" They had no answer because there was no authority for it, so they had to just say shut up and do what you're told, which is absolutism. Absolutism is foreign to American military service, but it has gone from the commander-in-chief down through the chairman of the joint chiefs, and everybody has said yes for so long that finally an E4 corporal asked the appropriate question that *either nobody above him thought to ask,* which is scary, *or they'd asked it and discarded it as a result of the failure to find any authority.*

JV: You bring out what every person should be espousing, and that is a vision, a higher call to higher principles, that man does not write, but comes from God. We're just seeing a complete blurring, this whole thing of community, this whole thing of reinventing government, this whole thing of the U.N. where it's the common good, everything that comes out of Bill Clinton's mouth basically is communism. And by the grace of God, I am able to recognize it, but Americans are not recognizing the philosophical shift that has occurred. They are deceived or asleep.

RR: It's interesting. It's a blurring of three things. First, it's international socialism. Remember, national socialism, or what came out of Germany in the 1930s, was called national socialism. Some called it fascism, which is interesting. Fascism goes back to the metaphor of a bundle of sticks bound very tightly together. There's your "community." They used to start fires when they burned people at the stakes, and they called them the fagots, facie, facie. It was the small sticks, bound tightly together, which would burn hotter and more brightly than a single log would burn. Fascism, or national socialism, had a Germanic or German base, but it wasn't communism. It was created as a bulwark against international communism because Germany still had private property in terms of large corporate ownerships. Those companies, like Krupp and IG Farben, worked in partnership with big government. This is national socialism or fascism. Communism, which says the state owns everything, has been proven not to work, so what we are seeing is the Third Way, the merger of the two worlds, which is international socialism because of the mega-multinational businesses in partnership with government.

JV: You read my book(Prince Charles the Sustainable Prince)!!

Chronology of Actions and Laws Which Have Reduced U.S. Sovereignty

This informational and informal chronology which I have been keeping has been added to many times as I have come across new and relevant material and dates. The purpose has been to understand how world government has evolved. While there may be more entries notating the evolution of the environmental agenda which is why we are losing our personal property rights, it also shows the other components—political, economical, and social. Not all of the information is uniform and not all the sources are noted. This is not an exhaustive list, nor does it include all of the dates that it should since research is ongoing. All U.S. environmental laws are italicized. All actions and laws which have to do with sustainable development are underlined. In some cases an activity may be italicized and underlined. Key activity is boldface.

1864—*The Yosemite Act of 1864 Yellowstone*—The world's first national park
1863—Britain passed the first broad-ranging air pollution legislation in the world and created the first pollution control agency. By 1971 there were still only twelve national environmental agencies in the world; today there are more than one hundred and forty.
1865—The world's first private environmental group (the Commons, Footpaths and Open Spaces Preservation Society) was found-

ed in Britain in 1865; today the world has more than fifteen thousand such groups, a third of them founded after 1972.

1886—The first international agreement on the environment was signed in 1886; today there are more than two hundred and fifty, three-quarters of which were signed after 1960 (McCormick, viii).

1891—*The Forest Reserve Act*

1893—Britain establishes The National Trust, a body to acquire and hold land and property for the nation to protect the nation's cultural and natural heritage from the standardization caused by industrial development (McCormick, 6).

1899—*The River and Harbors Act (RHA)*

1902—*Reclamation Act (RA)*

1902—Cecil Rhodes died and left instructions in his seven wills to find a way to reunite America with Britain.

1905—Rockefeller financed the first Communist Revolution through Jacob Schiff of Kuhn, Loeb & Co.

1910—*Glacier National Park established*

1910—*Insecticide Act (IA)*

1911—"Big Four" Convention for the Preservation and Protection of North Pacific Fur Seals (Russia, Great Britain/Canada, U.S., Japan)

1914—The Royal Institute of International Affairs established in London as the extension of Cecil Rhodes secret organization to bring America back under British rule.

1916—National Park Service Act—Woodrow Wilson passed it. "Preservationists congratulated themselves, was a clear-cut blueprint of what the national parks stood for and how they should be administered. Title to all existing and future national parks passed to the new agency, similarly, the Park Service took over each of the national monuments directly controlled by the Interior Department. Not until 1933 were the Forest Service and War Department also forced to give up the monuments under their jurisdiction" (Runte, 103).

1919—The International Chamber of Commerce (ICC) founded by

a group of international businessmen. As a group, they supported the creation of the United Nations in 1945, regional government or "New Federalism," Medicare, the voucher system for education, federal land use planning, the Equal Rights Amendment, and sustainable development. Local Chamber of Commerces support the ICC and usually mirror their goals.

1919—International Labor Conference created by the Peace Conference.

1921—The Council on Foreign Relations established by John D. Rockefeller in America. It is the counterpart to the Royal Institute of International Affairs.

1931—The Addison Committee was set up and presented a report in Great Britain that advocated the creation of national parks to protect the flora, fauna, and areas of exceptional natural interest and to improve public access. British national parks did not come until after the Second World War, and then took on a very different meaning. Instead of protecting wilderness, they preserved the countryside at large (McCormick, 6).

1934—*Taylor Garing Act (TGA)*

1935—President Franklin Roosevelt added to the great seal of the United States the pyramid topped by the all-seeing eye. Under the symbol is the Latin phase *Novus Ordo Seclorum*, the "New Order of the Ages."

1937—*Flood Control Act (FCA)*

1940—<u>**Washington-OAS Convention on Nature Protection and Wild Life Preservation in the Western Hemisphere—October 12, 1940—in Force 1942—Considered the start of the environmental movement.**</u>

1941—(UN) Food and Agriculture created as a result of the U.S. Nutrition Conference for Defense in 1941.

1945—The United Nations Charter is ratified by our Senate

1945—The United Nations Educational, Scientific and Cultural Organization (UNESCO) created

1945—The United Nations created the International Court of Justice

1945—The United Nations Economic and Social Development created

1945—The United Nations Commission on Human Rights created

1946—**Washington Convention for the Regulation of International Whaling**

1946—The United Nations established the Atomic Energy Commission with the purpose to eliminate all weapons—nuclear, biological, mass destruction, chemical, etc.

1946—The United Nations Economic and Social Council created

1948—The United Nations World Health Organization created

1948—The Inter-American Conference on the Conservation of Renewable Natural Resources in September 1948 was held in Denver and was convened at the request of the Pan-American Union and resolved to ask the Union to take the lead in helping the U.N. promote cooperation between Western governments in dealing with the conservation of natural resources. The twenty-one American governments represented were urged to set up national conservation bodies and to ratify the Western Hemisphere Convention (McCormick, 36).

1949—The Seventh Pacific Science Congress in New Zealand in February

1949—Rome Agreement for the Establishment of the Central Fisheries Council for the Mediterranean

1949—**The U.N. Scientific Conference on the Conservation and Utilization of Resources (UNSCCUR)**—Held at Lake Success, New York, August 17 to September 6, 1949. Organized jointly by FAO, WHO, UNESCO, and the ILO, it was attended by more than five hundred and thirty delegates from forty-nine countries. At fifty-four meetings held under sections on minerals, fuels and energy, water, forests, land and wildlife and fish, the conference discussed global resources questions having to do with increasing pressure on resources, the interdependence of resources, critical shortages of food, forests, animals and fuels, the development of new resources by applied technology, educational resource techniques for underdeveloped countries and the integrated development of river basins.

1950—Paris Convention for the Protection of Birds

1951—Rome International Plant Protection Convention

1951—The Treaty of Paris is signed by France and Germany which created the European Coal and Steel Community as a way to obtain greater economic strength.

1954—London Convention for the Prevention of Pollution of the Sea by Oil

1956—Britain passed the world's first "Clean Air Act"

1957—The Treaty of Rome brought the European Economic Community (EEC) into being with the initial goal of removing trade and economic barriers between member states and unifying their economic policies.

1957—Washington Interim Convention on North Pacific Fur Seals

1957—Geneva-European Agreement Concerning the International Carriage of Dangerous Goods by Road

1958—Geneva Convention on Fishing and Conservation of the Living Resources of the High Seas

1958—*Fish and Wildlife Coordination Act (FWCA)*

1959—Washington Antarctic Treaty

1962—President John Kennedy signs "Declaration of Interdependence"

1962—The Second World Conference on National Parks

1962—Rachael Carson writes *Silent Spring*, which brought together research and ecology. This book has been cited by environmentalists and U.N. supporters as a very important work.

1963—Vienna Convention on Civil Liability for Nuclear Damage

1963—Moscow Treaty Banning Nuclear Weapon Tests in the Atmosphere, in Outer Space,and Under Water—signed by U.S./ U.S.S.R./Britain

1963—**The Kennedy administration authorizes the Special Group —The Report from Iron Mountain**

1963—<u>John Kennedy addresses the annual International Monetary Fund meeting.</u> "Twenty years ago, when the architects of these institutions [Bretton Woods] met to design an international banking structure, the economic life of the world was polarized in overwhelming and even alarming measure, on the United States. So were the worlds monetary reserves. . . . Sixty percent of the gold reserves of the world were here in the United States. . . . There was a need for redistribution of the financial resources of the world. . . . All of this has come about. It did not come about by chance, but by conscious and deliberate and responsible planning. . . . We are now entering upon a new era of economic and financial interdependence. . . . Our gold reserves are . . . [now] forty percent of the world's holdings" (Cuddy, 22).

1964—The United Nations Conference on Trade and Development created

1964—Copenhagen convention for the International Council for the Exploration of the Sea

1964—*Wilderness Act (WA)*

1965—ICOMOS formed. ICOMOS is an international, nongovernmental, historic preservation organization composed of sixty-five national committees and fifteen international specialized committees. These committees form a worldwide alliance for the study and conservation of historic buildings, districts and sites. (Supports UNESCO—World Heritage Convention)

1965—*Solid Waste Disposal Act (SWDA)*

1965—*Water Resources Planning Act (WRPA)*

1966—The United Nations Development Program (UNDP) created

1966—The United Nations Population Fund created

1966—Rio International Convention for the Conservation of Atlantic Tunas

1966—*National Historic Preservation Act (NHPA)*

1967—Treaty on Principles Governing Activities of States in the Exploration and Use of Outer Space (London, Moscow,

Washington)

1967—Environmental Defense Fund formed to pursue legal solutions to environmental damage
(*http://www.edf.org/AboutEDF/d_history.html*)

1968—**The Biosphere Conference** (the Intergovernmental Conference of Experts on the Scientific Basis for Rational Use and Conservation of the Resources of the Biosphere) was held under the auspices of UNESCO in Paris from September 1–13, 1968. The biosphere was defined as "that part of the world in which life can exist, including therefore certain parts of the lithosphere, hydrosphere, and atmosphere." The conference discussed human impact on the biosphere, including the effects of air and water pollution, overgrazing, deforestation, and the drainage of wetlands. An important outcome of the biosphere conferences was the emphasis on the interrelatedness of the environment. **Delegates concluded that the deterioration of the environment was the fault of rapid population growth, urbanization, and industrialization. A massive rural exodus had led to the disappearance of traditions, customary rights, and changes in lifestyles, leading to particularly serious problems in less developed countries. The world "lacked considered, comprehensive policies for managing the environment. It is now abundantly clear that the national policies are mandatory if environmental quality is to be restored and preserved."** Recommendations 1 and 20 argued the case for a new international research program on man and the biosphere. The International Biological Programme was due to close in 1974. A successor to the IBP was discussed, and the Man and the Biosphere program (MAB) was eventually launched in November 1971 (McCormick, 89–90).

1968—Algiers African Convention on the Conservation of Nature and Natural Resources

1968—The Biosphere Reserve Network was established as one pro-

gram area of the Man and Biosphere program of UNESCO
which operates through independent national committees
in each of the participating countries. (*CRS Report for Congress,* June 6, 1996).

1968—*Wild and Scenic Rivers Act (WSRA)*

1968—Paul Erhlich publishes *Population Bomb* on the connection
between human population, resource exploitation, and the
environment. This work is instrumental in the population
reduction movement
(*http://www.pbs.org/population_bomb/*).

1969—Brussels International Convention on Civil Liability for Oil
Pollution Damage

1969—Brussels International Convention Relating to Intervention
on the High Seas in Case of Oil Pollution Casualties

1969—Bonn Agreement on Cooperation for Control of North Sea
Oil Pollution

1969—(US)—National Environmental Protection Act (NEPA)
"Starting with passage of the National Environmental
Protection Act of 1969 and continuing with the Clean Air
Act, Clean Water Act, Endangered Species Act, Surface
Mining Control and Reclamation Act, Coastal Zone Management Act, Superfund, and other laws, the federal government has acquired the means to force municipalities
and private industries to reduce and treat pollution discharges, assess the environmental impact of industrial development, restore lands degraded by mining and oil drilling, and dispose of hazardous waste. One of the linchpins
of these dramatic achievements has been NEPA. NEPA
has considerable influence on the way that federal agencies
and federally funded or approved projects deal with land.
After twenty-five years and some thirty thousand draft
and final environment impact statements, how well has
NEPA fulfilled its purpose and expectations? . . . Sixteen
state legislatures have adopted their own 'little NPAs' while
nineteen states have some level of environmental review

requirements established by statute, executive order, or administrative directors" (Diamond and Noonan, pp. 73–4)

1969—Friends of the Earth forms a non-profit advocacy organization dedicated to protecting the planet
(*http://www.foe.org/*)

1970—**Man and Biosphere (MAB) established at UNESCO general conference. The International Coordinating Council was chartered. MAB builds on the former International Biological Program (IBP).**

1970—Environmental laws passed in the U.S. include the *Clean Air Act (CAA) and Occupational Safety and Health Act (OSHA).*

1970—The First Earth Day held as a national teach-in on the environment.

1970—Executive J passed on March 19, which recognizes the United Nations as world government.

1971—*Convention on Wetlands of International Importance, Especially as Waterfowl Habitat (Wetlands Convention) (concluded at Ramsar, February 2, 1971)—Depository: UNESCO*

1971—Richard Nixon severed any connection the dollar had with the gold standard. From August 13, 1971, all currencies of the world floated against one another.

1972—**Convention for the Protection of the World Cultural and Natural Heritage—UNESCO** meeting in Paris from October 17–November 21, 1972—Entered into force—U.S.—Depositary: UNESCO—This convention was originally suggested by the U.S. in 1972 and the U.S. was the first country to ratify it in 1973. The convention came into force in December 1975 after twenty UNESCO member states had adhered to it. On signing the convention, each country pledges to conserve the cultural and natural sites within its borders that are recognized as being of exceptional and universal value. In return, the international community helps them protect these treasures. Currently there are three hundred and fifty-eight sites listed, of which two hundred and sixty are cultural; eighty-four, natural; and fourteen, mixed cultural and natural sites located in eighty-two countries.

1972—The U.N. created a new environmental program—The United Nations Environment Programme (UNEP); by 1980 almost all the major international organizations—from the World Bank to the European Community and the OECD—had taken policy positions on the environment (McCormick, viii).

1972—The first Green Party founded in New Zealand. By 1988, fourteen countries had functioning Green parties; eight had returned members to their national assemblies; and eleven Green members sat in the European parliament (McCormick, viii).

1972—**Stockholm "Earth Summit"—Mandate for the set up of eco systems in the Programme of Action**
(*http://www.www.unep.org/*)

1972—London Convention on the Prohibition of the Development, Production, and Stockpiling of Bacteriological and Toxin Weapons, and on their Destruction

1972—**Convention on Marine Waste Dumping**

1972—*Marine Mammal Protection Act*

1972—**Water Pollution Control Act (WPCA)**

1972—*Marine Protection, Research and Sanctuaries Act (MPRSA)*

1972—*Coastal Zone Management Act (CZMA)*

1972—*Home Control Act (HCA)*

1972—*Federal Insecticide, Fungicide and Rodenticide Act (FIFRA)*

1972—*Parks and Waterways Safety Act (PWSA)*

1972—**The Water Quality Act**

1972—**Club of Rome publishes "Limits to Growth," controversial because it predicts dire consequences if population growth is not slowed**
(*http://www.clubofrome.org/globis_develop_cont1.htm*)

1973—(February) The world currency markets closed due to the dollar dropping below set parameters. In May, President Nixon calls together the presidents/prime ministers and financial ministers of France, Germany, and Britain to meet to discuss the world economic situation. The Group of Five, which became the Group of Seven, birthed in 1975.

1973—The U.N. World Food Council established

1973—**Convention on International Trade in Endangered Species of Wild Fauna and Flora (CITES) in Washington D.C., March 3, 1973, entered into force for the U.S. July 1, 1975— Depository: Federal Department for Foreign Affairs of the Swiss Confederation, Bern**

1973—*The Endangered Species Act*
(*http://www.fws.gov/~r9endspp/esa.html*)

1973—**London International Convention for the Prevention of Pollution from Ships (MARPOL)**

1974—Geneva Convention Concerning Prevention and Control of Occupational Hazards Caused by Carcinogenic Substances and Agents

1974—Paris Convention for the Prevention of Marine Pollution from Land-Based Sources

1974—The concept of biosphere reserves as originated by a task force of UNESCO's Man and Biosphere Program in 1972 was launched in 1976, and as of March 1995 has grown to include three hundred and twenty-four reserves in eighty-two countries. The objective is achieving a sustainable balance between the sometimes-conflicting goals of conserving biological diversity, promoting economic development, and maintaining associated cultural values (Seville Strategy).

1974—The United Nations General Assembly called for the United Nations Environment Programme, the International Union for Conservation of Nature and Natural Resources (IUCN), now called the World Conservation Union, and the World Wildlife Fund (WWF) to "develop guidelines to help Governments in the management of their living resources through the formulation of a world conservation strategy" (U.N. General Assembly 38th Session, "Resolutions and Decisions adopted by the General Assembly during its Thirty-Eighth Session," September 20–December 20, 1983, and June 26, 1984, 129, A/38/47).

1974—**The U.S. Department of State established a U.S. National Committee for the MAB Program to guide the development of national research, education, and training activities. The long-term goal of the U.S. MAB Program is to contribute to achieving a sustainable society early in the twenty-first century (source: U.S. Man and Biosphere Program).**

1974—*Safe Drinking Water Act (SDWA)*

1974—*Energy Supply and Environmental Coordination Act (ESE-CA)*

1974—World Food Conference—Rome

1975—The first Group of Five met for the first time in Rambouillet, France. Participants included the presidents/prime ministers of the U.S., France, Germany, and England. They decided that a group of world leaders meeting to monitor the world currency markets was needed.

1976—The Group of Five became the Group of Seven with the invitation of Japan and Italy.

1976—Convention of Protection of the Rhine Against Chemical Pollution

1976—Barcelona Convention for the Protection of the Mediterranean Sea Against Pollution

1976—Habitat I—Canada

1976—*Toxic Substances Control Act (TSCA)*

1976—*Federal Land Policy and Management Act (FLPMA) (very key legislation)*—Gives the BLM an organic mandate that can be construed to impose some ecosystem management responsibilities. The FLPMA calls for managing the public lands to "protect the quality of scientific, scenic, historical, ecological, environmental, air and atmospheric, water resource and archaeological values." (*Ecosystem Management: Status and Potential—Resources Conservation and Recovery* [RCRA], 90).

1976—*The Magnuson Act*—Had a twofold purpose: to declare a fishery conservation zone for U.S. waters that go out to two hundred miles and to prevent over-sifting of the fish within that zone. It expanded the role of the National Marine Fisheries Service and created the system of eight other management councils which were to work with the industry, public and other agencies to development management plan. (*Ecosystem Management: Status and Potential*, 15).

1977—The Group of Seven agreed that the International Monetary fund should play a prominent role in the improved financial facilities in which the G-7 committed themselves to seeking additional resources. They said, "We will seek cooperation in appropriate international institutions, such as the U.N., the World Bank, the IMF, the GATT, and OECD."

1977—Geneva Convention Concerning Protection of Workers Against Occupational Hazards in the Working Environment Due to Air Pollution, Noise and Vibration

1977—*Clean Air Act Amendments*

1977—*Clean Water Act (CWA)*

1977—*Surface Mining Control and Reclamation Act (SMCRA)*

1977—*Soil and Water Resources Conservation Act (SWRCA)*

1978—Nairobi—Principles of Conduct in the Field of the Environment for the Guidance of States in the Conservation and Harmonious Utilization of Natural Resources Shared by Two or More States

1978—Ottawa Convention of Future Multilateral Cooperation in the Northwest Atlantic Fisheries

1978—*National Park and Recreational Act*—"Across the U.S., preservationists championed dozens of new parks under a wide variety of categories, from seashores and lakeshores to urban recreation areas. The impetus for park expansion reaches its peak in 1977 with the appointment of Rep. Phillip Burton of California to chair the House Subcommittee on National Parks and Insular Affairs. Burton, a strong promoter of local, regional and urban national parks, had pushed through Congress the largest single legislative package in national park history (Runte, 213).

1978—*Endangered Species Act Amendments (ESAA)*

1978—*Enviromental Education Act (EEA)*

1978—Amoco Cadiz Oil Spill

1979—**Geneva Convention on Long-Range Transboundary Air Pollution**

1979—Bonn Convention on Conservation of Migratory Species of Animals

1979—**Convention on Conservation of Migratory Species of Wild Animals (Migratory Species Convention)—Concluded at Bonn, June 23, 1979—Depository: Foreign Office of the Federal Republic of Germany, Bonn**

1980—The Monetary Control Act passed by Congress paved the way for money to flow "borderless" around the world without any constraints. For the first time in history, Americans can invest in any foreign country. Simultaneously other countries were passing similar laws which said they could now invest in other countries. This contributed to the $1.5 trillion which moves around the world today on a daily basis looking for the highest return.

1980—Nairobi Provisions for Cooperation between States on Weather Modification

1980—Canberra Convention on the Conservation of Antarctic Marine Living Resources

1980—*Comprehensive Environmental Response Compensation and Liability Act*

1980—**The World Conservation Strategy released by IUCN which discusses the main agents of habitat destruction as poverty, population pressure, social inequity on sustainable development.**

1980—Independent Commission on International Development Issues—publishes "North–South: A Programme for Survival.

1980—President Carter authorizes a study which led to the "Global

2000" report, which recognizes biodiversity for the first time as a characteristic for a properly functioning planet.

1981—Abidjan Convention for the Cooperation in the Protection and Development of the Marine and Coastal Environment of the West and Central African Region

1981—World Health Assembly adopts a Global Strategy for Health for All by 2000.

1981—The Group of Seven issued their first statement on terrorism.

1982—**The Group of Seven lined up the financial ministers of the seven countries to determine how they should interact with the International Monetary Fund.**

1982—**Montego Bay Convention on the Law of the Sea (U.S. has not ratified it)**

1982—Nuclear Waste Policy Act (NWPA)

1982—**U.N. Convention on the Law of the Sea is adopted.**

1982—The United Nations World Charter for Nature is published which adopts that every form of life is unique and should be respected irrespective of its value to humankind.

1983—Geneva International Tropical Timber Agreement

1983—Rome International Undertaking on Plant Genetic Resources

1983—**UNESCO and UNEP** joints convened the First International Biosphere Reserve Congress in Minsk (Belarus) in cooperation with FAO and IUCN. They developed "Action Plan for Biosphere Reserves" which was endorsed by UNESCO and UNEP. The Convention of Biological Diversity was signed at the Earth Summit in 1992.

1983—Bonn Agreement for Cooperation in Dealing with Pollution of the North Sea by Oil and Other Harmful Substances

1983—*Chesapeake Bay Agreement*—The Chesapeake Bay Commission, the governments of Pennsylvania, Maryland, Virginia, District of Columbia, and the U.S. EPA agreed to develop and implement coordinated plans "to improve and protect water quality and living resources of the Chesapeake Bay estuarine system." While non-specific, the 1983 Agreement launched a regional effort to manage the Bay as a whole—as an ecosystem (*Ecosystem Management: Status and Potential,* 179).

1984—Geneva Protocol (1979 LRTAP) for Long-Term Financing of Monitoring and Evaluation Programs

1984—The International Conference on Environment and Economics sponsored by OECD which concludes that the environment and economics should be mutually reinforcing. It helped to shape "Our Common Future" which coined "sustainable development."

1985—Nairobi-Montreal Guidelines for the Protection of the Marine Environment Against Pollution from Land-Based Sources

1985—**Vienna Convention for Protection of the Ozone Layer**

1985—Helsinki Protocol (1979 LRTAP) for Reduction of Sulfur Emissions

1985—Rome International Code of Conduct on the Distribution and Use of Pesticides

1985—**Farm Bill**—*established the Swampbuster Program to restrict farming in wetland areas.*

1985—**The Food Security Act**—The Food Security Act was significant in redirecting environmental policy in the U.S. The right of land owners to make independent decisions about use of land resources was challenged by federal policy. Society proclaimed that owners of agricultural land no longer could make decisions about land resources without consideration of the well-being of the rights of their members of society. (Ecosystem Management: Status and Potential", 246, summary of a workshop convened by the CRS 3/24 -25, 94. Prepared by the Environment and Natural Resources Policy Division of the CRS *for the Committee on Environment and public works—U.S. Senate).*

1985—Climate Change—The meeting of World Meteorological Society, UNEP, International Council of Scientific Unions reports on the build up of CO^2 and other "greenhouse gas-es". Predict global warming.

1986—Convention on Transboundary Movement of Hazardous Wastes (Basle)

1986—Convention on Early Notification of Nuclear Accidents

1986—The Geneva Convention Concerning Safety in the Use of Asbestos

1987—**The Chesapeake Bay Agreement** was expanded by a series of twenty-nine commitments signed December 1987. The commitment covered six areas: living resources, water quality, population growth and development, public information, education and participation, public access, and governance. With the Chesapeake Bay Agreement as a basic charter, the Chesapeake Bay Program grew to become a unique regional institution, guiding and coordinating bay-related activities of literally hundreds of federal, state, local, and interstate government agencies, and working with dozens of nongovernmental business, civic, and environmental organizations as well (*Ecosystem Management: Status and Potential*, 179).

1987—**Our Common Future—The Brundtland Report** by the World Commission on Environment and Development which weaves together social, economic, cultural, and enviromental issues and global solutions for "sustainable development." A key book and applauded by the environmental community and U.N.

1987—The Montreal Protocol on Substances that Deplete the Ozone Layer is adopted.

1988—The Royal Institute of British Architects and the American Institute of Architecture hold a joint conference in Pittsburgh entitled "Remaking the Cities," which is key in setting the tone for radical environmentalism as outlined in the United Nations Programme of Action Agenda 21.

1990—President George Bush uses the phrase "new world order" in calling for unifed action against Iraq in the Gulf War.

1990—**Farm Bill**—The conservation title of 1985 constrained land owner behaviors in a number of ways. Wetlands could no longer be drained for crop production, land could not be brought into crop production without a farm plan being developed to protect local ecosystems, and highly erodible cropland could not be cultivated without use of conservation practices. Landowners were subject to penalties for violation of these regulations. While penalties are relatively minor at this time, the fact that land tenure was challenged successfully is a tremendous change in methodologies of ecosystem management (ibid, 246). "The 1990 Farm Bill added a Wetland Reserve Program that provided easements and financial incentives for farmers willing to preserve and restore wetlands. (It is modeled on the Conservation Reserve Program. Also, the Farmers Home Administration became responsible for reviewing lands obtained through foreclosure and placing easements on lands deemed valuable for conservation. FmHa had placed 110,000 acres into easement as of 1993, authorized the transfer of 95,000 acres of land in fee title to the U.S. Fish and Wildlife Service and other federal and state agencies, and recommended another 200,000 be placed in easement" (Diamond and Noonan, 68–69).

1990—**National Affordable Housing Act**—Established the HOME program. Concomitant with HOME, the National Affordable Housing Act sparked the preparation of the Comprehensive Housing Affordability-Strategy (CHAS) documents, replacing the CDBG. (*Building Public-Private Partnerships to Develop Affordable Housing*, HUD)

1990—U.N. Summit for Children—Important recognition of the impact of the environment on future generations.

1990—Prince Charles holds the organization conference in Charleston, South Carolina, which is key in establishing the Prince of Wales Business Leaders Forum. At this conference chief executive officers from around the world discussed the role of business in the communities. **It concentrated on public-**

private partnerships, as Charles declared, "Governments can't do it by themselves."

1991—Prince Charles delivers a keynote address at a conference commending the Brundtland Commission for their report, "Our Common Future" and for "bringing the term sustainable development into all of our vocabularies." In June 1991 the Prince hosts a high level meeting with world leaders and nongovernmental organizations to determine how to get Agenda 21 (sustainable development) approved at the 1992 Rio Earth Summit.

1991—The theme of the Group of Seven meeting was "Building World Partnership." They stated: "We seek to build world partnership based on common values, and to strengthen the international order. Our aim is to underpin democracy, human rights, the rule of law, and sound economic management. . . . To achieve this aim, we will promote a truly multilateral system. . . . Central to our aim is the need for a stronger, more effective U.N. system, and for the greater attention to the proliferation and transfer of weapons." In addition, the G-7 added the environment to their list of priorities, "Our economic policies should ensure that the use of this planet's resources is sustainable and safeguard the interest of both present and future generations. . . ."

1991—The Third Congress of the European and North American MAB National Committees (EuroMAB) in Strasbourg, France, was held. More than half of UNESCO's recognized biosphere reserves were within the thirty-two countries which comprised EuroMAB.

1991—**The Spirit of Community by Amitai Etzioni is published, which is the "Rights, Responsibilities, and the Communitarian Agenda" for changing America. This book discusses what is needed for "sustainable communities."**

1991—**The U.S. Intermodal Surface Transportation Efficiency Act (ISTEA)** links transportation to land use planning. ISTEA builds on a history of federal planning and environmental review requirements that place a strong emphasis on proving a selected alternative is the most efficient and cost-effective means to address transportation. ISTEA lets states put federal funds where they are most needed, not where categorical slots dictate. It ties transportation investment to regional and local land use plans. ISTEA emphasizes long-range planning. The response of many states and regional planning organizations has been "visioning," an inclusive process that lets citizens, bureaucrats, and elected officials talk about the goals of a plan in a cooperative environment (Diamond and Noonan, 177–8). With ISTEA, Congress affirmed for the first time linkages between transportation and land use planning. Public participation and environmental concerns, including attainment of the Clean Air Act's standards for automobile emissions have gained much stronger standing. ISTEA requires state and local governments, through metropolitan planning organizations to develop comprehensive plans for any transportation projects receiving federal funding.

1992—**The United Nations Conference on the Environment and Development—Rio "Earth Summit"**—". . . Representatives from one hundred and seventy-eight nations met in Brazil in June 1992 to outline the environmental dimensions of a new world order" (Hemphel, 30). "The Rio summit was supposed to inaugurate a new era of international ecological responsibility, . . . but also the start of a global transition to a new century of sustainable development" (ibid, 42). The leaders of the Group of Seven made an effort to attend this conference. At the last minute George Bush changed his mind and attended for a brief period of time.

1992—**Biological Diversity Convention**—Biodiversity—"The principal provisions of the biodiversity treaty went to the heart of sensitive land-use, biotechnology, and sovereignty issues. Foremost on the minds of environmental leaders was the provisions that each part establish "in-situ" conservation measures (Article 8), including designation of protected areas and restoration of degraded ecosystems" (Hemphel, 34).

1992—**Framework Convention on Climate Change**

1992—**The U.S. Forest Service**—In June 1992 the Forest Service announced ecosystem management as the framework for managing the national forests and grasslands. This announcement followed a two-year experiment in ecological approaches to management that was called "New Prospectives." Although ecosystem management is a new **land management philosophy, the Forest Service is well positioned to develop ecological approaches building about nearly one hundred years of land management experience.** This effort is supported by the Organic Act, the Multiple Use-Sustained Yield Act, the National Forest Management Act, and the forestry provision of the 1990 Farm Bill.

1992—The Business Council for Sustainable Development is formed.

1992—The Earth Council is established in Costa Rica as focal point for implementing agreements reached in 1992 at the Earth Summit and linking national sustainable development councils.

(http://www.ecouncil.ac.cr/)

1992—Al Gore publishes *Earth in the Balance* in which he presents an environmental vision of the world in which earth has a greater value than man.

1993—United Nations Human Rights Conference

1993—**President Bill Clinton announces the creation of the President's Council for Sustainable Development.**

(http://www.whitehouse.gov/PCSD/)

1993—First meeting of the U.N. Commission on Sustainable Development—Established to ensure effective follow-up to UNCED, enhance international cooperation and rationalize intergovernmental decisionmaking.

(http://www.un.org/esa/sustdev/)

1993—President Clinton announces, "We intend to redesign, to reinvent, to reinvigorate the entire national government."

1994—*U.S.—Renewable Resources Extension Act (RREA)*—forest ecosystem grants, which are funding program to motivate private forest owners to practice good stewardship. **RREA is the most used line item for ecosystem management.**

1994—The Framework Convention on Climate Change was signed by over one hundred and fifty nations, and entered into force on March 21, 1994, ninety days after its fiftieth ratification had been registered. (Envir. Gov., 33).

1994—U.N. Conference on Population and Development—Cairo— reduce population/sustainable development—World Bank puts third world countries on notice that future loans will be granted based on what that country is doing to reduce their population.

1994—**North American Free Trade Agreement**—It established the North American Agreement on Enviromental Cooperation and the Commission for Environmental Cooperation. (*http://www.cec.org/*)

1994—First Summit of the Americas held in Miami to discuss a new economic bloc to be formed between the thirty-four countries of the Western Hemisphere.

1995—Secretary-General Boutros Boutros-Ghali publishes *An Agenda for Development and An Agenda for Peace.*

1995—**The Social Summit—Copenhagen**

1995—**Fourth Women's Conference—Beijing**

1995—World Business Council for Sustainable Development formed. Comprised of one hundred and twenty leading multinational and transnational corporations who support the United Nations environment agenda.

1996—**Habitat II—Istanbul**

1996—**World Food Summit—Rome**

1996—ISO 14001—International Standards Organization adopts as a voluntary international standard for corporate enviromental management systems.

1996—The United Nations General Assembly holds a special one-week session on the role of public administration which addressed areas of "sustained economic growth, the promotion of social development, facilitating infrastructure development, and protecting the environment, promoting public-private partnerships, managing development programmes and maintaining a legal framework for development."

1998—**The International Criminal Court established in Rome**

1998—April—The Free Trade Areas of the Americas formed in an official signing ceremony with the thirty-three presidents and prime ministers of the Western Hemisphere. This new economic union will ultimately merge these countries into one new unit similiar to what is happening in Europe.

1998—Clinton issues Executive Order 13083—Federalism—which redefines words like "state" so that it includes all types and levels of government, changes "sovereign powers granted to the states" so that the federal agencies have control over the states and allows the president to declare a national emergency which gives FEMA the power to direct federal, state, and local governments.

1999—The euro is launched on January 1, merging the economies and countries of Austria, Belgium, Finland, France, Germany, Ireland, Italy, Luxembourg, the Netherlands, Portugal, and Spain. By 2002, all national paper money will be exchanged for euro paper and coins.

1999—**Clinton issues Executive Order 13107 which establishes a federal agency to enforce compliance with all United Nations human rights treaties, even those which have not been ratified by the Senate.**

1999—**Vice President Gore holds the first global conference on reinventing government, which now is a worldwide movement.**

Appendix E

The President's Commission on Sustainable Development

Source: "The Road to Sustainable Development: A Snapshop of Activites in the United States of America" 3/97 prepared for Rio+5 Meeting called by the Earth Council and chaired by Mr. Maurice Strong, secretary-general of UMCTAD and Mr. Mikhail Gorbachev, president of Green Cross International.
"PPP"=Public Private Partnership

THE BUSINESS COMMUNITY	NONGOVERNMENTAL ORGANIZATIONS	THE FEDERAL GOVERNMENT
Extended Product Responsibility	**Great Printers Project**—NGOs work with small businesses to comply with environment	**White House Interagency Working Group on Sustainable Development**—Work with government agencies
The Evergreen Program—Manufacturers assume responsibility for product to end of useful life.	**Alliance for Environmental Innovation PPP**—Work in partnership with major corporation to reduce waste, prevent pollution, conserve resources. . . . Johnson Wax 1st.	**Other Federal Interagency Working Groups—** —Education for Sustainable Work. Group forum for federal agencies to coordinate/implement education.
Recycling Aerosols	**Sustainable Management of Forested Wetlands**—Nature Conservancy and G-P manage wetlands/ecosystem	—Working Group on Sus. Dev. Indicators change GNP/GDP, accounting, etc. —Working Group Materials/Energy Flows provides point contact for industry, academia, NGOs, state/local gov't who want to work with gov't agencies for energy/mat'l.
Vehicle Recycling Partnerships PPP—Chrysler, Ford, GM w/suppliers and vehicle recyclers	**Working with Communities—Architecture for the Future**—AIA—Committee on the Environment provides forum for SD	
ECO Industrial Parks 1. Zero-emissions eco-industrial park eliminates emissions/wastes, recycle water	**Education**—Arizona International Campus Integrating sustainable development into their liberal arts education	**Federal Offices of Sustainable Development** —Office Sus.Dev./Intergovernment Affairs Assist communities affected by fisheries

—Center of Excellence for Sus. Comm. Provide cities, villages, towns, parks, industrial parks with info on sus. dev.

—Agriculture Dept. Memo commits Agriculture "to balance production/profitability—rural areas

—Education—GLOBE PPP to link students, teachers, and scientists around the world to study the global environment.

Federal Technology Programs

"Technology is a powerful tool for making government more efficient, harmonize growth/environment . . ."

—Industries of Future Partners with industry in areas of scarce R&D resources—aluminum, steel, forest/paper, glass, chem., and petro. refining

—Manufacturing Extension Partnership DOC/TA Mgf. Ext. Partnership (MEP) helps sm./med. busi. adopt new tech.

—Rapid Commercialization Initiative Dept. of Comm./Tech. Admin w/DOD and fed. agencies to bring envir. tech. to mkt.

—National Environmental Tech. Strategy Council is cabinet level & chaired by Clinton. Coord. science, space, tech. in gov't. Builds on Tech. for Sus. Future

U.S. Business Schools—The World Resource Institute established the management institute for the environment and to work with business schools to "green" their curricula.

2. Virtual Eco-industrial Park—minimize impact on environment—supported by block grants

3. Eco-development—nonindustrial apply industrial ecology

Automotive Technology—New Generation of Vehicles (PNGV) **PPP**

LOCAL COMMUNITIES	METROPOLITAN DEVELOPMENT	FEDERAL GOVERMENT
1. Sarasota, FL—In mid-60s planning groups were organized to address economic and environmental concerns. In 1989, entered public-private partnership w/Sarasota County Coop. Ext. to est. nonprofit Florida House Foundation and Learning Center. Foundation offers low-cost mortgages for new houses. Learning Center is forum to discuss sustainability issues. 2. Pattonsburg, MO—Flooded town which received help to initiate sustainable development. 3. St. Louis, MO—The bi-state metropolitan planning organ. has developed a 20-year regional transportation plan. 4. Cleveland, OH—In 1982, CEO from 50 of region's largest co. formed "Cleveland Tomorrow"(CT) to develop initiatives to improve region's economy. Set up: Technology Leadership Council, Cleveland Advanced Manufacturing Campaign, Neighborhood Progress, Inc., a partnership of corps., banks, foundations, and governments to revitalize. Rec'd EPA grants and now new downtown with baseball park, new arena, and new inner harbor.	"Metropolitan regions have become the fundamental building block of the U.S. and are essential to prosperity in the global competitive marketplace. Over 80% of America's population lives/works in metropolitan regions. Gov't has designed the following (PPP): 1. Metropolitan Economic Strategy-PPP—HUD brought civil leaders and public/private sectors to improve air, water, transit, brownfields, parks. 2. Intermodal Surface Transportation Efficiency Act-PPP—ISTEA, DOT helps communities improve transportation. Strengthens regional partnerships—federal, state, local gov't, metropolitan planning, private sector. 3. Brownfields Economic Redevelopment Initiative-PPP—EPA developed "Brownfields Econ. Redev. Init." EPA awarded 78 pilots and will provide a tax incentive. 4. Overall Economic Development Program-PPP—30 years old. Help identify key issues, vision, set goals, improve comm. Multi-stakeholder process, works in partnership with gov't. 5. Empowerment Zones/Enterprise	**Eco-Efficiency Initiatives** 1. The Greening of the White House Improve buildings by new windows, state-of-art heating, ventilation, air conditioning. 2. Recycling Undeliverable Junk Mail Postal Service awarded 5-year contract to Southwest Paper Recycling to collect/recycle undeliverable junk mail. **New Approaches to Environmental Management** 1. Project XL (PPP)—The EPA has used strict command/control approaches to protect/improve environment. XL has been designed to respond to industrial communities and government agencies to implement environmental solutions. 41 facilities. 2. Common Sense Initiative (CSI) (PPP)—EPA sponsored to test innovative flexible solutions to environmental problems and improve cost effectiveness of regulatory systems. 3. Improving Environmental Performance (PPP)—DOD and EPA have launched program to demonstrate alternative environmental management.

Regional, State, and Community

1. Pacific Northwest Regional Council (PPP)—Community leaders established PNRC to implement PCSD's recommendations at regional level. Engaged in economic partnership with Canada and Pacific Rim countries. 28-member council with federal/state agencies, tribal governments, businesses, NGOs to promote sustainable development.

2. Minnesota—In 1993 governor + state envir. quality board appointed 105 people to develop long-term sustainable VISION. Wrote Challenges for Sus. MN which led to change in state legislature. Passed Sus. Forest Resources Act which calls for public-private partnerships to protect and manage MN forest ecosystems. Passed Metropolitan Livable Communities Act to redevelop brownfields/affordable housing. **MN first state to implement sweeping sustainability legislation for sustainable development.**

1. Oregon—Legislature set up Oregon Progress Board to develop a vision.

Communities-PPP—Fosters community-based partnerships w/fed/state to renew/revitalize urban/rural communities. HUD designed 6 empower zones, 4 enter-prise comm.

6. Sustainable Development Challenge Grant-PPP—EPA provides grants to local, state, or tribal gov'ts, NGOs, community groups, universities for regional projects, private/public help for sustainable development.

7. Northwest Forest Plan-PPP—Protects most of region's old growth forests for owl. Set aside parcels to be managed by community.

8. Mojave Desert Ecosystem Initiative-PPP—DOD and DOI initiated a major ecosystem mgmt. planning initiative. DOD does large-scale training and major weapons in desert. Ft. Irwin to be expanded to conduct joint military training. Provides framework for regional conservation. Will install GIS.

9. Farm Bill 1996—Implements PCSD, coordinates economic, envir. and social goals. (a) Environ. Quality Incentive Program (PPP) provides cost-sharing, incentives, assistance to producer for conservation systems. Partnership: USDA, Nat. Resources Conservation Serv., USDA

5. Chattanooga, TN—"Turn around" story on sustainable development. In 1984 city invited all community members to develop common vision and plan for economic, social, and environmental needs= SHARED VISION. Public Private Partnerships formed for downtown redevelopment, revitalizing neighborhoods, education, water pollution. U.N. "Best Practices" city and model for world.

6. Seattle, WA—"Many of Seattle's elected leaders and citizens have embraced concepts of sus. dev. Created three programs: Mayor's Env. Action Agenda, Seattle Comprehensive Plan, and Neighborhood Planning Project. Creating a "sus-tainable Seattle" and "urban village" while reducing urban sprawl.

7. Racine, WI—In 1996, S.C. Johnson, Chamber of Commerce commissioned a poll of residents on economic/environmental/social principles of sustainable development. In 7/96 Johnson sponsored a public forum to share results. 400 people out of 80,000 came. Interim Planning Group was set up and represented by twelve community reps. In process of (1) appointing advisory committee, initiating community visioning, and will report back by November 1997.

Farm Service, plus others. **Helps comply with environ. laws.** (b) Wildlife Habitat Incentives Program (WHIP) (PPP) authorizes $50 million over 7 years to local landowners and users who create/restore wildlife habitat. Participants will receive annual rental to enroll land in "conservation crops." (c) Wetland Reserve Program (PPP) is a voluntary program to restore wetlands on private property. Operated by USDA/NRCS, with other agencies, allows landowners to retire marginal agricultural land for financial incentives, can sell conservation easement or a shred cost contract.

10. Southern Appalachian Assessment-PPP— Cooperative, interagency analysis program designed to provide info. on biological, socio-economic resources in region. Partners: USDA, Forest Service, DOI Fish/Wildlife, National Parks, National Bio. Service, TVA, DOE, Oak Ridge National Laboratory, Georgia, NC, and TN.

11. Rebuilding Fisheries—Building sustainable fisheries means resources must be carefully balanced.

SUSTAINABLE COMMUNITIES NETWORK (SCN)—Partnership of 15 nonprofits to implement local sustainable development programs/approaches. Co-directed by CONCERN, Inc. in Washington, D.C. and Community Sustainability Resource Institute:

1. increase visibility of sustainability
2. facilitate access to timely information
3. provide forum for exchange ideas/information
4. mobilize citizen participation
5. Foster cooperative partnerships!

JOINT CENTER FOR SUSTAINABLE COMMUNITIES—Proposed by National Assoc. of Counties (NACO) and the U.S. Conference of Mayors (USCM) to address needs to promote sustainable development. Idea endorsed by Clinton and funding provided by NACO, USCM, EPA, and Depts. of Commerce and Energy. The JCSC will address economic, environmental, and social needs of cities, provide technical assistance, training, sustainable development information, and funding for community visioning.

Compiled by the Women's International Media Group, Inc., P.O. Box 77, Middletown, MD 21769

Appendix F
Perceived Global Components of World Government

THE BANK FOR INTERNATIONAL SETTLEMENTS
Basle, Switzerland—"The Central Bank's Bank"

GROUP OF TEN
Group of Seven + Switzerland, Holland, Sweden, and Belgium
(comprises the major money centers of the world)

GROUP OF SEVEN
United States, Britain, Canada, France, Italy, Germany, Japan + Russia

THE UNITED NATIONS
The countries left after G-7/G-10 which are called the "G-77,"
comprised of 122 of the remaining countries and considered developing countries.

THE FOUR PILLARS OF THE U.N. AGENDA FOR
implementing world government

| ENVIRONMENTAL | ECONOMIC | SOCIAL | MILITARY/POLITICAL |

I. ENVIRONMENTAL	II. ECONOMIC	III. SOCIAL	IV. MILITARY/POLITICAL

I. ENVIRONMENTAL

Implementing the "Agenda 21" Plans for the Environment (Based on environmental conferences in 1972 and 1992)

AGENDA 21	SUSTAINABLE DEVELOPMENT	THE BIODIVERSITY TREATY	PRESIDENT'S COMM. ON SUSTAINABLE DEVELOPMENT
The U.N. Conference on the Environment and Development in Rio de Janeiro, June 1992 —Established the U.N. Commission on Sustainable Development —Agreed for a bold mandate for change—to reorganize Western civilization —A number of non-legally binding agreements were signed for all types of forests, desertification, and climate change along with biological diversity around nature. **In the future, all personal property rights will change to conform with the environment, i.e. if you have an "endangered species" on your farm, you cannot farm your property. All rights are restricted to the government.**	The concept of sustainable development basically says that there are too many people on planet Earth and that the population of the world must be reduced in order to have enough resources for future generations. The U.N. should be the global custodian of the earth and all of its resources. This means that we will be measured by how much we produce and how much we consume as found in the "family dependency ratio." Every person will be valued according to their usefulness. In addition, the U.N. will control the earth's resources—energy, water, food, and so on. **The concept of sustainable development can be found in the Communist Manifesto and the 1977 U.S.S.R. Constitution.**	Part of Agenda 21 is biodiversity, which is a phrase coined to describe the variety of the genes, species, and ecosystems found on our planet. It embraces all life forms, from plant and animal life to micro-organisms and the water, land, and air in which they live and interact. . . . Al Gore wrote in his book, Earth in the Balance, "We must make the rescue of the environment the central organizing principle for civilization, . . . use every policy and program, every law and institution, every treaty and alliance, every tactic and strategy, every plan and course of action . . . to halt the destruction of the environment and to preserve . . . our ecological system." It moved 50% of the surface of America into protected "ecosystems." There are 47 biospheres in the U.S. occupying over 43.5 million acres of land.	The Senate did NOT ratify the U.N. Biodiversity Treaty, however, Bill Clinton through executive order set up the President's Commission on Sustainable Development, which is in the process of implementing the U.N. Biodiversity Treaty. This treaty will move human beings by 2025 into "protected islands" in which they will not be able to get out or move from. These islands will be surrounded by corridors and buffer zones. There are many laws which are being passed that are moving, bit by bit, thousands of acres into "protected" wildlife, heritage, and ecosystems."

I. ENVIRONMENTAL	II. ECONOMIC	III. SOCIAL	IV. MILITARY/POLITICAL

II. THE BRETTON WOODS MONETARY CONFERENCE
July 1944—Bretton Woods, New Hampshire

THE WORLD BANK	THE INTERNATIONAL MONETARY FUND	THE WORLD TRADE ORGANIZATION	THE GLOBAL SECURITY AND EXCHANGE COMMISSION
Birthed at the U.N. Monetary Conference in 1944, this organization was originally supposed to make reconstruction loans to develop countries after the war. They made two of them and then changed their mandate. Today, they are orchestrating world economic globalization. They have added, besides a number of regional banks in Africa, Latin America, and Asia, a loan guarantee company, and a company to establish stock markets around the world. In addition, they are an originator of loans to poor countries for development. There is much documented evidence that the World Bank is a heavy taskmaster and that Third World countries cannot develop infrastructure because of the debt load. The Bank is also a leader in lending based on sustainable development and population reduction.	The purpose of this fund was originally to help develop war-torn Europe. However, today they basically plan and orchestrate the economic development of countries of the world, looking to bring that development into harmonization and convergence with the U.N.'s overall plans. The Group of Seven finance ministers have agreed to change the direction of the IMF and provide it with the powers of a "world central bank" (U.N. Human Development Report 1994). These include: (1) stabilize global economic activity; (2) lender of last resort of financial institutions; (3) calm jittery financial markets; and (4) create and regulate new international liquidity. The first three are being put into motion now after agreement at the 1996 G-7 meeting in France and the spring IMF/World Bank meeting.	Originally recommended at the 1944 Bretton Woods Conference, the U.S. Senate refused to ratify a "world trading body" in 1948. However, after much lobbying, the GATT was signed into law in the U.S. by a lame duck congress in 12/94. On 1/1/95 GATT became the U.N. World Trade Organization. Lawmakers do not yet understand the extent of their actions when they signed the more than 25,000-page document. It is the goal of the U.N. to have a "world without borders." The WTO basically tears down tariffs, trade barriers, and copyright laws in favor of the global good and "free trade." The WTO will be meeting in December at their first ministerial conference to determine fines for countries who do not implement their 25,000 pages of global rules.	Due to the globalization process which is taking place in the world today, basically every country has established a stock exchange. The International Conference on Security Commissions—IOSCO—in Montreal is working with the Bank for International Settlements to set up and become a "global regulatory agency" which basically makes it a "Global Security and Exchange Commission." They currently think of themselves as a "United Nations of Security Commissions." They recently held their 21st annual meeting in which they have adopted more global regulatory measures that will standardize the regulatory laws worldwide. This encompasses banks, security firms, and exchanges, as well as insurance companies.

I. ENVIRONMENTAL	II. ECONOMIC	III. SOCIAL	IV. MILITARY/POLITICAL

III. SOCIAL

Population Reduction—Cairo 9/94	The Social Summit—Copenhagen 3/95	The Fourth Womens Conference—Beijing 9/95	Habitat II Conference—Istanbul 6/96	The Food Conference Rome 11/96
Here the U.N. passed a very large "Programme of Action" to reduce the population in the world through "family planning clinics and education" under the auspices of international Planned Parenthood, one of their imminent grassroots organizations. The women from the third world complained that all they could get from these clinics were condoms—not even aspirin.	The Social Summit was held under the guise of eliminating hunger, poverty, and social disintegration. However, the real agenda was a world tax for the U.N. This is still a goal, to find a source of funding which is "unlimited" so that they do not have to rely on contributions from member-states. Also, they recommended changes to the IMF, stated above, and are pushing for their own voluntary army. These are goals that they have been working toward basically since their inception in 1945.	This conference, while wanting to change the definition of "family" to include homosexuality, had a hidden agenda under the feminine rhetoric and that is the replacement of national laws with those of international law and sustainable development economics which would measure the production and consumption of every person in the world. Hillary Clinton has a Women's Commission at the White House in which they are advancing the Beijing agenda in the U.S.	This conference did much to show the extent of the U.N. agenda. Instead of the heads of governments making their speeches to the U.N., it was the ministerial level of every government which presented their goals on how they were going to conform with Habitat. The Habitat Agenda clearly and emphatically states that "personal property rights adds to injustice" and that they must be changed for the good of the public. Three mayors from U.S. cities were on the U.S. delegation. Kurt Schmoke from Baltimore said that he saw the participation of the grassroots level in the direct U.N. process as the "new wave of the future."	This conference, like others held before it in the '50s and '70s, is last in a series of mega conferences in which the U.N. was going after the definition of family and population control, not to mention trying to control the food supply in the world. This conference, along with the previous ones listed here, is part of the overall push for world governance through the U.N., negating in our case the U.S. Constitution and bypassing the Senate. International law is comprised of the consensus obtained at these conferences.

I. ENVIRONMENTAL	II. ECONOMIC	III. SOCIAL	IV. MILITARY/POLITICAL

IV. MILITARY/POLITICAL

DEMORALIZATION OF MILITARY

Gays in the military and women in combat.

DISARMAMENT

One of the chief goals of the U.N. is a complete disarmament of the forces and defense capabilities of the member-states so that in the end, the U.N. is dominant. There have been a number of laws and policies passed by the U.S. government toward this end. They are below:

1. FREEDOM FROM WAR—This would place our military under foreign command. State Department Publication 7277 which became Public Law 87-297 has provided for this possibility.
2. UPDATED AMENDMENT TO LAW 87-297—This is called the "Arms Control and Disarmament Amendments Act of 1989."
3. List of planks of the Communist Manifesto and their fulfillment in U.S. law.
4. The giving up of part of Holaman Air Force Base to the Germans—foreign soldiers training in the U.S., including Russians.
5. The establishment of many "Joint Law Enforcement" schools around the world.
6. The 40 points of terrorism agreed to by the G-7 in Lyon, France, which would join and bring our law enforcement under a central foreign command.

The Empowerment of the United Nations: The Teeth Are Added

Note: When I first wrote *Global Straitjacket* in January 1999, I discussed the fact that the "teeth" or major empowerments would be added at some future date to the United Nations structure. These "teeth" would give it absolute power over the countries of the world. In addition, these changes would provide the missing pieces to make it a true world government structure. The teeth were added at the Millennium Summit in September 2000. Here is my account of that meeting.

—Joan Veon, October 2000

On September 6–8, 2000, the presidents, prime ministers, kings, and princes of this world came together to add the teeth to the United Nations in the form of major empowerments and structures. Interestingly enough, the timing of this meeting was exactly nine months after the passing of the second millennium on December 31, 1999. Due to a fifty-year media blackout, most people don't realize that the skinny structure of 1945 has become, for the most part, a full blown government which lacked three necessary components: their own army, a taxing system, and a second chamber where the people of the world would be represented. Basically it was the objective of the 199 world leaders who met to add these "teeth" components. The Millennium Summit meetings basically comprise the beginning of a world parliament.

The United Nations Structure

The United Nations has its own charter (constitution), anthem, and oath. Every single secretary-general has been a communist, socialist, or Marxist. Besides the Secretariat, it has five organs: the International Court of Justice, the General Assembly, the Economic and Social Council, the Security Council, and the Trusteeship Council.

Global Changes Leading to the Millennium Summit

The world has changed dramatically since 1945. Instead of individual nation-states, we have become one as a result of globalization. As a result, we are told that globalization creates inequities and that is what the Millennium Document looks to change. Globalization has been defined many ways. Basically it is the tearing down of borders between countries. Over the last thirty years, political, economic, trade, electronic, and social barriers have been erased, rendering the world one and not separate nation-states, as most people still believe. This was followed by a philosophical change in how the world would be governed. What happened in New York was the merging of all of the various components of globalization.

Economic Globalization (see Chapter 5)

In 1975 the Group of Seven determined that the dollar was too strong and took measures to reduce the value of the dollar against the yen and the Deutsche mark. This agreement is called the "Plaza Accord." Over the years since that time, the dollar has consistently been devalued against these two currencies. As a result of the merging of eleven countries on January 1, 1999, into the Economic and Monetary Union (EMU) the euro was birthed, replacing the Deutsche mark. On January 1, 2000, the dollar, euro, and yen were at parity or within five percent difference in value. What his means is that we have a global currency called by three different names. In the future, they may decide to merge these three and rename what is in essence a global currency.

In 1980 President Carter started the integration of countries by passing the Depository Institution Deregulation and Monetary Control Act, also known as the 1980 Deregulation Act which erased laws prohibiting Americans from investing outside the United States and allowing foreigners to invest here. At the same time, the other Group of Seven countries—Britain, Italy, France, Canada, Japan, and Germany passed similar laws. This resulted not only in a flurry of global and foreign mutual funds investing in countries outside of America, but it created "a $2T borderless flow of money" which travels around the world daily looking for the quickest play or highest return. The finances of America are being integrated with the finances of the other countries of the world.

This was followed by end of the Cold War in 1989 and 1990 when communism was able to fall in Russia without one bullet being fired. With its fall, the world became one politically since we are told we have no enemies to fight. In an interview with Jim Garrison, president of the Gorbachev State of the World Forum, he told me that Gorbachev was driven from office when he tried to restructure the Soviet Union by dragging it, kicking and screaming, into the globalization age.

Interestingly enough, the Cold War has another aspect to it. It is credited for making the world one from a marketing standpoint. All of a sudden, multinational and transnational corporations had additional post-communist countries which could now buy their product. The world is one from a business standpoint!

To facilitate the business world, trade barriers between the countries of the world had to come down. They were eliminated in 1992 when Congress passed the 25,000-page General Agreement on Trade and Tariffs (GATT), now known as the World Trade Organization. Interestingly many other countries ratified the GATT that same year to birth borderless trade, which has given rise to a new powerful actor on the world stage: the transnational corporation which transcends borders.

GATT created a very powerful backlash. For the first time since the Tower of Babel, all the countries of the world were basically united economically. It is trade which allows money to flow and people to buy and sell! By making the world one, something happened: Joe Average farmer, baker, dentist, small manufacturer, etc. in South Africa started to compete with fellow farmers, bakers, dentists, and small manufacturers, etc. around the world instead of locally where he lives. Those who have the educational and market advantage like those in America, win. Those who don't, like Africa and South America, lose, while those who have the cheaper labor and product win over those whose product is priced higher to cover the costs of a standard of living. However, America loses, for it is our standard of living which has to fall in order to compete with the cheaper labor and priced products. This is the inequity of globalization. It is this inequity which requires a transfer of wealth from the U.S. remedy it. Unfortunately, this means a declining standard of living. It is doubtful that the situation in South Africa and Latin America will change. What will change is how we live.

Lastly, in a borderless world you need a global accounting system. Eventually a global stock exchange will emerge to compliment business. These are already in the offing.

The Political—Merging the National Level with the International Level

What is globalization? It is the blending together of economies, people, laws, politics, monies, and social ethics into one. The United Nations has stated that the founders in 1945 set up an open and cooperative system for an international world which has made globalization possible. The United Nations itself is a picture of globalization. When all of the nations of the world formed the UN, they also allowed it to form international governmental counterparts: finance with the International Monetary Fund and World Bank; education with the United Nations Economic, Scientific and Cultural Organization; Agriculture with the Food and Agriculture Organization; Labor with the International Labor Organization; the Supreme Court with the World Court; and Department of State with the General Assembly. Over the last fifty-five years, the United States has sent its own representatives from government to sit in plenaries and debate global issues of finance, agriculture, trade, food, health, education, and state issues. Our government has increasingly relinquished its power over these areas as it has participated in United Nations deliberations as they have rendered to the United Nations federal authority.

Reinventing Government through Public-Private Partnerships
(See Chapter 2)

In March 1993 President Clinton announced his program to reinvent our government. He said, "We intend to redesign, to reinvent, to reinvigorate the entire national government." To do this, the Administration set up the National Performance Review which said that power needed to be transferred from Congress to the executive branch and the bureaucracy. The new core of our own government is public-private partnerships.

A public-private partnership is a partnership (business arrangement which has profit as its goal) between government and business, along with nongovernmental organizations who perform the daily chores of the partnership. The word "public" refers to government—local, county, state, federal, and international levels of government—while "private" refers to nongovernmental groups such as foundations, non-profits, corporations, and individuals. For example, when a public-private partnership owns your sewer facility, that asset has just transferred from government (which you used to own) to this new partnership. As a taxpayer, you not only lose an asset, but the objective of that partnership changes from service to profit and you become a **customer** instead of a **citizen.** In this structure, it is the corporation which is being empowered as they take on "governance" responsibilities which used to be part of governments responsibilities. As power shifts to the deepest pockets (the corporation), the governmental structure of America has changed.

All across America public-private partnerships are being established that solidify the government/corporation as ruler. One of the organizations facilitating this change is the National Council for Public-Private Partnerships in Washington, D.C. Interestingly enough, public-private partnership has been the focus of the United Nations and was publically unveiled in 1996 at the Habitat II Conference and has been integrated since that time in future conferences and Programmes of Action. At Al Gore's First Global Conference on Reinventing Government in 1999, over a dozen countries came to testify how they were reinventing government—we are all doing the same thing. Public-Private Partnerships! You will see how public-private partnerships are now being used at the international level and how they are the core for "global governance."

Social and Environmental Globalization (See Chapter 4— Environment)

From a social and environmental stand point, the United Nations began laying the foundational shift for how the world is to be governed back in the 1970s when they hosted a series of international conferences on the environment, women's issues, population reduction, food, and housing/cities. Twenty years later, the UN revisited these issues with a new set of conferences on the same subjects. The Rio Earth Summit is pivotal.

In 1992 the United Nations sponsored the Conference on Environment and Development, called the "Rio Earth Summit." There, a very radical environmental agenda was unveiled—the effects of which are only now being felt and understood by the American people. In Rio, the United Nations presented their new environmental philosophy by which the world should be governed which basically points in the direction of world government, i.e. the United Nations as caretaker of the world and its resources. This document, known as "Agenda 21," perverts Genesis 1 by insisting that the earth has dominance over man instead of man having dominance over the earth. This new philosophy, known as "Gaia," is the worship of Mother Earth. These ideas now constitute the new way in which the world is being managed.

Electronic Globalization (See Foreword)

What was Y2K? As we have shown in the Foreword to this book, it was the electronic wiring of the world to facilitate world government.

Inequalities Cause by Globalization

Due to the fact that the political and economic barriers have fallen down between countries, this not only makes us ONE, but it also now makes every human being in the world my brother or sister and therefore, according to the United Nations, I am (you are) responsible for their health and well being. The UN Millennium Declaration states that inequalities have been created as a result of globalization. Therefore, they say we need to have a transfer of wealth—directly and indirectly—from us to them in order to make this equation equal.

Using the socialist tenant of transfer of wealth, the United Nations Millennium Declaration states

5. We recognize that developing countries face special difficulties in responding to this central challenge. Only through broad and sustained efforts to create a shared future, based upon our common humanity can globalization be made fully inclusive and equitable.

11. We will spare no effort to free our fellow men, women and children from the abject and dehumanizing conditions of extreme poverty.

12. We resolve to create an environment—at the national and global levels alike—which is conducive to development and to the elimination of poverty.

15. We call on the industrialized countries: to implement the enhanced programme of debt relief for the heavily indebted poor countries without further delay and to agree to cancel all official bilateral debts of those countries in return for their making demonstrable commitments to poverty reduction.

Highly Indebted Poor Countries (HIPCs)

Unfortunately, the 60 highly indebted poor countries, or HIPCs as they are called, include many of the African countries. The World Gold Council has identified half of the HIPCs as being gold producers. This is quite sad when you consider South Africa accounts for 40% of the world's chromium production; between the Congo and Zambia, they are the world's top producers of cobalt used in aircraft gas turbine engines and jet engines; South Africa produces 24% of the world's industrial diamonds, while Botswana, Ghana, Namibia, Angola, South Africa, and the Congo combined account for 49% of the world's gemstones; South Africa has 50% of all the world's gold resources, 80% of the world's manganese resources which is essential for people, animals and plants, 90% of the world's platinum, and about 85% of the world's vanadium.

The Raping of South Africa

We should ask ourselves what happened to Africa? The World Bank. Many of these countries are in dire straits as a result of taking World Bank advice over the years as to how to increase their revenues. They borrowed heavily to finance grandiose plans which the World Bank said would increase future income. Unfortunately 80% of these projects became "white elephants," leaving the country strapped with huge World Bank debts which are still in the process of being repaid. As a result, many of these countries cannot breathe as they do not have sufficient income from the sale of their own resources to erect the proper infrastructure in their countries such as hospitals, roads, schools, clean water plants, and electricity. For example, Ghana is the second largest gold producer in Africa. Gold mining equals 97% of their debt. This means they only have 3% left to run the government and provide services. Unfortunately due to the 30-year low gold prices in 1999, they had to sell 50% of the state-owned gold mine (the only one left) in order to keep the country running for a while. Now the developed countries of the world— you and me—are asked to bail these countries out. In essence, we are bailing out the World Bank! Lastly, the hoops these poor countries have to jump through in order to qualify for "debt reduction" creates another set of chains around their necks. I remember asking Tony Blair at the G-8 in England two years ago about the "new set of hoops these countries would have to jump through" and he took exception to my question and said there would be none. I will assume he was speaking out of ignorance! The World Bank has explained to me what these countries have to do to qualify—it is the worst nightmare you can imagine.

When you look at the state of the world, while most governments are bankrupt, the only people who have money and power are the multinational and transnational corporations! This is pretty scary, as public-private partnerships become a bailout of all levels of government and the United Nations is the organization which is fostering these arrangements. Again—we have to ask ourselves— "Is there a power behind the United Nations?"

A World Parliament Is Birthed

In order to understand the significance of the Millennium Summit—what was and was not said, and what was written—let us take a look at the U.N. 50th Anniversary in 1995.

In September 1995, at the United Nations 50th Anniversary, the presidents, prime ministers, princes, and kings of this world came to celebrate its existence and talk about their goals and concerns at the regular meeting of the General Assembly. At that time, Czech Republic President Vaclav Havel said:

> I have a vision of the UN General Assembly resembling one day *a parliament of the world*. I have a vision of the *UN Security Council assuming additional tasks*. One day it might become the focal point for the operational decision-making of this world organization. I have a vision of the UN one day establishing *a permanent strike force* capable of stopping aggressors as well as a permanent peacekeeping force with more of a policing role. Mine is a vision of a UN consisting not of divided nations but of *united people* [emphasis added].

Five years later, at the dawn of a New Millennium, presidents, prime ministers, princes, and kings came to discuss their vision for a new, empowered, and reformed international organization. What sets this meeting apart from all the others?

First, this meeting was a **special session** of world leaders to put in place a framework for how to reform it. Unlike the 50th anniversary, it had a Programme of Action. Since every mandate, memorandum of understanding, and General Assembly Resolution that is passed constitutes and adds to the body of international law (which governs above the law of the nation-states), the fact that the world's leaders endorsed it automatically incorporates it into international law. This action also constitutes the first time a World Parliament has met. Like our own Congress, the leaders of the world came, debated, and voted on action for the world body to take. Normally our ambassador to the United Nations would represent us as a sovereign country and vote according to how they were told. This time, the leaders of the countries came and directly consented by signing the United Nations Millennium Declaration. This action also sets precedence for the future!

Second, it constitutes a *follow up meeting to the first organizational meeting of the United Nations in 1945!* Interestingly enough none of the press packets included a copy of this very important Programme of Action, nor was it made clear until I asked if this meeting did indeed constitutes a historic follow-up to 1945. Let us review, the United Nation's Charter is not based on any of the principles or values in the United States Constitution. Alger Hiss, who served President Roosevelt as director of the State Department's Office of Special Political Affairs in charge of all post-war planning, led the American delegation to the founding UN conference. Others on the American delegation included Noel Field, Harold Glasser, Irving Kaplan, and Harry Dexter White (who founded the IMF and World Bank and who also was convicted as a communist spy). Alger Hiss became the first secretary-general of the United Nations and in 1950 was exposed and convicted as a Soviet spy. Because the statute of limitations had run out, he ended up being convicted of lying to Congress about his affiliation with the Communist Party. Upon his death several years ago, it was confirmed that he indeed was a communist spy.

Third, these actions make Kofi Annan, the Secretary General, supreme "commander" over all of the world's leaders! This paves the way for a supreme world leader with power over the nations of the world. Let us also remember that just as Kofi Annan is a figurehead, there is a power behind the United Nations which controls the secretary-general. It is interesting to note that Kofi Annan is now involved, along with other Middle East leaders and Bill Clinton, in "shuttle diplomacy" and in solving the violence between the Palestinians and Israelis. All of a sudden, the UN is now actively involved in peacekeeping—something we have not seen before.

The Millennium Declaration states in part:

> We, Heads of State and Government, have a collective responsibility to uphold the principles of human dignity, equality and equity at the global level. We reaffirm our commitment to the purposes and principles of the Charter of the United Nations, which have proved timeless and universal. We believe that the central challenge we face today is to ensure that globalization becomes a positive force for all the world's people.

While leaders spoke about their vision for the UN covering one or more of the above topics, two stood out very clear and indeed point to another major shift in world affairs not really highlighted: the negative side of globalization and the rapid deployment force. Unlike previous years, the leaders were quite candid and opinionated—something that normally occurs in free debates. Back in 1995, only three world leaders had the courage to criticize, thus making the Millennium Summit different.

With regard to a rapid deployment force, in 1995 Vaclav Havel was the only world leader to say the Utopian things he said. However, based on the reforms and goals in the Millennium Document, he was prophetic.

The testimony of two world leaders says it all:

Jacques Chirac, *France:* "Time has changed. A new world has emerged. A world taking shape before our eyes needs common rules, principles and ambition. That is why the time is right for this summit. We must work together to build a new international society that is more civilized, more caring, more just and better managed. The UN is the natural place to undertake this task."

Holy See: "It is the fervent hope of the Holy See that at the dawn of the third millennium the UN will contribute to the building of **a new civilization** for the benefit of all mankind."

Remember: words have meaning and meanings have words.

Key Millennium Documents

The key documents which support the restructuring and reinventing of the United Nations are:

"We the peoples: the role of the United Nations in the twenty-first century by the Secretary-General," dated 27 March 2000, document No. A/54/2000

This document basically sets the tone and provides the outline for what the Secretary-General wanted to accomplish at the Millennium Summit. Most people are aware that Kofi Annan from the time he was appointed in January 1997 until recently had a special adviser: Maurice Strong. Mr. Strong, a close friend of David Rockefeller (who is the originator of the Trilateral Commission and whose family started the Council on Foreign Relations which is the American counterpart to the Royal Institute for International Affairs in London), basically performed the same duties which Col. Mandell House performed for President Wilson. At one point Wilson said something to the effect, "If I said it, Col. House meant to say it, if he said it, I said it. He is my alter-ego." Col. House was affiliated with J. P. Morgan, a British banking family operating in America. Mr. Strong also headed up the first conference on the environment in Stockholm in 1972 and the Rio Earth Summit in 1992. He is a close friend of Mikhail Gorbachev and helped co-sponsor the Earth Charter.

The document has 369 action clauses. I came up with 44 categories. Of those categories the top three were: Global Stewardship: Building a New Ethic (this is the equivalent of changing how the world thinks and is run); Health and Public-Private Partnerships, which had 18 action clauses or double or quadruple the other categories!

"A Comprehensive review of the whole question of peacekeeping operations in all their aspects," Identical letters dated 21 August 2000 from the Secretary General to the President of the General Assembly and the President of the Security Council, document No. A/55/305-S/2000/809

This document is also referred to as "The "Brahimi Report" after the chair of the panel, former Foreign Minister of Algeria, Lakhdar Brahimi. It should make all Americans feel secure to know that the future structure of UN peacekeeping is based on a report from two generals (one who is a retired German officer and the other who is a general from Zimbabwe), two ambassadors from Trinidad and Tobago and the Russian Federation, a former member of Her Majesty's Inspectorate of Constabulary and government adviser on international policing matters from the United Kingdom, a former cabinet minister and permanent representative of New Zealand, a retired UN employee who served as director, Europe and Latin America Division of the Department of Peacekeeping Operations, and Brian Atwood from the United States (who formerly was administrator of USAID). Their recommendations include the following:

1. The Panel recommends a doctrinal shift in the use of civilian police, other rule of law elements and human rights experts in complex peace operations to reflect an increased focus on strengthening rule of law institutions and improving respect for human rights in post-conflict environments

2. Peacekeeping doctrine and strategy: once deployed, UN peacekeepers must be able to carry out their mandates pro-

fessionally and successfully and be capable of defending themselves, other mission components and the mission's mandate

3. The Secretariat must tell the Security Council what it needs to know, not what it wants to hear.

4. The UN should define "rapid and effective deployment capacities" as the ability, to fully deploy traditional peacekeeping operations within 30 days after the adoption of a Security Council resolution.

5. Member states should be encouraged, where appropriate, to enter into partnerships with one another, within the context of the UN Standby Arrangements System (UNSAS) to form several coherent brigade-size forces.

6. The Panel recommends that a revolving "on-call list" of about 100 military officers be created in UNSAS to be available on seven days' notice to augment nuclei of DPKO planners with teams trained to create a mission headquarters for a new peacekeeping operation.

7. Member states are encouraged to each establish a national pool of civilian police officers that would be ready for deployment to UN peace operations on short notice.

8. Member states are encourage to enter into regional training partnerships for civilian police in the respective national pools, to promote a common level of preparedness in accordance with UN guidelines, standard operation procedures and performance standards.

9. The Panel recommends that a revolving on-call list of about 100 police officers and related experts be created in UNSAS to be available on seven day's notice with teams trained to create the civilian police component of a new peacekeeping operation.

10. The Secretary-General should be given authority to draw up to $50 million from the Peacekeeping Reserve Fund.

11. The Panel recommends a substantial increase in recourse for Headquarters support of peacekeeping operations.

12. Peace operations could benefit greatly from more extensive

use of geographic information systems (GIS) technology, which quickly integrates operational information with electronic maps of the mission area, for applications as diverse as demobilization, civilian policing, voter registration, human rights monitoring and reconstruction.

Perhaps we should discuss what the United Nations means by "peace." I have defined it to be the "whole piece (world)" or "no opposition to their agenda." However, to understand the real intent, perhaps we should remember what happed in Katanga in 1961 when UN planes bombed hospitals, schools, administrative buildings, and private homes. Katanga was an anti-communist province of the Belgian Congo seeking freedom from its communist–controlled central government. We would do well to remember that the United States never came to its rescue. And we wonder what spiritual warfare is?

Draft resolution—"United Nations Millennium Declaration" dated 6 September 2000, document No. A/55/L.2;
The Declaration has eight sections: Values and Principles, Peace, Security and Disarmament, Development and Poverty Eradication, Protecting Our Common Environment, Human Rights Democracy and Good Governance, Protecting the Vulnerable, Meeting the Special Needs of Africa, and Strengthening the United Nations. Most of the key issues are addressed above in "We the peoples."

Missing Components Needed to be a World Government
As discussed, there are three missing components in order for the UN to be a world government: its own army, a global tax, and a "People's Chamber" or "International House of Representatives." The Millennium Declaration addressed these issues and confirmed the need for them.

Rapid Deployment Force
The Military Staff Committee of the Security Council has oversight

with regard to peacekeeping missions. According to writer Ted Flynn:

> In 1992 the UN had peacekeeping operations in eleven countries, with 11,496 personnel deployed. By 1994 that had dramatically risen to seven countries, with 73,393 personnel involved. The UN budget for peacekeeping had risen during the same period from $1.7 billion to $3.6 billion of which the U.S. was assessed about $1.2 billion.
>
> —Ted Flynn, *Hope of the Wicked,* MaxKol
> Communications, Herndon, 2000, p. 434

Flynn goes on to write:

> President Clinton has sent combat troops to Somalia, Haiti, Bosnia, Sudan, Afghanistan, East Timor and the Iraq area, all without obtaining advance congressional approval. In a related matter, Rep. Roscoe Bartlett (R-MD) has exposed President Clinton's improper, if not illegal, diversion of over $10 billion in military and other assistance to the UN by ordering U.S. agencies, including the Department of Defense, to implement UN Security Council Resolutions
>
> —Ibid, 435

In June 2000, H.R. 4453 was introduced to transfer 6,000 U.S. troops permanently to UN command, where they would take orders from the United Nations. They would join 36,000 troops from six other countries to comprise a rapid deployment force of 42,000. Bill Clinton called for UN peacekeepers "that can be rapidly deployed with the right training and equipment, missions well-defined and well led, with the necessary civilian police." Britain's Tony Blair said:

> We need UN forces composed of units appropriate for more robust peacekeeping that can be inserted quickly, rather than whatever the Secretary-General's staff has been able to garner from reluctant member states. This means a new contract between the

UN and its members. The UN must alter radically its planning, intelligence and analysis, and develop a far more substantial professional military staff.

We should remember that MacArthur, who was fighting the communists in Korea, could not understand why every time he planned a new offensive, the Chinese were there and he was defeated—not until he figured out that the military plans which he sent to Washington were being forwarded to the United Nations, which in turn was forwarding them to the communists! He was dismissed for disobeying orders—trying to defeat the communists when that was not the intent in the first place!

Bill Clinton: "Peacekeepers that can be rapidly deployed with the right training and equipment, missions well-defined and well-led, with the necessary civilian police." [Note: This is in conjunction with House Bill 4453 calling for 6,000 American soldiers to be placed under the direct control of the United Nations.]

Russia: "I am convinced that relying on [a] just world order and strategic stability shall guarantee sustainable development of the world. And today's Russia, as never before is open, responsible and ready for cooperation on an equitable partnership basis."

Global Taxation

I have been monitoring a "global tax" for six years. There is no doubt that they have been working hard to determine which is the best way to tax us. Should they levy a tax on international telephone calls, faxes, and airline tickets, or should they try and implement the "Tobin Tax," which would require great monitoring and sophistication? The Millennium Document has one clause which probably addresses taxation, "To ensure that the Organization is provided on a timely and predictable basis with the resources it needs to carry out its mandates."

People's Millennium Assembly

In May 2000, 100 nongovernmental organizations came together under the umbrella of the World Federalists. They hammered out a document which was presented to the General Assembly on Friday, September 9, which is a request to add a "People's Parliament" or "Upper Chamber" or "International House of Representatives" where their voices can be heard. They cite the protests in Seattle as one of the reasons why they need their own chamber. Two years ago when I was at the World Economic Forum in Davos, I asked both Kofi Annan and Maurice Strong about adding a "People's Parliament" and they told me then that there would be a "Millennium Assembly" when one would be added. My question was based on a picture which I found in the 1988 *Gaia Peace Atlas* in which Maurice Strong called for a "bicameral" or two chamber structure to be added to the United nations. I actually ran into Mr. Strong at the United Nations and had an opportunity to ask him about his prediction.

VEON: In 1988, the *Gaia Peace Atlas* had a future structure of what the UN should look like. We are there could you comment on arriving there?

STRONG: Yes, the very fact that more heads of state and government have gathered here today than have ever gathered here before underscores the importance they attach to the United Nations. They realize how necessary it is and I believe this assembly will reignite the flame which created the UN and give its members the sense of how much they need it, how much the future of their people and nations depends on a functioning global system because globalization is reducing the power of nations—even great nations like the United States—but there are the structures which the nations of the world can cooperate with each other and with other major stakeholders are very poorly developed. Our challenge is to develop them to the point where this world and this process of globalization can function for everyone. There is no organization that can do it without the UN. **It is the centerpiece of our world system. It's got to be strengthened to do the job that we all need it to do."**

Prince Charles Comes Out of His Closet

In my book, *Prince Charles the Sustainable Prince,* published by Hearthstone Publishing Ltd., I discuss the power behind the United Nations: the British royal family. I ended up writing a book on Charles because I found that he is a hidden power behind what is moving the world. He is responsible for getting passed the drastic Agenda 21 from the "Earth Summit," which brought us biodiversity and sustainable development and which changed the order on earth from God centered wherein man has dominance over the earth to one in which the earth has dominance over man! Charles is also responsible for working with 60 of the world's most powerful multinational and transnational corporations to set up public-private partnerships worldwide.

Charles came out of the closet at this historic Millennium Summit. First, at a meeting which correlates to the Summit, the sixth annual Gorbachev State of the World Forum, one of the Prince's organization, the Prince's Trust, was a co-sponsor. Second, his Prince of Wales Business Leaders Forum (PWBLF), which mobilizes 60 of the world's leading corporations, conducted several workshops. Third, although Charles was not present at either meeting, *The Earth Times,* the official UN newspaper, showed a picture of Charles in their September 5 edition. While the article did not specifically pertain to him, his picture was part of the article. Lastly, while his organization, The Prince of Wales Business Leaders Forum has written numerous workbooks and manuals on public-private partnerships," their latest book is on *The Business of Peace: The private sector as a partner in conflict prevention and resolution.* Bottom line: Peace is about to be privatized and turned over to the multinational and transnational corporations.

In an interview with Jim Garrison, president and founder of the Gorbachev State of the World Forum, I asked him (in light of the merger between business and government as seen in reinventing government, which is also what Mr. Gorbachev is facilitating), was it also part of Agenda 21, sustainable development, and a new compact for the 21st century? Garrison replied:

Absolutely, all of us have to change in this global economy. If we don't change, we are going to die. Governments have to change, corporations have to change, civil society has to change. No longer are we in a world of nation-states where we can depend on the government to take care of us. They are just not going to do it any more. The core function and implication of globalization is that it is democratizing power and if you look back 100 years the only action on the world stage was the nation-state. But at the beginning of the 3rd century, the nation-state is being weakened and global corporations and the civil society sector in the broadest sense of those terms are being strengthened so each of us individually and collectively, whether in the business sector, government or civil sector have to reevaluate the phenomena of globalization in which we are caught up and how we constructively engage with it and with each other in order to ensure that it works for as many people as possible.

Lastly, I asked Garrison of the agenda of his organization and that of the Prince of Wales Business Leaders Forum. He replied:

The PWBLF and the Forum have a close interactive relationship because we both stand for the same thing essentially. Namely the business sector in a global economy, in an era in which governments are being weaken and corporations are being strengthened have to look beyond the bottom line to two other bottom lines. There is now a triple bottom line challenging business right now. Of course (1) they have to have profits to survive but also need to look at the (2) community in which they exist and ensure that they are contributing to their community. Thirdly, they have to take note that the environment is important and there are certain environmental responsibilities. Even as the Forum and the PW-BLF work together we are bringing together several hundred business executives for a three-day track which is being organized by the Progressio Foundation in Holland in partnership with the Prince of Wales Trust to do a lot of these activities.

Conclusion

While no physical bomb was dropped on America, a philosophical and seemingly silent bomb was. Unfortunately, many Americans are fast asleep in their confidence that all is well. This philosophical bomb constitutes spiritual warfare of the greatest degree, not seen on planet Earth since Jesus the Messiah was crucified. We are at the beginning of THE END—the end of human history as we know it, the end of freedom as we have experienced it, and the beginning of trials which will try the hearts and souls of men and women everywhere. In all of this, we are also at an exciting time as well. We may be the generation which experiences the return of Christ. There is no doubt, in my opinion, that what happened on September 6–8, 2000, constitutes the **BEGINNING of WORLD GOVERNMENT.**

What does the Bible say about the orchestrations of men?

Behold, the nations are as a drop of a bucket, and are counted as the small dust of the balance: behold, he taketh up the isles as a very little thing. And Lebanon is not sufficient to burn, nor the beasts thereof sufficient for a burnt offering. All nations before him are as nothing; and they are counted to him less than nothing, and vanity.

—Isaiah 40:15–17

Have ye not known? have ye not heard? hath it not been told you from the beginning? have ye not understood from the foundations of the earth? It is he that sitteth upon the circle of the earth, and the inhabitants thereof are as grasshoppers; that stretcheth out the heavens as a curtain, and spreadeth them out as a tent to dwell in: That bringeth the princes to nothing; he maketh the judges of the earth as vanity.

—Isaiah 40:21–23

What we saw was Psalms 2 come alive:

Why do the heathen rage, and the people imagine a vain thing? The kings of the earth set themselves, and the rulers take counsel together, against the LORD, and against his anointed, saying, Let us break their bands asunder, and cast away their cords from us. He that sitteth in the heavens shall laugh: the Lord shall have them in derision. . . . Be wise now therefore, O ye kings: be instructed, ye judges of the earth.

—Psalm 2:1–4, 10

What should be our prayer at a time like this?

Hast thou not known? hast thou not heard, that the everlasting God, the LORD, the Creator of the ends of the earth, fainteth not, neither is weary? there is no searching of his understanding. He giveth power to the faint; and to them that have no might he increaseth strength. Even the youths shall faint and be weary, and the young men shall utterly fall: But they that wait upon the LORD shall renew their strength; they shall mount up with wings as eagles; they shall run, and not be weary; and they shall walk, and not faint.

—Isaiah 40:28–31

The LORD is on my side; I will not fear: what can man do unto me? . . . It is better to trust in the LORD than to put confidence in princes. . . . The LORD is my strength and song, and is become my salvation.

—Psalm 118:6, 9, 14

The nations are seduced! Their power is ONLY for a season. The greatest spiritual battle of all time is in the process of being fought. The question is, "Whose side will you be on?" If you do nothing, you have already determined the side you are on.

Index

BIBLIOGRAPHY

Arnold, Ronald and Alan Gottlieb. *Trashing the Economy*. Bellevue: Free Enterprise Press, 1994.

Bailey, Laura. "State Cop Retires—for Bosnia Beat." *The County Press,* March 2, 1999.

Barnaby Frank, General Editor. *The Gaia Peace Atlas*. New York: Doubleday, 1988.

Bank for International Settlement report, "Changes in the Organization and Regulation of Capital Markets." Published in March 1987.

Bastiat, Frederic. *The Law*. Irvington-on-Hudson: The Foundation for Economic Education, Inc., 1996.

Bennett, William J. *The Book of Virtues*. New York: Simon & Schuster, 1993.

Bonesteel, Joyce. "Bosnia Calls: Cop Takes New Job." *The County Press.* March 2, 1999.

Burstein, Daniel. *Euroquake*. New York: Touchstone Books, Simon & Schuster, 1991.

Boutros-Ghali, Boutros. *An Agenda for Development 1995*. New York: United Nations, 1995.

Broad, William J. and Judith Miller. "Pentagon Seeks Command for Emergencies in the U.S." *New York Times*, January 28, 1999.

Capital Markets Forum. *Modernizing Securities Ownership, Transfer and Pledging Law*. London, 1996.

Carlsson, Ingvar and Shridath Ramphal, Co-Chairmen, The Commission on Global Governance. *Our Global Neighborhood: The Report of the Commission on Global Governance*. New York: Oxford University Press, 1995.

Cheever, Daniel S. and H. Field Haviland, Jr. *Organizing for Peace*. Boston: Houghton Mifflin Co., 1954.

Childers, Erskine and Brian Urquhart. *Renewing the United Nations Systems*. Uppsala: Dag Hammarskjold Foundation, 1994.

Church, J. R. *Guardians of the Grail*. Oklahoma City: Prophecy Pub., 1989.

Cohen, Mitchell and Michael Wolzer. *Dissent,* Spring 1999. "Lost on the Third Way."

Conniff, Richard. *National Geographic*. "New Showdowns in the Old West: Federal Lands," February, 1994, Vol. 185, No. 2.

Cuddy, Dennis Laurence, PhD., and Robert Henry Goldsborough. *The Network of Power and Part II The New World Order: Chronology and Commentary*. Baltimore: The American Research Foundation. 1993.

Cuddy, Dennis Laurence, PhD. *Road to Socialism*. Highland City: Florida Pro Family Forum, Inc., 1998.

Dake, Finis Jennings. *Dake's Annotated Reference Bible*. Lawrenceville: Dake's Bible Sales, Inc., 1989.

de Bustamante, Antonio Sanchez. *The World Court*. New York: The MacMillan Company, 1925.

deStaint Phalle. *Federal Reserve—An International Mystery*. Washington: Praeger Press, 1984.

Dick, Edison W. "International Law and the Rule of Law" (speech delivered at the United Nations 50 Association Conference). Washington, D.C., September 1, 1995.

Diamond, Henry I. and Patrick F. Noonan. *Land Use in America*. Washington, D.C: Island Press, 1996.

Epperson, A. Ralph. *The Unseen Hand*. Tucson: Publius Press, 1985.

Etzioni, Amitai. *The Spirit of Community Rights, Responsibilities and the Communitarian Agenda*. New York: Crown Publishers, Inc., 1993.

Ferencz, Benjamin B. *New Legal Foundations for Global Survival*. Benjamin Ferencz self-published the paperback, while Oceana published the hardback, Boston: no date given.

Fernando, Maria Elena and Seri Horwitz. "As NATO Meeting Nears, Security Tops the Agenda in D.C." *Washington Post,* April 14, 1999.

Figgie, Harry E. Jr. with Gerald J. Swanson, Ph.D. *Bankruptcy 1995*. Boston: Little, Brown and Company, 1995.

Finer, S.E. *Five Constitutions*. New York: Penguin Books, 1979

Franchotte Pierre. Letter to Joan Veon. July 2, 1996.

From, Al. Speaker at the "Progressive Governance" roundtable discussion sponsored by the Democratic Leadership Council. April 25, 1999.

Gill, William J. *Trade Wars Against America*. New York: Praeger.

Heilbroner, Robert L. *The Worldly Philosophers*. New York: Simon and Schuster, 1953.

Henkin, Louis, Richard Crawford Pugh, Oscar Schachter, and Hans Smit. *International Law Cases and Materials Third Edition*. St Paul: West Publishing Company, 1993.

Hemphel, Lamont. *Environmental Governance*. Washington, D.C: Island Press, 1996.

Hilton Adrian. *The Principality and Power of Europe*. Rickmansworth: Dorchester House Publications, 1997.

Hyatt, Michael S. *The Millennium Bug*. Washington, D.C.: Regenery Press, 1998.

Jarrell, Frank P. and Kerri Morgan. *Charleston Post-Courier*. February 21, 1990, 3A.

Kettl Donald F. and John J. DiIulio, Jr. Editors. *Inside the Reinvention Machine: Appraising Governmental Reform*. Washington, D.C.: The Brookings Institution, 1995.

Lewin, Leonard C. *Report from Iron Mountain on the Possibility and Desirability of Peace*. New York: Delta Book, Dell Publishing, Inc., 1967.

Liotta, Linda. White Paper. *The United Nations—A World Government*. 1995.

Lodge, George C. *Managing Globalization in the Age of Interdependence*. San Diego: Pfieffer & Company, 1995.

Nelson, Jane. *Business as Partners in Development: Creating wealth for countries, companies and communities—"Executive Summary."* London: The Prince of Wales Business Leaders Forum, 1996.

Mullins, Eustace. *The Secrets of the Federal Reserve*. Bankers Research Institute, 1993

Murray, Jerome T. and Marilyn J. Murray. *Crisis: How to Avert the Coming Worldwide Computer Systems Collapse*. Petrocelli Books Inc., 1984.

Nash, Roderick. "Historical and Philosophical Considerations of Ecosystem Management." *Ecosystem Management: Status and Potential, Summary of a Workshop Convened by the Congressional Research Service*. March 24–25, 1994. (To order call 1-202-512-1800, ISBN: 0-16-046423-4).

McCormick, John. *Reclaiming Paradise*. Bloomington: University Press, 1991.

McLaughlin, Corinne and Gordon Davidson. *Spiritual Politics: Changing the World from the Inside Out*. New York: Ballantine Books, 1994.

Meyer, David J. *The Last Trumpet* newsletter. August 1998.

Pae, Peter, "Bank, Insurance giants set merger." *The Washington Post*, April 7, 1998, A13.

Paeman, Ambassador Hugo. "The State of the Union." Europe Special Report, *The European*, November 1996, 4-5.

Piekoff, Leonard. *The Ominous Parallels*. New York: Penguin/Putnam, 1982.

Prince Philip, Duke of Edinburgh. *Down to Earth*. Lexington: The Stephen Greene Press, 1988.

Prince of Wales Business Leaders Forum. *Business as Partners in Development*. London: Prince of Wales Business Leaders Forum, 1996.

Quigley, Carroll. *Tragedy and Hope.* New York: MacMillan Company, 1966.

Quigley, Carroll. *The Anglo-American Establishment From Rhodes to Cliveden.* New York: Books in Focus, 1981.

Ramphal Shridath and Ingvar Carlsson, co-chairmen. *Our Global Neighborhood.* New York: Oxford University Press, 1995. (To order call 1-800-451-7556.)

Rich, Bruce. *Mortgaging the Earth.* Boston: Beacon Press, 1994.

Ross, Robert Gaylong, Sr., *Who's Who of the Elite.* San Marcos, RIE, 1995 (phone: 512-396-7000).

Rotberg, Robert I. *The Founder: Cecil Rhodes and the Pursuit of Power.* New York: Oxford University Press, 1988.

Runte, Alfred. *National Parks, The American Experience. Second Edition.* Lincoln: University of Nebraska Press, 1987.

Ryan, Alan. *Dissent,* Spring 1999. "Britain: Recycling the 'Third Way.'"

Sachs, Moshe Y. editor and publisher. *Worldmark Encyclopedia of the Nations—United Nations.* New York: John Wiley & Sons, Inc., 1988.

Serageldin, Ismail. Interview with Linda Liotta, Istanbul, June 5, 1996.

Shaw, Gwen. *End-Time Maidens Magazine,* April 1999. "Kairos Time."

Solomon, Steve. *The Confidence Game.* New York: Simon & Schuster, 1995.

Tam, Henry. *Communitarianism.* New York: New York University Press, 1998.

Taylor, Ronald. *Washington Times.* "Government Waste Targeted." March 4, 1993.

United Nations Commission on the Status of Women. *Draft Platform for Action, The Fourth Women's Document.* 39th session, May 15, 1995, Item 232(d), 90.

United Nations Conference on Human Settlements (Habitat II). *The Habitat Agenda: Goals and Principles, Commitments and Global Plan of Action.* #A/C ONF.1645/L.1, April 12, 1996, 145.

United Nations Conference on Environment and Development (UNCED), June 3–14, 1992, Rio de Janeiro, Brazil. *Agenda 21: Programme of Action for Sustainable Development—Rio Declaration on Environment and Development—Statement of Forest Principles.* U.N.: 1992.

United Nations Development Programme, *Human Development Report 1993.* New York: Oxford University Press, 1993.

United Nations Development Programme, *Human Development Report 1994.* New York: Oxford University Press, 1994.

University of the Nations Catalogue 1996–1998, Youth With a Mission.

Valdmanis, Thor and Tom Lowry. "Exxon Mobil $74B deal largest ever." *USA Today,* B1.

Weiner, Tim. "The Man Who Protects America from Terrorism." *New York Times*, January 1, 1999.

Whitman, Christine Todd. *Washington Times*, January 25, 1995.

Wormser, Rene A. *Foundations: Their Power and Influence.* New York: The Devin-Adair Company, 1958.

Newspapers
Anaheim Bulletin
Baltimore Sun
Charleston Post-Courier
The European
Financial Times
New York Times
Wall Street Journal
Washington Post
Washington Times

Internet Websites:
Federal Bureau of Investigation: *www.fbi.gov*
Federal Emergency Management Agency: *www.fema.gov/about/femaorg.htm*
Global Emergency Management System: *www.fema.gov/cgi-shl/dbml.exe.*
Group of Seven/Eight: *http://www.library.utoronto.ca/www/g7*
International Chamber of Commerce: *www.iccwbo.org*
International Red Cross and Red Crescent Movement: *www.icrc.org/unicc/icrcnews.nsf/58*
United Nations Office for the Coordination of Humanitarian Affairs: *www.reliefweb.int/ocha_ol/programs/response/mcdunet/0jlogcen.html*
World Economic Forum: *www.weforum.org*
The Prince of Wales Business Leaders Forum: *http://www.oneworld.org/pwblf/*
U.S. Arms Control and Disarmament Agency: *www.acda.gov/link.htm*
U.S. State Department Office of the Coordinator for Counterterrorism: *www.state.gov/www/global/terrorism/index.html*
U.S. State Department, International Narcotics and Law Enforcement Crime Control: *www.state.gov/www/global/narcotics_law/crime.html*

Magazines:
Newsweek
Dissent

About the Author

Up until September 1994, Joan Veon was just a businesswoman. As a result of attending her first United Nations conference in Cairo, Egypt, she received her "wake-up call," as there was more going on at the global level than most Americans knew, understood, or were being told.

In her determination to understand the global level and what it really means for Americans, she has attended more than twenty-five U.N. and U.N.-related conferences since September 1994 on topics ranging from the social to the economic, the environment and reinventing the government. The level of conference has varied as well, from the U.N. mega-conferences in Cairo, Copenhagen, Istanbul, and Rome, to IMF/World Bank meetings, to Group of Seven/Group of Eight meetings, the International Organization for Security Commissions, the Rio plus Five in March 1997, the World Economic Forum in Davos, Switzerland, and the fiftieth anniversary of NATO.

Joan has reported for USA Radio Network, the Michael Reagan Show, the Jane Chastain Show, and the Lou Epton Show, to name a few.

As an international journalist, Joan has asked questions of presidents, prime ministers, key United Nations/IMF/World Bank officials, Bank for International Settlements executives, high officials in the Clinton administration, multinational CEO, and others in order to understand the global agenda and how it relates to the local level.

In her capacity as a businesswoman for fifteen years, Joan writes a quarterly economic newsletter which has become more global in its reporting in an effort to identify and name key economic players. Her firm, Veon Financial Services, Inc., is a Registered Investment Advisor.

In order to help with the expenses of covering international conferences, Joan started the Women's International Media Group, Inc., which is a 501(c)(3) educational corporation. Those looking to help inform others are welcome to support this endeavor.

Lastly, Joan has authored a number of briefing books documenting her research. Her book *Prince Charles: The Sustainable Prince,* which is in its third printing, discusses her view of world politics which states that when America signed the U.N. Charter we officially entered world government and reverted back to Britain. She documents the partnership between the Prince of Wales, the United Nations, and the World Bank. She shows the real Prince Charles as a very powerful man to watch!